Old Testament Wisdom

THIRD EDITION

Also from Westminster John Knox Press
by James L. Crenshaw

Ecclesiastes: A Commentary (The Old Testament Library)

Old Testament Wisdom

An Introduction

THIRD EDITION

James L. Crenshaw

WESTMINSTER
JOHN KNOX PRESS
LOUISVILLE · KENTUCKY

© 2010 James L. Crenshaw

First edition © 1981 John Knox Press
Revised edition © 1998 Westminster John Knox Press

Third edition
Published by Westminster John Knox Press
Louisville, Kentucky

10 11 12 13 14 15 16 17 18 19—10 9 8 7 6 5 4 3 2 1

Book design by Sharon Adams
Cover design by Pam Poll Graphic Design
Cover art: Sistine Chapel Ceiling (1508–12):
The Creation of Adam, 1511–12 (fresco) (post restoration)
by Michelangelo Buonarroti (1475–1564); Vatican Museums
and Galleries, Vatican City, Italy / The Bridgeman Art Library

Library of Congress Cataloging-in-Publication Data

Crenshaw, James L.
   Old Testament wisdom : an introduction / James L. Crenshaw.—3rd ed.
      p. cm.
   Includes bibliographical references and indexes.
   ISBN 978-0-664-23459-1 (alk. paper)
   1. Wisdom literature—Criticism, interpretation, etc.   I. Title.
   BS1455.C65 2010
   223'.061—dc22

                                                                    2009028361

PRINTED IN THE UNITED STATES OF AMERICA

♾ The paper used in this publication meets the minimum requirements
of the American National Standard for Information Sciences—Permanence
of Paper for Printed Library Materials, ANSI Z39.48-1992.

Westminster John Knox Press advocates the responsible use of our natural resources.
The text paper of this book is made from 30% postconsumer waste.

To Jerry and Hazel
and those dearest to them (Allan, Regina, Scott)
and the new generation

Contents

Preface to the First Edition

This book took shape in the classroom at Vanderbilt Divinity School, where for over ten years I have joined my students in trying to understand Old Testament wisdom. That common task was made more difficult by the lack of an adequate introductory textbook. With the publication of this present volume, I hope that need will finally be met. I have written this book as preparation for a more ambitious project, a study of the art of persuasion in Israelite wisdom, which I hope to complete in the near future.

Two grants, from The Association of Theological Schools in the United States and Canada and from the Graduate Research Council of Vanderbilt University, made possible a year's sabbatical study at Oxford University during 1978–79. I am deeply grateful for that opportunity to complete the writing of this book in such pleasant surroundings.

Several individuals have assisted me in the final stages of this work. Special thanks go to my colleagues, Walter Harrelson and Douglas Knight, and to the following students who have kindly read the manuscript and made helpful suggestions: Victoria Lynn Garvey, Andrea C. Barach, Thomas H. Lanham, and Laura Kelly York. I wish also to express appreciation to my wife and to Aline Patte, both of whom greatly assisted me with typing the manuscript.

This volume is dedicated to my brother and his wife, together with their larger family. My hope is that each of them will enjoy the search for wisdom as much as I have.

Preface to the Revised Edition

For more than a decade and a half readers have turned to *Old Testament Wisdom* to assist them in entering the intellectual and spiritual world represented by the books of Proverbs, Job, Ecclesiastes, and Sirach. During that time, an astonishing number of special studies have appeared, throwing new light on various aspects of biblical wisdom. While none of these publications necessitates a revision of my original analysis, it seems appropriate to update the notes and bibliography, add some special sections, and make minor revisions throughout the book. I hope readers will find the new edition a scintillating and trustworthy guide to ancient wisdom literature.

Preface to the Third Edition

The sustained interest in wisdom literature among scholars has prompted me to revise this introduction once more. This time I have done more than update the notes and reflect nuanced shifts in approach. More specifically, I have added a chapter on sages' understanding of the acquisition of knowledge. Its primary aim is to explore the reasons for revelatory knowledge to enter sapiential literature. I have also added a new section on wisdom literature at Qumran and an assessment of how the Gospels depict Jesus' teachings about the insights presented in the books of Job and Ecclesiastes. I have completely revised my treatment of psalms that have affinities with wisdom, focusing on Psalm 39 and Qoheleth. Finally, I have discussed remnants of wisdom literature from Syria, particularly Emar and Ugarit.

Abbreviations

AB	Anchor Bible
ABD	*Anchor Bible Dictionary*, ed. D. N. Freedman. 6 vols. New York: Doubleday, 1992
ABRL	Anchor Bible Religion Library
AEL	Miriam Lichtheim, *Ancient Egyptian Literature*. 3 vols. Berkeley: University of California, 1973–80
AJSL	*American Journal of Semitic Languages and Literature*
AnBib	Analecta biblica
ANET	J. B. Pritchard, ed., *Ancient Near Eastern Texts Relating to the Old Testament*, 3rd ed. Princeton: Princeton University, 1969
ANETS	Ancient Near Eastern Texts and Studies
ANQ	*Andover Newton Quarterly*
APOT	*Apocrypha and Pseudepigrapha of the Old Testament*, ed. R. H. Charles. 2 vols. Oxford: Clarendon, 1913
ASTI	*Annual of the Swedish Theological Institute*
ATD	Das Alte Testament Deutsch
ATSAT	Arbeiten zu Text und Sprache im Alten Testament
AzTh	Arbeiten zur Theologie
BA	*The Biblical Archaeologist*
BASOR	*Bulletin of the American Schools of Oriental Research*
BBB	Bonner biblische Beiträge
BBET	Beiträge zur biblischen Exegese und Theologie
BETL	Bibliotheca ephemeridum theologicarum lovaniensium
Bib	*Biblica*
BibOr	Biblica et orientalia
Bijdr	*Bijdragen*

BIS	Biblical Interpretation Series
BJRL	*Bulletin of the John Rylands Library*
BJS	Brown Judaic Studies
BKAT	Biblischer Kommentar: Altes Testament
BLS	Biblical Literature Series
BN	*Biblische Notizen*
BO	*Bibliotheca orientalis*
BS	Biblische Studien
BT	*Bible Translator*
BThSt	Biblisch-theologische Studien
BWANT	Beiträge zur Wissenschaft vom Alten und Neuen Testament
BWL	W. G. Lambert, *Babylonian Wisdom Literature*. Oxford: Clarendon, 1960
BZAW	Beihefte zur Zeitschrift für die alttestamentliche Wissenschaft
BZNW	Beiheft zur Zeitschrift für die Neutestamentliche Wissenschaft
CBQ	*Catholic Biblical Quarterly*
CBQMS	Catholic Biblical Quarterly Monograph Series
CJT	*Canadian Journal of Theology*
ConBOT	Coniectanea Biblica, Old Testament Series
COS	*Context of Scripture*, ed. W. W. Hallo. 3 vols. Leiden: Brill, 1997–2002
CThM	Calwer theologische Monographien
DBSup	*Dictionnaire de la Bible, Supplément*, ed. L. Pirot and A. Robert. Paris: Letouzey et Ané, 1928–
EBib	Études bibliques
EF	Erträge der Forschung
EHS	Europäische Hochschulschriften
EncJud	*Encyclopaedia Judaica*, ed. Cecil Roth and Geoffrey Wigoder. 16 vols. Jerusalem: Keter, 1971–72
ETL	*Ephemerides theologicae lovanienses*
EvT	*Evangelische Theologie*
ExpT	*Expository Times*
FAT	Forschungen zum Alten Testament
FOTL	The Forms of the Old Testament Literature
FRLANT	Forschungen zur Religion und Literatur des Altes und Neuen Testaments
FThSt	Freiburger Theologische Studien
HAR	*Hebrew Annual Review*
HAT	Handbuch zum Alten Testament
HO	*Handbuch der Orientalistik*
HSM	Harvard Semitic Monographs
HTKAT	Herders theologischer Kommentar zum Alten Testament

HTR	*Harvard Theological Review*
HTS	Harvard Theological Studies
HUCA	*Hebrew Union College Annual*
ICC	International Critical Commentary
IDB	*Interpreter's Dictionary of the Bible*, ed. George Buttrick. 4 vols. Nashville: Abingdon, 1962
IDBSup	*Interpreter's Dictionary of the Bible, Supplementary Volume*, ed. Keith Crim. Nashville: Abingdon, 1976
Int	*Interpretation*
IRT	Issues in Religion and Theology
IS	Bendt Alster, *The Instruction of Suruppak*. Copenhagen: Akademisk, 1974
JAAR	*Journal of the American Academy of Religion*
JANES	*Journal of the Ancient Near Eastern Society of Columbia University*
JAOS	*Journal of the American Oriental Society*
JBL	*Journal of Biblical Literature*
JBR	*Journal of Bible and Religion*
JCS	*Journal of Cuneiform Studies*
JNES	*Journal of Near Eastern Studies*
JNSL	*Journal of Northwest Semitic Languages*
JSem	*Journal for Semitics*
JSJSup	Journal for the Study of Judaism Supplements
JSOT	*Journal for the Study of the Old Testament*
JSOTSup	Journal for the Study of the Old Testament, Supplement Series
JSS	*Journal of Semitic Studies*
KAT	Kommentar zum Alten Testament
KJV	King James Version
LAE	W. K. Simpson, ed., *The Literature of Ancient Egypt*. 2nd ed. New Haven: Yale University, 1973
LHB/OTS	Library of Hebrew Bible/Old Testament Studies
LTPM	Louvain Theological and Pastoral Monographs
MHUC	Monographs of Hebrew Union College
NCB	New Century Bible
NEB	New English Bible
NIB	*New Interpreter's Bible*, ed. Leander E. Keck. 13 vols. Nashville: Abingdon, 1994–2004
NICOT	New International Commentary on the Old Testament
NIDB	*New Interpreter's Dictionary of the Bible*, ed. Katharine Doob Sakenfeld. 5 vols. Nashville: Abingdon, 2006–9
NIV	New International Version
OBO	Orbis biblicus et orientalis
OBT	Overtures to Biblical Theology

OLA	Orientalia lovaniensia analecta
OLZ	*Orientalische Literaturzeitung*
OTL	Old Testament Library
OTS	*Oudtestamentische Studiën*
PUE	Publications Universitaires Européennes
QR	*Quarterly Review*
RB	*Revue biblique*
REB	Revised English Bible
RevExp	*Review and Expositor*
RHPR	*Revue d'histoire et de philosophie religieuses*
RSR	*Religious Studies Review*
RSV	Revised Standard Version
SAIW	J. L. Crenshaw, ed., *Studies in Ancient Israelite Wisdom*. New York: Ktav, 1976
SB	Sources bibliques
SBLAB	Society of Biblical Literature Academia Biblica
SBLDS	Society of Biblical Literature Dissertation Series
SBLEJL	SBL Early Judaism and Its Literature
SBLSymS	SBL Symposium Series
SBS	Stuttgarter Bibelstudien
SBT	Studies in Biblical Theology
SOR	Studies in Oriental Religions
SOTSMS	Society for Old Testament Studies Monograph Series
SPOA	*Les Sagesses du proche-orient ancien*, ed. J. Leclant. Paris: Presses universitaires, 1963
SSP	Bendt Alster, *Studies in Sumerian Proverbs*. Copenhagen: Akademisk, 1975
SSU	Studia semitica Upsaliensia
ST	*Studia Theologica*
StBL	Studies in Biblical Literature
STDJ	Studies on the Texts of the Desert of Judah
Stp	Studia Pohl
SUNT	Studien zur Umwelt des Neuen Testaments
TDOT	*Theological Dictionary of the Old Testament*, ed. G. J. Botterweck et al., trans. G. W. Bromiley et al. 16 vols. Grand Rapids: Eerdmans, 1974–
TLZ	*Theologische Literaturzeitung*
TRev	*Theologische Revue*
TRu	*Theologische Rundschau*
TTS	Trierer theologische Studien
TZ	*Theologische Zeitschrift*
UAPQ	James L. Crenshaw, *Urgent Advice and Probing Questions*. Macon, Ga.: Mercer University, 1995
UF	*Ugarit-Forschungen*

UT	Urban Taschenbücher
VF	*Verkündigung und Forschung*
VT	*Vetus Testamentum*
VTSup	Vetus Testamentum Supplement
WBC	Word Biblical Commentary
WMANT	Wissenschaftliche Monographien zum Alten and Neuen Testament
WUNT	Wissenschaftliche Untersuchungen zum Neuen Testament
ZAW	*Zeitschrift für die alttestamentliche Wissenschaft*
ZDA	*Zeitschrift für deutsches Alterttum*
ZST	*Zeitschrift für systematische Theologie*
ZTK	*Zeitschrift für Theologie und Kirche*

Introduction

On Defining Wisdom

When *Old Testament Wisdom* appeared in 1981 Wisdom literature was beginning to attract considerable interest in the scholarly community, thanks to a combination of things—the influence of Gerhard von Rad's magisterial, but flawed, *Wisdom in Israel* (1972), the decline of neo-orthodoxy and biblical theology as the recital of divine acts, the increasing awareness among biblical critics of ancient Near Eastern texts resembling biblical wisdom, the emerging interest in the study of ethnic proverbs, or paramieology, dissatisfaction with any approach that emphasized "distinctive ideas in the Old Testament," and a growing secularism among contemporary scholars.

Past efforts at understanding the complex phenomenon labeled "wisdom" had achieved no real breakthrough, although Johannes Fichtner's *Die altorientalische Weisheit in ihrer israelitisch-jüdischen Ausprägung* (1933), gave a remarkable systematic analysis whose value persists to the present. Roger N. Whybray, *The Intellectual Tradition in the Old Testament* (1974), questioned the very existence of professional sages, and my prolegomenon to the collection I edited, *Studies in Ancient Israelite Wisdom* (1976), highlighted three unresolved issues in the research of that time: (1) affinities with other biblical literature, (2) literary forms, and (3) structure, particularly with regard to ideas about creation.

1

What a difference sixteen years have made! The popularity of research in wisdom can be judged not only by the numerous monographs and articles on the subject, but particularly by an editorial decision to concentrate on Wisdom literature when preparing a Festschrift for John Emerton (*Wisdom in Ancient Israel,* ed. John Day, Robert P. Gordon, and H. G. M. Williamson [1995]), when that was by no means the natural choice. Apparently, wisdom possesses a high degree of marketability, and the quality of the volume in question enables readers to appreciate the excitement being generated by contemporary interpreters.

We possess an embarrassment of riches today, but little certainty in crucial areas of research, as demonstrated by Claus Westermann's account of publications about wisdom covering the years 1950 to 1990 (*Forschungsgeschichte zur Weisheitsliteratur 1950–1990* [1991]). Stuart Weeks's contentious dismissal of what he calls a scholarly consensus (*Early Israelite Wisdom* [1994]) without offering a constructive alternative shows just how problematic the issues have become. From another perspective, Horst-Dietrich Preuss, *Einführung in die alttestamentliche Weisheitsliteratur* (1987), applies a theological criterion in reaching the conclusion that wisdom literature resides outside the pale of revelatory, and thus for him salvific, knowledge. The most balanced treatments, Roland E. Murphy, *The Tree of Life: An Exploration of Biblical Wisdom Literature* (2nd ed., 1996), and John J. Collins, *Jewish Wisdom in the Hellenistic Age* (1997), reveal the vast resources available for studying ancient wisdom and point to its rich legacy. On a more elementary level, Richard J. Clifford, *The Wisdom Literature* (1998), succeeds admirably in introducing students to the world of wisdom.

Not all of these treatments carry their presuppositions on their jackets, but two recent volumes assess wisdom literature in the light of particular ideologies: Diane Bergant, *Israel's Wisdom Literature: A Liberation-Critical Reading* (1997), and *A Feminist Companion to Wisdom Literature,* ed. Athalya Brenner (1995). John Eaton, *The Contemplative Face of Old Testament Wisdom in the Context of World Religions* (1989), widens the scope of comparison beyond the ancient Near East to embrace the desert fathers, Chinese contemplation, Indian philosophy, and Islamic Sufis.

Several specialists have concentrated on the theological views of biblical sages. Both Leo G. Perdue, *Wisdom & Creation: The Theology of Wisdom Literature* (1994), and Peter Doll, *Menschenschöpfung und Weltschöpfung in der alttestamentlichen Weisheit* (SBS 177; Stuttgart: Katholisches Bibelwerk, 1985), explore the function of creation in Wisdom literature, as well as its specific meaning. Lennart Boström, *The God of the Sages: The Portrayal of God in the Book of Proverbs* (1990), focuses attention on the sages' view of God, while Robert Davidson, *Wisdom & Worship* (1990), attends to the devotional life of the sages. Theology in general claims the imagination of Ronald E. Clements, *Wisdom in Theology* (1992). Joseph Blenkinsopp, *Wisdom and Law in the Old Testament: The Ordering of Life in Israel and Early Judaism* (rev. ed., 1995), investigates the relationship between two ways of shaping character. Franz-Josef Steiert, *Die Weisheit Israels—ein Fremdkörper im Alten Testament?* (1990), responds to the question in the title with a resounding no. In his view, wisdom is no alien body in the Old Testament.

The nature of education in ancient Israel has eluded detection. Nili Shupak, *Where Can Wisdom Be Found?* (1993), draws on Egyptian educational vocabulary to clarify biblical wisdom; and E. W. Heaton, *The School Tradition of the Old Testament* (1994) envisions a well-developed system of education in Israel. James L. Crenshaw, *Education in Ancient Israel: Across the Deadening Silence* (1998), ranges much more widely, exploring the larger issues of epistemology, pedagogy, and resistance to learning.

Several surveys of the entire field of research relating to wisdom have appeared, particularly *The Sage in Israel and the Ancient Near East*, ed. John G. Gammie and Leo G. Perdue (1990); *In Search of Wisdom*, ed. Leo G. Perdue, Bernard Brandon Scott, and William Johnston Wiseman (1993); *Wisdom, You Are My Sister*, ed. Michael L. Barré (1997); and *La Sagesse de l'Ancien Testament*, ed. Maurice Gilbert (2nd ed.; 1990). In addition, the collected writings of James L. Crenshaw, *Urgent Advice and Probing Questions* (1995), provide a window into scholarly research on biblical wisdom over nearly three decades.

An important study of wisdom texts from Qumran, Daniel J. Harrington, *Wisdom Texts from Qumran* (1996) has deepened our knowledge of the evolution of sapiential thought during the late Hellenistic and early Roman periods.

Such was the situation a little more than a decade ago when the revised edition of *Old Testament Wisdom* was published. Since then, a number of publications about ancient wisdom have appeared. I shall not try to be comprehensive, but a representative listing will show the vibrancy of current research.

I begin with introductions, collected works, and Festschriften. Leo G. Perdue, *Wisdom Literature: A Theological History* (2007); idem, *The Sword and the Stylus* (2008); and idem, ed., *Scribes, Sages, and Seers* (2008), take pride of place, if only for sheer volume. Alastair Hunter, *Wisdom Literature* (2006); Katharine Dell, *"Get Wisdom, Get Insight": An Introduction to Israel's Wisdom Literature* (2000); Kim Paffenroth, *In Praise of Wisdom: Literary and Theological Reflections on Faith and Reason* (2004); and Charles F. Melchert, *Wise Teaching: Biblical Wisdom and Educational Ministry* (1998), demonstrate the variety of these works.

Two volumes of collected essays have appeared: James L. Crenshaw, *Prophets, Sages, & Poets* (2006); and Otto Kaiser, *Gottes und der Menschen Weisheit* (1998). Several Festschriften have wisdom as their theme: *Shall Not the Judge of All the Earth Do What Is Right? Studies on the Nature of God in Tribute to James L. Crenshaw*, ed. David Penchansky and Paul L. Redditt (2000); *Seeking out the Wisdom of the Ancients: Essays Offered to Honor Michael V. Fox on the Occasion of His Sixty-fifth Birthday*, ed. Ronald L. Troxel, Kelvin G. Friebel, and Dennis R. Magary (2005); *Auf den Spuren der schriftgelehrten Weisen: Festschrift für Johannes Marböck*, ed. Irmtraud Fischer, Ursula Rapp, and Johannes Schiller (2003); *An Introduction to Wisdom Literature and the Psalms: Festschrift Marvin E. Tate*, ed.

H. Wayne Ballard Jr. and W. Dennis Tucker Jr. (2000); and *Intertextual Studies in Ben Sira and Tobit: Essays in Honor of Alexander A. Di Lella, O.F.M.*, ed. Jeremy Corley and Vincent Skemp (2005).

Publications centering on the sapiential texts at Qumran and apocalypticism include Matthew J. Goff, *Discerning Wisdom: The Sapiential Literature of the Dead Sea Scrolls* (2007); idem, *The Worldly and Heavenly Wisdom of 4QInstruction* (2003); Samuel L. Adams, *Wisdom in Transition: Act and Consequence in Second Temple Instructions* (2008); Grant Macaskill, *Revealed Wisdom and Inaugurated Eschatology in Ancient Judaism and Early Christianity* (2007); and Florentino García Martínez, ed., *Wisdom and Apocalypticism in the Dead Sea Scrolls and in the Biblical Tradition* (2003).

The larger geographical context is not neglected in sapiential research, as evidenced by a slim volume of essays edited by Richard J. Clifford entitled *Wisdom Literature in Mesopotamia and Israel* (2007). In addition, major commentaries and significant monographs on each of the five wisdom books in the canon have appeared. These will be referenced in the notes.

WHAT IS WISDOM?

The reasoned search for specific ways to ensure personal well-being in everyday life, to make sense of extreme adversity and vexing anomalies, and to transmit this hard-earned knowledge so that successive generations will embody it—wisdom—is universal. Until the second century BCE, biblical wisdom was silent about Abraham or any of the patriarchs, Moses, David, prophets, and priests, indeed anything specific to Israel. Within the Hebrew Bible, which is the subject of this book, wisdom expresses itself in several different forms: advice, often from parents to children, in brief sayings and longer instructions; questions relating to pressing problems, particularly suffering and life's meaning; numerical sayings, maledictions and benedictions, and existential observations aimed at labeling things and expressing judgments on types of character; praise of wisdom as a poetic(?) figure mediating divine rationality and of exceptional humans in whom she actively worked; anecdotal accounts, royal fiction, and personal biography; debate and diatribe; lists or catalogs of items; prayer and poem.

The goal of wisdom was the formation of character and to make sense of life's anomalies.[1] Instruction, which took place initially in a family setting,[2] focused on individuals rather than society in general. Mothers and fathers strove to shape moral character in their children by offering them the benefit of their accumulated insights. Their advice was traditional, conservative, and, for the most part, positive. When circumstances placed their teaching under a dark cloud of suspicion, however, they were capable of totally reformulating their understanding of the world. They could even question the "success orientation" that lay at the heart of the sapiential enterprise.

Proverbial sayings from widely different cultures have remarkable affinities, as specialists in paramieology, the study of proverbs, have made abundantly clear.[3] Some examples from African proverbs suffice to make the point.[4] "The earth is a beehive; we all enter by the same door but live in different cells." This saying recognizes the essential unity of humankind, but it also acknowledges varying life-styles. Sometimes criminal activity arises in surprising places, hence one must look beyond the obvious suspect: "Big-nose has not blown his nose; big-feet has not softened the road." Loose sexual morals militate against the establishing of a family: "A highway does not have grass on it; a highway does not grow mushrooms." Acute observation rests behind such sayings as the following: "Where there is more than enough, more than enough is wasted." "The journey of folly has to be traveled a second time." "Today's satiety is tomorrow's hunger." "Though you sweep the hut in a sand flat, the sand will not disappear." "Much silence has a mighty noise." "A butterfly that flies among the thorns will tear its wings." "Debts grow old, but they do not pass away." "One leg does not dance alone."

Highly reminiscent of biblical proverbs are these two: "Sticks in a bundle are unbreakable" and "A little bird does not fly into the arrow." The first resembles the observation in Ecclesiastes 4:12 that a threefold cord is not easily broken, and the second recalls a saying by the second-century sage, Ben Sira, to describe indiscriminate sexual activity (Sir. 26:12), although he places the blame on the young woman. Some of these Bantu sayings possess riddle-like qualities, increasing one's curiosity at the same time they obscure meaning. Their popularity in Africa led to the use of riddles as a greeting, their solution being given on departing, and as the decisive argument in legal disputes.[5] Biblical sages affirm the importance of riddles to their educational task, but none has survived in their literary corpus.

That body of literature consists of four books in Hebrew and one in Greek. Those written in Hebrew are Proverbs, Job, Ecclesiastes, and Sirach (also called Ecclesiasticus). Wisdom of Solomon, addressed to Jews living in Alexandria, uses Greek to communicate with those for whom Hebrew was no longer a viable language. Only the date of Sirach is known with reasonable certainty (c. 180 BCE);[6] the others require informed guesses. The book of Proverbs may not have been complete until Hellenistic times (332–198),[7] although containing much older literature. Its anthological character suggests that a distinction must be made between the origin of discrete collections and the final composition of the book. A sixth-century date for the book of Job seems likely,[8] and Ecclesiastes was probably written in the third century BCE.[9] Wisdom of Solomon derives from the first century CE or possibly about a century earlier.[10] Several psalms resemble these books in language and content to some degree, and these are often included in discussions of biblical wisdom (e.g., Psalms 1, 34, 37, 49, 73), usually with reservations of some kind.

Three of these books are attributed to King Solomon (Proverbs in large part, Ecclesiastes, and Wisdom of Solomon), just as the Psalter is associated with

King David and the Torah (Genesis through Deuteronomy) with Moses. Song of Songs is also attributed to Solomon, and its exclusive focus on human beings has led a few interpreters to label it wisdom. That view has been rejected by most critics. The book of Proverbs also links individual collections with other kings (chaps. 25–29 with Hezekiah, 31:1–9 with the mother of a foreign king, Lemuel). Similarly, in Egypt and in Mesopotamia Instructions were originally written by or for (potential) rulers, but with the rise of midlevel bureaucracy they were intended for a wider audience, finally, in Egypt, at least, becoming entirely democratized.

This early association of rulers with wisdom belongs to a hierarchical understanding in the ancient Mesopotamian world whereby the god Enki (also called Ea) possessed wisdom and revealed it to seven primordial sages, called *apkallu*, and to postdiluvian sages, called *ummanu*, who in turn transmitted it to scholars in the Babylonian *edubba*, or tablet house. In this view, all knowledge was mediated by a chain of tradition. Knowledge and the sacred were therefore inseparably joined, but the academy rather than the temple was the locus of education. Egyptian Instructions, and education more generally, were closely connected with the House of Life, situated near a temple and possessing religious features. In both regions, magic was integral to the task of sages.

Biblical wisdom seems not to have adopted this aspect of ancient Near Eastern wisdom, although Job definitely expected the curses uttered in desperation to bring about their intended disaster (chaps. 3 and 31), and Ben Sira certainly believed in the efficacy of the sacred dice, *'ûrîm* and *tûmîm*. Just as vestiges of a magical view persisted for millennia, the old notion of a chain of tradition guaranteeing authentic teaching continued into the Common Era, specifically in the rabbinic tradition underlying the second-century mishnaic tractate *Pirke Aboth*.

This ancient corpus of Wisdom literature lacks any specific designation such as "wisdom." The closest thing to that, the Egyptian expression *seboyet*, applies to a much wider group of texts than those specifically relating to wisdom. Modern scholars use biblical wisdom as the standard by which to assess texts in the neighboring areas, where the scope may have been considerably broader. In general, two types of texts are reckoned among Wisdom literature: (1) experiential wisdom, chiefly in the form of brief pragmatic sayings and longer instructions; and (2) theoretical wisdom, either as philosophical probing of life's inequities or as personal reflection on life's meaning in the light of death's inevitability.

The oldest Instructions are addressed to a king's son; they constitute a royal legacy intended to equip the prince for later responsibility in the court. The Sumerian ruler Shuruppak counsels his son Ziusudra, the Noah figure in the Sumerian flood story,[11] just as the Egyptian pharaoh Hardjedef (2450–2300) advises his son.[12] These texts, and others like them, concentrate on practical matters dealing with speech, social relationships, effective carrying out of one's responsibilities, correct exercise of authority, table manners and etiquette, sexual behavior, and so forth.[13] In addition, collections of proverbial sayings indicate that ordinary people also sought to profit from the experience of the group. As many as twenty-four Sumerian collections of aphorisms have survived from the Old Babylonian period (1800–1600 BCE),[14] and these include fables, witty sayings, and jokes. In addition, scribal texts discussing events at the educational establishment, both teacher/student relationships and rivalry among students, are known from the two cultural centers, Mesopotamia and Egypt. Some of these are particularly self-serving, exalting the scribal profession above all other types of occupation. From Phoenician Ras Shamra (Ugarit) comes an Akkadian text, *Counsels of Shube'awilum*, in which a father advises his son who is embarking on a journey, probably a metaphor for life itself.[15] Aramaean (Syrian) wisdom is attested in *The Sayings of Ahiqar*, a collection of Aramaic proverbs from roughly the eighth century and attributed to a Jew.[16]

Theoretical explorations of life's inequities and philosophical efforts at discovering meaning in the midst of randomness existed alongside the more pragmatic instructions and proverbial sayings. A Sumerian text, *A Man and His God*, examines the issue of undeserved suffering that finds its liveliest expression in the book of Job. Two additional Babylonian texts, *I Will Praise the Lord of Wisdom* and *Babylonian Theodicy*, examine the problem of the appropriate response to extreme suffering, whereas *A Dispute between a Master and His Slave* (*Dialogue of Pessimism*) entertains suicide as a way of escaping a situation where nothing seems to make any sense.[17] Egyptian texts also reflect on human misery. A brief section of *The Admonitions of Ipuwer* broaches the issue of theodicy, the defense of divine justice, as do *The Protests of the Eloquent Peasant*, and in their own way, *A Dialogue of a Man with His Ba (Soul)* and *The Songs of the Harper*.[18] The affinities with Ecclesiastes make these works essential reading as indicators of the sages' willingness to question everything despite their social conservatism.

Sumerian myth speculated about tablets of destiny, called *ME*, that the gods zealously guarded from anyone who would seize them for personal gain. Sages sought to read the future through various means, particularly the study of the livers of sacrificial animals, and to control fate by omen texts. In Egyptian myth, the gods implanted order in the universe; this principle, *ma'at*, was embodied in a goddess by that name and depicted as crouching with a feather on her knees or head. Sages studied nature and society to ascertain this principle of justice, order, and truth. Having found Ma'at, they expressed her nature in practical maxims.[19] An early saying in Proverbs 25:2 belongs to this worldview, according to which the Deity conceals valuable truth that must be sought after by humankind, especially by royalty.

Although much of the early wisdom revolved around professional, or scribal, interests—a *tupšarru* wrote, copied, and taught literature—the content and tone varied with the political and economic situation. Beginning with *The Instruction of Ani* (also spelled Any), a concern for the individual's inner peace comes to expression, a kind of personal piety[20] that persists from the Middle Kingdom (1550–1305) until *Papyrus Insinger* and *The Instruction of Ankhsheshonqy* (first century BCE). A growing sense of fate permeates the latter works, just as a similar concept, chance, pervades Ecclesiastes. In the face of such loss of control over one's destiny, sages resorted to prayer. This tendency can be seen in late biblical wisdom, particularly Sirach and Wisdom of Solomon.

The remarkable similarities between biblical wisdom and that of Israel's neighbors occasions little surprise when one considers the political situation over the centuries.[21] During its early years, Israel was surrounded by a number of small nations with populations closely related in language and culture, in particular to the north, Aramaean city states in the tenth–eighth centuries. Major powers shaped its destiny for centuries; to the east, Neo-Assyria (eighth–seventh), Neo-Babylonia (late seventh–early sixth), and Persia (539–333); to the south, Egypt. From 333 to 164 BCE Seleucid and Ptolemaic rulers exercised control over the small colony of Yehud, which finally achieved political autonomy, as a result of the Maccabean revolt, but this gave way before the Roman army in 63 BCE.

In summary, human survival depends upon an ability to study the complexity of human relationships and to cope with reality as it presents itself in the ordinary circumstances of daily existence. Generation after generation acquired fundamental insights into the difficult problem of male-female relationships, and these discoveries were etched into the collective memory through careful formulation of unforgettable sayings. Similarly, young people learned their parents' legacy concerning correct speech, proper table manners, control of one's temper, diligence, and the many things that enhance life. Not every mystery lent itself to convincing solutions. The suffering of innocent individuals has posed a vexing problem from time immemorial, for it has defied every effort at rational explanation. This difficult problem evoked one of the masterpieces of the religious spirit, the book of Job. Indeed, the tension between divine freedom and human claims to justice pervades much more than that book, so that this single issue looms large in any significant analysis of biblical wisdom.

Although it may seem that the scope of Israelite wisdom is beyond dispute, that is not the case. The highly informative passage and the most problematic in the wisdom literary corpus is chapter 31 in the book of Job, a defense of Job's ethical conduct constituting a moral code that soars to lofty heights not even surpassed in the Sermon on the Mount.[22] This is a good text to use in identifying wisdom.

SAPIENTIAL ETHICS

Having given up hope of attaining a hearing from his inept comforters, the suffering Job took his case to a higher court. Job's declaration takes the form of an oath: "I swear by El that if I have done X then let Y happen to me." Presumably, one who emerges unscathed after such a bold outcry cannot be guilty. Parallels for these imprecations exist in the Egyptian Book of the Dead (ch. 125) and the Code of Hammurabi from Mesopotamia. Normally, the result clause is omitted, possibly to increase the psychological dread by leaving the punishment unspecified. Job dares to defy tradition, stating four times the actual punishment envisioned (vv. 8, 10, 22, 40). The total number of offenses is unclear; the complete number fourteen (twice seven) may be intended. The entire confession, an ordered cacophony, teems with verbal links and rhetorical features, the most powerful of which is Job's defiant appeal for a divine weighing of his heart (against the feather representing justice) and the upheld defense, personally signed by a proud prince who is prepared to display an indictment on his shoulders. On two occasions Job's words carry barbs directed against the Deity, who in contrast to Job has abused a loyal servant and has neglected to set a guard over divine eyes.

Job's code of ethics is grounded in a primal bond akin to that of an infant for its mother. It is relational, not an abstraction of principles. An "I" has acknowledged a kinship with another, a "Thou." This bond extends to all others regardless of social status, and it reaches within the mind where motives and thoughts reside long before they issue in deeds. When a valued relationship fails, this code moves an individual to risk death in an effort to restore the lost ardor. The bond links all humankind in a single family, assuring protection for marginalized citizens—the widow, the orphan, and the resident alien in the Bible—and even producing good will for enemies. Nevertheless, even Job's code of ethics suffers from the controls exercised by all worldviews in at least two respects. It presents a proud man whose view of women needs refinement ("If I have committed adultery, let my wife become someone else's sex object," v. 10). It also indicts the Deity when virtue is not rewarded.

Job's list of offenses covers external deed and inner disposition, abuse of humans and affront to Deity, active misdeeds and passive acquiescence in wrongdoing. Outright adultery and its secret counterpart, seething lust, stand alongside one another as equally heinous conduct in Job's eyes. Without a moment's hesitation, he drew back the curtains to his heart and revealed uprightness with respect to avarice and deceit, as well as singleness of devotion before God. Devoid of deception, greed, and idolatry, Job refused to hoard his possessions for selfish ends, but distributed his goods to needy persons. He championed his servant's cause; clothed, fed, and sheltered widows, orphans, and the poor; provided hospitality to strangers traveling the dusty roads. Naturally, such a person acted out of his own understanding of justice rather than fear of the crowd, and possessed sufficient power to correct injustice. Even the land had no complaint against Job, who understood the necessity of allowing soil to replenish its nutrients. What is more, Job had never rejoiced over his enemy's misfortune.

The crucial question is not whether Job pulled the wool over the eyes of his companions, or even if he managed to trick God into thinking his servant was so pure that he had windows in his heart. We all know that nobody can be completely without fault. What really matters is that the poet describes his or her understanding of a *ṣaddîq* (righteous or upright person). This is what it means to be good, the poet writes, and proceeds to enumerate vices in such a manner as to indicate what he or she regards as virtue. The result constitutes a code of ethics.

But is the code Israelite and is it sapiential? Nothing in the catalog of vices falls into the category of distinctive wisdom behavior, and every item could appear in a non-Israelite declaration of innocence. Thus there is a fundamental problem at the outset: How can one determine what is distinctive of Israel's sages in the area of ethics, particularly when the wise share the general worldview that pervades the entire Hebrew Scriptures as well as Egyptian and Mesopotamian literature?

Our difficulties do not stop with shared viewpoints within the separate portions of the Hebrew Bible. What if the book of Job does not belong to Wisdom literature? After all, chapter 31 has the form of Egyptian ritual texts. Indeed, a case can be made against Job as a wisdom writing.[23] None can deny strong affinity between Job and complaints within the book of Psalms and related laments in Mesopotamian texts. The book can certainly be viewed as an example of an answered lament, a model for the appropriate manner of responding to suffering.[24] It also has the form of disputation, specifically, a mythological prologue, a debate, and a divine resolution. In addition, the book freely incorporates material from prophetic literature, especially Isaiah 40–55, and traditions concerning the divine self-manifestation.[25] The ending to the poetic dialogue, specifically God's approach to humans, belongs to prophetic and narrative texts but is ill at home within wisdom contexts.

At the same time, the book bears a striking resemblance to discussion literature in Mesopotamian wisdom, which in itself differs greatly from Israelite sapiential texts. This thematic continuity with wisdom concerns elsewhere, despite formal departure from the customary, poses an urgent question: Are form and content inseparable, or can one divorce the two? For the present, we shall assume the two are separate. Job 31 represents wisdom ethics, but not exclusively so. The latter qualification means that the prophets Amos and Hosea could subscribe to Job's standard of conduct without reservation. So could the Egyptian sage Amenemope and his Mesopotamian counterpart.

To understand how it is possible to include Job 31 within sapiential ethics, we need to define biblical wisdom. While there are various attempts to catch wisdom's essence—wisdom is "the ability to cope," "the art of steering"; it is "practical knowledge of the laws of life and of the world, based on experience"; wisdom constitutes "parents' legacy to their children"; it is "the quest for self-understanding and for mastery of the world"—no single definition suffices because of the variety of phenomena that employ the Hebrew word *ḥokmâ* and similar ideas in the ancient Near East.[26] Still, a beginning step toward an adequate definition can be taken.

A Literary Corpus

The first point concerns a scholarly convention. Wisdom signifies a literary corpus. However much the five biblical books enumerated above differ from one another, they retain a mysterious ingredient that links them together in a special way. This powerful bond prompts interpreters to use these works as a norm by which to connect certain psalms with the sages, despite the present context within which the "wisdom psalms" occur.

The same point applies beyond Israel's borders. Certain Egyptian texts identify themselves as "Instructions," that is, advice to prospective administrative officials from wise counselors.[27] Some texts stand apart from other literature by their subject matter, whether skeptical questioning of life's value or rhapsodic proclamations to live it up (*carpe diem*). Similarly, in Mesopotamia both subject matter and identifying vocabulary set off a significant body of literature that deserves the name "wisdom," even if certain features of that literary corpus differ sharply from Israelite and Egyptian wisdom. These are omen texts, which endeavor to regulate life so as to avoid activity that falls under menacing omens and to encourage business when favorable signs are visible; they are the magical foundation upon which Mesopotamian wisdom stood.[28]

Similar Texts in Egypt and Mesopotamia

The second observation about defining Israelite wisdom is that ancient Near Eastern parallels furnish an important clue that assists one in determining precisely what constitutes wisdom. Like all clues, this one must be interpreted, lest it thrust one along winding paths that lead astray. Distinctions within cultures must be honored if one wishes to profit from comparative analysis. For example, not a single example of omen wisdom has survived in Israel,[29] and the putative catalogs of nature wisdom in Job and Sirach scarcely resemble their Mesopotamian prototype.[30] Still, something unites these widely divergent texts.

A Special Attitude

The third point: Wisdom is a particular attitude toward reality, a worldview. That stance survives through time and reaches from one end of the Fertile Crescent to the other. It persists in Israel from the existence in small villages, through court circles, and into scribal settings. The prevalent attitude toward reality survived the collapse of the First Kingdom in Egypt (c. 2200 BCE) and the disappearance of Sumerians beyond the Euphrates (c. 1750 BCE). That way of looking at things begins with humans as the fundamental point of orientation. It asks what is good for men and women,[31] and it believes that all essential answers can be learned in experience, pregnant with signs about reality itself. That worldview assumes a universe in the deepest and richest sense of the word. The one God embedded truth within all of reality. The human responsibility is to search for that insight and thus to learn to live in harmony with the cosmos. To some degree, the sage knows the right time for a specific word or deed. It follows that wisdom is based on an optimism about predictability. Over the years this confidence in the world and human potential gives rise to profound skepticism, but such a heart-rending cry bears eloquent testimony to a grand vision of what ought to be, a vision that persists even though despair has overwhelmed the sage.[32]

Thematic Coherence

A fourth observation surfaces from such discussion of attitudes characterizing ancient sages: Wisdom expresses itself with remarkable thematic coherence. Wise men and women address common problems, whether the dangers of adultery, the perils of the tongue, the hazards of strong drink, the enigma of undeserved suffering, the inequities of life, or the finality of death.[33] In addition, these sages clothe their intuitions, confirmed by experience, in recognizable dress (proverb, sentence, debate, instruction). The style of the sages alternates between brief maxims and sayings, instructions, and dialogue. The perspective of teachers also varies from parental admonitions to courtier's political counsel and ultimately to religious dogmatism. Here too the supreme honor is bestowed upon wisdom: she gradually assumes separate existence. In female personification, Wisdom moves freely within two societies; she is truly a citizen of two worlds, the heavenly and the earthly.[34] A caution is in order at this point: many of the above-mentioned themes appear also in patently nonsapiential contexts. The circle is complete; once again the student of wisdom stands before the problem of form and content.

The conclusion reached from this multifaceted approach to defining wisdom is that formally, wisdom consists of proverbial sentence or instruction, debate, intellectual reflection; thematically, wisdom comprises self-evident intuitions about mastering life for human betterment, gropings after life's secrets with regard to innocent suffering, grappling with finitude, and quest for truth concealed in the created order and manifested in a feminine persona. When a marriage between form and content exists, there is Wisdom literature. Lacking such oneness, a given text participates in biblical wisdom to a greater or lesser extent.

A Search for Propriety

The situation is no less complex when reflecting upon the underlying premise of ancient wisdom. The fundamental assumption, taken for granted in every representative of biblical wisdom, consisted of a conviction that being wise meant a search for and maintenance of a stable society, in a word, a just order.[35] Propriety, then, is an essential ingredient in wisdom—the right time and place for each deed or word. It follows that the good act constitutes the appropriate one for a given situation. In truth, "for everything there is a time." The universe itself depended upon appropriate human conduct. A word untimely spoken or an act out of sequence threatened the harmony of nature, thus strengthening the forces of chaos that hovered over all creation.

It naturally follows that human actions had cosmic implications. This fact alone gave utmost seriousness to the search for insight, together with the dissemination of that valuable lore from generation to generation. At some moment in remote antiquity God had created the universe orderly, bestowing upon that creation the necessary clues to enable humans to assure their continued existence. From then on the Creator left human survival to its own devices. Those who used their intelligence to learn the universe's secrets and to live in accord with those secrets fared well; those who refused to do so suffered the consequences of their own folly. In such a world, grace played no role;[36] indeed, to ask for special consideration approached blasphemy, since individuals had the necessary equipment to assure their well-being.

Such an understanding of reality produced strong pragmatism. Life in harmony with the principles of the universe eventuated in the good things of society: health, wealth, fame, honor, longevity, progeny. Hedonism in its classical sense received divine sanction. Those who acted in such a way as to secure for themselves the above good things pleased God at the same time, for they demonstrated their approval of the creative act. Consequently, asking the important question, "What can I do to achieve happiness?" transcended self-centeredness. In fact, such egocentricity constituted genuine spiritual devotion.

In a society where pragmatism enjoyed religious undergirding, one could expect considerable emphasis upon moderation. The sages did not want anyone to rock the boat. Accordingly, they encouraged any means that would mollify anger, and they refused to become involved in efforts at social reform. Lacking political power, the sages quickly learned their place in the social world, recognizing the usefulness of bribes, obsequiousness, and general "yesmanship."[37]

Restraint prevailed in other matters as well and assisted greatly toward the formation of character. The wise saw the dangers of excessive drink and gluttony, just as they realized how readily too much talk could destroy individuals. Good things carried to excess became evil in their consequences. That included piety, which like all virtues carried, imbedded within, a seed of self-importance that could suddenly burst forth destructively. As Job knew from personal experience, and Qoheleth surmised, extreme piety came to no good end. Whether Israel's sages thought punishment for exceptional virtue or vice came from God or humans is uncertain; perhaps they envisioned both sources of evil.[38]

The Fear of the Lord

In some circles of the wise, the fear of the Lord functioned as the compass point from which they took moral readings. Originally this idea meant "religion," but in time it assumed a technical, restricted sense. Fear of the Lord thus stood at the beginning of all knowledge, and perhaps served as the crowning achievement in wisdom as well. In time *tôrâ*, that is, revelatory knowledge, became a legitimate subject for study, inasmuch as this sacred deposit contained all truth vouchsafed to Israel.

Authority

So long as wisdom represented human achievement, the authority conveyed to counsel and sapiential reflection lacked divine backing.[39] This does not imply that the sages' observations had no authority, for they carried the weight of parental standing and compelled assent through logical cogency. When their elders spoke, children were expected to listen. Similarly, when teachers summoned students to attention, the youngsters obeyed or suffered harsh consequences. To be sure, many proverbs by their very nature need no external reinforcing; because they ring true, they compel assent, and one wonders why it took so long to discover such transparent truth.

That is why the wise refused to reinforce their teachings by appealing to belief in creation. They could easily have said, "Do this because God created you and certain actions naturally follow." Instead, they appealed to a sense of self-interest and relied upon a capacity to reason things out. To assist others in recognizing the truth of sapiential discourse, the wise developed a rich repertoire of rhetoric. Whether admonition or warning, dialogue or sentence, narrative or poetry, the stylistic device adopted by sages enhanced the teaching and heightened its authority.[40]

Proverbs 6:20–35 illustrates this point. This textual unit focuses upon the threat posed by loose women, a favorite topic of Israelite sages whose passion matched that of most cultures. Here we have a discourse in which a teacher appeals to parental authority and invokes tôrâ (teaching) as well. Still, when he wants to make his point decisively this sage quotes a proverb, that is, relies on consensus, appealing to what everyone knows to be true. The argument runs as follows. Do not cavort with an adulteress, for unlike a common whore, she pursues a costly goal: life itself. Can a man carry live coals in his vest pocket without burning his clothes? Can one walk barefoot upon hot coals and not burn his feet?[41] The obvious, though unspoken, answer is no. Then neither can one commit adultery without suffering the consequences of such folly. Again the sage pushes the argument home: Do we not despise a thief who steals even if starving? How much more the hungry lecher will be stripped of all he has. With remarkable adroitness, the sage plays on the obscene meanings of fire, food, thief, go in, touch. In addition, he returns to the beginning by a clever pun on the similarity between the Hebrew words for "woman" and "fire"; otherwise the redundant reference to a man's committing adultery with a woman violates Hebrew syntax as grievously as an adulterer violates a marriage.

From Proverbs 9:13–18 it appears that Folly, also personified as a woman, had learned something from the sages' method of argument. In any event, she deigns to press her case with a vacillating individual by quoting a proverb: "Stolen water is sweet, and bread eaten in secret is pleasant." If the sage has given an accurate portrayal of this wanton, we can conclude that she chose to rely on commonly accepted knowledge. In truth, stolen water and bread signify sexual congress—as any fool knew. The simpleton also knew that forbidden fruit tasted better, at least in fantasy. In this particular unit, the sage has chosen to challenge the insight preserved in proverbial form. This time he appeals to personal authority achieved by means of fuller knowledge.

This appeal within an appeal demonstrates the sages' willingness to defy tradition when the evidence warrants such action. If true wisdom consists of the appropriate deed for the moment, then different situations called for varied responses. In this sense, biblical wisdom is immensely historical despite its complete disregard, until the second-century Ben Sira, for special moments in the history of Israel.

Anyone who is only remotely familiar with the content of the biblical book of Proverbs may wonder why I have ignored what occupies the center of the stage there—lengthy discussions of family relations, sexual ethics, political ethics, and general social relations. Without a doubt, the sages have bequeathed to us a partial code of conduct, which they never tired of promoting by every available means.

The family was the most important institution in ancient Israel.[42] Here values were acquired, and character was lovingly shaped. Respect for parents, obedience of their every command, and caring for them in old age functioned as cement to hold a complex society together. Discipline, freely rendered, signified the importance of learning and learner alike; a father disciplines those he loves. In such a closed social structure, brothers played a significant role. Any act that threatened fraternal peace was anathema. At the same time, the sages knew that friends could be closer than brothers. This perception prompted them to view every true friend as a potential brother or sister in difficult times. The chief threat to the family was sexual; the adulterer was loathsome because of the complete disregard for familial solidarity.

The wise never tired of discussing the dangers of sexual license. The foreign woman, who seems to combine features of ancient fertility religion and common adulterers, posed a health risk for young men, who were especially vulnerable to her blandishments. An Egyptian sage put the matter as follows: "Man is more eager to copulate than a donkey; his purse is what restrains him" (*Ankhsheshonqy* 24.10). As an antidote to this sickness, the sages suggested reflection upon the teachings; when all else failed, they resorted to poignant portrayal of the awful fate that befell victims who placed themselves in the hands of foreign women. Since the sages concentrated on sexual deviancy, we must glean from that discussion what was taken for granted. Marriage was the norm, departure from which is never mentioned except for eunuchs.[43] The latter were the subject of genuine sympathy in Sirach, where they are described as embracing lovely women and groaning (20:4; 30:20), and in Wisdom of Solomon, where they are promised special favor in God's sight to compensate for their grievous loss (3:14). Naturally, the goal of marriage was procreation, so important in a rural society.

A definite bias against women permeates biblical wisdom. Women are said to be responsible for perverting a good creation, and they "drink from any available fountain or open their quiver for every arrow," to paraphrase Ben Sira's coarse observation. At the same time, women are a gift of God and deserve praise from husbands and children, particularly because good wives enhance the reputation of a man in the community.[44] That is the point of the singular praise of a good wife in Proverbs 31, together with her rarity.

The latter point, reputation, calls attention to the larger society within which life unfolds. Honor and shame were powerful forces exercising control over behavior and assuring conformity, especially in sexual matters. The sages enjoined social responsibility for justice and encouraged truthful testimony. They conceded that bribes work effectively, and warned against heroic stands in the presence of powerful rulers. Life at court placed great demands upon young men, who had to learn proper table manners, discreet silence, and the art of eloquent reply. In general, the sages taught charity when one had sufficient means, but warned against involvement that might place one in financial jeopardy. They seem not to have objected to monarchy, although the wise knew that kings were subject to baser human emotions, leading to devastating fury.

A union of religion and ethics characterized ancient wisdom. The dichotomy between secular and sacred did not exist in the biblical world. Every act bore religious consequences and arose from a religious understanding of reality. Life with people was at the same time existence in God's presence. Whatever enriched one context enhanced the other; ethical behavior thus assumed ultimate significance.

The brief account of sapiential ethics concerning the family, sexual relations, politics, and so forth came last in this introductory analysis because nothing in it is exclusively wisdom. Although preserved within Wisdom literature, such views were shared by all Israel. Prophets, priests, and laypersons alike endorsed these teachings. So did biblical sages. Once again, a solid wall presents itself: the points of continuity between sages and the rest of society. Thus, the reason for beginning with observations about Job 31, a text that introduces the fundamental problem with which one struggles throughout any attempt to understand sapiential ethics.

What, then, characterizes wisdom's ethic as opposed to shared understandings? Belief in a just order, though pervasive and highly significant to sages, cannot qualify as distinctively sapiential. What does is a conviction that all men and women, Jewish and non-Jewish, possess the means of securing their well-being—that they do not need and cannot expect divine assistance. From this humanistic stance they achieved an amazing breakthrough: the recognition that virtue is its own reward. Disinterested righteousness emerged as a reality in biblical wisdom. If in truth this perception does capture the distinctive feature of wisdom, that understanding exploded all bounds, for it surfaces rarely in texts outside the wisdom corpus.[45] Conversely, the gracious wooing of subjects by the Creator intruded upon wisdom's self-sufficiency, until at last a wedding of Yahwism and wisdom took place. On the other hand, complete skepticism seems also to have characterized biblical wisdom. In this case, the book of Ecclesiastes, no comfort from beyond intrudes; instead, warm human arms suffice until death silences one and all.

It follows that wisdom is the reasoned search for specific ways to assure well-being and the implementation of those discoveries in daily existence. Wisdom addresses natural, human, and theological dimensions of reality, and constitutes an attitude toward life, a living tradition, and a literary corpus. Perhaps in the long run one can say about wisdom what a noted critic remarked with regard to a proverb, specifically that it possesses a certain indescribable quality.[46] This book is an attempt to clarify that "certain indescribable quality."

THE PLAN OF THIS BOOK

Chapter 1 will examine the world of wisdom, its language and literary forms. Did Israel's sages see themselves as a distinct group, and if so, what specific features characterized their self-understanding? Naturally, this investigation will concentrate on the wise as an elite class, and it will ask whether this group influenced others within Israelite society.

The second chapter will focus upon the sapiential traditions, hoping to discover central emphases which survived the several stages through which biblical wisdom passed. Since Solomon occupies center stage in this lore, we shall study his supposed role in composing and preserving canonical proverbs. In addition, we hope to demonstrate the way in which important themes arose and assumed increasing significance, especially the notion of personified Wisdom.

Chapters 3 through 7 will provide an analysis of the literary corpus: Proverbs, Job, Ecclesiastes, Sirach (Ecclesiasticus), and Wisdom of Solomon. Each of these discussions will treat the central themes of the book, characterize the chief literary features within each one, and attempt to place the book within the larger context of ancient wisdom. This section will also treat "wisdom" vocabulary and themes in some psalms.

The eighth chapter will examine the reciprocating touch of epistemology: divine disclosure and human discovery. It aims to clarify the presence of revelatory knowledge in sapiential discourse. Chapter 9 will isolate certain abiding contributions of biblical wisdom, specifically the insistence upon a fundamental realism that tests all convictions by experience itself, and the radical skepticism that kept the sages honest and enabled them to cope with unexpected turns in life. This chapter will also explore the sages' concept of God and piety, as well as the peculiar role of personified Wisdom.

The final chapter will place Israelite wisdom within the ancient Near Eastern setting. This discussion will examine sapiential texts from ancient Egypt and Mesopotamia. Its location at the end of the book suggests that such material functions best in Old Testament scholarship when it *helps to clarify biblical wisdom*, rather than serving as the *norm* by which all else is judged.

NOTES

1. William P. Brown, *Character in Crisis: A Fresh Approach to the Wisdom Literature of the Old Testament* (Grand Rapids: Eerdmans, 1996).
2. Claus Westermann, *Roots of Wisdom: The Oldest Proverbs of Israel and Other Peoples*, trans. J. Daryl Charles (Louisville: Westminster John Knox, 1995).
3. Friedemann W. Golka, *The Leopard's Spots: Biblical and African Wisdom in Proverbs* (Edinburgh: T & T Clark, 1993); Westermann, *Roots of Wisdom*; and Laurent Naré, *Proverbes salomoniens et proverbes mossi* (PUE 283; Frankfurt am Main: Peter Lang, 1986).
4. The following proverbs are taken from John Mark Thompson, *The Form and Function of Proverbs in Ancient Israel* (The Hague: Mouton, 1974), 29, 33–34;

M. Kussi, "Southwest African Riddle-Proverbs," *Proverbium* 23 (1969): 305–11; Westermann, *Roots of Wisdom*, 145–49; and Golka, *Leopard's Spots*.

5. Thompson, *Form and Function*, 33–34.

6. Ben Sira's grandson, who translated the Hebrew into Greek, mentions Pharaoh Euergetes, permitting scholars to date the translation after 132 BCE. In addition, Ben Sira praises the high priest Simon, who was in office from 216 to 196 BCE, as a contemporary whom he has witnessed in sartorial splendor. Ben Sira's teachings provide no evidence of the political turmoil instigated by the Maccabean revolt c. 165 BCE. The most probable date for his work is therefore between 190 and 180 BCE.

7. That date seems likely if Prov. 31:27 contains a pun on the Greek word for wisdom, *sophia*, as claimed by Al Wolters, "*Sôpîyyâ* (Prov 31:27) as Hymnic Participle and Play on *Sophia*," *JBL* 104 (1985): 577–87.

8. James L. Crenshaw, "Job, Book of," *ABD*, 3:858–68 (repr. In *UAPQ*, 426–48).

9. James L. Crenshaw, *Ecclesiastes* (OTL; Philadelphia: Westminster, 1986); Michael V. Fox, *Qoheleth and His Contradictions* (JSOTSup 18; Sheffield: Almond, 1989); Roland E. Murphy, *Ecclesiastes* (WBC 19A; Dallas: Word, 1992); and Thomas Krüger, *Qoheleth*, trans. O. C. Dean Jr. (Hermeneia; Minneapolis: Fortress, 2004). Choon-Leong Seow, *Ecclesiastes* (AB 18C; New York: Doubleday, 1997), opts for the fifth or fourth century BCE.

10. David Winston, *The Wisdom of Solomon* (AB 43; Garden City, N.Y.: Doubleday, 1979), argues for a date during the time of the Roman emperor Caligula (37–41 CE), largely on linguistic grounds and the apparent hostile treatment of Jews.

11. The texts are translated by Bendt Alster, *The Instruction of Suruppak: A Sumerian Proverb Collection* (Copenhagen: Akademisk, 1974); idem, *Studies in Sumerian Proverbs* (Copenhagen: Akademisk, 1975); and idem, *Proverbs of Ancient Sumer: The World's Earliest Proverb Collection* (Bethesda, Md.: CDL, 1997).

12. For Egyptian wisdom literature, see especially the three volumes by Miriam Lichtheim, *Ancient Egyptian Literature* (Berkeley: University of California, 1973–80); idem, *Late Egyptian Wisdom Literature in the International Context* (OBO 52; Göttingen: Vandenhoeck & Ruprecht, 1983); Helmut Brunner, *Die Weisheitsbücher der Ägypter* (Zurich: Artemis, 1991); William Kelly Simpson, *The Literature of Ancient Egypt* (2nd ed.; New Haven: Yale University, 1973). For various texts see *ANET*, 405–10, 412–25, 431–34; and *COS*, 1:61–68, 110–25.

13. Walter Harrelson, "Wisdom and Pastoral Theology," *ANQ* 7 (1966): 6–24, likens ancient wisdom to the court jester of recent times, current political satire, and advice to the lovelorn. In that sense, Amy Vanderbilt, Miss Manners, Ann Landers, Art Buchwald, and Dale Carnegie have carried on that tradition no less than Benjamin Franklin, Baltasar Gracian, and Blaise Pascal.

14. Edmund I. Gordon, *Sumerian Proverbs: Glimpses of Everyday Life in Ancient Mesopotamia* (Philadelphia: University Museum, University of Pennsylvania, 1959).

15. Jean Nougayrol et al., eds., *Ugaritica*, V (Paris: Geuthner, 1968), 779–84.

16. James M. Lindenberger, *The Aramaic Proverbs of Ahiqar* (Baltimore: Johns Hopkins University, 1983).

17. For these texts see respectively, *ANET*, 589–91, 596–600, 601–4, 600–601; and *COS*, 1:486–92, 492–95, 495–96, 573–75. See also *BWL*; Benjamin R. Foster, *Before the Muses: An Anthology of Akkadian Literature*, 2 vols. (Bethesda, Md.: CDL, 1993); idem, *From Distant Days: Myths, Tales, and*

Poetry of Ancient Mesopotamia (Bethesda, Md.: CDL, 1995); Willem H. Ph. Römer and Wolfram von Soden, *Weisheitstexte* I. Texte aus der Umwelt des Alten Testaments 3/1 (Gütersloh: Gerd Mohn, 1990).

18. Respectively, *ANET*, 441–44, 407–10, 405–7, 467; *COS*, 1:93–98, 98–104, 48–50.

19. On *ma'at* see Miriam Lichtheim, *Maat in Egyptian Autobiographies and Related Studies* (OBO 120; Göttingen: Vandenhoeck & Ruprecht, 1992); and Michael V. Fox, "World Order and *Ma'at*: A Crooked Parallel," *JANES* 23 (1995): 37–45.

20. Jan Assmann, *Weisheit, Loyalismus, und Frömmigkeit* (Freiburg: Herder, 1979); and James L. Crenshaw, "The Contemplative Life," *Civilizations of the Ancient Near East*, ed. Jack M. Sasson, 4 vols. (New York: Scribner's, 1995), 4:2445–57.

21. Richard J. Clifford, *The Wisdom Literature* (Interpreting Biblical Texts; Nashville: Abingdon, 1998): 23–41, and C. Wilcke, "Göttliche und menschliche Weisheit im Alten Orient," in *Weisheit: Archäologie der literarischen Kommunikation*, ed. A. Assman (Munich: Fink, 1991), 3:259–70.

22. Georg Fohrer, "The Righteous Man in Job 31," in *Essays in Old Testament Ethics (J. Philip Hyatt, in Memoriam)*, ed. James L. Crenshaw and John T. Willis (New York: Ktav, 1974), 3–22. On this text see the commentaries by Norman C. Habel, *The Book of Job* (OTL; Philadelphia: Westminster, 1985), Edwin M. Good, *In Turns of Tempest* (Stanford: Stanford University, 1990); and J. Gerald Janzen, *Job*, Interpretation (Atlanta: John Knox, 1985).

23. Claus Westermann, *Der Aufbau des Buches Hiob* (1956; CThM A6; Stuttgart: Calwer, 1977). The 1977 edition has a useful discussion of Joban research since 1956 written by Jürgen Kegler.

24. Hartmut Gese, *Lehre und Wirklichkeit in der alten Weisheit: Studien zu den Sprüchen Salomos und zu dem Buche Hiob* (Tübingen: Mohr [Siebeck], 1958), 63–78.

25. H. Bardtke, "Profetische Zuge im Buche Hiob," in *Das ferne und nahe Wort: Festschrift Leonhard Rost*, ed. Fritz Maass (BZAW 105; Berlin: Töpelmann, 1967), 1–10.

26. On this vexing problem, see my discussion in the prolegomenon to *SAIW*, 3–5; and in "Method in Determining Wisdom Influence upon 'Historical' Literature," *JBL* 88 (1969): 129–42 (also in *SAIW*, 481–94).

27. On Egyptian wisdom see Hellmut Brunner, *Altägyptische Weisheit* (Zurich: Artemis, 1988); idem, "Die Weisheitsliteratur," *HO*, 1/2 (Brill: Leiden, 1952), 90–110; and Ronald J. Williams, "The Sage of Ancient Egypt in the Light of Recent Scholarship," *JAOS* 101 (1981): 1–19; idem, "Wisdom in the Ancient Near East," *IDBSup*, 949–52; idem, "The Sage in Egyptian Literature," and "The Functions of the Sage in the Egyptian Royal Court," in *Sage in Israel and the Ancient Near East*, ed. Gammie and Perdue, 19–30, 95–98.

28. On Babylonian wisdom, see *BWL*; Samuel Noah Kramer, "The Sage in Sumerian Literature: A Composite Portrait," in *Sage in Israel and the Ancient Near East*, ed. Gammie and Perdue, 31–44; Ronald F. G. Sweet, "The Sage in Akkadian Literature: A Philological Study," and "The Sage in Mesopotamian Palaces and Royal Courts," in ibid., 45–66, 99–108.

29. Glendon Bryce, "Omen-Wisdom in Ancient Israel," *JBL* 94 (1975): 19–37, can find only traces of omens in canonical proverbs, and these are open to question.

30. Heinz Richter, "Die Naturweisheit des Alten Testaments im Buche Hiob," *ZAW* 70 (1958): 1–19. On the phenomenon of cataloging, see Yair Hoffman,

A Blemished Perfection: The Book of Job in Context (JSOTSup 213; Sheffield: Sheffield Academic, 1996).

31. Walther Zimmerli, "Concerning the Structure of Old Testament Wisdom," in *SAIW*, 175–207. This significant essay originally appeared in German as "Zur Struktur der alttestamentlichen Weisheit," *ZAW* 51 (1933): 177–204; see also idem, *Old Testament Theology in Outline*, trans. David E. Green (Atlanta: John Knox, 1978), 155–66.

32. Von Rad, *Wisdom in Israel*, 190–239, emphasizes trust and attack in such a way as to reveal the authentic struggle within the hearts and minds of ancient Israelite sages.

33. Johannes Fichtner, *Die altorientalische Weisheit in ihrer israelitisch-jüdischen Ausprägung* (BZAW 62; Giessen: Töpelmann, 1933), considers the following topics: the essential character of wisdom teaching, the goal, motive, and norm of action; and the understanding of God in ancient wisdom.

34. Bernhard Lang, *Frau Weisheit: Deutung einer biblischen Gestalt* (Düsseldorf: Patmos, 1975) and in revised form, *Wisdom and the Book of Proverbs: An Israelite Goddess Redefined* (New York: Pilgrim, 1986).

35. Roland E. Murphy, "Wisdom—Theses and Hypotheses," in *Israelite Wisdom: Theological and Literary Essays in Honor of Samuel Terrien*, ed. John G. Gammie et al. (Missoula, Mont.: Scholars, 1978), 35–42, especially 35–36, expresses caution with regard to emphasizing order. His desire to preserve an understanding of divine freedom is salutary, but the customary interpretation of order does not really threaten this principle. See James L. Crenshaw, "Murphy's Axiom: Every Gnomic Saying Needs a Balancing Corrective," in *The Listening Heart: Essays in Wisdom and the Psalms in Honor of Roland E. Murphy*, ed. Kenneth G. Hoglund et al. (JSOTSup 58; Sheffield: JSOT, 1987), 1–17.

36. J. Coert Rylaarsdam, *Revelation in Jewish Wisdom Literature* (Chicago: University of Chicago, 1946); and James L. Crenshaw, "The Concept of God in Old Testament Wisdom," in *In Search of Wisdom*, ed. Perdue et al., 1–18.

37. On the social world of the sages, see Michael V. Fox, "The Social Location of the Book of Proverbs," in *Texts, Temples and Traditions: A Tribute to Menahem Haran*, ed. Fox et al. (Winona Lake, Ind.: Eisenbrauns, 1996), 227–39; R. Norman Whybray, "The Social World of the Wisdom Writers," in *The World of Ancient Israel*, ed. R. E. Clements (Cambridge: Cambridge University, 1989), 227–50; Rainer Albertz, "Die sozialgeschichtliche Hintergrund des Hiobbuches und der 'Babylonischen Theodizee,'" in *Die Botschaft und die Boden: Festschrift H. W. Wolff*, ed. Jörg Jeremias and Lother Perlitt (Neukirchen-Vluyn: Neukirchener, 1981), 349–72; Frank Crüsemann, "The Unchangeable World: The Crisis of Wisdom in Koheleth," in *The God of the Lowly*, ed. Willy Schottroff and Wolfgang Stegemann, trans. Matthew J. O'Connell (Maryknoll, N.Y.: Orbis, 1984), 57–77; and the dissertation by Brian W. Kovacs, "Sociological-Structural Constraints upon Wisdom: The Spatial and Temporal Matrix of Proverbs 15:28–22:16" (Vanderbilt University, 1978). For an earlier discussion of the problem, consult Robert Gordis, "The Social Background of Wisdom Literature," *HUCA* 18 (1943–44): 77–118.

38. Klaus Koch, ed., *Um das Prinzip der Vergeltung in Religion und Recht des Alten Testaments* (Wege der Forschung 125; Darmstadt: Wissenschaftliche Buchgesellschaft, 1972); and O. S. Rankin, *Israel's Wisdom Literature* (1936; repr. Edinburgh: T & T Clark, 1954).

39. See my treatment of the problem in *Prophetic Conflict* (BZAW, 124; Berlin: de Gruyter, 1971), 116–23.

40. I have discussed the literary forms characterizing Wisdom literature in "Wisdom," in *Old Testament Form Criticism*, ed. John H. Hayes (San Antonio: Trinity University, 1974), 229–62 (*UAPQ*, 45–77) and in "Wisdom in the OT," *IDBSup*, 952–56. See also Roland E. Murphy, *Wisdom Literature* (FOTL; Grand Rapids: Eerdmans, 1981).

41. On this type of interrogative, see my essay, "Impossible Questions, Sayings, and Tasks," in *Gnomic Wisdom*, ed. John Dominic Crossan (Semeia 17: Missoula, Mont.: Scholars, 1980), 19–34.

42. See *Families in Ancient Israel*, ed. Leo G. Perdue, Joseph Blenkinsopp, John J. Collins, and Carol Meyers (Louisville: Westminster John Knox, 1997).

43. Jeremiah's abstention from marriage is a special instance. The prophet believed God had forbade him to take a wife because of the unusual historical circumstances in which he lived.

44. Trible, *God and the Rhetoric of Sexuality* (OBT; Philadelphia: Fortress, 1978), and Carol Meyers, *Discovering Eve: Ancient Israelite Women in Context* (New York: Oxford University, 1988), provide a stimulating analysis of positive roles played by Israelite women.

45. Hartmut Gese, *Essays on Biblical Theology*, trans. Keith Crim (Minneapolis: Augsburg, 1981), 34–59, develops a similar theory concerning belief in life after death, which he thinks the authors of Job and Psalm 73 put forth in a revolutionary way.

46. Archer Taylor, *The Proverb; and an Index to The Proverb* (Copenhagen and Hatboro, Pa.: Rosenkilde & Baggers, 1962), 3.

Chapter 1

The World of Wisdom

One can scarcely imagine a time when the adjective "wise" (*ḥākām*)[1] did not function in ancient Israel, like the word "good," to indicate morality. The same is true of the several related terms for sagacity, understanding, prudence, and insight.[2] By their actions certain people demonstrated wisdom, cleverness, skill, while others just as surely exemplified folly. To designate these individuals wise and foolish was not to identify them as members of a distinct class of professional sages or simpletons.[3]

As one might expect, the word "wise" and similar adjectives occur when signifying general ability or special skill at some craft. Those who possessed natural talent and who acquired expertise in weaving, shipbuilding, mourning, metalwork, and the like are designated "wise." Such persons possessed wisdom to accomplish a particular task. Similarly, animals are called "wise" because of their instinct for survival that leads them into profitable courses of action. Such uses of *ḥākām* and its derivatives have nothing whatever to do with a professional class of "the wise."

In some cases *ḥākām* seems to occur in contexts that imply a more narrowly defined clientele, as if to designate the special domain of a distinct group of people in Israel. According to Jeremiah 18:18, "the law shall not perish from the priest, nor counsel from the wise, nor the word from the prophet." Many critics have seen in this statement an allusion to three classes of leaders in ancient Israel: priests, prophets, and sages.[4] The essential function of each professional group is thus captured in a single word. Priests promulgate instruction (*tôrâ*), prophets proclaim the divine word (*dābār*), and sages give counsel (*'ēṣâ*).

A PROFESSIONAL CLASS

The existence of a professional class of sages in Israel has been postulated for various reasons: analogy with Egypt and Mesopotamia, the presence of a literary corpus that reflects sapiential concerns, attacks upon the wise within prophetic texts (cf. Isa. 5:21; 29:14; 31:2; Jer. 8:8–9), and general probability, that is, the likelihood that a royal court would need the special talents of learned scribes. Although such arguments are hardly decisive, they lend weight to the hypothesis that a professional class of sages existed in Israel.

A professional class of intelligentsia arose in the third millennium in ancient Egypt and Mesopotamia, somewhat later in Syria. In Egypt these courtiers instructed the children of pharaohs and other potential bureaucrats. The insights of such teachers concerning proper speech, correct etiquette, and interpersonal relationships proved indispensable to aspiring rulers. Consequently, a system of private education developed, and instructors soon composed texts that survived for centuries in a tradition-oriented culture. Similarly, schools in or near temples became the instrument by which Sumerian and Babylonian scribes acquired special skills that enabled them to assist the government in its various projects, and to provide numerous services for private citizens with sufficient capital to hire them.[5]

Such dependence upon learned individuals to carry out the ordinary requisites connected with transactions in business was largely due to the complex systems of writing in these two regions. Ancient Hebrew presented fewer obstacles to any reasonably intelligent person. For this reason, the argument from analogy lacks cogency, especially when one takes into consideration the relative simplicity of the Israelite court. Fundamental differences loom large—for example, the significant function of Babylonian sages, interpreting omens, is wholly missing from the Hebrew Bible.

The existence of a body of literature that reflects specific interests at variance with Yahwistic texts in general seems to argue strongly for a professional class of sages in Israel. Within Proverbs, Job, and Ecclesiastes one looks in vain for the dominant themes of Yahwistic thought: the exodus from Egypt, election of Israel, the Davidic covenant, the Mosaic legislation, the patriarchs, the divine control of history and movement toward a glorious moment when right will triumph. Instead, the reader encounters in these three books *a different world of thought*, one that stands apart so impressively that some scholars have described that literary corpus as an alien body within the Bible.[6]

Furthermore, that body of literature has achieved a high degree of artistic merit. Both the quality of the reflection and the beauty of expression testify to studied composition and arrangement. Now such accomplishment demands a unified worldview and ample leisure to master sapiential traditions. For this reason alone, several interpreters insist that a professional class of "the wise" must surely have existed in Israel.[7]

This hypothesis that the quality of Wisdom literature requires a distinct class may receive some support from the fact that certain prophets direct harsh criticism at "wise" persons who refuse to acknowledge God's control over political events.[8] Nothing within these texts, however, *requires* the assumption that the references have a special class of sages in mind. Such passages may inveigh against folly masquerading as wisdom, and thus have nothing to do with a professional group of "the wise."

Still, the several arguments seem to justify the conclusion that a group of professional sages existed in ancient Israel. That verdict does not rest upon the identification of counselors within the Davidic court. Even if Ahithophel and Hushai functioned solely as political advisors, which is probable, the subsequent appearance of "the men of Hezekiah" suggests that a distinctive class of sages existed in the eighth century. At least one function of these men must certainly have been the preservation of proverbs that expressed their own understanding of reality.[9] One noteworthy feature of Proverbs 25–29 is their general applicability: the narrow concerns of the royal court largely give way to more universal interest.

CONSCIOUSNESS OF DISTINCTIVENESS

Within the literary corpus preserved by the sages one discovers a strong conviction that "the wise" constitute a distinct group. The starting place in addressing this problem must surely be the comparison between the wise and persons engaged in other pursuits (Sir. 38:24–39:11). With painstaking care, the second-century poet describes the manner in which farmers, craftsmen, smiths, and potters carry on their work. Farmers concentrate singlemindedly on the care of oxen, the means of achieving straight furrows, and the best way to get maximum effort from animals. Similarly, craftsmen and designers labor until late at night, endeavoring to discover the right engraving and to obtain an exact copy of a desired image. So, too, smiths work long hours under intolerable conditions, hoping to achieve the correct pattern once the clamor of hammering is silenced and the intense heat has died away. Likewise, potters crouch over their wheels and race against time to achieve the required quota, and afterward they tarry to clean up the furnace.

Unlike its Egyptian parallel, *The Instruction of Khety*,[10] Ben Sira does not demean such workers. On the contrary, he admires them for their expertise and praises them as the mortar that holds civilization together. Nevertheless, these persons do not occupy positions of honor,[11] even if by work and prayer they maintain the fabric of society. Others sit in judgment within the governing assembly and discuss the complexities of legal proceedings or daily experience as reflected in maxims.

In contrast to these specialists in farming, craft, metals, and pottery, a scholar studies sacred literature, here described as law, wisdom, and prophets. This person "preserves the sayings of famous men and penetrates the intricacies of parables." He also "investigates the hidden meaning of proverbs and knows his way among riddles" (39:3). As a result, he advises rulers, and as one of many rewards bestowed upon him, often travels to faraway places. Such persons will not keep secret what they have learned, but they will transmit it to succeeding generations, both orally and in writing. Ultimately, these individuals will live in the memory of others, who recognize that they were a rare treasure—one in a thousand, to use a phrase preferred by sages.

According to this passage, the crucial difference between sages and persons in other occupations is leisure. Only those who have ample free time can afford to concentrate on intellectual pursuits. Taking this observation as their clue, several interpreters have suggested that Israel's sages belonged to the upper social class.[12] As wealthy owners of estates they possessed sufficient capital to enable them to cultivate the mind. If this observation is correct, wisdom remains an elite phenomenon.[13] The wise do not possess political power, hence their perceptions about justice cannot be implemented in the face of violence, nor do they claim membership in the oppressed class. When concern for justice surfaces in their teachings, it either registers a protest to God or merely observes the harsh facts of life. The slightest hint of prophetic outcry is wholly lacking in proverbs and maxims.

At the very least, Israel's sages see themselves as a distinct group standing over against fools. This consciousness of radical differences between wise persons and foolish ones has its corollary in the claim that the former are good, the latter, wicked. According to the wise, all people belong to one group or the other, there being no middle ground. Although this sharp division into two distinct camps may have grown out of antithetical parallelism, the preferred stylistic device characteristic of older proverbial collections, it persists relentlessly in sapiential thought. In fact, at least one modern scholar has viewed this feature of Israelite wisdom as distinctive within ancient Near Eastern texts that are related to the canonical Wisdom literature in form and content.[14] It should be noted, however, that the contrast between the silent one and the passionate one in Egypt functions in a comparable manner to the Israelite contrast between wise and fool, good and evil. A similar view is found in Psalm 1, which resembles the Egyptian moral contrast.

THE SAGES' GOAL

Another means of discovering the self-consciousness of Israel's sages is to analyze their stated goal in compiling a body of literature. Precisely what did they hope to achieve by coining proverbs and formulating observations about reality in all its mystery? A host of texts comment upon the aim that motivated the wise.

The canonical book of Proverbs has a carefully worded introduction that functions to set the several collections into a common framework. This valuable section (Prov. 1:2–7) uses many different words to characterize those who master the Solomonic proverbs: wisdom, instruction, understanding, intelligence, righteousness, justice, equity, discretion, knowledge, prudence, learning, and skill.[15] This heaping together of numerous ideas without further elucidation has been appropriately called stereometry. Those who truly listen detect multiple voices competing for attention, each of which rewards close hearing. Every pregnant concept triggers multiple images within the students' imaginations, which perceptive individuals grasp to their utter delight.

This passage mentions four kinds of sapiential teaching that students must understand: proverbs, parables, sayings, and riddles. The first of these, the "proverb" (*māšāl*) refers to a basic similitude or likeness[16] wherein a given phenomenon is set alongside another as illuminating it in some significant fashion. Perhaps, too, the original sense of the word shines through, signifying that proverbs are powerful expressions of truth. They therefore possess paradigmatic force, pointing beyond themselves to other verities. The second word, "parable" (*mĕlîṣâ*), seems to point in the direction of sayings that carry a sting hidden within their clever formulation, and may by extension refer to admonitions and warnings. The expression "wise sayings" (*dibrê ḥăkāmîm*) seems to function as a sort of general category, and consequently serves to identify certain collections within the present book of Proverbs. The final word, "riddles" (*ḥîdôt*), designates enigmatic sayings and perhaps even extensive reflections on the meaning of life and its inequities.[17]

Two further features of this programmatic introduction deserve comment. First, an implied distinction exists between wisdom and learning, intelligence and skill. It follows that learning is an art, and that one can become expert in the craft, so to speak. Second, hearing plays an important role in sapiential education, so much so in fact that "the hearing heart" becomes synonymous with an intelligent response in ancient Egypt. In Israel, the appeal to proper hearing or attention occurs with great frequency, both in prophetic literature and in wisdom.[18]

In still another passage within canonical Proverbs a father reflects upon the continuity of the wisdom tradition and his role in that important enterprise (Prov. 4:1–5). Wisdom almost constitutes a legacy transmitted from parents to children. Appealing to his son for a hearing, the teacher recalls his own instruction at the feet of his father, and repeats the earlier promise of long life and warning against intentional deafness. One can almost detect a tinge of nostalgia, in that direct quotation functions to demonstrate the value placed upon paternal teaching.

> He taught me, and said to me,
> "Let your heart hold fast my words;
>   keep my commandments, and live;
> Get wisdom; get insight;
> do not forget, nor turn away
> from the words of my mouth."
>   (4:4–5)

The glance backward employs a formula of self-abnegation ("I, too, have been a father's son" [my trans.]). This particular device recurs in Elihu's concession that he, like Job, was pinched from clay (Job 33:6) and in King Solomon's pious self-revelations within Wisdom of Solomon. The latter extends the formula in the direction of marital imagery, claiming that God endowed him with a pure soul and boasting that he had consequently wooed Wisdom for his bride.[19]

The reference to a mother within the text under consideration suggests that the words "father" and "son" function in their natural sense here, although an Egyptian text does exist in which a school boy is said to have been the recipient of tender maternal care.[20] That is, school contexts do not necessarily rule out mention of a mother. While scholars generally assume that "father" and "son" come to function metaphorically in canonical Proverbs, meaning "teacher" and "student," nothing prevents a literal understanding of these terms. Even the admonition to acquire wisdom at great cost (Prov. 4:7) does not invariably point to tuition, and thus to a school setting.[21] It could just as easily suggest the rigors facing anyone who wishes to become wise.

The book of Ecclesiastes closes with some brief observations about the intention lying behind the teacher's work (12:9–12). In this instance, the comments derive from someone other than the author of the sayings attributed to Qoheleth (the name used by the author). The description of the speaker's activity attempts to make his conclusions somewhat more palatable to the larger community.[22] Qoheleth taught what he knew to be true, this epilogue observes, and devoted considerable energy to packaging his teaching. Here we note the desire to present truth in pleasing form, and thus a hint of aesthetic interest on the part of Israel's sages.[23] In the opinion of the person commenting on Qoheleth's work, the sayings retain their sting even if clothed attractively. Indeed, he seems uncertain whether to praise the collected sayings or to warn against further efforts at writing and grasping the complexities of the written text. Still, the accuracy and sufficiency of Qoheleth's sayings are attested, inasmuch as they direct those assembled before him, just as goads spur animals on when wielded by any shepherd.

With regard to conscious articulation of pedagogic goals, Ben Sira makes up for what is lacking in the book of Job. The translator's preface compiled by Ben Sira's grandson, who rendered the work from Hebrew into Greek so as to make its teachings available to Jews in Alexandria, acknowledges that students of the Bible owe a debt to the outside world. Interestingly, this explanation for Ben Sira's intellectual effort breathes the same spirit as the book itself, where categories from wisdom mingle with legal ones. While the themes of discipline and wisdom accord with concerns of earlier sages, the means of achieving proficiency is said to be adherence to the law,[24] thus signaling a new note in sapiential texts.

The sufficiency of divine commandments prompted Ben Sira to warn against idle speculation about subjects that God had chosen to keep secret (3:17–24). Here one comes upon an astonishing attitude toward intellectual pursuits: do not try to discover the meaning of things that are too difficult for you, for what God withholds is of no concern.

> Do not meddle in matters that are beyond you,
>   more than you can understand has been
>   shown you.

> For their conceit has led many astray.
>   and wrong opinion has impaired their judgment.
>   (Sir. 3:23–24)

Apparently, danger from apocalyptic movements and Greek philosophical speculations caused Ben Sira at this point to lose all contact with a legitimate stream within ancient wisdom, the probing of riddles and all kinds of enigmas. Elsewhere he opposes the practice of predicting the future by means of dreams, but the effectiveness of his observations suffers through a qualifying concession that dreams sent by God do possess significance.

What changes have occurred within society that prompted some to devote so much attention to the future? The earlier principle of act-consequence has been pushed into the next life. This eschatology was likely the consequence of two books, Job and Ecclesiastes. In both, the expected reward for a good deed and punishment for an evil one has collapsed, leaving a sense of anomie (lawlessness). The authors of both books staunchly oppose such eschatologizing, and they are joined by the later Ben Sira. The forces driving this future orientation were powerful enough to overcome their resistance, and the new view that reward and retribution will take place after death gains momentum in apocalyptic works under the names of Enoch and Ezra in a wisdom text (1QSapiential Text) from Qumran that combines apocalyptic and sapiential themes.[25]

Omen wisdom, which had thrived in ancient Mesopotamia, now threatens to invade biblical wisdom in disguise. Ben Sira's warning against this threat, like so many other teachings, never really achieves consistency. In 14:20, for example, he declares the one who ponders wisdom's secrets to be happy indeed.

In another setting Ben Sira reflects upon the long line of tradition by which fathers pass their teachings along to their children (8:8–9). In this instance he focuses upon the high office of counselors to princes, which befalls those who master the art of appropriate reply. Learned maxims should be studied diligently, inasmuch as they embody truths that past generations have tested and found reliable before transmitting them to succeeding ones. Elsewhere he concedes that much effort has gone into formulating proverbs (13:26), a point forcefully put forth in the epilogue to Ecclesiastes.

Ben Sira's contrast between scholars and persons in other occupations, which we discussed earlier, concludes with a glowing description of the advantages enjoyed by sages (38:34–39:11). As students of the entire Hebrew canon (here presented in the unusual sequence "Law, Wisdom, and Prophets," with wisdom occupying the second rather than its customary third position), Israel's sages preserve the sayings of famous men and penetrate the intricacies of parables; "they investigate the hidden meaning of proverbs and know their way among riddles" (39:2–3, my trans.). The terminological affinities between this text and the prologue in Proverbs indicate a desire to demonstrate continuity with past scholarship. With justifiable pride, Ben Sira writes that God willing, the devout sage will be inspired to put out his own wise sayings, something that Ben Sira takes pains to demonstrate by his own life and teachings. More than once he confesses that his own wise sayings threaten to overflow their banks like a raging flood. Having finished his inspired utterance, he proceeds to identify himself and to urge attention to his book just as one would study the other sacred texts (50:27–29). Only here do we encounter an expression comparable to modern pride of authorship. All previous wisdom books in Israel remain anonymous to this day, with the exception of two foreign treatises, which have been attributed to Agur (Prov. 30:1–4) and Lemuel's mother (Prov. 31:1–9). For the rest, it sufficed to call them "Solomonic" due to the belief expressed in 1 Kings 4:32–34 (Heb. 5:12–14) that King Solomon uttered three thousand proverbs and a thousand and five songs or to ignore the issue of authorship altogether.

The concluding thanksgiving prayer in Sirach 51:1–12 trails off into a long self-congratulatory account in which Ben Sira connects piety and wisdom in such a way as to present himself as a worthy teacher. Naturally, Ben Sira invites prospective students to dwell in his house of learning so that their thirst will be slaked without going on a long journey to acquire wisdom, perhaps to Alexandria, with its outstanding library of more than four hundred thousand books. This is the first reference to an actual school in Israelite literature; whether this institution had newly arisen in the early second century remains a disputed point. The possible objection to the high cost of tuition and lodging may have prompted the reminder that gold will come in return for silver expended. The religious dimension echoes throughout this highly mundane appeal for means of livelihood. Demonstrating his familiarity with Scripture, Ben Sira alludes to Deutero-Isaiah's rhetorical invitation to "buy without money" and thereby to quench thirst (Isa. 55:1–2). Noting the metaphorical imagery in Deutero-Isaiah and Proverbs, some interpreters think Ben Sira may actually have been referring to his book, metaphorically "my house of learning."[26]

LITERARY FORMS

If we are correct in assuming that the wise constituted a distinct class within Israel, we may make another assumption: these sages used a characteristic mode of discourse. It follows that the literary forms within Job, Proverbs, Ecclesiastes, Sirach, and Wisdom of Solomon comprise a special world of communication which can only be understood in terms of its own categories.[27] What were the peculiar wisdom forms? We shall examine eight literary categories: proverb, riddle, allegory, hymn, dialogue, autobiographical narrative, catalogs or noun lists, and didactic narrative (poetry and prose).[28]

The simple saying registers a conclusion that has arisen through observation of nature, animal behavior, or human conduct. Its form is succinct, epigrammatic, and metaphorical. Such *proverbs* need not include a pedagogic intent, since the desire to teach others seems to have arisen at a secondary stage in the process of proverbial composition. Once the impulse to teach became dominant, syntax was altered so as to include motivation clauses, warnings, and the like. In the process, a distinct type of proverb emerged: instruction. Both sentence and instruction aimed at brevity and placed a premium on their capacity to be retained through memorization. Imagery that made a lasting impression ranked high in the eyes of those who composed proverbs; naturally, similes possessed a remarkable power to linger in the memories of those who valued instruction. Who could easily forget the comparison of sluggards on their bed with a door on its hinges, or the likening of a beautiful woman lacking discretion to a pig with a gold ring in its snout?

Although no pure *riddle* has survived within the wisdom corpus, there can be little doubt that ancient sages coined enigmas. We have seen that Ben Sira thought the solving of riddles belonged to the essential tasks of the wise. The ingredients of a riddle are (1) code language that (2) simultaneously informs and conceals. It follows that riddles function both as clue and snare. Within Wisdom literature certain vestiges of cipher language have survived, particularly in allegorical contexts.

Two *allegorical* texts stand out as worthy links with riddles; these are the poignant description of old age in Ecclesiastes 12:1–7, which contains a few allegorical images, and the exquisite advice about marital fidelity in Proverbs 5:15–23, where a wife is likened to a cistern from which one drinks life-giving water. In both instances ciphers function on two levels at the same time, so that one must distinguish between general and special language. "Cistern," for example, has two distinct meanings, and only those who possessed special knowledge grasped the cipher's full sense.

Although the sages did not invent the category of *hymn*, they fashioned their own particular kinds of song about personified Wisdom or about human achievements despite the inaccessibility of wisdom. In Job 28 daredevils are extolled for exploring the inner recesses of the earth in search of rare metals, but at the same time the hymn recognizes human limits. Thus it concludes by praising God, who alone has access to wisdom. The hymns in Proverbs and Ben Sira concerning God's self-revelation through personified Wisdom resemble those hymnic texts throughout the Hebrew Bible that rejoice in God's goodness and power. In the case of wisdom hymns, emphasis falls upon the role of wisdom in creation and in making known God's will to humans. Similarly, prayers take on special features when sages utter them, which is rare, particularly in those cases where the acquisition of wisdom is under discussion.

Perhaps the supreme achievement of sapiential rhetoric was the *disputation* or *dialogue*. Its peculiar characteristics, as distinct from prophetic disputes, include a mythological introduction and conclusion, the dialogue proper, and a divine resolution. The book of Job has all three of these formal features, which also characterize comparable discussions of the problem of undeserved suffering in ancient Babylonia. One text, *I Will Praise the Lord of Wisdom*, lacks a dialogue between friends, but this feature occurs in *The Babylonian Theodicy*. A variant of the disputation, imagined speech, occurs frequently in Israelite Wisdom literature. Once again, prophetic texts have similar passages, although the content differs notably from the sapiential texts.[29]

The sages developed a special type of *autobiographical narrative* that allowed them to communicate a lesson from personal experience. Wisdom's firm roots in experience provide the occasion for profiting from what one sees, even if that object lesson is played out in someone else's life. By chance sages observe significant features of the environment and portentous behavior on the part of human beings, later putting that knowledge to effective use (Prov. 6:6–11; 24:30–34).

The literary category known as *noun lists* (onomastica) has not survived as such in the Old Testament, but certain numerical proverbs indicate that the type of thinking that produced exhaustive lists of flora, fauna, and the like has given rise to a secondary stage in which this information has been put to work in the service of instruction concerning morals. Some critics think the divine speeches within the book of Job contain echoes of ancient onomastica, and the same goes for the description of the different occupations in Sirach.[30] Evidence for viewing these texts as a late form of noun lists is scant, even if they represent the same kind of thinking that produced comprehensive catalogs of various phenomena.

Another important literary form that the sages adapted to their own purposes is the *didactic narrative*. An exquisite example of the homily in story form exists in Proverbs 7:6–23, where a seductress leads an unfortunate young man to his ruin. The author of such texts uses every available means to heighten the impact of the story. Naturally, appeal to personal experience and superior knowledge occurs with regularity. Didactic poetry aims at the same kind of edification, although it often shows signs of real personal struggle, especially when reflecting on divine justice.

This brief discussion of forms within Wisdom literature has indicated the difficulty of isolating specific categories that were the peculiar domain of sages. The difficulty is exacerbated when one tries to identify exclusive sapiential vocabulary.

Since Israel's sages did not dwell in isolation, and consequently spoke the language of everyday use, such attempts at discovering the special terminology of the wise inevitably abort. For this reason, we shall not try to identify sapiential vocabulary. In truth, all such investigations stumble over their own circular reasoning,[31] for the favorite expressions in Wisdom literature also functioned in a nontechnical manner throughout Israelite society. This observation applies, above all, to such words as "wise," "intelligent," "understanding," "knowledge," and the like.[32]

WISDOM INFLUENCE

The attempt to recognize wisdom influence in canonical texts other than Proverbs, Job, and Ecclesiastes encounters the same problems. Since that pursuit of a larger sapiential corpus has resulted in far-reaching claims in recent literature, I shall describe that endeavor, without trying to be exhaustive.[33]

Within certain liturgical passages in Isaiah (9:6 [Heb. 5]; 11:2, 9), but also in nonliturgical texts (28:23–29; 31:2), emphasis falls upon wisdom and understanding, so much so that some interpreters have thought that Isaiah was originally a member of the sages,[34] but submitted to a prophetic summons and turned his back upon old friends. Not all critics who recognize wisdom influence upon Isaiah assume that he once was a professional sage; instead they claim that the prophet has made free use of sapiential vocabulary, especially with regard to agricultural data and the Torah.[35]

Similar conclusions have been reached concerning Amos, whose hometown, on dubious grounds, is said to have been a center of wisdom.[36] Various types of argument have been mustered to place Amos squarely within clan wisdom: linguistic phenomena, such as the peculiar kind of numerical sayings; theological emphases, for example, the universalistic message that submits all peoples to God's judgment; special vocabulary, like Sheol, "right," and so forth; unusual rhetorical devices, for instance, the "woe" sayings. This sort of reasoning has also led to the claim that Micah should be understood against the background of clan wisdom.[37] Similarly, Jonah is thought by some to have been written under wisdom influence, since its message endorses universalism and the entire book wrestles with the problem of divine justice. Moreover, the literary form that the book takes, that of a *māšāl,* is at home among sages.[38] Because Habakkuk, like Jonah, struggles with the issue of theodicy, this book has also been understood as closely related to ancient wisdom.[39]

Within historical literature, the succession narrative (2 Samuel 9–20; 1 Kings 1–2) has been attributed to a wisdom writer who sought to illustrate the teachings of various proverbs by telling a story in which eternal truths find embodiment.[40] The same goes for the Yahwistic narrative, which at least one author thinks constitutes a conflation of wisdom and history.[41] Such an astonishing conclusion derives much of its inspiration from the claim that the Joseph narrative was composed by a sage in the royal court who sought to provide a model for professional courtiers.[42] The association of court tales with wisdom has also led to the observation that Esther was written by a sage who wished to demonstrate the rewards that accrue to those who combine wisdom and integrity.[43]

Even the primeval history (Genesis 1–11) has been broken up to make way for wisdom influence in specific units, especially the story of the fall, which alludes to a tree of knowledge and refers to the knowledge of good and evil.[44] One interpreter has gone so far as to see the entire primeval history as a product of the sages.[45]

Beyond these larger units, wisdom influence has been found in numerous verses and individual chapters. For example, the majestic description of God's attributes in Exodus 34:6–7, which is alluded to in Jonah, is thought to derive from a sage.[46] This trend has caught on so widely that the entire Hebrew canon is in danger of being swallowed. For example, the book of Deuteronomy, despite extensive covenantal language and election categories, has been attributed to sapiential authorship,[47] and the claim has arisen that wisdom gave birth to apocalyptic.[48] Clearly, such widening of the net threatens to distort the meaning of wisdom beyond repair. In every instance these claims rest upon circular reasoning. Therefore, this discussion will restrict itself to those literary works that are widely acknowledged to be the legacy of the sages.[49] That legacy constitutes a tradition that Israel's sages endeavored to conserve and to transmit from generation to generation.

NOTES

1. See M. Saebø, "ḥkm to be wise," *Theological Lexicon of the Old Testament*, ed. Ernst Jenni and Claus Westermann, 3 vols. (Peabody, Mass.: Hendrickson, 1997), 1:418–24; Hans-Peter Müller and M. Krause, "chākhām," *TDOT*, 4:364–85; Georg Fohrer, "Sophia," in *SAIW*, 63–83; and R. N. Whybray, "Slippery Words, IV. Wisdom," *ExpT* (1978): 359–62. The word "wisdom" (*ḥokmâ*) occurs 147 times in the Old Testament, and the adjective "wise" (*ḥākām*) appears 135 times. The verb "to be wise" (*ḥākām*) is used 26 times, and the variant nominal form *ḥokmôt* can be found four times. Over half of the uses of *ḥokmâ* and *ḥākām* occur in three books: Proverbs, Job, and Ecclesiastes. In this literary corpus and elsewhere a number of additional words occur in parallelism with specific vocabulary for wisdom, thus enriching the discourse about wisdom manifold. The most common such parallels are *bîn* (to perceive), *nābôn* (perceptive, skillful), *bînâ* (insight) and *těbûnâ* (insight, skill), or *dāʿat* (knowledge), *yādaʿ* (to know), and so forth.
2. Shupak, *Where Can Wisdom Be Found?* examines the language of education, words and phrases indicating either positive or negative character, terms for industrious and lazy students, and vocabulary denoting parts of the body involved in learning. In drawing up a list of words used in sapiential contexts, she casts the net widely. Her primary interest is the relationship between Egyptian and biblical language. She finds eight direct borrowings of Egyptian expressions, four literal translations (*ʾîš ḥēmâ*, heated man; *qar rûaḥ*, shorttempered; *tōkēn libbôt*, the one who weighs the hearts; *taḥbulôt*, guidance),

and four modifications (*ḥadrê bāṭen*, chambers of the heart; *'erek 'appāyim*, patient; *qĕṣar 'appāyim*, impatient; and *qĕṣar rûaḥ*, quick-tempered).

3. A text from Ras Shamra has the goddess Athirat say to El: "You are wise indeed. . . . The gray of your beard has truly instructed you." In two eighth-century inscriptions Azitawadda is said to have been treated as a father by every king because he possessed righteousness, wisdom, and graciousness, and Barrakib says that his father, Panammuwa II of Jaudi grasped the hem of Assyrian overlords' garments in his wisdom and righteousness. A text from Jeremiah points to the complexity of distinguishing between a technical use of *ḥākām* and other nontechnical uses ("Thus says the LORD: Do not let the wise boast in their wisdom, do not let the mighty boast in their might, do not let the wealthy boast in their wealth"; Jer. 9:23 [Heb. 22]). Although the first two references could indicate professional classes, sages and soldiers, the third cannot. Parallelism seems to imply that all three instances are nontechnical. In the Aramaic portion of the book of Daniel, clear examples of a special profession, diviners, are indicated by the root *ḥkm*.

4. Whybray, *Intellectual Tradition*, 24–31, challenges their conclusion. His view is accepted by Weeks, *Early Israelite Wisdom*, 75–91 ("It [*ḥākām*] is never used as a technical term for a class of Israelites," p. 90). Weeks considers it truly remarkable that "the wise" never appears in any of the lists of officials throughout the Bible.

5. See above all the essays in part 1 of John G. Gammie and Leo G. Perdue, eds., *The Sage in Israel and the Ancient Near East*: Rivkah Harris, "The Female 'Sage' in Mesopotamian Literature (with an Appendix on Egypt)," 3–18; Ronald J. Williams, "The Sage in Egyptian Literature," 19–30; Samuel Noah Kramer, "The Sage in Sumerian Literature: A Composit Portrait," 31–44; Ronald F. G. Sweet, "The Sage in Akkadian Literature: A Philological Study," 45–66; Loren R. Mack-Fisher, "A Survey and Reading Guide to the Didactic Literature of Ugarit: Prolegomenon to a Study on the Sage," 67–80; James R. Russell, "The Sage in Ancient Iranian Literature," 81–92. In addition, part 2 includes important articles on the social location of sages in Egypt and Mesopotamia: Ronald J. Williams, "The Function of the Sage in the Egyptian Royal Court," 95–98; and Ronald F. G. Sweet, "The Sage in Mesopotamian Palaces and Royal Courts," 99–108. Important discussions can also be found in Jack M. Sasson, ed., *Civilizations of the Ancient Near East*, vol. 4 (New York: Scribner's, 1995), especially Edward Wente, "The Scribes of Ancient Egypt," 2211–22; and Laurie E. Pearce, "The Scribes and Scholars of Ancient Mesopotamia," 2265–78. Overviews of Egyptian literature (Donald Redford), Sumerian literature (Piotr Michalowski), and Akkadian literature (Jean Bottéro) and a study of memory and literacy in ancient Western Asia (Herman Vanstiphout) also appear in this valuable opus. See also James L. Crenshaw, "The Contemplative Life in the Ancient Near East," 2445–58 (*UAPQ*, 250–64); and Ronald J. Williams, "Scribal Training in Ancient Egypt," *JAOS* 92 (1972): 214–21.

6. Gese, *Lehre und Wirklichkeit in der alten Weisheit*, 2. Horst-Dietrich Preuss, *Einführung in die alttestamentliche Weisheitsliteratur*, goes one step further; since Wisdom literature lacks salvation history, it is for him devoid of inspiration and belongs alongside pagan texts (cf. also idem, "Erwägungen zum theologischen Ort alttestamentlicher Weisheitsliteratur," *EvT* 30 [1970]: 393–417; and idem, "Das Gottesbild der älteren Weisheit Israels," in *Studies in the Religion of Ancient Israel* [VTSup 23; Leiden: Brill, 1972], 117–45). Preuss's extreme views have elicited strong resistance (Steiert, *Die Weisheit Israels—ein Fremdkörper im Alten Testament?*).

7. Von Rad, *Wisdom in Israel*, 24–50.
8. William McKane, *Prophets and Wise Men* (*SBT* 1/44; London: SCM, 1965). The key texts are Isa. 5:19–24; 10:13ff.; 19:11–13; 29:14–16; 30:1–5; 31:1–3; Jer. 49:7; Ezek. 28:2ff. Weeks, *Early Israelite Wisdom*, 70–72, discounts the evidence, pointing out that some of the charges concern attitudes wholly alien to Wisdom literature. Weeks's point would be persuasive if polemicists always accurately described the views they opposed. That they did not can be seen from Elihu's clumsy attributions of words to Job that he did not utter (e.g., Job 34:5–6) and from the caricature of Qoheleth's teaching by the author of Wisdom of Solomon in 2:1–20.
9. Preservation, rather than composition, appears to be the function of Hezekiah's men indicated by the verb *he'tîqû* (Prov. 25:1).
10. Miriam Lichtheim, *AEL*, 1:184 considers this instruction humor in the service of literary satire. A prologue and an epilogue frame the actual instruction, which treats eighteen professions. A few examples illustrate the humor. The smith has fingers like claws of a crocodile and stinks more than fish roe; the potter grubs in mud more than a pig; the farmer wails more than a guinea fowl; the weaver is worse off than a woman; the cobbler is well if one is well with corpses.
11. Oda Wischmeyer, *Die Kultur des Buches Jesus Sirach* (BZNW 77; Berlin: de Gruyter, 1995), discusses the stratification of Jewish society in Ben Sira's day: rulers, the rich, the high priest, physicians, scribes, merchants, artisans, and peasants.
12. Whybray, *Intellectual Tradition*, passim; and von Rad, *Wisdom in Israel*, 17.
13. The matter is considerably more complex, however, as R. N. Whybray, *Wealth and Poverty in the Book of Proverbs* (JSOTSup 99; Sheffield: JSOT, 1990), indicates. He discerns four types of social milieu: the court, educated urban society, prosperous farmers, and small farmers earning a precarious living. The sentence literature (10:1–22:16; chaps. 25–29; 24:23–34; 5:15–23; 6:1–19) derives from small farmers for whom life was precarious, whereas the instructions in 22:17–24:22 and chaps. 1–9 come from a well-to-do urban society, one eager to get to the top. The view expressed in 31:1–9 is that of someone already at the top; similarly, 31:10–31 describes a family that has achieved success.
14. Hans Heinrich Schmid, *Wesen und Geschichte der Weisheit* (BZAW 101; Berlin: Töpelmann, 1966), 155.
15. The formal similarity between this preface and Egyptian Instructions, particularly *Amenemope*, does not extend to function and addresses. Both Prov. 1:2–7 and *Amenemope* use infinitives, but the Egyptian text addresses courtiers while Prov. 1:2–7 reaches out to everyone, beginner and advanced thinker alike.
16. George M. Landes, "Jonah: A *Māšāl?*" in *Israelite Wisdom*, ed. Gammie et al., 137–58.
17. On riddles, see my entry, "Riddle," *IDBSup*, 749–50; and *Samson: A Secret Betrayed, a Vow Ignored* (Atlanta: John Knox, 1978), 99–120. A genuine riddle uses ciphers (or symbolic language) that furnish a clue to the riddle's meaning but include a hidden trap at the same time.
18. Shupak, *Where Can Wisdom Be Found?* 55–57, 277–80. The epilogue of *The Instruction of Ptahhotep* focuses attention on the necessity of hearing, that is, obeying.
19. See Wis. 7:1–6 in particular, where the infancy of Solomon is recalled, and 9:10–18, where a Hellenistic view of the body as a heavy intellectual burden to the spirit surfaces.

20. *The Instruction of Ani* (*ANET*, 420–21). See also *The Instruction of Dua-Khety*, or *The Satire on The Trades*: "Praise God for your father, your mother, who set you on the path of life!" (*COS* 1:125).

21. Would the thought of purchasing wisdom have arisen if such a practice did not exist in the wider environment? On schools in Israel, see David M. Carr, *Writing on the Tablet of the Heart: Origins of Scripture and Literature* (New York: Oxford University, 2004); James L. Crenshaw, *Education in Ancient Israel* (New York: Doubleday, 1998); idem, "Education in Ancient Israel," *JBL* 104 (1985): 601–15 (*UAPQ*, 235–49); Graham I. Davies, "Were There Schools in Ancient Israel?" in *Wisdom in Ancient Israel*, ed. Day et al., 199–211; and less cautiously, Heaton, *School Tradition*.

22. Svend Holm-Nielsen, "On the Interpretation of Qoheleth in Early Christianity," *VT* 24 (1974): 168–77; G. T. Sheppard, "The Epilogue to Qoheleth as Theological Commentary," *CBQ* 39 (1977): 182–89; and Martin A. Shields, *The End of Wisdom: A Reappraisal of the Historical and Canonical Function of Ecclesiastes* (Winona Lake, Ind.: Eisenbrauns, 2006).

23. In the area of aesthetics the distance between modern tastes and those of ancient peoples increases sharply. Note that the remark about Qoheleth's aesthetic interest does not state that he actually succeeded in finding pleasing words. It merely says that "Qoheleth sought to find pleasing words."

24. Surprisingly, Ben Sira never points to specifics of ritual law, and even his allusions to ethical teachings are somewhat random. He does, however, encourage financial support of priests.

25. See above all the excellent discussions by Samuel L. Adams, *Wisdom in Transition: Act and Consequence in Second Temple Instructions* (JSJSup 125; Leiden: Brill, 2008); and J. Edward Wright, *The Early History of Heaven* (Oxford: Oxford University, 2000).

26. Wischmeyer, *Die Kultur des Buches Jesus Sirach*, 175–76.

27. This statement does not imply that such forms have no affinities with nonwisdom texts, for prophets employed aphorisms and allegories, priests and lyrical poets wrote laments and hymns, genealogists and historiographers compiled lists. Therefore, form alone cannot suffice to set Wisdom literature off from all the rest.

28. A fuller discussion of these forms appears in my essay, "Wisdom," in *Old Testament Form Criticism*, ed. John H. Hayes (San Antonio: Trinity University, 1974), 225–64; especially 229–62. See also von Rad, *Wisdom in Israel*, 24–50; Roland E. Murphy, *Wisdom Literature* (FOTL; Grand Rapids: Eerdmans, 1981); and Philip Johannes Nel, *The Structure and Ethos of the Wisdom Admonitions in Proverbs* (BZAW 158; Berlin: de Gruyter, 1982).

29. For discussion of tension between form and content, see James L. Crenshaw, "When Form and Content Clash: The Theology of Job 38:1–40:5," in *Creation in the Biblical Tradition*, ed. R. Clifford and J. J. Collins (CBQMS 24; Washington, D.C.: Catholic Biblical Association, 1992), 70–84 (*UAPQ*, 455–67).

30. Von Rad, "Job XXXVIII and Ancient Egyptian Wisdom," in *SAIW*, 267–77, and Albrecht Alt, "Solomonic Wisdom," in *SAIW*, 102–112.

31. Whybray, *Intellectual Tradition*, 155, concedes this danger. Use of themes to identify the particular concerns of sages also runs this risk, inasmuch as some concerns were shared by representatives of several groups.

32. The most extensive investigation of sapiential vocabulary is that of Shupak, *Where Can Wisdom Be Found?* She isolates twenty-four expressions and collocations that occur only in Wisdom literature (pp. 338–40). Perdue, *Sword and Stylus*, 161–65, lists what he considers wisdom terminology in the Psalter.

33. See James L. Crenshaw, "Method in Determining Wisdom Influence upon 'Historical' Literature," *JBL* 88 (1969): 129–42 (*UAPQ*, 312–25); and Donn F. Morgan, *Wisdom in the Old Testament Traditions* (Atlanta: John Knox, 1981).

34. Johannes Fichtner, "Isaiah Among the Wise," in *SAIW*, 429–38.

35. J. William Whedbee, *Isaiah and Wisdom* (Nashville: Abingdon, 1971); and Joseph Jensen, *The Use of Tôrâ by Isaiah* (CBQMS, 3; Washington, D.C.: Catholic Biblical Association of America, 1973).

36. Amos's connection with this town has been interpreted as evidence that he came under the influence of sages. The argument depends on a questionable reading of the adjective *ḥākām* that describes the woman of Tekoa as well as the assumption that the town must have been a center of the wise. Neither seems likely. For discussion, see Samuel Terrien, "Amos and Wisdom," in *SAIW*, 448–55; Hans Walter Wolff, *Amos the Prophet: The Man and His Background*, trans. Foster R. McCarley (Philadelphia: Fortress, 1973); idem, *Joel and Amos*, trans. Waldemar Janzen et al. (Hermeneia; Philadelphia: Fortress, 1977); and James L. Crenshaw, "The Influence of the Wise upon Amos," *ZAW* 79 (1967): 42–52.

37. H. W. Wolff, "Micah the Moreshite—The Prophet and His Background," in *Israelite Wisdom*, ed. Gammie et al., 77–84.

38. Landes, "Jonah: A *Māšāl?*" in *Israelite Wisdom*, ed. Gammie et al., 137–58; Phyllis Trible, "Studies in the Book of Jonah," Ph.D. diss., Columbia University, 1963.

39. Donald Gowan, "Habakkuk and Wisdom," *Perspective* 9 (1968): 157–66. Theodicy actually permeates prophetic literature, on which see James L. Crenshaw, "Theodicy and Prophetic Literature," in *Theodicy in the World of the Bible*, ed. Antii Laato and Johannes C. de Moor (Leiden: Brill, 2003), 236–55; and idem, "Theodicy in the Book of the Twelve," in *Thematic Threads in the Book of the Twelve*, ed. Paul L. Redditt and Aaron Schart (BZAW 325; Berlin: de Gruyter, 2003), 175–91.

40. R. N. Whybray, *The Succession Narrative* (SBT 2/9; London: SCM, 1968), has understood this literary complex as an attempt to illustrate truths resting in canonical proverbs. Wisdom, in his view, provides the impetus for this material.

41. Hans J. Hermisson, "Weisheit und Geschichte," in *Probleme biblische Theologie: Gerhard von Rad zum 70. Geburtstag*, ed. Hans Walter Wolff (Munich: Kaiser, 1971), 136–54.

42. Von Rad, "The Joseph Narrative and Ancient Wisdom," in *SAIW*, 439–47. T. A. Perry, *God's Twilight Zone: Wisdom in the Hebrew Bible* (Peabody, Mass.: Hendrickson, 2008), 3–91, thinks that Genesis reflects extensive sapiential influence (he sees a similar influence in the stories about Samson and Saul).

43. Shemaryahu Talmon, "Wisdom in the Book of Esther," *VT* 13 (1963): 419–55. See also L. Wills, "The Court Legend in Post-Exilic Judaism," Ph.D. diss., Harvard University, 1987.

44. Luis Alonso Schökel, "Sapiential and Covenant Themes in Genesis 2–3," in *SAIW*, 468–80.

45. John McKenzie, "Reflections on Wisdom," *JBL* 86 (1967): 1–9.

46. R. C. Dentan, "The Literary Affinities of Exod. XXXIV 6f.," *VT* 13 (1963): 34–51.

47. Moshe Weinfeld, "The Origin of Humanism in Deuteronomy," *JBL* 80 (1961): 241–47; "Deuteronomy—The Present State of Inquiry," *JBL* 86 (1967): 249–62; idem, *Deuteronomy and the Deuteronomic School* (1972;

repr., Winona Lake, Ind.: Eisenbrauns, 1992); C. Brekelmans, "Wisdom Influence in Deuteronomy," in *La Sagesse de l'Ancien Testament*, ed. Gilbert, 28–38, takes an opposing view.

48. Von Rad, *Wisdom in Israel*, 263–83, and Armin Lange, *Weisheit und Prädestination: Weisheitliche Urordnung und Prädestination in den Textfunden von Qumran* (STDJ 18; Leiden: Brill, 1995).

49. For research in Wisdom literature, see Crenshaw, *UAPQ*, 1–140 (indeed, 1–596); Roland E. Murphy, "Wisdom in the Old Testament," *ABD*, 6:920–31; idem, "Hebrew Wisdom," *JAOS* 101 (1981): 21–34; Holger Delkurt, "Grundprobleme alttestamentlicher Weisheit," *Verkündigung und Forschung* 36 (1991): 38–71; Westermann, *Forschungsgeschichte zur Weisheitsliteratur*; Brunner, *Altägyptische Weisheit*; R. J. Williams, "The Sages of Ancient Egypt in the Light of Recent Scholarship," *JAOS* 101 (1981): 1–19; Gammie and Perdue, eds., *The Sage in Israel and the Ancient Near East*; Perdue et al., eds., *In Search of Wisdom*; Day et al., eds., *Wisdom in Ancient Israel*; Collins, *Jewish Wisdom in the Hellenistic Age*; and Barré, ed., *Wisdom, You Are My Sister*. The following surveys of research in Wisdom literature provide further information about the course of scholarship: Walter Baumgartner, "The Wisdom Literature," in *The Old Testament and Modern Study*, ed. H. H. Rowley (Oxford: Oxford University, 1951), 210–37; Crenshaw, "Prolegomenon," in *SAIW*, 1–45 (46–60, bibliography); idem, "The Wisdom Literature," in *The Hebrew Bible and Its Modern Interpreters*, ed. D. A. Knight and Gene Tucker (Chico, Calif.: Scholars, 1985), 369–407; John Emerton, "Wisdom," in *Tradition and Interpretation*, ed. George W. Anderson (Oxford: Oxford University, 1979), 214–37; Maurice Gilbert, "Avant-propos," in *La Sagesse de l'Ancien Testament*, ed. Gilbert, 7–13; Roland E. Murphy, "Assumptions and Problems in Old Testament Wisdom Research," *CBQ* 29 (1967): 102–12 (407–18); and R. B. Y. Scott, "The Study of Wisdom Literature," *Int* 24 (1970): 20–45.

Chapter 2

The Sapiential Tradition

The thesis that Israel's sages made up a distinct professional class gains further support from a consciousness that the wise endeavored to transmit a valued tradition. Job's friend, Eliphaz, interjects the following remark:

> I will show you, listen to me;
>> what I have seen I will declare
> What sages have told,
>> and their ancestors have not hidden. . . .
>> (Job 15:17–18)

The sense of urgency that prompted a desire to pass along vital insights underlies the father's plea to be heard, which occurs frequently in Proverbs. Even a sage like the author of Ecclesiastes, who stands in open opposition to "school" tradition,[1] finds it impossible to *ignore* that sapiential tradition. The central figure in that tradition was King Solomon. In what follows, we shall examine the traditions about Solomon as Israel's greatest sage. Clarification of this significant elevation of a royal figure should enable us to grasp the manner in which other sapiential traditions emerged.

SOLOMON AS SAGE PAR EXCELLENCE

Tantalizingly enigmatic language characterizes the story describing the unnamed Queen of Sheba's visit to Jerusalem for the purpose of testing Solomon's wisdom (by means of riddles [*bĕḥîdôt*] 1 Kgs. 10:1–13). Certain phrases tease the imagination in extraordinary fashion. Drawn by the legendary language of hyperbole, the references to gold, precious stones, spices, and the allusion to "the half has not been told," Jewish weavers of fantasy readily seized upon these provocative expressions and turned Solomon into a king on the make.[2] The summary statement, "And King Solomon gave to the Queen of Sheba all that she desired," explodes with eroticism when set alongside the comment that "there was no more strength in her" and "there was nothing hidden from the king." Later fantasy substituted a son for the queen's squandered energy, and identified him with Israel's notorious enemy, Nebuchadnezzar.

The queen's loyal subjects engaged in flights of fantasy too, hoping to capitalize on the result of honor's compromise. In Ethiopian legend Solomon had his way with the queen through subterfuge, and the son born to their brief union brought divine favor and presence with him to Ethiopia. Two different traditions tell of the deceitful way Solomon gained access to the queen. In both she agreed to share Solomon's bedroom if he would not force her, but promised that if she ate anything during the night he could cohabit with her. Each story describes Solomon's treachery. In one, he served an exceedingly salty meal, making her thirsty for water conveniently placed by her bed. In the other, he suspended honey from the ceiling, and its fragrance eventually enticed her to reach out for it. The young son born from Solomon's act of lust and deceit later visited his father in Jerusalem; after a short stay at the court, he returned to Ethiopia, and a retinue of Hebrew sages were so impressed by Solomon's son that they followed him to Ethiopia and took along the sacred ark.

Arabic and Christian legend embellished the story even more, now at the expense of Sheba's queen. In these stories she appears as a demon, and Solomon used his wits to discover her true nature. In some versions he applied a special depilatory and removed ugly hairs from her feet; in others the ass-footed demon refused to cross a bridge because she knew that the cross on which Jesus was to be slain would come from its wood. In medieval legend riddles were supplied for the story, and the scene depicting the queen's visit adorns tapestries and tavern walls throughout Europe. Even the oldest collection of Germanic riddles, the Strassburg Book of Riddles,[3] contains a woodcutting that depicts Solomon and the Queen of Sheba. The latter presents him with two bouquets of flowers, one real and one artificial, asking him to identify each. Hovering over the genuine flowers is a bee, a messenger of truth to Solomon.

An impregnable mountain called Fantasy stands between biblical interpreters and the historical Solomon.[4] In all his glory King Solomon compares unfavorably with lilies of the field, but none born of woman can compel him to stand aside when awards for fame are passed out. If Solomon were to accompany the goddess Inanna into the underworld, perhaps we could finally observe the real Solomon, stripped of all trappings of wealth.[5] Sheol, unfortunately, is not peopled with creatures who function to remove pieces of apparel. The task, it follows, is to scale the mountain of tradition.

Disregarding the aforementioned Jewish, Ethiopic, Christian, and Arabic legends, we come to yet earlier speculation about Solomon's wisdom, a theme running through the apocryphal Wisdom of Solomon. The association of his name with a text written in Greek is a derivative tradition. The legend, by this time full blown, prompts talk about a marriage between Solomon and Wisdom, now understood as divine hypostasis, the earthly expression of God's intelligence. "I loved her and sought her from my youth, and I desired to take her for my bride, and I became enamored of her beauty" (Wis. 8:2). Here and throughout this section is a midrash upon a legend in 1 Kings 3:3–14, God's unlimited offer to Solomon and the young king's request for wisdom.

Another book, Ecclesiastes, halfheartedly attempts the literary fiction of Solomonic authorship, although his name is never given. Instead, the author adopts the title Qoheleth, perhaps with reference to Solomon as a gatherer of women, and speaks of himself as "the son of David, king in Jerusalem" (Eccl. 1:1). In this same vein, Solomon's name is associated with the superlative songs celebrating the joys of sex. Here one reads in the opening line: "The Song of Songs, which is Solomon's." Elsewhere Solomon is mentioned, however, in the third person (1:5; 3:7, 9, 11; 8:11–12).

Certain superscriptions in collections of biblical Proverbs derive from an earlier period, though still looking back upon the era of Hezekiah when wisdom flourished. Information gleaned from the book of Isaiah confirms the presence of an active group of sages at this time, prompting considerable discussion of Isaiah and wisdom. Essentially three forms of superscription occur in Proverbs: (1) "The proverbs of Solomon" (10:1); (2) "The proverbs of Solomon, son of David, king of Israel" (1:1); and (3) "These also are proverbs of Solomon that the men of Hezekiah king of Judah copied" (25:1, my trans.). Perhaps these men of Hezekiah who presumably transmitted and copied proverbial collections link up with a phrase uttered by the Queen of Sheba (1 Kgs. 10:8). That expression, "Happy are your men," need not be emended. David surrounded himself with his own entourage, skilled warriors with special responsibilities, and Hezekiah seems to have done the same thing. Since mastery of one's emotions is preferable to physical prowess (Prov. 16:32), Hezekiah's men may indeed have been sages rather than warriors.

Mention of Solomon within at least one of the superscriptions (Prov. 25:1) to the various collections of Proverbs postdates Hezekiah. Another derives from a period sufficiently removed from Solomon's monarchy to necessitate an identifying qualification ("son of David, king of Israel," 1:1). Only one superscription (10:1) has any claim to an earlier period than Hezekiah, and it can hardly be dated. In short, nothing within the superscriptions demands a date prior to the eighth or seventh century. This fact must be kept in mind when raising the larger question of compositional dates for the several proverbial collections.

Positive proof of a tenth-century date for certain proverbs still would not require us to ascribe Solomonic authorship to them, although making it a live option. Thus far no demonstration of a tenth-century date for Proverbs has appeared, even if the trend to consider the major collections to derive from the period of the monarchy seems correct for all but the first (Proverbs 1–9).[6]

Solomon in the Deuteronomistic History

The Deuteronomistic Historian preserves three further narratives that throw considerable light on the tradition of Solomonic wisdom. In each of these, Solomon's dream at Gibeon (1 Kgs. 3:4–15), the royal judgment in a case of disputed parentage (3:16–28), and the king's literary activity (4:29–34 [Heb. 5:9–14]), Deuteronomistic language and vocabulary that is typical of predominately late literary works abounds. In addition, each story makes copious use of stylistic traits and motifs typical of legend. Any attempt to peel away legendary accretions in search of historical record cannot succeed unless these fictional aspects of the stories are taken with utmost seriousness.

The account of Solomon's dream at Gibeon constitutes an early defense of that cult center. Its preservation in the Deuteronomistic History is astonishing, since exclusive worship at a central sanctuary in Jerusalem plays such an important role in that work. This special plea in Gibeon's behalf reflects the practice of incubation, by which a devotee of a particular deity slept at a sanctuary hoping to receive a visit from the god in question. The story teems with features that do not belong within wisdom texts, suggesting that the gift of wisdom is either a secondary development or more probably that the language about wisdom is used in a general rather than a technical sense. Within wisdom literature only in the early second-century Sirach do we encounter the description of Israel as God's chosen people who are so numerous they cannot be counted. What is more, dreams play virtually no role in sapiential texts, although this particular incident may explain Ben Sira's ambivalence toward them.[7] On the one hand, he knows they pose a threat to individuals, but he also recognizes that God may use dreams to accomplish his will.

Actually, the putative "wisdom" language belongs to royal ceremony. The clue to such an understanding of the passage is provided by Solomon's formula of humility: "I am a little boy; I don't know how to go out or to come in" (1 Kgs. 3:7, my trans.).[8] Like kings throughout the ancient Near East, Solomon confesses his dependence on his god. Other features of this text recall Egyptian literature as well. In response to the blank check that God offered Solomon ("Ask what I shall give you" [my trans.]), the young king requested a *hearing heart* to judge God's people, discerning good and evil.[9] When a pleased God announced the gift that he intended to grant the pious ruler, he varied the language significantly: "I give you a wise heart and unparalleled understanding" (my trans.). Naturally, Solomon received as bonus those things on which he was discreetly silent: riches and honor.

The story about two harlots (1 Kgs. 3:16–28), intricately connected with this account of God's gift to Solomon, demonstrates the king's hearing heart to judge God's people.[10] Even those individuals having no social status stand boldly before the divine representative, who disseminates pure justice. The tale, a polished narrative, begs to be analyzed in depth. Such an explication would begin with the excessive wordiness of the two women, which undoubtedly signifies their extreme nervousness in the presence of royalty. The first harlot takes great pains to rule out the possibility of a guilty third person: "We two were together in the same house, and there was no one else, just the two of us" (my trans.). Later both harlots press their claims with complete abandon, provoking the king to describe the dilemma facing him in their own words: the one says "the living child is mine, and the dead one hers" (my trans.) and the other says, "No, for your child is dead and mine is alive" (my trans.).

The story demonstrates rare psychological insight in yet another way. Solomon's verdict relies upon maternal instinct, a compassion for the fruit of the womb that rarely abandons mothers. Strangely, the narrator seems compelled to explain this reality, lest simpleminded persons miss it. Nevertheless, a curious silence reigns with regard to the reasons prompting the original exchange of the dead boy for the living one under cloak of darkness, for one can assume that a child was no great blessing to a harlot. The story is entirely consistent, for it also explains why the mother of the live child woke up early in the morning; she was motivated by a desire to nurse the infant.

Solomon's test brought out the basest and noblest feelings within the two women. The threat of cutting the child into two halves, each to be presented to one of the harlots, evoked tender compassion from the true mother, but it also provoked bitter resentment within the woman who had accidentally smothered her own son. Here is a singular example of a king's hearing heart for judging between good and evil. Such a wise king can speak with utter confidence: "Give her the living child, and by no means kill it; she is his mother" (my trans.).

Now all Israel saw evidence that God's wisdom rested upon King Solomon. In all fairness, we must acknowledge that the basic story antedates Israel's king by quite some time and surfaces in many different cultures. As many as twenty-two variants of the story have been located, the earliest of which is thought to come from India.[11] Like the pregnant motif of the "third day," which also occurs in this story and often elsewhere to signify a significant liminal moment, a point of transition in ancient literature,[12] this incident was popular far and wide, since it honored the ruler and assured everyone that justice lay within his or her grasp. It follows that this story has been adapted by the Israelite narrator and secondarily applied to Solomon. Hence it hardly supplies authentic material about Solomon.

The third narrative alludes to Solomon's skill at coining proverbs and songs, praising him as superior to all peoples of the East and of Egypt (4:29–34 [Heb. 5:9–14]). Four persons renowned for their wisdom are mentioned (Ethan the Ezrahite, Heman, Calcol and Darda, sons of Mahol). The number of proverbs ascribed to Solomon is three thousand; his songs are set at one thousand and five. Their subject matter includes trees, beasts, birds, reptiles, and fish. Within canonical Wisdom literature we search in vain for proverbs and songs that deal with these topics. The brief miscellaneous collection of numerical proverbs in Proverbs 30 constitutes the single exception. In short, Solomon's literary works either were nonexistent or have disappeared.

Another text throws indirect light upon traditions about Solomon. Deuteronomy 17:14–20 warns against enthroning a king who will multiply horses, wives, silver, and gold. Few scholars today doubt that Solomon sat for this portrait, one that must have appealed greatly to King Hezekiah, who, thanks to the Assyrian military machine, no longer had a rival on the throne at Samaria and, like Solomon, was free to dream great things. Since wisdom is missing from this passage reflecting the Solomonic tradition, perhaps we should discount the text altogether. Silence with regard to the function of wisdom at the royal court, however, may be more significant than it appears on the surface.

Scattered stories within the Hebrew Bible register suspicion about wisdom, since it can be used to accomplish dubious ends.[13] The old story about the crafty serpent who seduced the first woman (and indirectly man) to rebel against external authority demonstrates an awareness of wisdom's questionable features from ancient times. Similarly, the description of Jonadab as clever enough to devise a means for Amnon to obtain his dishonorable wishes with Tamar, his half sister, shows the widespread knowledge of wisdom's devious ends in Israel. When one also considers the incidents involving the wise woman of Teqoa[14] and the wise mother in Abel,[15] both of whom use their craftiness to achieve at the very least questionable goals, it is clear that the negative attitude toward wisdom made its presence felt in the Israelite community. The prominence that foreign powers gave to its sages, and the conflicts arising within the political arena, naturally strengthened this suspicion with regard to wisdom. Small wonder wisdom was not viewed as an attribute of God until quite late in the Hebrew Bible,[16] for those humans who acquired *ḥokmâ* did not always use it to accomplish noble goals.

Now the Deuteronomist may have known this negative attitude toward wisdom and subscribed to it. If so, his failure to mention wisdom in this portrait of Solomon may indicate that the legend about that king's mastery of wisdom had not yet arisen.

In sum, our examination of the biblical traditions about Solomon's wisdom discovers no shred of evidence deriving from the era of that king. Instead, every account teems with material typical of popular legend and folklore. The only possible authentic allusion, Solomon's reputation for composing proverbs and songs with a subject matter vastly different from those preserved within the canon, is so full of legend that fact cannot be separated from fiction.

Explanations for Solomon's Reputation as a Sage

Our ascent of the mountain constructed by biblical legend has led us to a vantage point from which we perceive still another peak obscured by low-lying clouds. That range of mountains has been erected by scholars reflecting upon biblical materials. For a brief moment the burning sun penetrates the clouds and illuminates one pathway that leads directly to the top. Signs along the way read "Le mirage salomonien" and "Solomon's posthumous reputation for wisdom."[17] One well-known traveler along this route refuses to mention Solomon at all in a comprehensive study of ancient oriental wisdom in its Israelite-Jewish configuration.[18] To these journeyers, the legendary mountain poses no obstacle. Wisdom and Solomon have nothing to do with one another.

For others, the reality of the mountain is beyond question, having been founded on solid fact rather than legend.[19] Accordingly, new mounds of dirt and stone are forever brought to the mountain. Let us examine this glorification of Solomon by modern exegetes.

Perhaps the least satisfactory view is that which attributes proverbs and songs to Solomon, but explains their disappearance as the result of their inferior quality. When judged against standards that later sages achieved, Solomon's attempts at composition paled. More importantly, by the time the various proverbial collections were taking final shape, the Solomonic songs and proverbs had become archaic beyond comprehension.[20] The essential flaw in this argument lies in the consequent loss of an explanation for the son of David's reputation for exceptional wisdom. If Solomon's contribution to the literary heritage of the ancient sages possessed only momentary value and if the compositions were mediocre, why did the wise honor him as sage par excellence?

A more attractive hypothesis draws heavily on parallels in Egypt and Mesopotamia, where noun lists (onomastica) functioned as a means of ordering the vast store of knowledge achieved by students of nature.[21] The subject matter of Solomon's proverbs and songs, according to 1 Kings 4:33 (Heb. 5:13), resembles these noun lists more than so-called Solomonic proverbs within the Bible.

"He would speak of trees, from the cedar that is in the Lebanon to the hyssop that grows in the wall; he would speak of animals, and birds, and reptiles, and fish." With the exception of a few numerical sayings in Proverbs 30, the proverbial teachings of the wise manifest little interest in categorizing natural phenomena. It follows that the Israelite beginnings in natural science were lost to posterity, although not as a result of their inferiority. On the contrary, Solomon adapted such noun lists to his own use, transforming them into poetic compositions. This demonstration of originality, daring, and ability explains the honor bestowed upon Israel's king, who surpassed the renowned sages of the east.

While such an explanation for the disparity between the tradition in 1 Kings 4:32–33 (Heb. 5:12–13) and the actual content of canonical proverbs is inherently plausible, it rests upon several dubious assumptions. The first concerns the nondidactic character of our lists as opposed to the moralizing tendency within biblical proverbs that allude to animals, insects, and the like. What precludes an interpretation of Solomon's proverbs and songs from the background of these sayings that draw lessons from the world of nature? Stated another way, what requires a jump from natural phenomena to noun lists? The supposed onomastica within the divine speeches recorded in the book of Job[22] function as a powerful lesson that those who think they can tell God how to govern the universe should master their own little world before trying to branch out to the remote reaches of space.

Another objection centers on the claim that Solomon's superiority over other sages arose from poetic craft. Nothing supports the view that Solomon freely rendered noun lists into poetic form. On the face of it, the text suggests that his superiority derived from the vast number of proverbs and songs, for the clear emphasis lies there rather than on their external form.

A third objection presents itself as particularly forceful: such proverbs and songs may have constituted riddles and fables that became lost over the years. Since animals, trees, and insects are essential to these literary forms, and Israel's sages undoubtedly composed enigmatic sayings, this explanation is more natural than resorting to onomastica for which no clear evidence exists within biblical wisdom. In short, why appeal to Egyptian and Mesopotamian texts for clarification of 1 Kings 4:32–33 when a better explanation can be formulated on the basis of Israel's sapiential literature?

These observations demonstrate the difficulties accompanying every attempt to view 1 Kings 4:32–33 as reliable information about King Solomon. A negative decision with regard to the historicity of this text does not preclude Solomonic literary activity, although it renders such unlikely. One could still associate Solomon with Israel's sages in another manner. He may very well have functioned as "patron of the arts," and in this capacity the full weight of royal privilege and resources may have become accessible to the sages. Solomon's bold attempt to establish a government faintly resembling the Egyptian pattern lends credibility to this hypothesis of royal patronage for wisdom, but the case is by no means established beyond reasonable doubt.

If in truth the king did take an active interest in promoting the intellectual life of his court, the era may have become significant in shaping the literary traditions of ancient Israel, as many interpreters believe.[23] Such a burst of activity may have vastly extended the scope of knowledge in tenth-century Jerusalem, particularly with respect to models for conduct, a cultivation of the individual, a nursing of rhetoric, and scientific interests. Naturally, this new departure would have maintained an openness to knowledge acquired from all peoples, so that a humanistic spirit emerged and focused upon psychological insights into what it means to be truly human. Perhaps such humanism gave birth to a radically new understanding of God's activity among the people. No longer breaking into ordinary events, God's actions could now be perceived only by eyes of faith, and a distant Lord accomplishes his purpose through human agents. Hidden within this understanding of divine activity was the seed that soon sprouted and grew into full-blown skepticism.[24]

While this elevation of the Solomonic era may be reasonably accurate, it remains a hypothesis for which little supportive evidence exists. For that reason alone, the phrase "Solomonic enlightenment" seems inappropriate.[25] In short, the theory of a Solomonic enlightenment claims that the old view of things, that is, pansacralism, vanished with this era, and in its place a fresh breeze of humanism swept through the royal court. In truth, secularistic and sacral thinking existed alongside each other from the very beginning. The most that can reliably be asserted is that the emphasis may have shifted appreciably in Solomon's day, but even the literature that supposedly dates from this period bears distinctive signs of sacral thinking. Clearly, the conviction that God honors certain sacred acts thrives within the Succession Narrative (2 Samuel 9–20; 1 Kings 1–2) and the Joseph story. Nevertheless, the Samson saga provides strong evidence that secularism invaded the bastion of pansacrality long before the era of Solomon, for the earlier form of Samson's heroic exploits must surely antedate the tenth century. When this datum is added to the sacral emphases within the Succession Narrative (for example, David's consulting the Lord at crucial times, his submission before the power of a curse, obedience to a prophetic oracle, agonizing in prayer before God on behalf of his sick child, and his devoted servants' selfless act in pouring out water acquired at great peril), the weakness of the claim that the sacral interpretation of reality disappeared with the Solomonic era becomes apparent.

Even the thesis that a fresh wave of humanism and concern for the individual characterized the period overlooks harsh reality, for Solomon stopped at nothing to fill the royal coffers. The era of his rule was almost unrivaled for tyranny in ancient Israel; oppression of subjects who were forced to perform the labor of slaves and from whom exorbitant taxes were exacted ruled the day. While such cruelty could go hand in hand with scholarly activity of an unprecedented nature, this suppression of human beings demands that one use the word "enlightenment" cautiously if at all.

Although Solomon's connections with Egypt were sealed through royal marriage, the leap to sponsorship of sapiential activity is a major one. Supportive evidence does not necessarily come from royal liturgies within Isaiah 9 and 11, for such texts inevitably emphasize a king's exceptional wisdom. Canaanite concepts reflected in Ezekiel 28 furnish a satisfactory background for convictions that the ruler possesses wisdom sufficient for the task committed to him. As for the presence of counselors in David's court, nothing requires an interpretation of the word *yôʿāṣîm* (counselors) as a technical term for sages.[26] As a matter of fact, Ahithophel and Hushai function in a purely political role.

To recapitulate, biblical traditions about Solomon's extraordinary wisdom are late legends, while the fame he enjoys among biblical interpreters is equally undeserved. How did Solomon's connections with wisdom arise? One answer is that such legends grew because they were grounded in fact. The decisive factor in this view has been the disparity between biblical proverbs and the reputed character of Solomon's literary compositions. Another explanation for the legends can be given, one so simple that it conceals its cogency. According to the fundamental premise of the wise, the orderliness of creation (or stated another way, belief in the calculable quality of reality), wisdom leads to life, folly to death. In a word, wisdom secures one's being, granting wealth and happiness.

The significance of this profound faith cannot be exaggerated for the entire wisdom corpus, even if it functions as a foil for Ecclesiastes.

Now the equation of wisdom and wealth in old wisdom leads naturally to the conclusion that since Solomon was the wealthiest man in Israel's history, it follows that he must have been the wisest. Legends about his prowess in wisdom constitute the faith of the wise in their universe. These legends take as their point of departure the ancient claim about royal wisdom, originally understood in a general sense. From here they move to wondrous legendary wisdom and make of Solomon the sage par excellence. Indeed, they leave strong clues behind, particularly in the story about the Queen of Sheba's visit. Here wisdom and wealth have kissed each other and consummated their marriage. Therefore the strange emphasis upon wealth in the legend about Solomon's wisdom does not clash with the rest of the story after all.

Once Solomon is thought of as a sage surpassing all others, he embraces all types of wisdom. Accordingly, legends grow up demonstrating his skill in drawing lessons from natural phenomena, his judicial wisdom, and his ability to discover the mysteries of life. About Solomon as sage par excellence it can be said:

> It is the glory of God to conceal things,
>> but the glory of kings is to search things out.
>> (Prov. 25:2)

Over time the canonical principle latches onto this glorification of Solomon, attaching to his name the third division of the Hebrew Bible. Moses dispenses law, Solomon, wisdom.

THE ANCIENT NEAR EASTERN CONTEXT

A single feature of the Solomonic tradition strikes readers as strange beyond measure: the comparison of Solomon's wisdom with that of non-Israelite sages. One can hardly imagine a prophetic narrative that placed a Yahwistic prophet alongside a Baalistic one, even if Yahweh's spokesman were ranked first. This unusual feature of wisdom furnishes a clue to the international character of the sapiential tradition. We shall examine non-Israelite wisdom later on, but wish at this time to paint that phenomenon in broad strokes.

Both Egypt and Mesopotamia had a flourishing wisdom tradition, consisting of professional sages who composed extensive literary works that manifest remarkable thematic and formal coherence.[27] In Egypt those writings included instructions and reflections upon life's deeper mysteries. Such texts functioned within the royal court as a means of educating future courtiers, and in time produced a scribal profession that looked upon other vocations as inferior to their own exalted one. Similarly, texts from Mesopotamian wisdom preserve valiant gropings with the problem of human suffering, but they also contain collections of popular proverbs.

This literature manifests an international spirit, inasmuch as it speaks about truths that present themselves to persistent inquirers regardless of the historical context. Moreover, a strong humanism pervades the tradition, although that optimism regarding human potential springs from a conviction that God has created the universe orderly. Furthermore a tinge of eudaemonism, or indulgent self-interest, persists in the sapiential worldview, since the created order has been programmed to reward virtue and punish vice. Naturally, this wisdom tradition had no place for special revelation beyond the secrets of the universe implanted there at the moment of creation.

We shall see that the sapiential tradition throughout the ancient Near East was sufficiently uniform to permit the probable incorporation of a section from an Egyptian Instruction into the biblical book of Proverbs, and to prompt modern critics to label Mesopotamian texts a "Sumerian Job" and a "Babylonian Ecclesiastes." To be sure, significant differences exist among the three cultural contexts, but the idea of a sapiential tradition in the ancient Near East has considerable merit.

The locus of the sapiential tradition in Egypt was the pharaonic court, while Mesopotamian sages functioned primarily in a school, at times located in or near a temple. It follows that the different settings affected the character of the wisdom literature emerging from each group. Whereas Egyptian wisdom concentrated on providing instruction for successful life at the royal court, its Mesopotamian counterpart gave special consideration to assuring the good life by means of cultic practices. In Egypt a propagandistic tendency inserts itself into the literature, and in Mesopotamia expertise at interpreting signs or omens was cherished by the sages who earned their livelihood from such activity and from scribal duties that they performed for wealthy individuals.

What, then, was the setting for Israel's sapiential activity? We have seen that the Solomonic court left its mark on a tiny portion of canonical proverbs, although the allusion to the "men of Hezekiah" (Prov. 25:1) suggests that learned scribes, at least, must surely have functioned at the court in Jerusalem. The vast majority of biblical proverbs seems to have arisen in a context other than the royal court. That setting for numerous proverbs was the family, where parental instruction was very much at home. This ethos saw the virtual union of law and instruction, both of which carried the full authority of the patriarch. During this premonarchic and early monarchic period in Israel's history, careful observation of the immediate world paid significant dividends in the form of proverbs and maxims. Such sayings focused upon the agrarian enterprise, personal relationships, particularly sexual ones, self-control, and the many ways one could enrich or impoverish life. It seems likely therefore, that most biblical proverbs arose as folk sayings and were transmitted in a family setting.

To be sure, some canonical proverbs could easily have arisen within a court setting, although references to a king hardly demand such a conclusion. Many older proverbs could have been adapted for use in the royal court, however, since self-mastery was as much a desideratum in this setting as it was in the family. It follows that an origin in the family for most canonical proverbs does not necessarily exclude a subsequent function at the Jerusalemite court.

A third setting for sapiential activity manifests itself in Sirach, where one reads about a house of learning that stood in readiness for those who wished to pursue the scholarly vocation. From Ben Sira's remarks, such education was undoubtedly costly. Perhaps we can also conclude that the curriculum represented a convergence of sapiential and sacred traditions.[28] Whether that house of learning was distinct from the place of worship, or formed a vital part of the holy place, we cannot say with any confidence. In any case, the prominence of the school in the Hellenistic world probably stimulated the growth of a similar educational institution among Jews.[29]

To recapitulate, Israel's sapiential tradition seems to have arisen initially among ordinary people in small villages, perhaps flourishing subsequently at the royal court and eventually in houses of learning.

The question arises, then, about the actual dates of the various literary complexes that make up the wisdom corpus. Some canonical proverbs may have preceded the monarchy, others flourished during the exile, and the latest collection, Proverbs 1–9, may be postexilic. As we have seen, we cannot establish the dates of Job and Ecclesiastes with certainty, but Job was probably composed in the sixth century and Ecclesiastes in the late third. The situation is different with Sirach, for Ben Sira is known to have lived in the early second century. Since he includes a eulogy of the high priest Simon II, he must have composed his work between 190 and 180 BCE. Wisdom of Solomon comes from an even later time, perhaps the first century CE.

We shall discuss the themes that characterize the wisdom tradition in connection with the individual analyses of Proverbs, Job, Ecclesiastes, Sirach, and Wisdom of Solomon. Certain themes take on increasing significance within these books: the fear of the Lord, Yahweh's self-manifestation through personified Wisdom, the problem of innocent suffering, the meaning of life, the justification of God's ways, the limits of human knowledge, and the inevitability of death. Given the range of this literature, we may conclude that Israel's sages struggled with life's fundamental questions. Their way of addressing these issues, and the solutions they reached, stand as a perpetual witness to a remarkable group of people.

AN ENDLESS SEARCH

In a sense, the characteristic features of this significant class was its *pursuit* of insight, its search for the unknown. Indeed, the sages believed that God had hidden precious secrets from human eyes: God's glory was to conceal things. Over against this fact, sages juxtaposed human striving for knowledge, especially a king's attempt to fathom such mystery.

Where then does wisdom come from?
   And where is the place of understanding?
It is hidden from the eyes of all living,
   and concealed from the birds of the air.
Abaddon and Death say,
   "We have heard a rumor of it with our ears."
                       (Job 28:20–22)

This majestic poem goes on to say that God alone has access to wisdom, ultimately identifying religion with wisdom. Now if God has sole possession of wisdom it can be dispensed at will. The few persons who beat a path to wisdom's door come by way of prayer, as "Solomon" proclaims mightily in the wisdom book by his name.

I went about seeking how to get her for myself. . . .
But I perceived that I would not possess wisdom unless
   God gave her to me—
and it was a mark of insight to know whose gift she was—
so I appealed to the Lord and implored him,
and with my whole heart I said. . . .
                       (Wis. 8:18, 21)

The author of Tobit took issue with the sages' depiction of reality in terms of competing wills to conceal and to search out the hidden. Here the angel Raphael introduces a different contrast between God and kings. In his view, kings' secrets should remain closely guarded mysteries, whereas divine truth ought to be proclaimed far and wide. Twice the angel announces this variant to Proverbs 25:2.

It is good to conceal the secret of a king, but to acknowledge and reveal the works of God, and with fitting honor to acknowledge him. (Tob. 12:7, 11)

In this text two different kinds of secrets seem to be envisioned. Prudence dictates caution with regard to what kings desire to conceal from others, for the spreading of forbidden knowledge can serve no good purpose. By way of contrast, God's marvelous works should not be closely guarded secrets among a faithful few, but deserve royal heralds who will announce glad tidings throughout the universe.

These two texts deal with different realities. In one, the king clutches precious data to his chest while God allows free proclamation of divine works; in the other, kings eagerly search for what God presses to the bosom. Both perceptions capture distinct features of reality with which the sages wrestled. Some truths freely surrendered to royal search, while others refused to budge an inch. Perhaps that inconsistent response to the sages' quest arose from God's desire to guard sacred mystery while divulging partial knowledge. In any event, both texts point to a reality that complicates all attempts to understand ancient wisdom: the awareness that wisdom eludes those who search for her, and the conviction that she gives herself freely to those who love her. Ben Sira sums up this paradox in tantalizingly enigmatic fashion:

> For wisdom is like her name,
>   she is not readily perceived by many.
>   (Sir. 6:22)

While Proverbs 25:2 specifies kings as those upon whom the quest for hidden things falls, other texts extend that hunt to all subjects of kings. Indeed, the idea of searching for wisdom as for precious metals occurs again and again in Wisdom literature. Wisdom makes herself known

> if you seek it like silver,
>   and search for it as for hidden treasures.
>   (Prov. 2:4)

She is worth more than red coral or precious jewels; gold and silver are like sand compared to her. To acquire wisdom one should gladly give up a fortune in silver, for she will pay dividends in gold.

Still other texts change the image from precious metals to that of a bride. Wisdom is to be pursued like a beloved, for in her hands are long life and happiness.

> Wisdom is radiant and unfading,
>   and she is easily discerned by those who love her,
>   and is found by those who seek her.
> She hastens to make herself known to those who desire her.
> One who rises early to seek her will have no difficulty,
>   for she will be found sitting at the gate . . .
> because she goes about seeking those worthy of her,
>   and she graciously appears to them in their paths,
>   and meets them in every thought.
>   (Wis. 6:12–14, 16)

> I loved her and sought her from my youth;
> I desired to take her for my bride,
>   and became enamored of her beauty.
>   (Wis. 8:2)

Considerable emphasis falls on wisdom's initiative. Not only does she meet her lover halfway, but she also actively invites people to search for her. Those who love her are loved in return, and whoever finds her discovers life. At first her discipline may seem unusually harsh, but in time her fetters will take on a wholly different appearance. In retrospect, lovers will consider her price a trifling sum.

Like the quest to discover the mystery of a lover, the search for wisdom never ends. In a moment of poetic flourish, Ben Sira compares wisdom to several kinds of trees, and invites his readers to feast heartily.

> Come to me, you who desire me
>   and eat your fill of my fruits.
> For the memory of me is sweeter than honey,
>   and the possession of me sweeter than the honeycomb.
> Those who eat of me will hunger for more,
>   and those who drink of me will thirst for more.
>
> (Sir. 24:19–21)

Like a fire, a parched land, an empty womb, and Sheol, knowledge never cries out, "Enough" (Prov. 30:15–16). Qoheleth's familiar adage, "The more one knows, the more sorrow" (Eccl. 1:18, my trans.), has its corollary in, "The more people know, the more they are eager to learn what remains hidden."

Perhaps this allusion to unquenchable thirst is Ben Sira's way of expressing *wisdom's essential hiddenness*. Although she may give herself freely to those who seek her, wisdom also withdraws until she is wholly outside human reach. Like the Creator who delighted in her presence before the creation of the world, wisdom is both present and hidden. The poet who composed the poem that has been inserted into chapter 28 of the book of Job painted a detailed picture of men searching the darkest recesses of the earth for valuable ore, only to highlight their inability to discover wisdom. Similarly, Qoheleth laments God's withholding of vital knowledge from human beings (Eccl. 3:11) and defiantly challenges sages who claim success in finding wisdom (Eccl. 8:16–17).

> Even though a wise man claims to know, he cannot find it out. (Eccl. 8:17 RSV)

This emphasis on a royal search within Wisdom literature may underlie the well-known text in which the pursuit of wisdom leads to kingship, a passage that uses a Greek device known as sorites, in which ideas are strung together like pearls on a necklace.

> The beginning of wisdom is the most sincere desire for instruction,
> and concern for instruction is love of her,
> and love of her is the keeping of her laws,
> and giving heed to her laws is assurance of immortality,
> and immortality brings one near to God;
> so the desire for wisdom leads to a kingdom.
>
> (Wis. 6:17–20)

In Sirach 14:20–27 one comes upon the image of a hunter who stalks his prey, in addition to those of camping alongside wisdom's house and resting under her shade.

> Happy is the person who meditates on wisdom
>   and reasons intelligently,
> who reflects in his heart on her ways
>   and ponders her secrets,

pursuing her like a hunter,
　　and lying in wait on her paths;
who peers through her windows
　　and listens at her doors;
who camps near her house
　　and fastens his tent peg to her walls;
who pitches his tent near her,
　　and so occupies an excellent lodging place;
who places his children under her shelter,
　　and lodges under her boughs;
who is sheltered by her from the heat,
　　and dwells in the midst of her glory.

In the quest for wisdom one adopts whatever means are necessary to accomplish the goal, whether these happen to be appropriate social conduct or not. Wisdom's elusiveness is signaled by shifting images. She first appears as a wild animal; later she is described as a house and a tree, and ultimately she assumes human form.

In a word, Israel's sages envisioned themselves actively hunting for precious wisdom, and they described that search in rich imagery. These lively metaphors for the object of hot pursuit adorn wisdom texts at every stage of their composition, indicating that the search for wisdom was no passing fad.

THE OBJECT OF THE SEARCH

For what, then, did ancient sages search from dawn to dusk? Perhaps nothing suffices to answer this important question but the word "life." Canonical sages went in pursuit of the good life in all its manifestations: health, wealth, honor, progeny, longevity, remembrance. These teachers never seemed to grow tired of promising such bounty to faithful listeners and of threatening fools with loss of life itself. In their eyes sufficient proof existed that life's goods accompanied wisdom, so that the few seeming discrepancies did little to alter this conviction until Job and Qoheleth registered mighty protests.

I shall use several different ideas in describing the object of the search represented by Proverbs, Job, Qoheleth, and Sirach. In essence, Proverbs is a search for *knowledge*, for the aim of the many attempts to grasp reality seems to be the acquisition of sufficient understanding about nature and human beings to enable persons to live wisely and well.

The object of Job's search was not so much knowledge about how to cope with the enigmas of ordinary existence, although he certainly achieved vital information that called all previous knowledge into question, as a burning quest for God's *presence*.[30] Having known God's gracious presence in the past, Job could not endure a *Deus absconditus*, a hidden God. Therefore, he searched the darkest depths of despair in pursuit of his God, and eventually risked death to achieve restored communion. To Job, God was the highest good; life itself paled by comparison.

Qoheleth endeavored to find some sense in existence under the sun. He raised the ultimate question of *meaning* in a silent universe. Like Job, he could not affirm life as the supreme good, but unlike him Qoheleth did not enter into dialogue with a living Presence.[31] The shadow of death hovered nearby,[32] and chance reigned on earth. Lacking confidence in life's goodness, and hardly drawn by the presence of divine mystery, Qoheleth searched in vain for some meaning that would enable him to endure the few days of his empty existence.

In the Hellenistic environment within which Ben Sira found himself, he launched a vigorous search to discover a means of presenting Jewish teaching to sophisticated audiences. In doing so, he embarked upon a significant quest for *continuity*.[33] Facing two entirely different fronts, he endeavored to show that Wisdom literature actually continued Israel's venerable sacred traditions, and to convince youthful Jews that Greeks were not the only ones who boasted a magnificent intellectual heritage. His goal was tantamount to survival of the Jewish faith.

To sum up, Proverbs searched for knowledge, Job for presence, Qoheleth for meaning, and Ben Sira for continuity. Significantly, the temporal focus differs in each instance. The eyes of those who compiled the book of Proverbs were fixed upon the *primeval age* when God established an order that enabled life to endure. They endeavored to understand the true character of reality and to live in harmony with that discovery. Job's incredible suffering increased the urgency to find relief from suspicion that God had suddenly become his enemy. It follows that his concern was wholly *present*. The ache within Qoheleth's soul arose from an inability to discern any *future* at all, since death silenced both human and beast. On the other hand, Ben Sira glanced backward upon a glorious *past*, which he hoped to salvage for his pupils.

Invariably, Israel's seekers, whatever their goals, arrived at a closed door that resolutely refused to swing open. Behind this door lay profound mystery, but none held the key to this room except God. That is what Proverbs 25:2 professed when it declared that God's glory lies in the tendency to conceal essential reality. At times this restriction of what could be known caused considerable chafing, but in the end it gave birth to marvelous reflection concerning a gracious opening of the door by God, primarily through means of personified Wisdom. The tension between self-reliance, on the one hand, and hope in divine mercy, on the other, bestows immense pathos upon biblical wisdom. Indeed, one can even say that the relentless search oscillated between these two extremes: trust in one's ability to secure existence, and dependence upon God's mercy. Divine compassion has the final word, whether communicated by Wisdom, God's gracious turning to humans, or simply affirmed, as so often occurred in Sirach.

In Proverbs 7:6–27 and 24:30–34 anecdote functions as an effective teaching aid, hence the following story. A little girl once wandered away from home and became hopelessly lost. After trying unsuccessfully to retrace her steps, at last she gave up, and exhausted from her effort and from the growing fear that tore at her insides, she lay down beside a log and fell asleep. Meanwhile the girl's parents had missed her and had begun to search the woods nearby. Eventually the father came upon the sleeping child, but in doing so he stepped on some dry twigs that snapped explosively, awaking her. Seeing her father, the girl cried out, "Daddy, I've found you."

Israel's wise men and women searched diligently too, but in the end they became the willing objects of a greater pursuit. The search became truly Royal, one in which God came in search of humans. In what follows, we shall attempt a search of our own, hoping to understand ancient wisdom. In doing so, we shall heed Ben Sira's counsel:

> Put your feet into her fetters,
>   and your neck into her collar.
> Bend your shoulders and carry her,
>   and do not fret under her bonds.
> Come to her with all your soul,
>   and keep her ways with all your might.
> Search out and seek, and she will become known to you;
>   and when you get hold of her, do not let her go.
> For at last you will find the rest she gives,
>   and she will be changed into joy for you.
> Then her fetters will become for you a strong defense,
>   and her collar a glorious robe.
> Her yoke is a golden ornament,
>   and her bonds are a purple cord.
> You will wear her like a glorious robe,
>   and put her on like a splendid crown.
>
> (Sir. 6:24–31)

NOTES

1. R. E. Murphy, "Qoheleth's 'Quarrel' with the Fathers," in *From Faith to Faith: Essays in Honor of Donald G. Miller on His Seventieth Birthday*, ed. Dikran Y. Hadidian (Pittsburgh: Pickwick Press, 1979), 234–45, is the latest of several critics to discuss this important topic.
2. Lou H. Silberman, "The Queen of Sheba in Judaic Tradition," in *Solomon and Sheba*, ed. James B. Pritchard (London: Phaidon, 1974), 65–84; W. Hertz, "Die Rätsel der Königin von Säba," *ZDA* 27 (1883): 1–33; Moses Gaster, "Story of Solomon's Wisdom," *Folklore* 1 (1890): 133–35; and E. Ullendorff, *Ethiopia and the Bible* (London: Oxford University, 1968).
3. *Strassburger Räthselbuch. Die erste zu Strassburg ums Jahr 1505 gedrucket Deutsch Räthselsammlung*, ed. A. F. Butsch (Strassburg: K. J. Trübner, 1876). This unusual collection of riddles, on which I did considerable study during a sabbatical in Heidelberg from 1972 to 73, has 326 difficult questions and answers. Although written by a monk, the riddles are sometimes blasphemous, and they often achieve appreciable humor.
4. R. B. Y. Scott, "Solomon and the Beginnings of Wisdom in Israel," in *Wisdom in Israel and in the Ancient Near East: Presented to Professor Harold Henry Rowley*, ed. M. Noth and D. Winton Thomas (VTSup 3; Leiden: Brill, 1955),

262–79 (*SAIW*, 84–101); and R. N. Whybray, "Wisdom Literature in the Reigns of David and Solomon," in *Studies in the Period of David and Solomon and Other Essays*, ed. Tamoo Ishida (Winona Lake, Ind.: Eisenbrauns, 1982), 13–26. E. W. Heaton, *Solomon's New Men: The Emergence of Ancient Israel as a National State* (New York: Pica, 1974); and Walter E. Brueggemann, "The Social Significance of Solomon as a Patron of Wisdom," in *The Sage in Israel and the Ancient Near East*, ed. Gammie and Perdue, 117–32, credit the historical Solomon with radical changes, a virtual Enlightenment, to use von Rad's unfortunate term. Brueggemann writes of an abiding memory of a vital connection between Solomon and wisdom, a relationship both emancipatory and ideological. His claim rests on sociocultural reconstructions for which only conjectural evidence exists. Ronald E. Clements, "Solomon and the Origins of Wisdom in Israel," in *Perspectives on the Hebrew Bible*, ed. James L. Crenshaw (Macon, Ga.: Mercer University, 1988), 23–35, views the glorification of Solomon as a sage in the light of the Deuteronomist's desire to validate the Davidic dynasty. Two things, in Clements's view, make this possible: the unique nature of royal wisdom and the association of wisdom and wealth.

5. For a translation of this myth concerning Inanna's descent into the netherworld, see S. N. Kramer, *ANET*, 52–57.

6. The dating of these chapters in exilic or postexilic times rests on two foundations: the nature of the theological views and the character of personified Wisdom. The warning against the foreign or strange woman may reflect the era of Ezra and Nehemiah.

7. Hans-Peter Müller, "Magisch-mantische Weisheit und die Gestalt Daniels," *UF* 1 (1969): 79–94. Both Eliphaz and Elihu refer to revelatory dreams, but these differ greatly from ancient Near Eastern mantic wisdom by the absence of magic.

8. Siegfried Herrmann, "Die Königsnovelle in Ägypten und in Israel," *Wissenschaftliche Zeitschrift der Universitäts Leipzig* 3 (1953–54): 53–57.

9. The Egyptian *Instruction of Ptahhotep* concludes with a lengthy pun on the word for hearing (*ANET*, 414).

10. On this story see Trible, *God and the Rhetoric of Sexuality*, 31–34. See also Stuart Lasine, "Solomon, Daniel, and the Detective Story: The Social Functions of a Literary Genre," *HAR* 11 (1987): 247–66; and idem, "The Riddle of Solomon's Judgment and the Riddle of Human Nature in the Hebrew Bible," *JSOT* 45 (1989): 61–86.

11. Hugo Gressmann, "Das salomonische Urteil," *Deutsche Rundschau* 130 (1907): 212–28.

12. George M. Landes, "The 'Three Days and Three Nights' Motif in Jonah 2:1," *JBL* 86 (1967): 446–50.

13. Henri Cazelles, "Les debuts de la sagesse en Israel," in *Les sagesses du proche-orient ancien*, ed. Leclant, 27–39, especially 34–35; George Mendenhall, "The Shady Side of Wisdom: The Date and Purpose of Genesis 3," in *A Light unto My Path: Old Testament Studies in Honor of Jacob Myers*, ed. H. M. Bream, R. D. Heim, and C. A. Moore (Philadelphia: Temple University, 1974), 319–34.

14. On the basis of this story, Teqoa has been seen as a center of sapiential activity—despite the explicit statement that Joab instructed the woman on what to say to David. G. G. Nicol, "The Wisdom of Joab and the Wise Woman of Tekoa," *ST* 36 (1982): 97–104, stresses Joab's role in instructing the woman; but J. Hoftijzer, "David and the Tekoite Woman," *VT* 20 (1970): 419–44, insists that she used her own ingenuity in guiding David to radical self-analysis.

15. Whybray, *Succession Narrative*. Such a negative attitude toward wisdom does not depend upon a technical use of the adjective "wise" in the stories about Abel and the women from Teqoa and Abel.

16. Martin Noth, "Die Bewährung von Salomos 'Göttlicher Weisheit,'" in *Wisdom in Israel*, ed. Noth and Winton Thomas, 225–37.

17. Scott, "Solomon and the Beginnings of Wisdom," 263, cites these opinions and documents them in the writings of Anton Causse and H. Wheeler Robinson.

18. Fichtner, *Altorientalische Weisheit*.

19. Heaton, *Solomon's New Men*; and Walter Brueggemann, *In Man We Trust* (Richmond: John Knox, 1972). See n. 4 for a different view.

20. W. F. Albright, "Some Canaanite-Phoenician Sources of Hebrew Wisdom," in *Wisdom in Israel*, ed. Noth and Winton Thomas, 13, writes that a Solomonic nucleus is probable for Proverbs, but those didactic materials credited to Solomon "failed to meet later standards of literary taste—or were simply so archaic in content that they were no longer understood."

21. Albrecht Alt, "Solomonic Wisdom," in *SAIW*, 102–12.

22. Von Rad, "Job XXXVIII and Ancient Egyptian Wisdom," in *SAIW*, 267–80.

23. Brueggemann, *In Man We Trust*; and Whybray, *Succession Narrative*.

24. Von Rad, "The Joseph Narrative and Ancient Wisdom," in *SAIW*, 439–47.

25. The reasons for my misgivings about this phrase appear in an extensive review of von Rad's analysis of Israelite wisdom and in a book on his thought. See *"Wisdom in Israel* by Gerhard von Rad," *RSR* 2, no. 2 (1976): 6–12; and *Gerhard von Rad* (Waco: Word, 1978).

26. Whybray, *Intellectual Tradition*.

27. R. J. Williams, "Wisdom in the Ancient Near East," *IDBSup*, 949–52; Brunner, *Altägyptische Weisheit*.

28. Johannes Marböck, *Weisheit im Wandel: Untersuchungen zur Weisheitstheologie bei Ben Sira* (BBB 37; Bonn: Peter Hanstein, 1971).

29. Bernhard Lang, "Schule und Unterricht im alte Israel," in *La Sagesse de l'Ancien Testament*, ed. Gilbert, 186–201.

30. I have pursued this theme in an article entitled "In Search of Divine Presence (Some Remarks Preliminary to a Theology of Wisdom)," *RevExp* 74 (1977): 353–69; see also Samuel Terrien, *The Elusive Presence* (New York: Harper & Row, 1978).

31. Von Rad, *Wisdom in Israel*, 232–33.

32. On the centrality of death to Qoheleth's thought, see my essay, "The Shadow of Death in Qoheleth," in *Israelite Wisdom*, ed. Gammie et al., 205–16 (*UAPQ*, 573–85).

33. Wisdom of Solomon falls into the same category as Sirach.

Chapter 3

The Pursuit of Knowledge

Proverbs

Israel's sages seem to have discerned a fundamental order hidden within the universe; this ruling principle applied both to nature and to humans.[1] Discovery of this "rational rule" enabled the wise to secure their existence by acting in harmony with the universal order that sustained the cosmos. Conduct, it follows, either strengthened the existing order or contributed to the forces of chaos that continually threatened survival itself.

This decisive order permeating the universe constituted God's gift to those who bore the Creator's image. As a sign of divine favor, the principle governing the universe was subject to God's will: the Lord of the universe always spoke the final word. No *concept* of order held that sovereign will in subjection.[2] Israel's sages recognized this significant fact and acknowledged the ultimate veto over every attempt to control their existence by living in harmony with the principle that God had bestowed on the universe. At the same time, they believed that God did not exercise the right of veto arbitrarily, and thus the wise confidently endeavored to discover the principle by which they should live.

The task facing ancient sages was not simply that of ferreting out every signpost that pointed to an underlying principle. Once this important clue presented itself forcefully upon human imaginations, it had to be transferred from the realm of nature to the human sphere. The chief means of accomplishing this goal was analogy.[3] Comparisons proceeded on the level of essential reality; surface differences vanished before functional similarities. Close observation of nature and the animal kingdom convinced Israel's sages that the world was truly a harmonious *universe*.

The search for proper analogies had as its single purpose the securing of life. Those who successfully achieved correct knowledge purchased long life for themselves, together with other indications of divine approval. Knowledge was therefore a means to an end, not the end itself. This fact should be kept in mind as one examines the book of Proverbs.

LITERARY ANALYSIS

Like wisdom, the term "proverb" is difficult to define. The Hebrew word *māšāl*, the plural form of which identifies the book of Proverbs, points to two possible meanings: a similitude or a powerful word.[4] The first sense of *māšāl* derives from the verb that means "to be like," the second, from the meaning, "to rule." The former emphasizes the analogy that lies at the heart of every proverb, while the latter stresses its paradigmatic or exemplary character. A particularly apt description captures the second of these senses: a proverb is "a 'winged word,' outliving the fleeting moment."[5]

Etymology alone cannot suffice to define "proverb" in ancient Israel, for the word *māšāl* occurs with reference to a wide range of literary forms: similitudes, popular sayings, literary aphorisms, taunt songs, bywords, allegories, and discourses. Attempts to characterize proverbs on the basis of form and function encounter similar ambiguities. Since Israel's sages seem never to have adopted a single notion of proverb, we should be content with a broad definition. For this reason, "saying" best retains the openness of the Hebrew word *māšāl*.

All proverbs, whether similitudes or paradigms, were grounded in experience. A modern writer has captured this singular feature of proverbs in an observation that approaches the proverbial itself: a proverb is a short sentence founded upon long experience, containing a truth.[6] Brevity characterizes all proverbs; they say a great deal in a few, carefully chosen words. Observation also belongs to the intrinsic character of a proverb, which announces an important discovery in "sentence," or statement, form. The weight of tradition rests behind proverbs; they do not represent the isolated view of one person, however intelligent that individual may have been. Above all, proverbs embody truth. On hearing a proverb for the first time, "It is as though, within the depths of human consciousness, we perceived the proverb's content to be true."[7]

An incommunicable quality distinguishes proverbs from sayings that lack paradigmatic value. Perhaps that unknown and unknowable aspect derives from the distance separating the ancient world from contemporary scholars. In one sense, the distinguishing mark of a proverb is forever lost to modern critics, forcing scholars to impose their own understandings on texts from bygone days. In another sense, interpreters engage in the search for analogies between then and now, confident that at the deeper levels of human existence continuity exists between people of today and those forebears who left a legacy for them to treasure. In reality, humankind participates in a quest for knowledge comparable to the one occupying Israelite sages.

Proverbs encapsulated truth, and this valuable information was not private property; instead, it belonged to everyone. To be sure, a single individual was responsible for the form that a given proverb took, but the entire community profited from each discovery. A didactic quality clings to those proverbial statements that seem to be completely neutral, for every single recognition of "the way things are" signaled a step toward mastering the universe. That task was everybody's responsibility.

The primary function of proverbs seems to have been the linking of two realms and two ages. In short, the winged word transcended time and space. It joined together nature and humans by isolating a vital correspondence between the natural realm and the social order. In addition, the proverb linked past generations to the present. By this means traditional values survived the passing of time, and ethos emerged. "Ethos" refers to a system of cherished values, presuppositions, aspirations, linguistic usage, and so forth.

To accomplish this union that defied space and time, proverbs needed to be transparent. They had to ring true. The combined wisdom of many and wit of one entrusted proverbs with persuasive capacity. Fundamentally, proverbs relied on their typicality for immediate cogency. They could be tested in daily experience over and over with unchanging results. Such verifiability arose from investment of cultural values. It follows that proverbs constitute the best single source for discovering cherished values in ancient Israel.[8] These succinct sayings introduce modern readers to deeply rooted ways of life; in familiarizing oneself with them, one goes a long way toward fathoming an ancient people's understanding of good and evil.

The transparency inherent within a given proverb was reinforced by means of poetic imagery and stylistic devices, all of which seem to have aimed at aiding memorization and enhancing enjoyment. The chief poetic feature was parallelism, although a few sayings lack this feature entirely. It cannot be ascertained whether these single-line proverbs antedate the bilinear proverbs, which by far outnumber the rest, or whether they represent a later corruption of the two-line saying.

Three types of parallelism occur with great regularity: antithetic, synonymous, and progressive.[9] Antithetic parallelism depends upon the juxtaposition of opposites:

> A false balance is an abomination to the LORD,
>   but an accurate weight is his delight.
>   (Prov. 11:1)

An important variation is the excluding proverb, often called a "better saying." For example,

> Better is a dinner of vegetables where love is
>   than a fatted ox and hatred with it.
>   (Prov. 15:17)

This saying sets one reality over against another in complete opposition. The contrast implied in such proverbs suggests that the oft-used descriptive term "comparative proverb" is less satisfactory than "excluding proverb," which acknowledges an antithesis.[10] The saying does not attempt to determine the better of two good things; instead, it announces that one is good and its opposite bad.

Synonymous parallelism reinforces an astute observation by repetition of the essential point in different words.

> Hear, my child, your father's instruction,
>   and do not reject your mother's teaching;
> for they are a fair garland for your head,
>   and pendants for your neck.
>   (1:8–9)

This example of synonymous parallelism uses a positive and a negative, both of which mean the same thing. Naturally, shades of meaning add variety amid synonymity. Strictly speaking, the phenomenon of ascending or accumulative parallelism lacks exact synonyms or antonyms but builds upon an earlier idea after the fashion of stairsteps. For instance,

> The beginning of wisdom is this: Get wisdom,
>   and whatever else you get, get insight.
>   (4:7)

This saying advances beyond the two similar notions (wisdom and insight to whatever one obtains), an entirely new idea. A variant of the progressive proverb is the following formulation, where the second line is essential for the meaning of the proverb.

> Like a war club, a sword, or a sharp arrow
>   is one who bears false witness against a neighbor.
>   (25:18)

Examples of these three basic kinds of parallelism could be multiplied indefinitely. The following proverbs illustrate the great variety that arose within the three fundamental types.

> If you close your ear to the cry of the poor
>   you will cry out and not be heard.
>   (21:13)

> Do not rob the poor, because they are poor,
>   or crush the afflicted at the gate;

for the LORD pleads their cause
    and despoils of life those who despoil them.
                (22:22–23)

Train children in the right way,
    and when old, they will not stray.
                (22:6)

Leave the presence of a fool,
    for there you do not find words of knowledge.
                (14:7)

The first of these shows how a conditional clause in the first line is followed by its natural conclusion. The second example expands the proverb to twice its normal length, and the second half of the proverb gives the reason for the advice in the first half. The third illustration shows how the result of a given course of action can be presented in the second half of a proverb, while the final example demonstrates the use of second person in proverbial statements.

Two further forms deserve special recognition. The first is the numerical proverb.

Three things are stately in their stride;
    four are stately in their gait;
the lion, which is mightiest among wild animals
    and does not turn back before any;
the strutting rooster, the he-goat,
    and a king striding before his people.
                (30:29–31)

The second type is the listing of comparable phenomena without numerical heightening.

Four things on earth are small,
    yet they are exceedingly wise;
the ants are a people without strength,
    yet they provide their food in the summer;
the badgers are a people without power,
    yet they make their homes in the rocks;
the locusts have no king,
    yet all of them march in rank;
the lizard can be grasped in the hand,
    yet it is found in kings' palaces.
                (30:24–28)

Just as diversity characterizes Hebrew parallelism within proverbial literature, multiplicity of patterns adds abundant variety. At least seven different patterns have been isolated: (1) identity, equivalence, invariable association; (2) nonidentity, contrast, paradox; (3) similarity, analogy, type; (4) contrary to right order, futile, absurd; (5) classification and clarification; (6) value, relative value or priority, proportion or degree; (7) consequences of human behavior or character.[11]

THE INDIVIDUAL COLLECTIONS

Variety in parallelism and patterns extends to the several collections within the book of Proverbs. Four extensive collections and five short ones can be recognized on the basis of superscriptions and content.

1. 1:1–9:18   The proverbs of Solomon son of David, king of Israel
2. 10:1–22:16   The proverbs of Solomon
3. 22:17–24:22 The sayings of the wise
4. 24:23–34   More sayings of wise men
5. 25:1–29:27   More proverbs of Solomon transcribed by the men of Hezekiah, king of Judah
6. 30:1–14   Sayings of Agur son of Jakeh from Massa
7. 30:15–33   (no superscription)
8. 31:1–9   Sayings of Lemuel, king of Massa, which his mother taught him
9. 31:10–31   (no superscription)

The international character of Hebrew wisdom is reflected in three collections that are attributed to (or borrowed from) foreign sources (numbers 3, 6, 8 above). *The Instruction of Amenemope*, from which eleven of thirty sayings in collection three probably derive, originated in Egypt.[12]

The first collection (chaps. 1–9) differs greatly from the others, with respect to both form and content. Formally, it makes use of the short poem that links individual sayings together loosely. As a result, certain themes surface, particularly the dangers posed by an adulteress.[13] In addition, poetic personification functions pedagogically. Wisdom woos her followers, inviting them to a banquet in her house, which she has built by innate expertise, and Folly lurks in the night, actively seducing simpletons to their ruin.[14] The entire collection breathes a deeply religious spirit, for the individual sayings adopt as their motto: "The fear of the Lord is the beginning of knowledge."[15] Furthermore, they consciously seek to instruct, both by exhortation and admonition.[16] Forever holding out the promise of reward or threat of punishment, these poems endeavor to shape character much more self-consciously than the other collections do.[17]

In some instances a real proverb lies encased within a brief poem (1:10–19; 6:20–35; 9:13–18). The first poem warns against joining criminals who devise schemes to get rich at the expense of helpless individuals. It reinforces the warning by citing a proverb:

> For in vain is a net baited
>   while the bird is looking on.
>   (1:17)

Similarly, the second poem exposes the risks involved in sexual debauchery:

Can fire be carried in the bosom
    without burning one's clothes?
Or can one walk on hot coals
    without scorching the feet?
                    (6:27–28)

This short poem (6:20–35) argues that fire inevitably burns, and only fools
think they can dally with another man's wife with impunity. The third poem
(9:13–18) demonstrates Folly's skill at citing appropriate proverbs that reinforce
her smooth words of invitation to forbidden pleasures:

Stolen water is sweet,
    and bread eaten in secret is pleasant.
                    (9:17)

The initial collection of proverbs, to use the last word in its loose sense,
manifests a tendency toward sophistication in poetic technique. Here one discovers direct appeals for attention, rhetorical questions, extended metaphors
approaching allegory, vivid description, anecdote, and related rhetorical devices.
The combination of style and content suggests that this collection derives from a
different setting than the one(s) that produced the other larger collections.

Ten instructions and five interludes may be discerned in this opening collection.[18] They are:

Lectures
I.   1:8–19   The seductive gang
II.   2:1–22   The path to wisdom
III.   3:1–12   The wisdom of piety
IV.   3:21–35   Winning favor with God and man
V.   4:1–9   Loving wisdom; hating evil
VI.   4:10–19   The right path
VII.   4:20–27   The straight path
VIII.   5:1–23   The promiscuous woman
IX.   6:20–35   The promiscuous woman
X.   7:1–27   The promiscuous woman

Interludes
I.   1:20–33   Wisdom's condemnation of fools
II.   3:13–20   Praise of wisdom
III.   6:1–19   Four epigrams
IV.   8:1–36   Wisdom's self-praise
V.   9:1–18   Invitations issued by Wisdom and Folly

The second major collection is clearly divisible into two smaller entities (10:1–
15:33; 16:1–22:16). The first of these differs from the other in its preference
for antithetic parallelism. Only one (19:7) of the 375 proverbs lacks the dis-
tich balanced by two halves, and it uses the tristich form (three units). So far
no principle of arrangement has been discovered for these individual sayings,

although here and there signs of intentional sequence present themselves. For instance, 16:10–15 and 25:2–7 discuss kings, 26:1–12 treats the misdeeds of fools, 26:13–16 deals with lazy people, 16:27–29 begins with '*îš*, the letter *mem* begins 18:20–22, the letter *beth* joins together 11:9–12, and the Hebrew words *lēb* (heart) and *ṭôb* (good) connect the sayings in 15:13–17.[19]

It naturally follows from an absence of thematic arrangement in this major collection that description of its contents must necessarily remain hopelessly general. Covering a wide range of everyday occurrences, the proverbs pass judgment on various kinds of conduct ranging from secret actions like bribery to open vilification of poor victims of society's indifference.[20] These brief maxims offer astute observations on the folly of pride, laziness, passion, deceit, gossip, and similar vices, and they cast their ballot in favor of acknowledged virtues such as generosity, faithfulness, self-control, industry, and sobriety.

In some respects *the third collection* (22:17–24:22) resembles the first, in which considerable Egyptian influence is also visible. For example, a tiny step toward the clustering of related sayings occurs in this brief collection, where paragraph units emerge rather distinctly.[21] Second-person address sets apart the material resembling several teachings from the *Instruction of Amenemope*, greatly increasing the urgency of these sayings. Unlike collection two, this one rarely employs the various types of parallelism by which Israel's sages reinforced their striking insight into one small facet of reality. Most conspicuous within this third collection is a brief poem in which the miserable plight of drunkards is described with enormous pathos (Prov. 23:29–35). One other feature of this section resembling *Amenemope* is the use of exquisite metaphors; in this regard, the collection seems to indicate an advanced stage in poetic reflection beyond that found in Proverbs 10:1–22:16.[22]

The fourth major collection (chaps. 25–29) resembles the second in its fondness for antithetic parallelism, but it makes lavish use of comparative statements. These similitudes cover a wide spectrum of topics and demonstrate keen powers of perception.

> A word fitly spoken
>   is like apples of gold in a setting of silver.
>   (25:11)

> Like snow in summer or rain in harvest,
>   so honor is not fitting for a fool.
>   (26:1)

> Like a roaring lion or a charging bear
>   is a wicked ruler over a poor people.
>   (28:15)

The last of these comparisons introduces a favorite subject within this collection: the king. Here as nowhere else the powerful individual with whom all subjects had to reckon is acknowledged, although occasional allusions to royalty surface in other collections.[23]

The first minor collection (24:23–34) lacks parallelism (except in vv. 30, 32, 34) but employs both exhortation and admonition. It shows an unusual relationship with Proverbs 1–9, inasmuch as a single proverb from this extensive collection (6:10–11) has been taken over and used as the "traditionally sanctioned message" that undergirds a brief poem on laziness.[24] Assuming the rare form of anecdote, this passage concludes with a marvelous metaphor.

> I passed by the field of one who was lazy,
>   by the vineyard of a stupid person;
> and see, it was all overgrown with thorns;
>   the ground was covered with nettles,
>   and its stone wall was broken down.
> Then I saw and considered it;
>   I looked and received instruction.
> A little sleep, a little slumber,
>   a little folding of the hands to rest,
> and poverty will come upon you like a robber,
>   and want, like an armed warrior.
>   (24:30–34)

The second incidental section (30:1–14) comprises, in the view of some interpreters, a dialogue between a skeptic and a believer, to which has been affixed a profound prayer to be spared either extreme, poverty or riches.[25] Verse 9 concludes:

> or I shall be full, and deny you,
>   and say, "Who is the Lord?"
> or I shall be poor, and steal,
>   and profane the name of my God.

The third minor collection (30:15–33) is largely composed of numerical sayings[26] and simple listing of related phenomena.[27] It brings together things that resist all efforts to stifle desire for more, phenomena that defy explanation, situations in which certain persons become unbearable, insignificant things that achieve unexpected results, and proud parading on the part of animals and humans. *The fourth minor collection* (31:1–9) takes the form of advice offered by a queen mother to her young son. The strong warning against sexual profligacy and drunkenness comes perilously close to harangue, although the intimate language points to genuine affection. In addition, the final appeal for fairness in exercising royal judgments links up with similar ideas throughout the ancient Near East.[28] *The fifth minor collection* (31:10–31) supplies an appropriate ending[29] to the book of Proverbs, which sings Wisdom's praises and confesses that a good wife is a gift from God. The alphabetic poem extols the virtues of a capable wife, the mistress of a household (cf. 9:1–6). Whereas the basis of her unparalleled reputation is wholly secular, a religious note erupts toward the end:

Charm is deceitful, and beauty is vain,
  but a woman who fears the LORD is to be praised.
            (31:30)

Efforts to divide the older Solomonic proverbs into an architectonic structure
have not been altogether successful.[30] One significant hypothesis of four sections with thematic coherence may be noted.[31] According to it, the following
divisions apply:

1. Chapters 10–15   Righteousness versus Wickedness
2. 16:1–22:16   Yahweh and the King
3. Chapters 25–27   Nature and Agriculture
4. Chapters 28–29   The King or Potential Rulers

Another approach to the vexing problem of overall structure in the book of
Proverbs takes its cue from the two primary forms of Egyptian proverbial wisdom. Into the category of Instruction fall chapters 1–9; 22:17–24:22; 31:1–9.
The remaining proverbs belong, in this view, to the Sentence (10:1–22:16;
24:23–34; chaps. 25–29).[32]

Within the extensive collection of Solomonic proverbs, one group gives the
impression of moral neutrality, a feature that has often led to the conclusion that
such purely secular sayings indicate great antiquity.[33]

Some give freely, yet grow all the richer;
  others withhold what is due, and only suffer
    want.
                (11:24)

From the fruit of the mouth one is filled with good things,
  and manual labor has its reward.
                (12:14)

Some pretend to be rich, yet have nothing;
  others pretend to be poor, yet have great wealth.
Wealth is a ransom for a person's life,
  but the poor get no threats.
                (13:7–8)

The poor are disliked even by their neighbors,
  but the rich have many friends.
                (14:20)

The appetite of workers works for them;
  their hunger urges them on.
                (16:26)

A gift opens doors;
  it gives access to the great.
                (18:16)

The poor use entreaties,
>   but the rich answer roughly.
>   (18:23)

"Bad, bad," says the buyer,
>   then goes away and boasts.
>   (20:14)

The glory of youths is their strength,
>   but the beauty of the aged is their gray hair.
>   (20:29)

Such observations about "the way things are" scarcely pronounce judgment upon one or the other phenomenon being described. We must guard against an assumption that Israel's maxims underwent a gradual development from wholly secular proverbs to fervently religious precepts. Presumably, even the most devout sage was capable of describing reality without always feeling obligated to affix a moral. In any event, religious sayings belong to the oldest collections and appear with great frequency.[34]

A PEDAGOGICAL INTENT

The mere placing of these neutral observations into larger collections with didactic intent transforms the maxims in some small way, for they then take on the persuasive spirit of the whole unit. As a result of the new setting, a wry observation about the advantages rich people enjoy over the poor cannot be understood properly apart from the sages' attitude to poverty and riches.[35] Modern interpreters face an added peril—the temptation to assess wealthy individuals in the light of later suspicion about the virtue of those upon whom fortune smiles.

The *didactic impulse* manifested itself in many different ways. Perhaps the most noticeable expression of a desire to teach was the shift from observation to exhortation or admonition, and the resulting disintegration of the proverb form. The simple addition of motive clauses and energetic warnings signaled an unwillingness to allow the proverb to communicate its own message. The consequences of a given action come to the forefront, and direct address punctuates the discourse. In addition, value judgments reflecting this all-consuming passion pervade the steady stream of advice. We note further the introduction of an arsenal of rhetorical devices: paranomasia, assonance, alliteration, puns, repetition, rhyme, and synonymy.

Nothing in this account of the shift from sentence to instruction demands a school setting, although many scholars seem inclined to posit such a transformation in the actual context of learning.[36] All of the conscious educational techniques mentioned above lay within reach of sages who studied at their parents' feet. In short, we must be alert to distortion from two different fronts. On the one hand, the temptation to date all proverbs late if they possess elaborate teaching aids;[37] on the other hand, the assumption that only persons trained in professional schools had an ounce of literary expertise. One does not have to endorse the theory of a noble savage or its corollary, the gifted *Volk*, to recognize that perceptive members of Israelite villages could have coined exquisite proverbs and persuasive instructions.[38]

It follows from these observations that we lack sufficiently sophisticated analytic tools to date the individual proverbs, or even the larger collections, with any confidence. Although these sayings, by and large, reflect life as it is known from other sources, they remain completely silent with regard to the great historical events that must have been taking place simultaneously with their compilation. Whoever wrote these proverbs knew that the truths they proclaimed remained unchanged regardless of the ceaseless jockeying for territorial sovereignty in the ancient world. Israel's proverbs do not contain a single reference to a recognizable historical person or event, with the exception of the editorial superscriptions that mention Solomon and Hezekiah's men.[39] The sages searched for universal truth; in assessing reality they acknowledged no geographical boundaries, at least prior to Ben Sira.

THEMATIC ANALYSIS

At the very heart of the wise's search for knowledge lay a value judgment: *life* was the supreme good. The word "life" is used here in its pregnant sense—a long existence characterized by robust health, an abundance of friends, a house full of children, and sufficient possessions to carry one safely through any difficulty. Naturally, the sages reckoned with death as a real factor, but the book of Proverbs never utters so much as a sigh over the prospect of natural death. The lack of any anxious lament over the universal decree, "You must die," becomes all the more astonishing when we consider that these wise men and women entertained no hope of life beyond the grave.

A comparison of the sages' attitude to death in the book of Proverbs with that of some psalms that are often labeled "wisdom" or said to be influenced by sages is instructive. For example, Psalm 39 comes close to the attitudes expressed in the books of Job and Ecclesiastes about life's brevity and the need for respite from divine surveillance (cf. Psalms 62 and 90).

Perhaps this limitation of life to existence on this side of the tomb explains why images like "tree of life" and "fountain of life" recur with such frequency in the sayings. Indeed, like the Egyptian goddess Ma'at, Wisdom is even pictured with long life in her right hand, riches and honor in her left hand. Or again, she is called a staff of life to those who grasp her, and a refuge for all who cling to her (Prov. 3:16–18).

Another image that plays an important part in the vocabulary of Israel's sages who composed the book of Proverbs is the *path* or *way* to life.[40] The significance of this terminology depends on the double sense with which the word for way was used: path and sovereignty. A singular example of the reliance upon this double meaning for the Hebrew word *derek* (way) is found in Proverbs 30:18–19.

> Three things are too wonderful for me;
>   four I do not understand:
> the way of an eagle in the sky,
>   the way of a snake on a rock,
> the way of a ship on the high seas,
>   and the way of a man with a girl.

Here the incomprehensible feature of the four movements concerns the lack of any "tracks" or telltale signs of progress.[41] The eagle (or vulture) splits the air without leaving any trail; the snake slithers along a rock, leaving behind no sign of its movement; the ship parts the ocean's floor momentarily; young people cohabit and no one can ascertain that such conduct has taken place (alternatively, the emphasis falls on the wondrous mystery of birth resulting from the union of male and female).

The notion of a path was particularly appropriate in the thinking of Israel's wise men and women, for at birth everyone had embarked on a journey that led to a full life, or lamentably, to premature departure. Useful road maps existed; they were the fruit of long effort. Those who relied on their own ingenuity soon became hopelessly lost along winding footpaths. Often God overruled human itineraries, leaving helpless individuals somewhere off the beaten path. From this encounter with human finitude, sages learned an important lesson.

> All our steps are ordered by the LORD;
>   how then can we understand our own ways?
> (20:24)

Nevertheless, the wise journeyed toward their ultimate destination with sure confidence that they would reach that place safely, whereas fools would lose their way.

On this path of life two distinct groups of pilgrims walked toward different goals. They were known as *the wise and the foolish*; all people fell into one or the other category. In the view of sages, no middle ground existed for those who participated in folly, or in wisdom, only minimally. Moreover, an ethical understanding of the two categories prevailed. The wise were righteous, and fools wicked.[42] This surprising conclusion arose from the operative assumption that anyone who strengthened the order upholding the universe belonged to God's forces, while those who undermined this harmony were enemies of the Creator.

Although the wise did not allow for a middle ground between wisdom and folly, they did make careful distinctions among fools, achieving this by varying their language when characterizing fools. Eight different terms for "fool" occur within canonical Proverbs.[43]

1. *petî*—the naive, untutored individual
2. *kĕsîl*—one who is innately stupid
3. *'ewîl*—a person characterized by obstinacy
4. *sākāl*—one who persists in folly
5. *bā'ar*—the behavior of a crude individual
6. *nābāl*—a brutal, depraved person
7. *hōlēl*—an irrational madman
8. *lēṣ*—a foolish talker who values his opinions overmuch

Naturally, not all of these persons were beyond help. The *petî*, for example, presented a real challenge, inasmuch as he or she could readily be influenced for good or ill. Like an inexperienced young girl, whose vulnerability offered a rare opportunity for preying individuals, the *petî* could easily be swayed. For the rest, the wise had nothing but contempt. Believing them to be God's enemies, who schemed to overthrow the principle governing the world, the sages could hardly have adopted a tolerant attitude toward fools.

Now if all humans belonged to two camps, each of which was clearly distinguishable, we should be able to describe two different lifestyles. One pattern of behavior secured existence, and its opposite led to destruction. To a certain extent, any attempt to characterize life-sustaining conduct and its counterpart is hampered by the sages' tendency to speak in general categories. For instance, they enjoin *right action* and *justice*, which pleases God more than sacrifice (Prov. 21:3), and encourage *goodness* with confidence that their meaning leaves no ambiguity. In short, these teachers take for granted a common understanding of good and evil, one that modern interpreters must construct with great care in order to guard against erroneous conclusions.

CONDUCT THAT SECURED EXISTENCE

Perhaps a word of caution should be registered at this point. Placing various themes in an orderly sequence inevitably gives the impression of priority. Whatever receives first treatment must surely have been most important, and the farther down the scale something appears, the less significant it must have been. No such intention prompts the order into which kinds of conduct appear in this discussion, for the nature of the book of Proverbs rules out any such attempt to place relative values upon topics that are treated in isolated sayings. We may even be misled into thinking that frequent treatment implies special fondness, whereas it may only result from accident in the process of selecting what proverbs would be preserved. Still, certain things stand out impressively as the means by which the wise secured their existence.

Obedience to parents occurs as a cherished good; no individual who walks roughshod over those who gave him or her life can hope to enjoy its bounty. Proper respect extends beyond childhood to later years when age alters a father and mother's appearance and behavior, and when senility creeps into family relationships. Children honor their parents by heeding advice, that is, through listening to instruction and putting it into practice in their daily conduct.

Corporal punishment reinforced obedience to parents. Israel's sages never tired of urging vigorous lashings for children and fools. It seems that they almost thought a sound thrashing accomplished wonders.

> Blows that wound cleanse away evil;
> > beatings make clean the innermost parts.
> > > (20:30)

Convinced that young persons who were pointed in the right direction would forever retain their bearings, the sages freely used chastisement as a means of orientation. This bodily punishment must have been particularly harsh, for warnings against *killing* children and slaves are sprinkled throughout the proverbs. Loving parents sought justification for such cruelty in the belief that discipline sprang from love. They even elevated this principle to a higher realm.

> My child, do not despise the LORD's discipline
> > or be weary of his reproof,
> for the LORD reproves the one he loves,
> > as a father the son in whom he delights.
> > > (3:11–12)

But bodily punishment was wasted on fools, who obstinately clung to their folly, and intelligent persons, for whom a tongue-lashing accomplished wonders. Verbal rebuke therefore functioned as an alternative mode of discipline for certain individuals, and knowing when to apply this option was a sign of intelligence.[44]

The Hebrew word *mûsār* (discipline) embraced far more than simple thrashings or verbal rebuke. It also signified a whole body of teaching whose purpose was to bestow life. Naturally, such precepts and instructions had to be learned. Israelite children looked on endless study no more enthusiastically than did their Egyptian counterparts, despite promises of reward and threats of punishment.[45] Such discipline resembled a yoke by which animals were forced to work for their master's good, but in time it transformed itself into a garland of honor or a beautiful necklace. Hence, not surprisingly, like God and human parents, Wisdom submits individuals to an uncommon discipline (Sir. 6:23–31).

One consequence of disciplined action is *self-control*. Perhaps the most difficult task of all was mastering the tongue. This tiny member possessed remarkable power for healing, just as it could also destroy innocent victims. The sages recognized the value of eloquence[46] and cherished words fitly spoken. An ability to present a case well was indispensable to the sapiential enterprise. Eloquence consisted of more than artful expression; it also demanded a sense of timeliness—the ability to discern the right occasion for a given word. Even melodious notes and beautiful words did not commend themselves at all times and in every circumstance.

> Like vinegar on a wound
>   is one who sings songs to a heavy heart.
> Like a moth in clothing or a worm in wood.
>   (Prov. 25:20)

Mastery of the tongue meant one further thing—the ability to remain silent when speech would produce harmful results.

Another sign that discipline had achieved its target was the *subordination of the passions.*[47] The honor due soldiers in the ancient world was considerable, but the sages believed self-mastery deserved more praise.

> One who is slow to anger is better than the mighty,
>   and one whose temper is controlled than one who
>   captures a city.
>   (16:32)

Rampaging passions brought nothing but dishonor and destruction; small wonder Egyptian sages developed this distinctive mark of wisdom and folly into technical vocabulary. Virtuous persons were "silent ones," whereas the foolish were "passionate ones."[48] In Israel this distinction never produced surrogate designations for opposing factions, but the heated person was certainly one who camped squarely in the midst of fools. Those who kept their passions in check, even when anger seethed within, soon learned the definite advantages residing in calculated, rational action.

A good wife assisted in the endeavor to gain control over passions. Perhaps more than any other divine gift, a faithful companion filled a man's days with sheer ecstasy.

> House and wealth are inherited from parents,
>   but a prudent wife is from the LORD.
>   (19:14)

> He who finds a wife finds a good thing,
>   and obtains favor from the LORD.
>   (18:22)

Anyone unfortunate in marriage wandered about aimlessly and sighed (Sir. 36:30).

Besides these values that secured existence in the ancient world, about which the sages readily conversed, other values, though equally cherished, occur in the sayings less frequently. In some instances, they almost have to be deduced from the way something is expressed. For example, a good name is actually mentioned far less often than it forms the unspoken presupposition of what is being proclaimed.

A different problem relates to the way certain givens are used, particularly wisdom, kindness, and truth. Here virtues appear whose worth none would question in theory, but in practice the wicked trampled on them all. Whoever hoped to find life beat a path to wisdom's door. Possessing her, they learned kind treatment of friends *and enemies*. Modern interpreters may quibble about the selfish motive for refusing to repay evil deeds in the same coin, but the pragmatic ethical basis for all sapiential ethics should be kept in mind constantly.[49] Behind such pragmatism stood God's will.

> Truthful lips endure forever,
>> but a lying tongue lasts only a moment.
>>> (12:19)

> Lying lips are an abomination to the LORD,
>> but those who act faithfully are his delight.
>>> (12:22)

Generosity also caused a smile to form on the divine countenance, especially when acts of kindness caused alms to fall into pockets of poor men and women.

> Those who oppress the poor insult their Maker,
>> but those who are kind to the needy honor him.
>>> (14:31)

So far we have examined important means by which sages achieved life, without noting that even good things sometimes participate in ambiguity. Wealth is one sign of favor that carries concealed within its train the possibility of great spiritual deprivation. The author of Proverbs 30:7–9 saw this with exceptional clarity, and on the basis of this insight, asked to be spared excessive riches lest he forget that creaturely existence is characterized by dependence upon the Creator at every moment.

This ever-present ambiguity extended to other things besides possessions and gave rise to the notion of propriety.[50] The deed had to be matched with the occasion. To answer a fool according to his folly only dignified his remark, but not to respond to him strengthened the folly itself. As a result of these two possible interpretations of silence, sages had to choose which answer addressed the actual situation in an appropriate manner. Even silence possessed a measure of ambiguity, particularly when it arose from lack of courage.

Israel's teachers believed that inner resolve on their part was matched by external forces that assisted them in the struggle for life. They viewed the accumulated wisdom tradition as a social force that enhanced their own efforts significantly:

> Prudence will watch over you;
>> and understanding will guard you.
> It will save you from the way of evil,
>> from those who speak perversely.
>>> (2:11–12)

Elsewhere they developed the notion of wisdom as a guard who watched over the sages while they slept. With this idea they arrived remarkably close to the modern concept of culture or ethos, that powerful network of sanctions that all individuals unconsciously assimilate just as naturally as they eat and breathe.[51] This acknowledgment that individual effort plugged into a power that depended upon communal achievement places the sages' notion of self-reliance in an altogether new light. It follows that we should balance individualism with group influence when trying to characterize wisdom.

CONDUCT THAT LEADS TO DESTRUCTION

The vivid descriptions of *the adulteress* within the first major collection of Proverbs leave no doubt about the arch-villain in that author's view. Indeed, the previously cited allusion to prudence and understanding as guards who watch over obedient children concludes with the promise that these two qualities will also give protection from the seductive words of the loose woman. This text goes on to point out that she travels a direct path to death, so that anyone who falls victim to her blandishments abandons the path to life. By means of such language, the teacher confronted hot-blooded young men with stark reality: anyone who fools around with an adulteress, regardless of the smooth talk with which she presents her case, has by that very decision opted for death. To her, the act comes as naturally as eating.

> This is the way of an adulteress:
>   she eats, and wipes her mouth,
>   and says, "I have done no wrong."[52]
> (30:20)

But her husband takes quite a different view, and no amount of money will satisfy his lust for revenge.

> For jealousy arouses a husband's fury,
>   and he shows no restraint when he takes revenge.
> He will accept no compensation,
>   and refuses a bribe no matter how great.
> (6:34–35)

The husband's wrath is not the only factor to be reckoned with once the adulteress's enticements have caught their prey. Shame, loss of wealth, starvation, and dreaded disease may befall him as well. In the end his pitiful lot will evoke a painful concession that he should have listened to his teacher's advice.

That valuable counsel took many forms: direct appeal, extended metaphor, and autobiographical narrative, to name only three. An exquisite short poem on fidelity likens adultery to drinking from a stranger's cistern, and letting one's own springs flow into the streets. This text uses several metaphors for a wife—cistern, fountain, a lovely doe, a graceful hind—and pictures her as a protective garment wrapped around her husband. The image of clothing then becomes a leitmotif that returns to the original idea of marital fidelity. Why should you be *wrapped up* in the love of an adulteress, the teacher asks, until you reach your destination, *wrapped* in a funeral shroud (5:15–23)?

Another poem in autobiographical style resembles this one in its descriptive power (7:6–27).[53] The narrative purports to describe what a teacher has observed from a window, although the omniscient narrator takes great liberty by exposing the conversation that the author imagines must have taken place between the adulteress and her foolish young man. The time is naturally twilight, when dark deeds multiply. Dressed like a harlot, the eager wife accosts a youth, who has already taken a step in the direction of her corner, and assures him that her husband has gone on a journey and has sufficient funds to keep him away for some time. Her appeal combines beauty and seductive speech; the foolish lad cannot reject her promise of a whole night devoted to love-play, for the fantasy of drowning himself in pleasure overwhelms him. So he takes her hand, and she leads him to his death like an ox to the slaughterhouse.

> Right away he follows her,
>   and goes like an ox to the slaughter,
> or bounds like a stag toward the trap
>   until an arrow pierces its entrails.
> He is like a bird rushing into a snare,
>   not knowing that it will cost him his life.
>   (7:22–23)

While the greatest danger confronting young men was undoubtedly another man's wife, prostitutes also lured them into wayward paths. Proverbs 6:26 seems to imply that sexual relations with a harlot are a peccadillo when compared with adultery, although the point may simply be that a prostitute's price is a pittance when set over against what a married woman demands for her favors. In the small collection that shows striking affinities with *The Instruction of Amenemope*, we find the following observation about a prostitute.

> For a prostitute is a deep pit;
>   a strange woman is a narrow well.
> She lies in wait like a robber
>   and increases the number of the faithless.
>   (23:27–28)

Apparently, Israel's sages did not feel constrained, like their Mesopotamian counterparts, to warn against marrying a prostitute, whose husbands are legion.[54]

It is difficult to determine which posed a greater threat to the pursuit of life's nectar: *drunkenness* or *laziness*. At least, the sayings treat both with considerable vigor. To be sure, wine enhanced life when used wisely.[55] But like so many good things, excessive use of wine and strong drink brought ruin without delay. One saying goes so far as to claim that anyone who loves wine and oil, the symbols for pleasurable living, will never grow rich (21:17). Such austerity must have struck a solitary note in a society that placed a premium on life's good things. Be that as it may, the following picture of a drunkard's wretched plight rings true.

> Who has woe? Who has sorrow?
>   Who has strife? Who has complaining?
> Who has wounds without cause?
>   Who has redness of eyes?
> Those who linger late over wine,
>   those who keep trying mixed wines.
> Do not look at wine when it is red,
>   when it sparkles in the cup
>   and goes down smoothly.
> At the last it bites like a serpent,
>   and stings like an adder.
> Your eyes will see strange things,
>   and your mind utter perverse things.
> You will be like one who lies down in the midst of the sea,
>   like one who lies on the top of a mast.
> "They struck me," you will say, "but I was not hurt;
>   they beat me, but I did not feel it.
> When shall I awake?
>   I will seek another drink."
>
> (23:29–35)

Numerous sayings denounce sluggards and describe the dismal lot that befalls lazy persons. Matchless imagery compares a sluggard tossing on his bed with a door's turning on its hinges (26:14). Sometimes an element of ridicule surfaces, as in the observation that a sluggard is too lazy to lift a spoon to his mouth (26:15). The flimsy excuses that he offers for inactivity present themselves as ludicrous, for example, when he stays in the house for fear a lion might lurk outside (26:13). The consequences of such laziness lacked the slightest tinge of humor—since the sluggard had failed to plow his fields and plant a crop, starvation would raid his pantry. One saying almost personified poverty and want.

> A little sleep, a little slumber,
>   a little folding of the hands to rest,
> and poverty will come upon you like a robber,
>   and want like an armed warrior.
>
> (6:10–11)

The point may have been that poverty will overpower its hapless victim, rather than taking him by surprise. In any event, Israel's sages tried their utmost to reduce the possibility that any sluggard could interpret his miserable fate as wholly unexpected.

Alongside these three (the adulteress, drunkenness, and laziness), *gossip* and other misuse of the tongue worked to bring destruction and to undermine society itself. So universal was this evil that one saying almost equates talkativeness and sin:

> When words are many, transgression is not lacking,
>> but the prudent are restrained in speech.
>>> (10:19)

Given the strong attraction of privileged information concerning forbidden conduct, one is not surprised to read:

> The words of a whisperer are like delicious morsels;
>> they go down into the inner parts of the body.
>>> (18:8)

Some individuals reinforced their insidious vocabulary with appropriate body language:

> winking the eye, shuffling the feet,
>> pointing the fingers.
>>> (6:13)

For such persons, violence was food and drink (4:17).

Those who became adept at body language transformed their entire being into an organ of speech—one that succeeded in communicating wickedness from head to toe.

> There are six things that the LORD hates,
>> seven that are an abomination to him:
> haughty eyes, a lying tongue,
>> and hands that shed innocent blood,
> a heart that devises wicked plans,
>> feet that hurry to run to evil,
> a lying witness who testifies falsely,
>> and one who sows discord in a family.
>>> (6:16–19)

Here as elsewhere (8:13) the subversive power of the tongue gets equal billing to actual physical violence. In this instance the enormity of abusive and lying words lingered in the author's imagination so powerfully that the saying returns to this theme after completing a clever poem about various parts of the body.

These *four kinds of threats to existence—adultery, drunken debauchery, laziness, and gossip*—were by no means the only dangers that lured young people and adults away from the path to life, but the numerous other temptations elicited less picturesque attacks. In most cases, the teachers simply name the villain: folly, pride, greed, presumption, and so forth. Often a theological refutation of such behavior is offered. False scales are an abomination to God; mockery of the poor is an affront to their Creator; pride is detestable to the Lord.

Another kind of annoyance, a nagging wife, evoked considerable comment.

> To restrain her is to restrain the wind
>> or to grasp oil in the right hand.
>>> (27:16)

The masculine viewpoint of this and other sayings is obvious, for nothing is said about verbally or physically abusive husbands, who obviously existed.[56] In short, both at home and in the open streets mighty foes poised in readiness to attack innocent prey, eager to drag still one more victim into their lair.

THEOLOGICAL SYNTHESIS

To combat such foes, self-reliance hardly sufficed. Instead, one donned the armor forged by the entire wisdom tradition (28:26). Whether that suit of armor fashioned wholly by human hands could withstand the poisonous arrows whistling from every direction was a debatable point. At least one teacher advised against dependence upon one's own understanding (presumably however much it was informed by the wisdom tradition) in favor of complete trust in the Lord (3:5). At a much later time this tension between self-reliance and trust in God crops up in the teaching of a single individual.

> Whatever you are doing, rely on yourself,
>   for this too is a way of keeping the commandments.
>   (Sir. 32:23 NEB)

> But also trust your own judgement,
> for it is your most reliable counsellor.
>   (Sir. 37:13 NEB)

In both instances, these strong affirmations of self-reliance within Sirach give way to a religious impulse: trust the Lord, and above all pray to the Most High.

The struggle to assert the sufficiency of human effort, on the one hand, and to defend a conviction that divine aid was essential, on the other hand, turned Israelite wisdom into an exciting contest.[57] We shall soon discover that these competing comprehensions of reality ultimately transformed the essential character of wisdom. For now, let us take a close look at this theologization of wisdom within the book of Proverbs.

To begin with, the common assumption that old wisdom, as it is usually called, lacked religious content altogether does not commend itself. Anyone who accepts the hypothesis of an earlier secular wisdom must reckon with the fact that a conscious editing process has infused later piety into the old wisdom texts so thoroughly that the additions can be removed only by sheer conjecture. Alternatively, the person who opts for secular wisdom must be compelled grudgingly to admit that it never existed. The truth residing within this attempt to isolate secular wisdom is that a definite editing of earlier sayings has taken place, one in which deeply felt religious sentiments were consciously allowed to interpret older texts.[58] However, this editing process must surely have found a kindred base upon which to work. It follows that wisdom contained a religious element from the beginning. That ingredient must have focused upon the limits imposed upon human beings by the Creator.

> No wisdom, no understanding, no counsel,
>   can avail against the Lord.
> The horse is made ready for the day of battle,
>   but the victory belongs to the Lord.
>   (Prov. 21:30–31)

> The plans of the mind belong to mortals,
>   but the answer of the tongue is from the Lord.
>   (16:1)

In attempting to trace the evolution of wisdom thinking in ancient Israel, one should not posit a movement from pure secularism to theological reflection. But how else can one tackle this vexing problem? Perhaps by distinguishing three fundamental manifestations of that phenomenon called wisdom: family, court, and theological wisdom. These three distinct types of thinking differ with regard to the goal envisioned, the stance, and the method adopted to achieve that purpose.

Family wisdom, or folk proverbs, aimed to accomplish a single goal: the mastering of life.[59] As a means of achieving this valuable ambition, observant individuals combined their talents in order to understand nature and human relationships. That is, they developed insights from nature and practical wisdom. The former consisted of the study of natural phenomena and the compilation of lists in which comparable actions were placed alongside one another. The fruits of such labor now exist in the numerical proverbs and enumeration of kindred things that have been collected, for the most part, in Proverbs 30. Possibly, such texts lie behind other passages in the larger corpus of Wisdom literature, particularly the divine speeches in Job, as well as the description of the wonders of nature in Sirach 43. Practical, or experiential, wisdom was an elementary ordering of life in all its dimensions. It entailed close study of human behavior in every conceivable situation, from which certain basic principles for successful conduct were formulated. Such lessons assumed proverbial form— brief, pregnant, and paradigmatic.

The chief disseminator of such succinct aids to successful living was the father. Presumably, he was assisted in this task by the mother. The two terms, "father" and "mother," occur with sufficient regularity to warrant the conclusion that popular wisdom had its original context within individual families. Emphasis upon the formation of character belongs naturally to this intimate circle, specifically strong admonitions to industry, sobriety, and control of the tongue. Here sharp divisions serve to remove any possibility for error where good and evil, truth and falsehood, wisdom and folly are concerned. The hortatory stance arose as an appropriate means of reinforcing parental authority for sayings that in themselves lacked motivations and warnings to undergird their cogency. At this early stage legal formulations and sapiential instruction probably resembled one another, especially in style.[60]

Although the vast majority of canonical proverbs seem to have arisen among the populace in small villages, a few of them *may* derive from the *royal court*.[61] There is no reason for the tradition to arise associating Hezekiah with wisdom unless a historical basis for such thinking existed, although legends do seem to cling to this king (cf. Isaiah 36–39) just as they do to Solomon, whom Hezekiah sought to resemble.[62] To be sure, no single proverb demands a court setting, for persons who resided far away from palaces could reckon with royal power and the mystery of a king's personality. Conversely, members of a court could easily have reflected on the concerns described under popular wisdom above.

Court wisdom had a limited clientele; it was restricted to a select group of potential rulers and advisors to persons in power.[63] Such activity that enabled the government to survive endless attack from without and ruthless insiders who hungered for power had to be unflinchingly realistic[64] and at times unscrupulous. This kind of wisdom was noticeably more secular than religious. The chief means of communicating court wisdom was didactic. Here the teachers seem much more conscious of pedagogical technique; thus they attach motive clauses and reasons to their sayings. In addition, they use rhetorical questions freely and often rely upon exhortation and admonition.

Their basic interests reflect the situation of the court: proper table manners, eloquence, propriety, humility before superiors, fidelity, and so forth. Naturally, court wisdom instructs future court personnel about ways to behave around kings and warns against presumption with respect to royal dispositions. This wisdom stresses the ruler's responsibility for ensuring justice and recognizes that his throne is founded on righteousness. Perhaps the royal court gave special urgency to the universal problem of passion, inasmuch as temptations to adultery may have increased the closer one came to the royal court. Advice about business investments and truthful witness had its place here. Eloquence may even have included the art of entertaining nobles; certainly this interest in lively dialogue comes to prominence in late wisdom.[65] The "Contest of Darius's Guards" preserved in 1 Esdras 3:1–5:3 bears eloquent testimony to such entertainment.[66] We cannot be absolutely certain that riddles and impossible questions belonged at the royal court, although biblical legend about the Queen of Sheba and a tradition within Josephus's *Antiquities* make it highly likely that these sages sometimes busied themselves with life's enigmas.[67]

The third type of wisdom differs fundamentally from these two predecessors. *Theological wisdom*[68] spreads its net widely, hoping to catch as many subjects as possible. Its goal is to provide education for everyone, regardless of social standing or vocational intention. The primary means of reaching this target are dialogue and admonition, a direct appeal that rests upon religious foundations. Argument accompanies exhortations or warnings, and themes constitute brief poems. A religious dogmatism concerning proper conduct before God and humans underlies the whole system of instruction. To a certain extent, even God is caught up in this system, especially in the notion of exact reward and retribution.[69] Conscious didactic concern gives rise to numerous stylistic niceties and eventually produces a powerful means of relating God to creatures without relying upon direct revelation to prophets, priests, or poets.

Fear of the Lord

Possibly the most distinctive feature in theological wisdom is the notion concerning proper "fear of the LORD." This idea changes over a period of time, so that its use differs considerably in Job and Ecclesiastes from that in Proverbs.[70] For now, we are concerned only with the usage in the book of Proverbs. Here the "fear of the LORD" amounts to "religion" as we understand it today. By "fear of the LORD" these sages called attention to religious devotion in the richest sense of the phrase. It meant, purely and simply, that which every human being owes the Creator. That is why the editor who wrote the motto for the first collection of Proverbs can affirm that religious devotion constitutes the beginning and fundamental principle of all knowledge. Without a vital relationship with God, no one could possibly attain sufficient wisdom to merit the adjective "wise," for the source of all knowledge was divine.

Initially, the phrase "fear of the LORD" seems to have amounted to religious devotion or proper awe in the face of divine mystery, but as time passed the idea became considerably broader. In the older collections within Proverbs, particularly those designated Solomonic, the term has this narrow sense of religious duty. The initial collection uses the phrase "fear of the LORD" in such a way as almost to suggest *the laws and statutes* that God had made known to Israel. To be sure, the sages who edited and compiled these discourses never quite identify the old idea, "fear of the LORD," with covenantal obligations, but one senses that these teachers would have claimed Ben Sira as an authentic heir to their specific tradition.[71] In him the implicit assumptions underlying Proverbs 1–9 become entirely explicit. "Fear of the LORD" consists of the ancient covenantal obligations, and no genuine conflict exists between wisdom and sacred history.

Personification of Wisdom and Folly

The second feature of theological wisdom is by far the liveliest theme in Proverbs—the personification of wisdom and folly. This remarkable development in theological reflection arose from frequent talk about limits imposed upon human knowledge and ability, as well as from the recognition that men's and women's fates lay in their own hands. The silence of heaven was a terrible burden; so was the lack of certainty about the vast accumulation of knowledge. Did it, or did it not, accord with the will of God? In short, frail humans acknowledge a need for contact with the universal Lord, particularly as the idea of exact reward and retribution for good and evil gradually eroded. Personified Wisdom achieved that purpose for these teachers.[72]

It naturally follows that prophetic influence intrudes where personified Wisdom is concerned, for inspired utterance had been equated with prophecy from time immemorial. Thus we are not surprised to hear Wisdom berating those who spurn her invitation; even her language is drawn from prophetic indictment (Prov. 1:20–33). Here a spurned woman complains that no one heeded when she stretched out her hand in invitation, so now she will laugh when calamity strikes. Furthermore, she will withdraw so that no one can find her and persuade her to intercede during the time of punishment. This dreadful moment is described with language faintly resembling futility curses—the fruit and surfeit of their labor will hardly be something for enjoyment.[73] We should note the scene for Wisdom's activity: she proclaims her message in the crowded marketplace, daring to compete with one and all for the attention of the people. At one point this remarkable individual goes beyond what any prophet would have said. She promises life to those who listen to her. Amos, for example, could speak in God's name: "Seek me and live" (5:4). But it is unthinkable that he would have spoken this way in his own name.

Some of these same themes characterize Proverbs 8, but this passage introduces some wholly new concepts. The location for Wisdom's proclamation is the same, that is, the busy places where people carry out their daily activities. Wisdom emphasizes the reliability of her teaching and promises that it is priceless. In addition, she boasts considerable authority—kings and governors, princes and rulers, derive their nobility from her. All this is just what one expects Wisdom to say, right down to the brief description of things she despises: pride, presumption, evil courses, subversive talk. But she does not end her speech with characterizations of her present task or invitation. Instead, she reflects upon the beginning when she played in God's presence prior to the creation of the world.[74]

Wisdom was the first of God's creative works; she was fashioned long before earth and sea came to be and before the mountains and hills settled into their place. She stood beside the Deity and watched while God constructed the heavens, girdled the ocean with the horizon, fixed the clouds, prescribed limits for the sea, and knit earth's foundation together. Playing before God, Wisdom was a daily delight, a little child bringing great pleasure. Once the earth was created she changed her playground and began to delight in men and women. Therefore, she issues her invitation to life, and pronounces blessings upon those who find her. Although Wisdom possesses a lofty position in this poem, the emphasis rightly falls on divine majesty.

Once upon earth Wisdom does some fashioning of her own (9:1); after completing a house with seven pillars, she invites simpletons and fools to dine with her. Maidens assure these unlikely prospects for knowledge that all is not hopeless in their case. A few sips of her spiced wine and several morsels of her food, together with resolve to abandon folly, will accomplish wonders.

For now, we shall postpone discussion of the rich development in the sages' understanding of personified Wisdom, particularly as they describe her in Job 28, Sirach 24, and Wisdom 7–8.[75] However, one further word needs to be said about an interesting variation in Proverbs. Just as wisdom is pictured as a woman, so folly is also portrayed in human form. Folly, or Stupidity, is set over against Wisdom, each competing for the lives of individuals.

> The foolish woman is loud;
>   she is ignorant and knows nothing.
> She sits at the door of her house,
>   on a seat at the high places of the town,
> calling to those who pass by,
>   who are going straight on their way,
> "You who are simple, turn in here!"
>   And to those without sense she says,
> "Stolen water is sweet,
>   and bread eaten in secret is pleasant."
> But they do not know that the dead are there,
>   that her guests are in the depths of Sheol.
>   (Prov. 9:13–18)

Here, as also in Genesis 3, knowledge is closely associated with forbidden fruit.[76] Although no mention of knowledge occurs in this harsh caricature of Wisdom, Folly must surely be understood as an opponent who boasts a better kind of knowledge than Wisdom can offer. For some strange reason, later sages do not develop this highly interesting character of a seductress. Such reluctance to speak further about personified Stupidity surely arose from the attractiveness of fertility goddesses in the ancient world, even to Israelites.[77]

So far in this discussion nothing has been said about the source for this personification of Wisdom and Folly. Perhaps the Hebrew plural form *ḥokmôt* offers a clue that a Canaanite goddess by that name existed,[78] but convincing proof for this hypothesis is lacking. On the other hand, considerable evidence for an Egyptian provenance for this portrayal of Wisdom has been assimilated.[79] The striking similarities between Wisdom and the Egyptian notion of Maʿat, particularly with regard to the cosmological speculation (existence before creation, the darling of God, the possession of life and right dealing in her hand), are offset by the monotheism in Proverbs and the initiative of Wisdom in wooing the young. Israel's psalmists and poets expressed themselves at times by means of personified virtues. From pictures of righteousness and truth kissing each other, or prudence and understanding watching over someone, it is a tiny step to personified Wisdom. But the further jump to cosmological speculation probably came as the result of outside influence. The erotic dimension may derive from hymnic speculation about Ishtar, the goddess of love in Mesopotamia.

Regardless of the provenance for this personification, the picture of Wisdom possessed remarkable didactic power. Besides vividness, the portrait had sex appeal, which must have captured young men's fantasies immediately. The highly erotic language associated with Wisdom certainly justifies this understanding of the image. Most importantly, the idea enabled sages to talk about a heavenly messenger without unduly compromising their conviction that they themselves controlled their fate. By means of Wisdom, these teachers were able to say that God does more than conceal truth at the moment of creation. Through her, God communicates life-giving knowledge in the living present.

This amazing development within canonical Proverbs means that the sages understood the tension between their own quest for knowledge and wisdom's readiness to be found, which implied in their thinking that God really desired to communicate life-giving knowledge despite a propensity toward concealing precious data. Thus they wrestled increasingly with a fundamental problem: Am I for myself, or is someone else for me? That is, must I secure my existence through my own ingenuity and right conduct, or does the Creator bestow favor upon me because my own achievements do not suffice? This question became an existential one for the author of the book of Job.

NOTES

1. The appropriateness of this concept of order has been questioned, largely on grounds of Yahweh's supreme authority, but nothing requires the subjection of the Deity to this principle. How else can one acknowledge the sages' attitude toward mastering life by studying the secrets hidden in nature and human behavior? They believed that rules of conduct could be ascertained by careful observation, and they devoted considerable energy to spelling out these rules by which to live. The primary concern, however, is moral development, not knowledge of the universe.

2. Klaus Koch's language with reference to Yahweh's role in reward and punishment, as well as his extreme view of an act producing its own consequences, has resulted in energetic resistance. Few scholars concur in his view that Yahweh's sole function was that of a midwife assisting in birthing the inevitable consequence of behavior (see Koch, "Is There a Doctrine of Retribution in the Old Testament?" in *Theodicy in the Old Testament*, ed. James L. Crenshaw [IRT; Philadephia: Fortress, 1983], 42–56). Adams, *Wisdom in Transition*, argues that tension always existed throughout the ancient Near East between actions and their inevitable consequences, on the one hand, and the deity's freedom to act with disregard for human merit, on the other hand.

3. Von Rad, *Wisdom in Israel*, 115–24.

4. Landes, "Jonah: A *Māšāl?*" 139; and William McKane, *Proverbs: A New Approach* (OTL; Philadelphia: Westminster, 1970), 22–33, reject the latter possibility.

5. Quoted in Aage Bentzen, *Introduction to the Old Testament*, 2 vols. (Copenhagen: Gad, 1948), 1:168.

6. This definition has been attributed to Cervantes.

7. Thompson, *Form and Function of Proverbs*, 23.

8. Roger D. Abrahams, "On Proverb Collecting and Proverb Collection," *Proverbium* 8 (1967): 181–84. Katharine J. Dell, *The Book of Proverbs in Social and Theological Context* (Cambridge: Cambridge University, 2006), endeavors to integrate Wisdom literature into the wider canon by demonstrating influence on the sages from prophecy and Deuteronomy. In her view, the theological beliefs of the general culture were also shared by the sages, and there is no basis for considering wisdom outside the realm of biblical theology.

Perdue, *Sword and Stylus*, 100–16, emphasizes the administrative function of those responsible for the book of Proverbs. He also stresses the theological and cultic features of their thought.

9. Thompson, *Form and Function*, 59–68; Scott, *Proverbs. Ecclesiastes* (AB 18; Garden City, N.Y.: Doubleday, 1965), 18–20; James L. Kugel, *The Idea of Biblical Poetry Parallelism and Its History* (New Haven: Yale University, 1981); and Robert Alter, *The Art of Biblical Poetry* (New York: Basic Books, 1985).

10. Schmid, *Wesen und Geschichte der Weisheit*, 159 n. 69. In many instances, particularly within Qoheleth, a comparison certainly occurs.

11. R. B. Y. Scott, *The Way of Wisdom in the Old Testament* (New York: Macmillan, 1971), 59–63.

12. The exact relationship between this section of proverbs and the Egyptian text has generated extensive discussion. Some interpreters posit a prior work from which both may have drawn, while others insist that the canonical author borrowed eleven sayings from *Amenemope* (see A. Niccacci, "Proverbi 22:17–23:11," *Studii Franciscani Liber Annuus* [Jerusalem] 29 [1979]: 42–72; and D. Römheld, *Wege der Weisheit. Die Lehren Amenemopes und Proverbien 22:17–24:22* [BZAW 184; Berlin: de Gruyter, 1989]). Niccacci argues that 22:17–23:11 is an earlier work of ten instructions and that 22:17–24:22 comprises two separate collections. Römheld insists that 24:14–24:22 contains thirty sayings edited to resemble *Amenemope*. The complexity of the issue is illustrated by R. N. Whybray's recent analysis, particularly *The Composition of the Book of Proverbs* (JSOTSup 168; Sheffield: JSOT, 1994), 132–47; and "The Structure and Composition of Proverbs 22:17–24:22," in *Crossing the Boundaries: Essays in Biblical Interpretation in Honour of Michael D. Goulder*, ed. S. E. Porter et al. (BIS 8; Leiden: Brill, 1994), 83–96. Whybray does not find thirty sayings in this unit; hence he rejects the emendation of Prov. 22:20 to "thirty."

13. This seems to be the primary warning in Proverbs 1–9 ("Seduction is the main [indeed, almost the only] peril warned against in the lectures," Michael V. Fox, "Ideas of Wisdom in Proverbs 1–9," *JBL* 116 (1997): 620. Joseph Blenkinsopp, "The Social Context of the 'Outsider Woman' in Proverbs 1–9," *Bib* 71 (1991): 457–73; and Harold C. Washington, "The Strange Woman of Proverbs 1–9 and Post-Exilic Judean Society," in *Second Temple Studies, 2: Temple and Community in the Persian Period*, ed. Tamara C. Eskenazi and Kent H. Richards (JSOTSup 175; Sheffield: JSOT, 1994), 217–42, view the sages' concern to reject the seductive invitation of the strange woman against the background of the situation confronted by Ezra and Nehemiah.

14. J.-N. Aletti, "Séduction et parole en Proverbs I–IX," *VT* 27 (1977): 129–44, emphasizes the mechanism of seduction, the eloquence, by which the strange woman overcomes young men's resistance to her overtures.

15. Von Rad, *Wisdom in Israel*, 53–73.

16. Carol A. Newsom, "Woman and the Discourse of Patriarchal Wisdom: A Study of Proverbs 1–9," in *Gender and Difference in Ancient Israel*, ed. Peggy L. Day (Minneapolis: Fortress, 1989), 142–60, discerns the dominant voice of patriarchy in these instructions, a voice that drowns out that of the sons as well as all feminine voices. See also James L. Crenshaw, "The Missing Voice," in *A Biblical Itinerary: In Search of Method, Form and Content. Essays in Honor of George W. Coats*, ed. E. E. Carpenter (JSOTSup 240; Sheffield: Sheffield Academic, 1997), 123–43.

17. William P. Brown, *Character in Crisis*; and H. Delkurt, *Ethische Einsichten in der alttestamentlichen Spruchweisheit* (BThSt 21; Neukirchen-Vluyn: Neukirchener, 1993).

18. Fox, "Ideas of Wisdom in Proverbs 1–9"; Whybray, *The Composition of the Book of Proverbs*; and idem, *Proverbs* (Grand Rapids: Eerdmans, 1994). According to Fox, whose analysis is followed here, the two voices are heard in counterpoint, and in the interludes Wisdom says the same things about herself that the father says about her in the lectures. Fox understands personified Wisdom as a universal of which the particulars of human wisdom are imperfect images or realization.

19. There has been growing attention to this problem, with little result other than the many insights into the meaning of specific sayings. See Raymond C. van Leeuwen, *Context and Meaning in Proverbs 25–27* (SBLDS 96; Atlanta: Scholars, 1988); Scott R. Harris, *Proverbs 1–9: A Study of Inner-Biblical Interpretation* (SBLDS 150; Atlanta: Scholars, 1995); Ruth Scoralick, *Einzelspruch und Sammlung: Komposition im Buch der Sprichwörter Kapitel 10–15* (BZAW 232; Berlin: de Gruyter, 1995); Ted Hildebrant, "Proverbial Pairs: Compositional Units in Proverbs 10–29," *JBL* 107 (1988): 207–24, J. Krispenz, *Spruchkomposition im Buch Proverbia* (EHS 349; Frankfurt: Peter Lang, 1989); K. M. Heim, *Like Grapes of Gold Set in Silver: Proverbial Clusters in Proverbs 10:1–22:16* (BZAW 273; Berlin: de Gruyter, 2001); and Otto Plöger, "Zur Auslegung der Sentenzensammlungen des Proverbienbuches," in *Probleme biblischer Theologie: Gerhard von Rad zum 70. Geburtstag*, ed. H. W. Wolff (Munich: Kaiser, 1971), 402–16. Seenam Kim, *The Coherence of the Collections in the Book of Proverbs* (Eugene, Or.: Pickwick, 2007), launches a fresh approach, the tabulation of words that are unique to each collection as well as of vocabulary that is shared among the various collections. Kim claims to have isolated distinctive wisdom features for each collection, demonstrating coherence in the entire book of Proverbs. Even those who do not share Kim's assumptions about such exhaustive lists will surely appreciate the light he has thrown on sapiential use. In some ways, his study resembles that of Daniel C. Snell, *Twice-Told Proverbs and the Composition of the Book of Proverbs* (Winona Lake, Ind.: Eisenbrauns, 1993).

20. The sages' attitude toward poverty and wealth is elusive, partly because of their assumption that one controls his own destiny, which often complicated matters when poverty actually struck an individual. On the problem, see James L. Crenshaw, "Poverty and Punishment in the Book of Proverbs," *QR* 9 (1989): 30–43 (*UAPQ*, 396–405); Harold C. Washington, *Wealth and Poverty in the Instruction of Amenemope and the Hebrew Proverbs* (SBLDS 142: Atlanta: Scholars, 1994); and R. N. Whybray, *Wealth and Poverty in the Book of Proverbs* (JSOTSup 99; Sheffield: JSOT, 1990).

21. A convenient analysis is that of Whybray, *Composition*, 132–45, who finds ten instructions in 22:17–23:11 and five more in 23:12–24:22 (23:12–18; 23:19–28; 24:3–9; 24:10–12; 24:13–22; and 24:1–2). A. Meinhold, *Die Sprüche* (2 vols.; Zurich: Theologischer Verlag, 1991), argues for thirty units in 22:17–23:11 and thirty more in 23:12–24:22.

22. Westermann, *Roots of Wisdom*; and idem, "Weisheit im Sprichwort," 73–85 in *Schalom: Studien zu Glaube und Geschichte Israels. Festschrift A. Jepsen*, ed. K.-H. Bernhardt (AzTh 1/46; Stuttgart: Calwer, 1971), considers systematic thought about the order of the world and human behavioral traits a late development. He thinks wisdom thought passed through three stages: first a preliterate one in villages and representing tribal life; second, an educational one profoundly influenced by foreign wisdom; and third, systematic reflection. Dell, *Book of Proverbs*, emphasizes orality as a factor to be reckoned with in studying the emergence of the proverbial collections.

23. Udo Skladny, *Die ältesten Spruchsammlungen in Israel* (Göttingen: Vandenhoeck & Ruprecht, 1962), 25–46, views 16:1–22:16 as instruction directed at royal officials. Perdue, *Sword and Stylus*, 86–89, locates the earliest collections in the period of the monarchy. He thinks the addition of smaller collections and the overall introduction, 1:2–9, took place somewhat later, perhaps in the Ptolemaic and Hellenistic eras.

24. See Snell, *Twice-Told Proverbs*. In terms of scope, this brief collection leans toward rural interests, even if introduced by a judgment about forensics.

25. For my own view of this intriguing unit, see "Clanging Symbols," in *Justice and the Holy: Essays in Honor of Walter Harrelson*, ed. Douglas A. Knight and Peter J. Paris (Atlanta: Scholars, 1989), 51–64 (*UAPQ*, 371–82). The translation of this difficult text continues to baffle the experts. The most daring approach comes from E. Lipiński, "Peninna, Iti'el et l'Athlète," *VT* 17 (1967): 68–75. He thinks not of an exhausted speaker but of a boastful athlete who claims to have attained superhuman insights. Some interpreters do not separate this collection from the following observations based on numerical sequence (e.g., Bruce K. Waltke, *The Book of Proverbs: Chapters 15–31* [NICOT; Grand Rapids: Eerdmans, 2005], 454–501).

26. On numerical sayings, see Wolfgang M. W. Roth, *Numerical Sayings in the Old Testament: A Form-Critical Study* (VTSup 13; Leiden: Brill, 1965); and Georg Sauer, *Die Sprüche Agurs: Untersuchungen zur Herkunft, Verbreitung und Bedeutung einer biblischer Stilform unter besonderer Berucksichtigung von Proverbia c. 30* (BWANT 84; Stuttgart: Kohlhammer, 1963). The latter stresses Canaanite influence; the phenomenon is virtually absent from Mesopotamian wisdom.

27. Yair Hoffman, *A Blemished Perfection: The Book of Job in Context* (JSOTSup 213; Sheffield: Sheffield Academic, 1996), emphasizes the significance of catalogs, or lists, to the author of Job; but Michael V. Fox, "Egyptian Onomastica and Biblical Wisdom," *VT* 36 (1986): 302–10, questions the appropriateness of this category in describing canonical material.

28. James L. Crenshaw, "A Mother's Instruction to Her Son (Proverbs 31:1–9)," in *Perspectives on the Hebrew Bible: Essays in Honor of Walter J. Harrelson*, ed. Crenshaw (Macon, Ga.: Mercer University, 1988), 9–22 (*UAPQ*, 383–95). On royal ideology, see Leonidas Kalugila, *The Wise King* (ConBOT 15; Lund: Gleerup, 1980). The expectation that rulers would attend to the needs of widows, orphans, and the poor knew no geographical boundaries. Such royal ideology was promulgated by the court but also represents popular longing for justice.

29. Together with chaps. 1–9, where Wisdom is personified and aggressively seeks a following, 31:10–31 provides a frame for the entire book (Whybray, *Composition*, 159–65). The superhuman qualities of the woman have led scholars to conclude that the final poem also personified Wisdom, while at the same time stressing her earthiness lest she be understood as a goddess (see Claudia V. Camp, *Wisdom and the Feminine in the Book of Proverbs* [BLS 11; Sheffield: Almond, 1985], 90–92, 186–91; see also T. P. McCreesh, "Wisdom as Wife: Proverbs 31:10–31," *RB* 92 [1985]: 25–46).

30. Patrick W. Skehan, "The Seven Columns of Wisdom's House in Proverbs, 1–9," *CBQ* 9 (1947): 190–98, and in revised form in *Studies in Israelite Poetry and Wisdom* (CBQMS 1; Washington, D.C.: Catholic Biblical Association of America, 1971), 9–14, envisions the seven columns of Wisdom's house as the seven poems in Proverbs 2–7, while chaps. 8–9 constitute the house's frame.

31. Skehan, *Studies in Israelite Poetry*, 9–45.

32. McKane, *Proverbs*, 7, 11.

33. McKane, *Prophets and Wise Men;* idem, *Proverbs,* 1–47; and Whybray, *Wisdom in Proverbs: The Concept of Wisdom in Proverbs 1–9* (*SBT* 1/45; London: SCM, 1965). The question today appears to be this: How deeply immersed in ordinary Yahwism were the sages? At the very least, they used the name Yahweh (with the exception of Qoheleth). They also used such vocabulary as fear of Yahweh, abomination of Yahweh (a preferred term in the book of Deuteronomy), covenant, and torah. Do these expressions have the same sense in Proverbs that they do in the nonsapiential books? I think not.

34. Perhaps historical circumstances led to a growing sense of personal piety in Israel resembling that in ancient Egypt beginning with the *Instructions of Ani* and *Ptahhotep,* on which see Miriam Lichtheim, *AEL,* 2:146–47; Jan Assmann, *The Search for God in Ancient Egypt,* trans. David Lorton (Ithaca: Cornell University, 2001), and Rainer Albertz, *Persönliche Frömmigkeit und offizielle Religion: Religionsinterner Pluralismus in Israel und Babylon* (1975; reprint, Atlanta: Society of Biblical Literature, 2005).

35. Rainer Albertz, *A History of Israelite Religion in the Old Testament Period,* trans. John Bowden (2 vols.; OTL; Louisville: Westminster John Knox, 1994), conjectures that a division arose in the postexilic upper class over the poor, one group insisting that they should be treated kindly and another group opposing such indications of solidarity. Class conflict seems to have increased the more vulnerable an individual became as the result of shifting economic circumstances.

36. Views range from the positing of an extensive system of formal education, most recently by Heaton, *School Tradition,* to cautious acceptance of educational establishments by Graham I. Davies, "Were There Schools in Ancient Israel?" in *Wisdom in Ancient Israel,* ed. Day et al., 199–211; Crenshaw, *Education in Ancient Israel;* Carr, *Writing on the Tablet of the Heart;* and even to an emphatic no by Stuart Weeks, *Early Israelite Wisdom,* 132–56.

37. The neat form-critical assumption that simplicity of form requires an early date, and vice versa, comes to grief over the late *Instruction of Ankhsheshonqy.*

38. Carole Rader Fontaine, *Traditional Saying in the Old Testament* (BLS 5; Sheffield: Almond, 1982). Fontaine draws upon paroemiological studies in general to clarify the traditional saying in ancient Israel. She focuses on the following texts: (1) Judges 8:2 ("Is not the gleaning of the grapes of Ephraim better than the vintage of Abiezer?"); (2) Judges 8:21 ("For as the man is, so is his strength"); (3) 1 Samuel 16:7 ("Man looks on the outward appearance, but the LORD looks on the heart"); (4) 1 Samuel 24:14 (Eng. 13) ("Out of the wicked comes forth wickedness"); (5) 1 Kings 20:11 ("Let not him that girds on his armor boast himself as he that puts it off"). Other texts are often cited in this connection, for example, Ezek. 18:2 (Jer. 31:29), "The fathers have eaten sour grapes, and the children's teeth are set on edge," and Ezek. 16:44 ("Like mother, like daughter").

39. On the problems attending a historical reading of this reference to Hezekiah's men, see M. Carasic, "Who Were the Men of Hezekiah (Proverbs XXV I)?" *VT* 44 (1994): 291–300. The studies by Katharine Dell, *Book of Proverbs,* and Leo Perdue, *Sword and Stylus,* illustrate the impenetrable world resting behind sapiential literature. Their conclusions, although often plausible, are largely fiction. Nevertheless, their fertile imagination throws considerable light on the ancient world of the sages. See James L. Crenshaw, "Love Is Stronger than Death: Intimations of Life beyond the Grave," in *Resurrection: The Origin and Future of a Biblical Doctrine,* ed. James H. Charlesworth (New York: T & T Clark, 2006), 53–78; and Edward W. Wright, *The Early History of Heaven* (New York: Oxford University, 2000).

40. Norman Habel, "The Symbolism of Wisdom in Proverbs 1–9," *Int* 26 (1972): 131–57. Kim, *Coherence of the Collections*, 5–8, discusses the five different words for path and their occurrence in the several collections.

41. Wisdom 5:9–14 adapts this saying and suggests that its meaning concerns the absence of any trace of movement. This example of intertextuality raises the fundamental problem of such readings that have become something of a trend. Did the author of Wisdom of Solomon learn this saying from studying a canonical text or from popular tradition? There is no way of answering that important question.

42. The textual basis in Proverbs 10–15 for this identification of fools with the wicked is minimal, according to Scoralick, *Einzelspruch und Sammlung*, 67–73. She isolates five units in Proverbs 10–15, with 12:14–13:2 as a nodal point. Sapiential ethics has been studied by Eckart Otto, *Theologische Ethik des Alten Testament* (Theologische Wissenschaft 3/2; Stuttgart: Kohlhammer, 1994), 117–74; and Miriam Lichtheim, *Moral Values in Egypt* (OBO 155; Fribourg: University Press, 1997).

43. W. O. E. Oesterley, *The Book of Proverbs* (Westminster Commentaries; London: Methuen, 1929), LXXXIV–LXXXVII. In addition, locutions such as *ḥăsar lēb*, "intellectually deficient," point to behavior that is unacceptable to the wise. Shupak, *Where Can Wisdom Be Found?* 339, considers this expression genuinely Israelite despite its similarity to a phrase in Egyptian.

44. The Aramaic *Proverbs of Ahiqar* observes: "Spare not your son from the rod; otherwise, can you save him [from *wickedness*]?" (# 3). The Syriac version reads more strongly: "My son, withhold not thy son from stripes; for the beating of a boy is like manure to the garden, and like rope to an ass (or any other beast) and like tether on the foot of an ass" (Lindenberger, *Aramaic Proverbs of Ahiqar*, 49).On the harsh punishment associated with ancient education, see my *Education in Ancient Israel*, 147–49, 165–67.

45. See chapter 5, "Resistance to Learning," in my *Education in Ancient Israel*.

46. Walter Bühlmann, *Vom Rechten Reden und Schweigen* (OBO 12; Fribourg: Universitätsverlag, 1976); and Antoon Schoors, *The Preacher Sought to Find Pleasing Words* (2 vols.; OLA 41, 43; Leuven: Peeters, 1992–2004). The title of this magisterial work derives from an observation by the first epilogist to Ecclesiastes in 12:10.

47. A certain irony adheres to the idea that one must suppress the passions although the God of Israel, Yahweh, was supremely passionate. The outbursts of Job and Elihu indicate that sages could vent their anger when the circumstances called for it, although most interpreters think Elihu's anger is satirized. Moreover, the erotic attachment to personified Wisdom gave legitimacy to sexual desire in the service of knowledge. On Yahweh's passion, see James L. Crenshaw, "Who Knows What YHWH Will Do? The Character of God in the Book of Job," in *Fortunate the Eyes That See: Essays in Honor of David Noel Freedman in Celebration of His Seventieth Birthday*, ed. A. B. Beck et al. (Grand Rapids: Eerdmans, 1995), 185–96.

48. Brunner, "Weisheitliteratur," 96.

49. The sages did not want to upset the status quo, for their success depended on the approval of those in positions of power and influence. The author of Ecclesiastes chose the persona of Solomon, but he could only utter a feeble lament when observing tears of the oppressed (Eccl. 4:1). Nevertheless, those who coined proverbial sayings and composed poetic explorations of life's mysteries engaged in a quiet revolution, a reorienting through disorienting. On this aspect of aphorisms, see James G. Williams, *Those Who*

Ponder Proverbs: Aphoristic Thinking and Biblical Literature (BLS 2; Sheffield: Almond, 1981).

50. Kovacs, *Sociological-Structural Constraints upon Wisdom.*

51. On ethos in sapiential discourse, see James L. Crenshaw, "Wisdom and Authority: Sapiential Rhetoric and Its Warrants" (*Congress Volume: Vienna 1980*, ed. J. A. Emerton [VTSup 32; Leiden: Brill, 1981], 10–29 [*UAPQ*, 326–43]). This exploration of rhetoric employs the terms "logos," "pathos," and "ethos" to indicate rational exposition, passionate argument, and appeal to the speaker's character, respectively.

52. The sexual connotation of eating is also found in Gen. 39:6, 9, for Joseph takes pains to explain that Potiphar's wife is the food that is forbidden the servant. The Joseph narrative has been associated with wisdom by von Rad, "The Joseph Narrative and Ancient Wisdom," in *SAIW*, 439–47; and George W. Coats, "The Joseph Story and Ancient Wisdom: A Reappraisal," *CBQ* 35 (1973): 285–97; idem, *From Canaan to Egypt: Structural and Theological Context for the Joseph Story* (CBQMS 4; Washington, D.C.: Catholic Biblical Association of America, 1976).

53. Jack Miles, *God: A Biography* (New York: Vintage Books, 1995), 298–99, attributes this description to a feminine voice. His argument is hardly persuasive: the *virtual* consistency of Old Testament descriptions of someone observing a scene from a window—the mother of Sisera in Judg. 5:28, Michal in 2 Sam. 6:16, and Jezebel in 2 Kgs. 9:30, with Abimelech in Gen. 26:8 the lone exception. See also Athalya Brenner, "Some Observations on the Figurations of Woman in Wisdom Literature," 50–66, and Meike Heijerman, "Who Would Blame Her? The 'Strange' Woman of Proverbs 7," 100–109, in *Feminist Companion to Wisdom Literature*, ed. Brenner. Carole R. Fontaine, "The Social Roles of Women in the World of Wisdom," in ibid., 37–38, notes that one would expect to hear more about abusive and drunken husbands if women had written many of the proverbs.

54. *ANET*, 427.

55. Its power for good and ill is described in 1 Esd. 3:18–24.

56. The possibility of violence against the offender is raised in Prov. 6:34–35, but nothing is said about retaliation against the wayward wife, for that lies outside the teacher's concern. Claudia Camp's reading of Prov. 7:6–27 as a wife's picking up some extra money by sleeping with a wealthy patron gives insufficient weight to spousal jealousy, especially on being cuckolded ("What's So Strange about the Strange Woman?" in *The Bible and the Politics of Exegesis: Essays in Honor of Norman K. Gottwald on His Sixty-Fifth Birthday*, ed. David Jobling et al. [Cleveland: Pilgrim, 1991], 31).

57. See Boström, *God of the Sages*; and Crenshaw, "Concept of God," in *UAPQ*, 191–205.

58. An extreme position is taken by McKane, *Proverbs*, but the evidence for such an evolution of theological concerns as he posits cannot stand close scrutiny. Furthermore, Egyptologists no longer interpret early instructional texts as secular, even if piety became more explicit with *Ani* and *Amenemope*, eventuating in the fatalism of *Papyrus Insinger*.

59. Westermann, *Roots of Wisdom*, considers biblical wisdom a beginning in philosophical investigation, but he thinks the latter differed in its elitism and spiritualizing of existing matter. In his view, wisdom contrasts with science in that sages had a view of the whole whereas science has lost this notion, focusing on the particular (135–37).

60. Jean-Paul Audet, "Origines comparées de la double tradition de la loi et de la sagesse dans le Proche-Orient ancien," *Akten des 25 Internationalen Orientalistenkongresses* (Moscow, 1962), 1:352–57.

61. W. Lee Humphreys, "The Motif of the Wise Courtier in the Book of Proverbs," in *Israelite Wisdom*, ed. Gammie et al., 177–90. Fox, "Social Location," favors the hypothesis of composition in and for the court.

62. Given ancient historiographic ideology, it may be more accurate to say that a later historian made associations between the two kings. Moving from literature to history is problematic at best.

63. Brunner, *Altägyptische Weisheit*, identifies only two short proverbial collections and one long one, the *Instruction of Ankhsheshonqy*, whereas seventeen Instructions have survived. Here and in Mesopotamia these Instructions were primarily a father's counsel to a son, although they are often associated with a royal court.

64. McKane, *Prophets and Wise Men*, stresses this fact, although he may press the idea too far.

65. *A Pessimistic Dialogue between a Master and His Slave* links dining with intellectual stimulation, and this association becomes prominent in later Greco-Roman circles (cf. also Ben Sira and *Testaments of the Twelve Patriarchs*). On symposia, see Fox, "Ideas of Wisdom in Proverbs 1–9," 626 n. 27.

66. Crenshaw, "The Contest of Darius's Guards in 1 Esdras 3:1–5:3," in *UAPQ*, 222–34. This powerful description of wine, the king, and woman probably rests on antecedent topoi that provided lively entertainment on numerous occasions.

67. *Antiquities* 8.5.

68. Von Rad, *Wisdom in Israel*, passim; and Christa Bauer-Kayatz, *Einführung in die alttestamentliche Weisheit* (BS 55; Neukirchen-Vluyn: Neukirchener, 1969), 36–92. Perdue, *Wisdom Literature: A Theological History*, endeavors to write a historical theology of wisdom, a daunting task given the paucity of such data in the texts themselves.

69. From this perspective, one could argue that the author of Job defends God's freedom, just as some interpreters insist that Qoheleth guards divine prerogative.

70. Egon Pfeiffer, "Die Gottsfurcht im Buche Kohelet," in *Gottes Wort und Gottes Land: Hans-Wilhelm Hertzberg zum 70. Geburtstag*, ed. Henning Graf Reventlow (Göttingen: Vandenhoeck & Ruprecht, 1965), 133–58.

71. To which one must add the second epilogue in Qoheleth; see Gerald T. Sheppard, "The Epilogue to Qoheleth as Theological Commentary," *CBQ* 39 (1977): 182–89.

72. The many interpretations of this concept can be seen in the following works. Von Rad, *Wisdom in Israel*, 144–76; Lang, *Frau Weisheit*, 168–84; Burton Lee Mack, *Logos und Sophia: Untersuchungen zur Weisheitstheologie im hellenistischen Judentum* (SUNT 10; Göttingen: Vandenhoeck & Ruprecht, 1973); Camp, *Wisdom and the Feminine*; idem, "Woman Wisdom as Root Metaphor: A Theological Consideration," in *Listening Heart*, ed. Hoglund et al., 45–76; Roland E. Murphy, "The Personification of Wisdom," in *Wisdom in Ancient Israel*, ed. Day et al., 222–33; McKinlay, *Gendering Wisdom the Host*; Susanne Gorges-Braunwarth, *"Frauenbilder-Weisheitbilder-Gottesbilder" in Spr 1–9: Die Personifizierte Weisheit im Gottesbild der nachexilischen Zeit* (Exegese in unserer Zeit 9; Münster: LIT, 2002); Christine R. Yoder, *Wisdom as a Woman of Substance: A Socioeconomic Reading of Proverbs 1–9 and 31:10–31* (BZAW 304;

Berlin: de Gruyter, 2001); Alice M. Sinnott, *The Personification of Wisdom* (SOTSMS; Aldershot: Ashgate, 2005); and Silvia Schroer, *Wisdom Has Built Her House: Studies on the Figure of Sophia in the Bible*, trans. Linda M. Maloney and William McDonough (Collegeville, Minn.: Liturgical, 2000). Schroer thinks "*Ḥokmâ* is a counterpart for YHWH, a divine counterpart . . . the God of Israel in the image of a woman and in the language of the goddesses" (p. 29).

73. Delbert R. Hillers, *Treaty-Curses and the Old Testament Prophets* (BibOr 16; Rome: Pontifical Biblical Institute, 1964), 28–29.

74. R. N. Whybray, "Proverbs VIII 22–31 and Its Supposed Prototypes," in *SAIW*, 390–400; Samuel Terrien, *Till the Heart Sings* (Philadelphia: Fortress, 1985).

75. The absence of this concept in wisdom at Qumran is surprising, especially in light of personified Wickedness in *The Wiles of the Wicked Woman*.

76. Luis Alonso Schökel, "Sapiential and Covenant Themes in Genesis 2–3," in *SAIW*, 468–80.

77. The exact order of this development, the tendency to personify both folly and wisdom, has not been established. One could argue that Folly preceded Wisdom (see Boström, *The God of the Sages*, 56, for the suggestion that Folly may be older and Wisdom serves as a "competitor for the attentions of men").

78. William F. Albright, "Some Canaanite-Phoenician Sources of Hebrew Wisdom," in *Wisdom in Israel*, ed. Noth and Winton Thomas, 8.

79. Christa Kayatz, *Studien zu Proverbien 1–9* (WMANT 22; Neukirchen-Vluyn: Neukirchener, 1966), 76–134.

Chapter 4

The Search
for Divine Presence
Job

The book of Job comprises a poetic dialogue, or debate, which has been inserted into a narrative framework.[1] As a result of this strange union of incompatible literary strata, tension between the prose and poetry mounts. The pronounced differences dissuade many scholars from interpreting the dialogue by means of clues provided within the story.[2] Nevertheless, the poetry requires an introduction of some kind; otherwise it begins in medias res and forces readers to supply a proper beginning that would illuminate the subsequent dialogue. The epilogue, however, can be dispensed with altogether, since the poem ends appropriately with Job's acquisition of firsthand knowledge about God by means of the divine self-manifestation for which Job risked everything, and the prologue has arrived at a satisfactory solution of the problem under discussion without the happy ending.

STRUCTURE

To some extent the shape of the book depends on one's predisposition, but three different ways of viewing the structure commend themselves. Readers may emphasize (1) the diction, (2) the dramatic movement, and (3) the individual components in outline form. By discounting brief prosaic introductions and observations, the first approach yields two parts, prose and poetry. The second perspective uses narrative introductions—and to some extent conclusions—to distinguish three divisions, specifically 1:1–2:10; 2:11–31:40; 32:1–42:17. The third approach divides the book into five discrete sections: chapters 1–2; 3–31; 32–37; 38:1–42:6; 42:7–17.

On the Basis of Diction

Perhaps the most noticeable feature of the book is its use of a story to enclose a poetic center. This device was widely employed among sages of the ancient Near East to provide a specific historical framework within which to interpret teachings that had broad application, whether philosophical ruminations about innocent suffering and the governance of the universe or collections of aphorisms to enable others to make wise decisions. For example, Ahiqar and Anksheshonqy have left significant proverbial sayings for posterity, but in each instance an account of the teacher's personal adversity encloses the collection of maxims. Little effort to connect this prose framework with the poetic teachings is evident, so that both story and poetry stand on their own. Nevertheless, the juxtaposition of the two parts of the book offers a way of understanding the teaching that would otherwise not occur. Just as a simple frame enhances a painting, delineating its original features and drawing attention away from itself to the art, so these brief biographies give vital data about the hero's words and character.

In a sense, the Joban poetry interrupts the story, which suspends Job's destiny in midair until the poetry has reached its goal; only then does the tale resume and achieve closure. The narrator of the story, who freely intrudes twice to pass independent judgment on the hero (1:22; 2:10), recedes in the poetry so that other voices may be heard. The lyrical poetry of Job, whose threatened ego fights for survival against overwhelming odds, the confident assurances of Eliphaz and his companions, Elihu's brash rebuttal of all four, and the divine interrogation— all this takes place while the narrator creates a story within an earlier story, the folktale. The narrator's resumption of the tale after Job's claim to have seen the Deity gives the impression of returning to reality, at least a realm that ordinary people comprehend. *Do ut des* (I give in order to receive) still functions in this land of Uz, for divine anger departs as a result of Job's obedient deed, and God restores Job at this time. Prologue elicits dialogue, and epilogue terminates it. The epilogue does more than end the dialogue, for the force of "antiwisdom" within the poetry evaporates under the heavy hand of the narrator. Viewpoints collide everywhere, not just in the dialogue. The prose framework and that in the poetic core speak opposing views: the former ultimately seems to affirm the reward of the innocent (Job is at least compensated for his suffering, if not rewarded for his virtue), while the latter proclaims most persuasively that the innocent are not rewarded. To this day no satisfactory harmonization has been found.

On the Basis of Dramatic Movement

Introductions at 1:1–5, 2:11–13, and 32:1–5 suggest another way of dividing the book. The first introduces Job and gives essential insights into his character, which will soon be assailed mightily. The second introduction identifies Job's three friends and sets up expectations about their role as comforters, whereas the third introduction describes Elihu's boldness in venturing to address his elders without their consent and justifies his fury at the level of discourse so far. Thus understood, the book of Job becomes a drama consisting of three episodes: God afflicts Job, Job challenges God, God challenges Job. Another way of stating the drama is the hidden conflict, the conflict explored, and the conflict resolved.[3] This interpretation depends on an understanding of narration through dialogue, so that the fundamental category of the book is said to be prose with the poetic dialogues retarding the movement of plot and heightening the emotional pitch.

This approach encounters difficulties other than the brevity of the first part, since Job's laconic confessions in this section differ from his outpouring of resentment in the second unit, although his two repentant statements in part three balance the shorter confessions nicely. More to the point, the narrator's commendation of Job's conduct (1:22; 2:10) marks two closures, and although section two ends appropriately (31:40, "The words of Job are ended"), the third section concludes reluctantly. God's first speech evokes Job's final words, or so he says (40:4–5), only to give way to a second divine speech and an additional response from Job (42:2–6). Each indecision necessitates further brief introductions of speakers, but these comments play no role in the suggested structuring of the book. The description of plot development also presents difficulty, for Elihu's speeches hardly contribute to resolving the conflict between Job and God. Indeed, the epilogue alone describes the resolution, the divine speeches functioning as disciplinary chastening of the hero.

On the Basis of Individual Components

Yet another means of structuring the book derives its clues from the distinctive components in it: (1) a story about Job's affliction, (2) a dispute between him and three friends, (3) the speeches of Elihu, (4) divine speeches punctuated by Job's submission, and (5) a story about Job's restoration. The second division fails to qualify as a consistent dispute, for the third cycle breaks off without Zophar's final speech and thereafter Job appears either to address the divine enemy or to enter into nostalgic monologue. This approach does not disparage the dialogue by labeling it an almost interminable retardation of the plot, since the poetic speeches possess value in their own right apart from any progress they may signal toward some unspoken telos. Because the action moves toward a divine pronunciation of Job's innocence in the debate between Job and his friends, the dialogue gives an impression of progress, particularly the emergence of references to the figure of an "advocate" or "redeemer." Emotional changes and high points mark still another kind of movement in the poetry, indicating that progress does occur even when opposing intellectual positions come no closer together than at the beginning. One should view the book as a triptych (prologue, dialogue, and theologue) with Job's two monologues in chapters 29–31 as the hinge connecting the three panels.[4]

THE NARRATIVE

Emphasizing the historical gap between the time of the hero and the subsequent narrating of the events, the narrative sets the action in (pre-)patriarchal times.[5] Job's possessions, like those of the patriarchs, consist of cattle and servants; not only his three friends but also his enemies (nomadic Sabeans and Chaldeans) come from the greater environment associated with Abraham's wanderings; the monetary unit, qĕśîtâ (42:11), belongs to that ancient era (cf. Gen. 33:19); Job's life span exceeds that of the patriarchs; and his sacrifice of animals corresponds to the practice prior to official priests. The name Job recalls a folk hero associated in Ezekiel 14:14 and 20 with Noah and Daniel, probably the Dan'el of Canaanite epic texts. Although the meaning of Job's name is uncertain, similar forms are attested from early times in Egypt and Mesopotamia with the meanings "Where is the divine father?" and "Inveterate Foe/Hated One." In accord with the universality typical of early wisdom, the hero seems to have been an Edomite, famous for the wisdom of its inhabitants, and the setting in the land of Uz echoes the noun 'ēṣâ (counsel).[6]

The theme underlying what has been called an epic substratum,[7] the didactic narrative perhaps chosen to give the story the appearance of antiquity, concerns the search for a single instance of *disinterested righteousness*. The Adversary (haśśāṭān is not a personal name here, but an office) formulates the problem in his initial conversation with God: "For *naught* does Job serve God?" The cynical charge that Job's piety depended on favorable external circumstances struck at the heart of ancient religion. The radical denial of genuine religious devotion was met by an equally adamant claim on God's part that his servant Job rose above selfish interests in relating to his Creator. The suffering that befell God's servant provided the means by which to adjudicate the two opposing convictions. It follows that innocent suffering functions as a *secondary* theme of the story,[8] inasmuch as Job demonstrated the *proper manner of responding to undeserved suffering*.

The prologue (1:1–2:10b) consists of *five scenes* in which action alternates between earth and heaven.[9] The opening scene (1:1–5) sets the stage in the distant past when legendary heroes roamed the earth. The folktale beginning introduces a seminomadic sheikh named Job who enjoyed preeminence in the land of Transjordanian Uz, just as King Solomon is reputed to have surpassed the wisdom of the easterners and Egyptians. Job's exceptional qualities have four foci; he was "blameless and upright, one who feared God and turned away from evil." Naturally, his family circle was complete. He had seven sons and three daughters, who enjoyed one another's company on festive occasions, particularly birthdays.[10] He also had impressive holdings: seven thousand sheep, three thousand camels, five hundred yoke of oxen and an equal number of she-asses, and, of course, innumerable servants.[11] Only one thing marred this idyllic existence: Job seemed overly anxious that his *sons* (or children) may inadvertently have sinned against God. So the suspicious father took proper precautions to ward off an angry Deity.[12]

While Job's children gathered together for the purpose of eating and drinking, a heavenly assembly of God's *sons* also took place (1:6–12).[13] Into their presence came the Adversary;[14] the Hebrew *gam* (also) almost identifies *haśśāṭān* as an intruder. An inquiring God learns that this figure has been traveling hither and yon[15] to see whether a single individual worshiped God with purity of heart. The Adversary's occupation had left him an utter cynic, resulting in the following creed: "Touch Job's possessions and he will curse you openly." Curiously, the Adversary's eyes had not fallen on Job during his investigations of human conduct, so that God had felt obliged to call attention to his faithful servant and to inform the Adversary about Job's fourfold virtue. In doing so, God differs appreciably from that earthly father Job, who thought the worst about his own sons. (The sins of his daughters are not mentioned.) Instead, God could not imagine Job's departing from genuine piety. That trust was soon to undergo the ultimate test, for God consented to allow the Adversary to strip Job of all worldly possessions. In a single stroke the protective hedge would vanish completely, and Job would prove one of these heavenly figures a liar. To accomplish this worthy end, Job's life had to be spared. At this point, God manages to preserve Job's health as well.

The next scene occurs back on earth, where God's bounty flowed freely (1:13–21). The description of the Adversary's activity achieves unusual dramatic power, particularly through repetition of certain phrases. A reference to the sons and daughters eating and drinking offers a *false sense of security*, which is soon exposed when that allusion recurs in a report that knocks Job to his knees and elicits the profound confession; "Naked I came from my mother's womb, and naked shall I return there; the LORD gave and the LORD has taken away; blessed be the name of the LORD."[16] Between those two references to sons and daughters who went about enjoying life's goodness two refrains drone away, shattering Job's protective hedge bit by bit. The first is the messenger's comment, "I alone have escaped to tell you," and the second is the transitional remark, "While he was still speaking, another came and said." The substance of these messages concerns four decisive blows, two from earthly powers and two from heavenly forces. The Sabeans stole Job's oxen and asses; divine fire consumed the sheep; Chaldeans made off with the camels; and a mighty wind felled a house upon Job's children. Naturally, Job's many servants perished in a vain attempt to save the cattle, and only the bearers of horror survived. Confronted with such news, Job gave full vent to his grief, but earned God's approbation. Lest the point be missed, the narrator enters the story momentarily and underlines Job's integrity: "In all this Job did not sin or charge God with wrongdoing" (1:22).

The fourth scene (2:1–6) returns to heaven, where another assembling of God's children occurred. Again the Adversary presented himself before God, who repeated the earlier inquiry concerning the intruder's activity. This time God reminded the Adversary that Job has held securely to his integrity, "although you incited me against him, to destroy him for no reason." This allusion to the absence of any reason for destroying Job's "hedge" recalls the Adversary's initial question, "Does Job fear God for naught [that is, without cause]?" and amounts to a triumphant shout. Still, the Adversary refused to concede that he has misjudged humanity; instead, he cited what sounds like an old proverb, perhaps related to barter: "Skin for skin! All that people have they will give to save their lives." Accordingly, the Adversary urged God to smite Job's skin and bones, confident that the afflicted one would curse God to his face. The divine confidence in Job equals the tempter's faith in his own creed, and once again God's servant falls into compassionless hands. This time, too, a qualification occurs, and the Adversary is entrusted with the ironical task of *watching over* Job's life. The same verb was also used to connote the protection that God's statutes provided from the notorious loose woman in Proverbs.

The second, third, and fourth scenes began with a single Hebrew verb; that consistency explodes in the fifth scene (2:7–10b) in order to focus on the Adversary's hasty departure from God's presence. The narrative wastes no time in recounting the consequences of the awful declaration, "Very well, he is in your power." Stricken with grievous sores from head to toe, God's trusted servant sat on an ash heap and scraped the infected skin with sherds. His wife exacerbated his misery by imploring Job to curse God and die; the use of the same verb to indicate blessing and cursing God increases the ambiguity of the text.[17] Whereas God had complimented Job for holding on to his integrity, she reprimanded her husband for doing so—without cause, one might add. Maintaining his integrity in the face of this deepest cut of all, Job endeavored to instruct this woman who had uttered folly at the precise moment when her husband deserved a compassionate spouse. The lesson he taught was simple but profound at the same time: "Shall we receive the good at the hand of God, and not receive the bad?"[18] At this decisive point the *narrator intrudes* for a second time, preempting any rejoinder from Job's companion. Instead, we are told again that "in all this Job did not sin with his lips."[19] The final three verses in chapter 2 make the necessary transition from this remarkable story to the poetry, where the hero dares to challenge God just as Job's wife had wanted him to do. They introduce the three friends who came to comfort Job in his misery.

The epilogue (42:7–17) tidies up the story by degrees, placing God's servant once again within a protective wall and securing his existence until death came to gather a contented Job to his ancestors. Naturally, Job's friends stood in need of his intercession,[20] for Job himself had maintained his integrity to the end. This negative judgment on Eliphaz, Bildad, and Zophar must arise from another story that has not survived, since we cannot imagine that what they said in the poetry would have been dismissed as lies.[21] In any event, twice God praises Job for speaking the truth about the Lord, presumably the necessity of receiving both good and evil from him. Job's restoration followed his intercessory prayer; friends and relatives dined with Job as before and bestowed gifts on him. In the end he had twice as much property as before, and the same number of children as previously. The three daughters came in for special notice, since their beauty surpassed that of all other women, and they were the recipients of a generous—and exceptional—inheritance from their father.[22] In this idyllic scene of God's favorite servant surrounded by four generations, only one jarring note is sounded: the reminder that the Lord brought all the misfortunes that necessitated comforting words from Job's companions.[23] The reader has already been informed by God that such provocation came *without cause*.

Whoever pauses to assess this narrative from a theological perspective[24] discerns that discordant sounds produced by a seemingly amoral Deity are balanced by melodious chords occasioned by God's unshakable faith in Job's integrity. To be sure, the prologue depicts a God who permits wanton destruction of innocent victims just to prove a point. Job's sons and daughters fell in their youthful innocence, as did countless servants, and nowhere does God seem to take these "Joban possessions" into consideration as differing essentially from camels, sheep, oxen, and asses. In addition, the Lord of the epilogue fulminates over Job's friends' inaccurate understanding of God and requires cultic means of atonement. Above all, this guilty Lord ties all loose ends together neatly, totally oblivious to the misery resulting from entering into dialogue with the Adversary.[25]

Nevertheless, the prologue addresses the fundamental questions of human existence: Does disinterested piety exist, and what explains innocent suffering? The story affirms pure religion, labeling the magical assumption that pervades most religion[26] the lie that it is, and lays undeserved suffering on God's majestic shoulders. No attempt to explain either enigma is made; the story seems content to affirm disinterested righteousness and to acknowledge vexing instances that lack a positive correlation between sin and punishment.

The tension between profound questions and naive theology[27] prevents one from dismissing the story as trite, even if one cannot tell whether the narrator is characterized as trustworthy. Precisely because evil is somehow bound up with God, the matter of disinterested piety assumes vital significance. Given the painful reality that some persons suffer without reason, the narrative asks, can that undeserved misery find a corollary in devotion that refuses to count the cost? Without such integrity, how could faith survive the unfathomable ways of the Lord? The poetic dialogue probes the depths to which an innocent sufferer was driven by an arbitrary Deity who hedged Job round about with violence and provoked an authentic curse on the lips that had remained sinless in the story.

THE POETIC DIALOGUE

Job's powerful lament begins and ends with a *curse*—but not upon God.[28] To be sure, the initial curse that Job pronounced against the day of his birth (chap. 3) calls God's wisdom and goodness into question, although indirectly. This curse upon day and night achieves unusual poetic quality, particularly in such metaphors as "eyelids of dawn" (v. 9, my trans.). Job wishes to erase the day of his birth from the calendar; how he envies those skilled in magic, for if he possessed their power he could blot out all memory of that fateful day on which he was born. Alternatively, he reckons that he would have been fortunate if he had perished at birth or been exposed to die. Having been permitted to live, and consequently to endure untold misery, he now seeks death eagerly, inasmuch as God has hedged him round about (cf. 1:10) with adversity.

The final curse within chapters 29–31 represents Job's endeavor to achieve God's declaration of innocence, for such vindication has not come from the three friends. Despising the present, Job reminisces about the good old days when signs of divine favor abounded. In those days he dwelt securely, his children by his side, and presided over assemblies at the city gate like a beloved elder statesman. All who knew him had cause to rejoice; he served as eyes for the blind, feet for the lame, and a father to orphans. Because of him, widows' hearts leapt for joy. Job's present misery saw brigands mocking him, but worst of all, God cruelly pursued the one whose harp had been tuned for a dirge. Unable to make any sense of God's behavior, Job's confusion mounts because of belief in punishment for evil and conviction that God sees everything. Since Job knows that he is innocent, he can only believe God culpable. Therefore, he pronounces a self-imprecation, an oath of innocence,[29] and challenges God to prove otherwise. In short, Job asks that his life serve as a witness to his innocence, with the understanding that false testimony is punishable by death. Perhaps Job's knowledge that lying accusation carried the same penalty strengthened his plea that God write out the crimes for which he is being punished.

Between Job's two curses a dialogue with three friends takes place. It consists of *three cycles of speeches*, the last of which is in mutilated form.[30] Job enjoys favored status literarily, for he responds to each of the three friends. In some respects the comforters speak in unison, so that it is difficult to characterize the individual viewpoints held by Eliphaz, Bildad, and Zophar. In addition, the various responses frequently ignore the addressees they purport to answer, giving the impression that Job and friends talk past one another.

The Speeches of Job and His Three Friends

Two assertions lie at the center of Eliphaz's speeches (chaps. 4–5, 15, 22). The first is stated both negatively and positively; however it is formulated, the point stands in tension with the second claim. Since no innocent person has ever perished, wicked individuals will die, for their destruction is certain. The other assertion concerns the nature of God: human virtue is no asset to the One who refuses to concede that mortals can be more righteous than God. Now if right conduct does not benefit God, why does the Deity punish wickedness, which presumably does not harm God either? Recognizing this problem, Eliphaz claims that Job is being punished because of *excessive* wickedness. Elevation of God at human expense prompts Eliphaz to view virtue as powerless to nullify the consequences of being human (born of woman). His argument runs from the greater to the lesser: if God cannot trust heavenly beings, how much less must God trust those who dwell in houses that can be torn down? The literal sense of this metaphor must have cut Job to the heart, despite Eliphaz's overtures toward kindness. Perhaps he understood this allusion to Job's fallen children as beneficial, for Eliphaz thought God wounded and healed in disciplinary action. The children, however, were beyond healing, as were Job's loyal servants who perished defending his possessions.

Both points that Eliphaz forced upon Job were fully endorsed by Bildad, who makes no real advance in the argument except to provide matchless imagery for the destruction of the wicked (chaps. 8, 18, 25). For example, he likens divine punishment to the extinguishing of a lamp and a plant's destruction, pictures a hunter's powerful trap, and envisions disease and death as divine agents. It follows that such ample aids for punishment completely blot out evil, destroying its offspring without mercy. Bildad is certain, however, that none born of woman can be innocent. Even heavenly bodies lack purity in God's sight; how much more man, the maggot, and mortal man, the worm. Such convictions should have led Bildad to answer his own question, "Does God pervert justice?" with a resounding yes. How can one talk about justice when humans are by nature guilty?

Zophar concentrates fully on the fate of the wicked, which he describes with considerable enthusiasm (chaps. 11; 20; 27:11–23). The wicked flourish temporarily, but their food soon turns to poison within the body. They then become God's enemies, whom the Deity attacks mightily, demolishing their houses, destroying their sons, and handing over wicked persons' possessions to the righteous. Oblivious to Job's suffering, Zophar insists that God exacts less than Job deserves. It naturally follows that he thinks Job's claims regarding innocence stray far from the truth. All is not lost, however, for repentance alters one's fate appreciably. Therefore Zophar appeals to Job to turn from his evil ways.

Job comes perilously close to the view that human conduct does not affect God in the slightest degree, but he differs sharply from his friends with regard to the fate of the wicked (chaps. 6–7, 9, 12, 16, 19, 21, 23, 26, 27). He asks how his supposed sin injured the "watcher of humanity" (7:20), as if he thought God's majesty insulated the Deity from all adverse effects of evil. Nevertheless, Job is absolutely sure that God destroys the innocent and sinners alike, for no other explanation made sense of his own suffering. Indeed, he even maintains that God maliciously mocks those who have fallen victim to undeserved misery, and implies that a conspiracy exists between God and the forces of evil. From beginning to end Job refuses to yield an inch in his conviction that God has made a grievous error in Job's case; this certainty of his own innocence leads him to interpret God's conduct as malice. God, it follows, has become Job's personal antagonist.[31]

The sheer imbalance of power between him and God thrusts Job forward to new horizons of thought: Is it conceivable that someone will come forward to arbitrate our dispute? At first the idea merely looms on the horizon as the remotest of possibilities, but eventually it recurs as if the thought has now entered the realm of the credible. Ultimately, Job stands firmly upon a conviction that his vindicator exists on high and will call God to task for unfair and malicious treatment of Job. Thus he wishes that his words could be inscribed on a rock as a permanent witness, which the umpire could use to win a declaration of Job's innocence. If only Job can find God, he knows his vindication will follow, for no sinner can stand in the divine presence.

The bitter realization that virtue has not reaped its appropriate rewards in his own experience brings with it a readiness to question morality itself. "Why be good," Job asks, "if God reckons one to be wicked?" The most sacred convictions of the devout crumble one by one, and Job dares to parody familiar assertions of the faithful. The comforting thought that God watches over men and women (Psalm 8) fails to console Job, who longs for a moment's relaxation of that watchful eye. He dares to accuse God of creating him solely for the purpose of catching him in an evil act, which would justify subsequent punishment.

At times Job thinks his own suffering will be as pointless as Abel's and utters a poignant appeal that earth refuse to cover his blood (Job 16:18). Behind this wish lurks the notion that innocent blood cried to heaven until bringing about a vindication of wrongdoing. At other times Job seems certain that he is being tested in a furnace of affliction, just as smiths purify ore in fire, and that he will come forth as pure gold. Job also recognizes the frailty of life and the hard lot of humankind, but he knows that his own misery cannot be explained solely by the appeal to finitude. Job certainly sings about God's grandeur just as readily as his three friends do,[32] but knowledge that mortals touch only the fringes of God's power brings no relief. Absolute power turned malicious threatened Job's very existence.

Job's physical suffering paled in comparison with his mental agony over this unfathomable face of God, which no longer smiles on him but now contorts itself angrily before him. It seems to Job that this God actively destroys all hope, wearing it away like the slow erosion of rocks brought about by flowing water. Job perceives an element of unfairness in the natural order of things that grants sure expectation that a tree will put forth new growth after it has been cut down, provided sufficient water reaches the stump, but denies similar hope to humans. Memory of previous relationship with God evokes an astonishing declaration: God will remember me when it is too late, eventually longing for the faithful servant. On one occasion Job recalls the reciprocity that characterized their relationship. It seems that whenever Job called upon God, he could count on an answer, but now he contrasts that memory with the present moment when God seems bent on disgorging a former friend. One critic puts it this way: "But here is a new tone which has never been sounded before—God as the direct enemy of men, delighting in torturing them, hovering over them like what we might call the caricature of a devil, gnashing his teeth, 'sharpening his eyes' . . . and splitting open Job's intestines."[33]

Job's lament unfolds a curious situation that bristles with irony. On the one hand, he endeavors to escape God's constant vigilance, while, on the other hand, he longs to find God, who conceals the divine self from a faithful devotee. Job cannot believe God capable of such personal antagonism, although his eyes tell him that such misfortune can come only from God. Death alone will afford relief from the "Hound of Heaven," so he earnestly begs God to look away for a brief moment into which the messenger of death can insert itself. The realization that death cancels any opportunity to vindicate himself gives Job renewed resolve to find God at any cost, for only by doing so can he obtain the divine declaration of innocence. That is why Job complains bitterly that he cannot discover God and desperately states his case before the heavenly court.

> Oh, that I knew where I might find him,
>   that I might come even to his dwelling!
> I would lay my case before him
>   and fill my mouth with arguments.
>
> If I go forward, he is not there;
>   or backward, I cannot perceive him;
> on the left he hides, and I cannot behold him;
>   I turn to the right hand, but I cannot see him.
>   (Job 23:3–4, 8–9)

The three rounds of speeches indicate a change in Job's response to God. In the first speech he addresses God directly, but in the second and third speeches his comments sink to the level of talking about the Deity.

The Divine Speeches and Job's Responses

The two faces of God manifest themselves in two distinct speeches from the tempest,[34] each one of which reduces Job to silence. The first speech extols the mysteries of nature,[35] while the second indirectly acknowledges the force of Job's attack upon God.[36] Both speeches remove Job from the center of the picture, destroying his illusion that he occupies the central position in the universe.[37] The expulsion of Job from the thrust of the speech is accompanied by a similar ignoring of the charges he has laid against the Deity. As a result, the divine speeches seem completely irrelevant, for they fail to provide any answers to the problem of innocent suffering and divine injustice.[38]

The first speech resembles a majestic harangue, for God mockingly asks Job where he was during the creation of the world, and challenges him to govern nature's powerful forces and to tame those creatures who dwelt beyond the

regions of human habitation.[39] The animals and winged creatures serve to demonstrate the sheer stupidity in Job's Titanism, but an element of humor softens
the rebuke. God asks Job whether he can summon lightning, elicit from it a
submissive response, "At your command!" (38:35), or whether he can force a
mythical monster representing chaos to plead with him for mercy (41:3 [Heb.
40:27]). The absence of any explicit reference to humans in the entire speech is
calculated to teach Job the valuable lesson that the universe can survive without
him. In truth he cannot perform midwife service at the birth of the sea, dispense
dew and rain, send the sources of light on their respective journeys, provide food
for wild animals, or control the instincts of creatures like hawks and vultures.
Lacking the ability to perform a single act that God isolates for his consideration, Job reluctantly admits that he cannot rule the universe. In the face of such
sublime irrelevance, who would not be speechless?

The second divine speech addresses Job's complaint somewhat more directly
and comes very close to an admission that God found the task of ruling the
world a difficult one. This time God rebukes Job for justifying himself at God's
expense, inasmuch as Job's vindication could only come as the result of God's
pleading guilty to the charge of perverting justice. In self-defense God challenges
Job to conquer pride within those who thought too highly of themselves and to
overthrow the wicked. Only when Job's might succeeds in vanquishing overt
and covert evil will God admit that the lowly creature's right hand can save him.
The detailed description of the king of the beasts, in this case a metaphor for a
crocodile-like creature,[40] reminds Job just how ludicrous his verbal attacks upon
God have been.

For a second time Job attempts a proper response now that his search for
God has ended in dialogue, but the shift in subject matter leaves him unprepared to do anything except acknowledge God's power, which had never been
questioned. What follows can only puzzle readers who have been led to believe
Job's earlier relationship with God throbbed with vitality. Now Job claims that
all previous knowledge stemmed from secondary report, whereas the present
moment corrects partial knowledge through immediate sight. Earlier he had
spoken things that he did not fully understand, for which Job despises himself
and repents in dust and ashes. No reading of this final speech by Job removes the
perplexing features[41] nor explains why he feels obliged to repent over incomplete
knowledge. Where has Job's integrity gone?

> Then Job answered the LORD:
> "I know that you can do all things,
>   and that no purpose of yours can be thwarted.
> 'Who is this that hides counsel without knowledge?'
> Therefore I have uttered what I did not understand,
>   things too wonderful for me,
>   which I did not know.
> 'Hear, and I will speak;
>   I will question you, and you declare to me.'

I had heard of you by the hearing of the ear,
     but[42] now my eye sees you;
therefore I despise myself,
     and repent in dust and ashes."
                              (42:1–6)

The Speech of Elihu

Between Job's negative confession (chap. 31) and God's response (chaps. 38–41) another speech (chaps. 32–37) attempts to provide a more adequate answer to Job than the three friends had managed. The speaker, an Israelite named Elihu (meaning "He is my God"), is introduced in a prose section (37:1–6) that emphasizes his intense anger at Job for making himself more righteous than God and at the friends because they failed to give a convincing refutation of Job. The intrusive character of this speech[43] is reflected in God's silence concerning this brash young man who thinks he has the final word on every question. Similarly, Job ignores him altogether, for he has already grown tired of human words.

Since Elihu's speech represents an addition to the debate, it utilizes the content of the previous arguments. This youth may have thought he had a furrow to plow, but his fundamental line of reasoning borrowed heavily from others. Essentially, Elihu emphasized God's majesty, which removed the Deity from human criticism, and divine justice. Since God is greater than mortals, no one can condemn the Creator. After all, sin touches humans only, and is a matter of small consequence to God; but Elihu insists that God pays everybody exactly what they earn, although using suffering to instruct people in the way they should walk, and overlooking sin to allow time for repentance. From such firm convictions it naturally follows that Job is a sinner and a rebel. Therefore he stands no chance of winning his case in the heavenly court, even if he were able to find the Almighty. Instead, he must rely on the angelic mediator's intercession, together with his own repentance and confession of sin. Naturally, this leaves no place for pointing an accusing finger at God.

The Poem on Wisdom's Inaccessibility

The tempest that brought God to Job swept all rumor concerning the Deity far away. In wisdom's case no such correction of secondary knowledge takes place, and it remains known only to God, who dispenses it to humans. Such is the thesis of the exquisite poem that concludes with an observation about wisdom's inaccessibility (chap. 28) that has somehow found its way into the debate between Job and his friends. The poem paints a detailed picture of human efforts to discover precious metals and rare gems within the innermost recesses of the earth, contrasting this dangerous activity with the peaceful growth of grain far above. In this search for valuable minerals human ingenuity overcomes every obstacle, achieving resounding success. No victorious shout accompanies the quest for wisdom, whose price far exceeds that of gold and silver. Desperately seeking a clue about its whereabouts, mortals question the abyss and the sea, only to be told that wisdom does not reside with them. The closest humans come to it is a report from Abaddon and Death that they know wisdom by rumor. God alone has access to it, but he distills wisdom to humans in religion and piety. True wisdom, the poem asserts, consists in the fear of the Lord.[44]

WARRANTS FOR VARIOUS VIEWS

The poetic section has been described by such words as "debate" and "argument," although one expects a lament from Job and comforting assurances from his three friends.[45] The reason good intentions quickly faded arises from the disparity in starting points. Job's insistence that God was at fault could hardly be reconciled with the friends' conviction that the Deity could not trample upon justice. They rested their case on the general truth that God rewards virtue and punishes vice, whereas Job based his argument on the particular instance that he knew best, his own situation. Naturally, each position had much to commend it, which explains the copious arguments in defense of the general truth and the specific instance. The two sides struggled to produce authoritative warrants for their claims.[46]

The three friends appealed to at least *eight different kinds of authority* in their vain attempt to justify God's ways. They argued from universally accepted truth, for example, when claiming that the triumph of the wicked is short-lived, or when reinforcing that position with an argument from consensus. Personal experience prompted them to say, "I have seen such and such," while careful inquiry led to certainty regarding some matters.

> See, we have searched this out; it is true.
> Hear, and know it for yourself.
>
> (5:27)

Access to tradition, particularly paternal legacies, afforded still another means of acquiring authoritative information.

The three friends did not stop with these easily verified warrants for their argument, but pressed forward into dimensions not subject to validation. Eliphaz mentions a terrifying theophany that made his hair stand up, and he insists that God spoke a decisive word to him on that memorable occasion.

> Now a word came stealing to me,
>   my ear received the whisper of it.
> Amid thoughts from visions of the night,
>   when deep sleep falls on mortals,
> dread came upon me, and trembling,
>   which made all my bones shake.
> A spirit glided past my face;
>   the hair of my flesh bristled.

> It stood still,
>> but I could not discern its appearance.
> A form was before my eyes;
>> there was silence, then I heard a voice:
> "Can mortals be righteous before God?
>> Can human beings be pure before their Maker?"
>>> (4:12–17)

The question, "Can mortals be more righteous than God?" (an alternative to the above translation), indicates that the Deity perceived the real issue being debated and endeavored to incline the scales in a particular direction. Elsewhere Eliphaz refers to God's spirit that whispers within the ear as sufficient directive, and mockingly inquires whether Job has stood within God's secret council. Zophar, too, thinks God actively declares a word and expounds wisdom's secrets. Finally, both Bildad and Eliphaz rely on age as an accurate indication of intelligence.

> The gray-haired and the aged are on our side,
>> those older than your father.
>>> (15:10)

The warrants for Job's argument do not differ appreciably from those employed by his friends to refute him. He appealed to universally acknowledged fact, for example, when insisting that an ass does not bray when its belly is full, and he did not shrink from the bold claim, "This I know!"[47] when it corresponded to general truth such as the impossibility of winning a case against God. Job also used the sages' customary language with reference to personal validation of information ("I have seen, heard, and understood") and mentioned wisdom derived from observing nature as a significant source of truth, for cattle, birds, creatures, and fish bear witness to God's heavy hand. In addition, Job recommended the acquisition of information from travelers abroad, who can tell what occurs on wider perimeters of human experience. He did not hesitate to challenge one important sign of wisdom, inasmuch as he had not lived nearly so long as his friends had. Therefore Job conceded that age gives wisdom, but he noted that God turns people into idiots, which may be a polite way of accusing the friends of early senility. Above all, Job insisted that personal experience possessed the power to call dogma into question. In his view every theory, however pious, was subject to personal confirmation or disconfirmation.

> Look, my eye has seen all this,
>> my ear has heard and understood it.
> What you know, I also know;
>> I am not inferior to you.
>>> (13:1–2)

Elihu agreed with Job about the positive correlation of wisdom with age, since he too lacked seniority. The warrants for his argument constitute a happy union of personal conviction and divine inspiration. Confident that God instilled his spirit in him at birth, Elihu also claimed that God kept that inspiration up to date by means of dreams and visions. As if such ready access to God were not sufficient grounds for his rebuke, the angry Buzite even relied on universal truth, for instance, when insisting that one who hates justice could in no way hold the reins, and alluded to wisdom based on observation of nature, although disparaging what can be learned from beasts and birds.

God's careful avoidance of such warrants for the speech from the whirlwind is entirely in character. Everything contributes to divine majesty, which needs no justification for action. Even the Hebrew syntax underlines this fact, for the questions function as strong declarations. "Were you present when I established the foundations of the world?" really means, "You were not present on that auspicious occasion." Perhaps Job's grasp of this fundamental truth partly explains his ready acquiescence to God's might, for he finally realized the futility of arguing with one who rose above the law.[48]

A HARP TUNED FOR A DIRGE

Job's spiritual crisis evokes a similar one within modern readers, who find it exceedingly difficult to sustain an objective attitude to the book.[49] In this pitiful victim of divine indifference they sense a finely tuned instrument being forced to emit unaccustomed sounds. For no reason of his own, Job's praise has changed to lament, and weeping fills the hours that drag themselves toward dawn's portals. At some time during the dark night of the soul this obedient servant launches an offensive against God.[50] What led to his bold enterprise?

The first step toward answering this question requires one's recognizing the exemplary character of Job, who must surely stand for all the innocent sufferers in Israel, but his sufferings also particularize the universal situation enveloping humanity. For that reason his cries seem to arise in the depths of our being, and his longing for God who withdraws farther and farther away strikes a familiar chord in us. This means that Job's exemplary character extends to the present, transcending time and space, for his suffering resembles our own.

Now the thesis that Job exemplified is that the spiritual crisis in his life was no private affair, but represented a decisive stage in Israel's dealing with its God. The belief in divine justice threatened to collapse because of the burdens placed upon it by historical events. The older simplistic understanding of divine providence hardly reckoned with powerful empires led by deities other than the Lord, nor did it take sufficiently into account the status of individuals making up the collective whole. The convenient explanation for suffering—that adversity arose as punishment for sin—may have sufficed for a brief interval, but eventually this idea produced a mighty outcry.[51]

That protest surfaced in various literary strata of the Old Testament, as if it had reached the nooks and crannies of daily reflection. The patriarch Abraham became its spokesman for a brief moment, formulating the basic issue in a passionate question: "Shall not the Judge of all the earth do right?" (Gen. 18:25).[52] Wholesale slaughter of cities no longer seemed appropriate activity for a moral Deity, and Abraham dared to suggest that the leavening presence of a few righteous persons ought to count for something in God's eyes. Similarly, Jonah sulked outside Nineveh's walls because God had blatantly ignored justice's requirements,[53] and Jeremiah complained bitterly that God could not be trusted.[54] The same suspicion overwhelmed Gideon, who called attention to a gaping disparity between belief and reality, and Habakkuk, who observed sufficient evidence to justify belief in divine blindness. The unknown author of Psalm 73 illumined the problem posed by the prosperity of the wicked in a manner that detailed his own internal struggle to survive among the faithful.[55] Together these voices and hundreds like them raised a mighty wail in the name of justice.

Guardians of the theory that virtue is rewarded and vice punished in exact measure championed God's justice, sparing no effort in their zeal to secure cherished belief. As a consequence of this intense search for appropriate responses to the hue and cry of spiritual rebels, several explanations for suffering presented themselves with varying degrees of adequacy.[56] The essential conviction that adversity arose as divine retribution for sin took on various colorations, two of which undermined the fundamental theory. Suffering often was God's means of disciplining wayward or foolish children; it functioned to test the quality of faith; or it fell into the category of an illusion that would quickly disappear like a dream. Adversity, according to some critics, belonged to the human condition and thus was inevitable. Therefore attaching moral blame to those whom misfortune had struck could only be viewed as a grievous error. Others acknowledged a mysterious element within suffering and humbly abandoned the attempt to explain it. Still others preferred to see something arbitrary at the center of the phenomenon, divorcing suffering from moral considerations completely. One daring poet, Deutero-Isaiah, discerned a redemptive capacity within adversity, insisting that others benefited from undeserved suffering, freely endured.

Now haphazard misfortune and vicarious suffering fall outside a theory of exact retribution; the one demeans God, and the other exalts humans. We have seen the same sort of tension within the attacks on God's justice, for God's appeal to Jonah rests on a passionate belief that mercy should transcend justice's strict requirements, and the author of Psalm 73 takes comfort in the touch of God's hand despite the continued prosperity of the wicked. A readiness to take personal experience into account seems to have adopted permanent residence in both groups, hence the whole truth dwelt at neither extreme. The same judgment applies to Job and his detractors, for truth and error intermingle freely as they do in real life.

Despite this intrinsic flexibility, the conflict between proponents of these two viewpoints achieved incredible harshness. Close friends stooped to personal vilification when it became clear that neither Job nor his companions would relinquish cherished beliefs. A youth threw off restraint, claiming superior insight to gray-haired ones and implying that those who disagreed with him were fools. A distraught wife felt constrained to encourage her miserable husband to precipitate the death sentence, and one is left to wonder about her motive for suggesting an unusual form of euthanasia. Such taking leave of one's senses extended to heaven, where God deigned to show a face that inspired terror in an obedient servant who had hitherto rested in the shadow of solicitous care. As a result of this new face, innocent sons and daughters fell victim to fatal blows wielded, with God's express permission, by a member of the heavenly court.

Job's friends cherished religious conviction more than a vital relationship with the living God, for they believed in a rational Deity who was enslaved by a greater principle: justice. According to them, two principles ruled the universe, and the first was not God.[57] In such a theological system, the Deity was reduced to the category of *reaction*. Suffering invariably exposed guilt, and grievous misfortune signified heinous offense. Nothing justified human visions of grandeur, for decisions by men and women, however selfless and wise, made little if any difference with God, whose ways were unfathomable. Vast regions of space separated creatures from their Creator, and essential differences as well kept them at safe distance. The Lord of the universe had more important things to do than watching over puny earthlings. God's unflinching commitment to a certain kind of justice assured restoration for properly repentant individuals but ruled out all questioning of divine integrity even when that reputation was purchased at the expense of a great man's honor.

Job's miserable condition soon extinguished the philosophical question, "Why does God *permit* me to suffer?" and set afire the bold formulation, "Why does God *make* me suffer these injustices?"[58] The shift from suffering to God as the real problem reveals the depths of Job's agony. Torn by the discrepancy between past memory and present reality, Job strove mightily to reconcile the two faces of God. The present fury directed against him made no sense in the light of clear recollection of divine favor in bygone days. A single question burned itself into Job's anguished spirit: "Is God for me or against me?" Intuition told him that nobody could force a claim upon God, but reason insisted that virtuous individuals laid up dividends that a just God dispensed fairly. Unless this latter belief accorded with reality, Job's complaint that he had been wronged lacked force. Paradoxically, his attack on God destroyed the ground on which he stood. Nothing in Job's present experience gave the slightest reason to believe that God acted justly.

Perhaps Job could have endured God's fury if it had not been followed by withdrawal, which shut off all dialogue.[59] An eclipse of God took place at the precise moment of Job's pressing need for answers. Faced with silence from his former partner in dialogue, and confronted with empty words from human substitutes, the distraught father adopted extreme measures of provocation. The bold charges against God aimed at a single goal: to evoke God's response at any cost. Confident that a sinner dared not take a stand before God, Job aspired to personal vindication by overcoming divine silence.

THE ROOT OF THE MATTER

Placing the book of Job within the context of a spiritual crisis in ancient Israel is only the first step in the demanding task of interpretation and appropriation. Like all great literary works, this one rewards readers who come to it from vastly different starting points. What follows will attempt to indicate the rich variety of viewpoints that exists today with regard to Job.

Perhaps the only area in which something resembling consensus has formed concerns the sui generis nature of the work, despite comparable discussions in Mesopotamian literature. Nothing that has survived from the ancient world achieves such sublimity of thought and expression, a combination that explains the singular influence of this work to the present day. Poets, artists, philosophers, psychologists, and playwrights are drawn to Job like bees to fresh blossom's nectar, and each one who wrestles with the book captures new insights that had previously eluded readers.

Occasionally, such new readings of Job filter down to the populace and provoke lively discussion of existential issues from people who possess little theological sophistication but who care deeply about life's essential questions. Archibald MacLeish's Broadway play, *J.B.*, introduced religious thinking into the lives of countless thousands who found his brand of humanism attractive indeed.[60] This modernization of Job conveys the spirit of the original with remarkable accuracy and power, although *J.B.*'s God lacks the ambiguity—and passion—of the biblical work. For this reason alone, *J.B.* fails to re-create the scandal that pervades Job: the tension within God between love and justice. *J.B.*'s God does not really matter, for he simply *is*; Job's God is both more majestic and more terrifying.

The uncanny ability to capture the spirit of the canonical work without doing justice to its ambiguity is also true of Carl Jung, whose *Answer to Job* represents a powerful emotive statement concerning injustice in high places.[61] Naiveté with respect to ordinary historical-critical issues detracts from the many fresh insights throughout this book, so that its cumulative effect scarcely reaches the heights achieved by the biblical masterpiece. Nevertheless, Jung's protest against divine disregard for human questions and his insistence that God respond more fully by embracing the human problem touch base with the concerns expressed by the source of his inspiration, however differently that author formulated them.

Other works deriving their inspiration from Job deserve some acknowledgment in this context. In most instances these examples surrender to the modern spirit so fully that they distort the sense of the original in one way or another. Goethe's *Faust* borrows the idea of a wager with the devil and creates a situation that permits him to discuss life's futility arising from the problem of evil. Classical Greek ideas and romantic philosophy suppress whatever Hebraic features may have informed the work, and the necessity for a happy ending mars this masterful discussion of the two souls residing within the human breast. A similar surrender to contemporary political philosophy or to the ideas of the counterculture has rendered recent attempts to appropriate Job less than satisfactory, despite much that is worthwhile.[62]

Literary analysis of Job confronts difficulty at the outset. What genre best describes the book? Answers vary, partly because scholars cannot agree whether to disregard the prose tale. If one takes the book as it stands, the most appropriate category would seem to be debate or dispute, particularly as this genre occurs in Mesopotamian wisdom. This form consists of a mythological introduction and conclusion, a dispute proper, and a theophany in which God resolves the debate. If one disregards the prose framework, two solutions to the problem of genre commend themselves: dialogue and lament. Of these two choices, the first takes account of the fact that Job's speeches are matched by comparable ones from several individuals, so that they form a dialogue concerning human response to suffering and the character of God. Still, the dialogue opens with Job's curse and closes with his submission, so that a genre that concentrates on Job's singular position must not be ruled out in principle. That being so, the category of lament naturally comes to mind. One can further refine such attempts to isolate the peculiar genre that best characterizes Job. The book may thus be viewed as a paradigm of an answered lament, which implies that it served as a model to teach people how to respond during suffering.

Resemblances between laments within the Psalter have not escaped notice, for many of Job's speeches register the same complaints that occupied the authors of individual psalms. These similarities are so striking at times that they have generated discussion of Job's dependence upon the Israelite cult, particularly with respect to repentance, confession, and forgiveness. In addition, the theophany has seemed to corroborate such thinking, since God's self-manifestation within the cult played a significant role in Israelite religion. Complaints do not necessarily point to the cult, however, for laments occurred widely in daily life, just as repentance and restoration did. The same goes for theophanies, which took place wherever God chose to lift the curtain concealing holiness from human eyes.

Further cause for caution in this endeavor to relate the book of Job closely with the cult arises from the careful avoidance of anything that would identify Job as an Israelite.[63] To be sure, this tendency derived from the sages, who had acquired international tastes. For this reason, the search for historical allusions within Job is not likely to produce positive results, in that Job's experience does not signify the main events of Israel's history. Nevertheless, resemblances between Job and certain canonical works, specifically Deutero-Isaiah[64] and the hymnic passages in Amos,[65] attest to a desire to link Job more closely with Israel's religious thought. In their own way, these two literary entities were just as radical as Job, for the doxologies of Amos praise God despite a death sentence, and the prophet of deliverance views vicarious suffering in a redemptive light.

Such affinities between Job and other canonical works complicate matters when it comes to determining the ethos within which this powerful discussion of innocent suffering and divine character arose. Prophetic elements, psalmic features, legal language, and wisdom occur. Thus far silence has prevailed with regard to striking references to a trial before the heavenly tribunal. This explicit language permeates Job's speeches, suggesting that the debate may more properly be described as a legal dispute.[66] The difficulty with this attractive hypothesis is that Job longs for the opportunity to confront his accuser in court but despairs of doing so. His final imprecatory oath certainly belongs to a legal dispute, but ritualistic and cultic associations seem to prevail. The divine speeches make a mockery of human notions concerning a trial, as also do baseless accusations by Job's three friends and Elihu.

Despite these elements from various literary strands, the dominant one is surely wisdom. That judgment does not depend wholly upon analogy with Mesopotamian wisdom literature[67] but finds reinforcement from closer to home. The theophany preserves choice examples of wisdom based on the observation of nature, while the entire book owes its inspiration and much of its language to the sapiential tradition. We need not assume that the poem culminating in a statement restricting wisdom to God derives from the same hand that wrote the dialogue, but we ought to congratulate the unknown person who inserted this unusual poem, for it certainly catches the spirit of the greater literary entity. True wisdom, like God, defies human reason.

AN UNRESOLVED QUESTION

The partial nature of all answers to ultimate questions can find no more eloquent testimony than the book of Job. Who speaks for the author? Since Job is given free rein to respond after each of his friends, it has been claimed that the scales tilt in his favor. That sort of reasoning cannot suffice if we consider the Elihu speeches, to which Job proffers no reply. Surely we must not suppose that the poet intended for Elihu to be his, or her, mouthpiece. By the nature of the case, God supplied the definitive word, which crushed Job's Titanism like a caterpillar under the wheels of a steamroller. But does God speak for the poet?[68] The answer is unclear. Job's friends definitely do not speak for the poet, since they succeeded only in earning God's scorn—if the narrative ending can be heeded.

In determining the poet's sentiments, the reader must ask whether the ancients appreciated spiritual rebels any more than officials of institutionalized religion do today. The answer to that question may not be quite so significant after all, for the wisdom tradition was itself a witness to a different understanding of reality from the one that characterized Israel's religious community. Nor should one overlook the remarkable tolerance within prophetic, legal, and narrative texts. At times it appears that the biblical God welcomes a good debate, eagerly awaiting lively dialogue. In the light of numerous instances of rebellion against God in the Hebrew Scriptures, together with accounts in which the Lord of the universe is said to have entered into discussion with troubled souls, Job was not automatically labeled a rebel without cause. Ancient readers must surely have responded positively to his cry and therefore could have heard the poet's voice in Job.[69]

This judgment does not lead to denigration of Job's friends (but see 42:7–9), for these men endeavored, initially in a pastoral manner, to lead Job on the path to repentance. While their conviction that a just God ruled the universe brought extreme spiritual consternation to Job, we must not forget that they suffered considerable abuse from their friend. In addition, who can say that adherence to religious conviction in the face of contradictory evidence is wholly wrong? Only shallow faith would result if the dimension of mystery departed and we clung solely to what could be verified. In a way, Job's friends are partly victimized by the literary genre in which they appear, but they also exceed proper bounds when praising God at the expense of human beings. Surely no sage wished such sentiments to be mistaken for his or her own.

To a certain degree, modesty would have prevented the poet from putting his own words in God's mouth. To be sure, the divine speeches communicate effectively for the poet, but his sympathies lie with Job rather than with his attacker. At the same time, the poet's own feelings surface in God's painful concession that the human realm posed acute problems to divine rule, if that is really the meaning of the challenge to conquer pride and wicked conduct among humans. Therefore Job's final remark should not be understood ironically. Neither Job nor the poet showed contempt for the kind of God who parades before him wild creatures and recalls the taming of nature. Such a God must surely have inspired awe—would God have been God if accomplishing less when becoming manifest?

What, then, has Job learned from this firsthand encounter with God? Perhaps the first thing he discovered concerned the mistaken reason for Job's quest. The consuming passion for vindication suddenly presented itself as ludicrous once the courageous rebel stood in God's presence. By maintaining complete silence on this singular issue that had brought Job to a confrontation with his maker, God taught this servant the error in assuming that the universe operated according to a principle of rationality. Once that putative principle of order collapsed before divine freedom, the need for personal vindication vanished as well,[70] since God's anger and favor show no positive correspondence with human acts of villainy or virtue. Job's personal experience had taught him that last bit of information, but he had also clung tenaciously to an assumption of a just moral order. Faced with a stark reminder of divine freedom,[71] Job finally gave up this comforting claim, which had hardly brought solace in his case.

Job's loss may have been accompanied by significant gain—the ability to cherish God's presence for naught, to quote the Adversary's language, but God seems not to have encouraged Job along these lines, perhaps because presumption with regard to personal relationship can be equally as wrong as presuming that God bows before a principle of human justice. That is why Job's sole recourse was to melt away before divine mystery.[72] Nevertheless, enforced silence in the presence of one who has just spoken, even in rebuke, surpasses speechless indifference from on high. Unlike Job, Qoheleth never so much as provoked a personal reprimand from the silent heavens.

NOTES

1. For a survey of recent approaches to the book of Job, see James L. Crenshaw, "Job, Book of," *ABD*, 3:858–68 (*UAPQ*, 426–48). Older accounts can be found in Hans-Peter Müller, *Das Hiobproblem* (EF 84; Darmstadt: Wissenschaftliche Buchgesellschaft, 1978); and Jürgen Kegler, 9–25, in Claus Westermann, *Der Aufbau des Buches Hiob* (CThM A6; Stuttgart: Calwer, 1977). The Colloquium Biblicum Lovaniense 42, which was held on August 24–26, 1993, concentrated on the book of Job; the papers have been edited by W. A. M. Beuken, *The Book of Job* (BETL 14; Leuven: Leuven University, 1994). An Academy Colloquium in Amsterdam in April 2002 on "The Book of Job: Suffering and Cognition in Context," resulted in the publication *Job 28: Cognition in Context*, ed. Ellen van Wolde (BIS 64; Leiden: Brill, 2003). Maria Gorea, *Job: Ses précurseurs et ses epigones ou comment faire du nouveau avec de l'ancien* (Orient & Méditerranée 1; Paris: De Boccard, 2007), treats the antecedents to the book of Job and later adaptations, especially the *Testament of Job*. In three volumes Stephen J. Vicchio has discussed the image of the biblical Job: *Job in the Ancient World, Job in the Medieval World*, and *Job in the Modern World* (Eugene, Or.: Wipf & Stock, 2006). See also L. Besserman, *The Legend of Job in the Middle Ages* (Cambridge: Harvard University, 1979); and R. Eisen, *The Book of Job in Medieval Jewish Philosophy* (Oxford: Oxford University, 2004). *Job ou le drame de la foi*, ed. Maurice Gilbert and Françoise Mies (Paris: Cerf, 2007), contains thirteen essays by Jean Lévêque on the book in context, the development of the problem, and the basic themes. A valuable commentary by Samuel E. Balentine (*Job* [Macon, Ga.: Smyth & Helwys, 2006]) richly illustrates the biblical book from art and literature. See also Roy B. Zuck, ed., *Sitting with Job: Selected Studies on the Book of Job* (Grand Rapids: Baker Book House, 1992); Ronald J. Williams, "Current Trends in the Study of the Book of Job," in *Studies in the Book of Job*, ed. Walter E. Aufrecht (Waterloo, Ont.: Wilfrid Laurier University, 1985), 1–27; Leo G. Perdue and W. Clark Gilpin, eds., *The Voice from the Whirlwind: Interpreting the Book of Job* (Nashville: Abingdon, 1992); and Samuel Terrien, *Job in Literature and Art* (University Park: Pennsylvania State Press, 1997).
2. Nevertheless, a tendency to stress the editorial unity of the book and thus to try to make sense of its present shape can be detected in several recent commentaries and monographs, particularly Norman C. Habel, *The Book of Job* (OTL; Philadelphia: Westminster, 1985); Edwin M. Good, *In Turns of Tempest* (Stanford: Stanford University, 1990); David J. A. Clines, *Job 1–20* (WBC 17; Dallas: Word, 1989); Carol A. Newsom, "The Book of Job," *NIB*, 4:319–637, Yair Hoffman, *A Blemished Perfection: The Book of Job in Context* (JSOTSup 213; Sheffield: Sheffield Academic, 1996); and David W. Cotter, *A Study of Job 4–5 in the Light of Contemporary Literary Theory* (SBLDS 124; Atlanta: Scholars, 1989), on a microlevel.
3. Ellen van Wolde, *Mr and Mrs Job* (London: SCM, 1997), 89.
4. Habel, *Book of Job*, 27–35.
5. "But the author has so convincingly located his narrative in the patriarchal period that there are no clear contemporary allusions of any kind to the period contemporary with the author" (Clines, *Job 1–20*, lvii).
6. The actual date of composition of the book cannot be determined. The vocabulary has been judged to be no earlier than the sixth century (Avi Hurwitz, "The Date of the Prose Tale of Job Linguistically Reconsidered," *HTR* 67 [1974]: 17–34). The silence about the fall of Jerusalem in 587 BCE accords

with the sages' usual practice of ignoring particular historical events. A change came only with Ben Sira in the second century. The allusion to incising a message in rock (19:24) may indicate knowledge of the Behistun Rock on which Darius, King of Persia, commemorated his achievements. The mention of caravans from Teman and Sheba (6:19) and nomenclature for officials (kings, counselors, and princes) in 3:14–15 corresponds to Persian hierarchy. Use of the definite article with "the Adversary" (*haśśāṭān*) implies a stage prior to the Chronicler (fifth century BCE) and coterminus with Zechariah (521–516). The rare vocabulary derives, at least to some extent, from artistic subtlety (a single example illustrates the point; in 4:10–11 five different words for "lion" stretch modern translators' wits to the breaking point).

7. Nahum M. Sarna, "Epic Substratum in the Prose of Job," *JBL* 76 (1957): 13–25. See also Hurwitz, "Date of the Prose Tale."

8. Georg Fohrer, *Das Buch Hiob* (KAT 16; Gütersloh: Gerd Mohn, 1963), passim. Gustavo Gutiérrez, *On Job*, trans. Matthew J. O'Connell (Maryknoll, N.Y.: Orbis, 1987), thinks the primary issue of the book concerns the question, "How are we to talk about God in the midst of so much poverty and suffering?" Gutiérrez overstresses Job's solidarity with the poor and his contemplative nature. René Girard, *Job: The Victim of His People*, trans. Yvonne Freccero (Stanford: Stanford University, 1987), interprets the book of Job as a sacrificial drama, with Job as a scapegoat for the community's guilt. In doing so, Girard takes excessive liberty with the text.

9. Meir Weiss, *The Story of Job's Beginning* (Jerusalem: Magnes, 1983), offers a perceptive analysis of the literary and psychological dimensions of this narrative. Wolf-Dieter Syring, *Hiob und sein Anwalt: Die Prosatext des Hiobbuches und ihre Rolle in seiner Redaktions- und Rezeptionsgeschichte* (BZAW 336; Berlin: de Gruyter, 2004), provides a thorough examination of the idea of a just sufferer in the ancient world.

10. The Hebrew word *yômô* (his day) probably refers to birthdays and does not indicate a ceaseless round of partying on the part of the seven sons.

11. The numbers suggest wholeness (sevens and threes, as well as the totals, ten thousand and one thousand).

12. Ironically, Job's exceptional goodness led to the death of his children. Renate Egger-Wenzel, *Von der Freiheit Gottes, anders zu sein: Die Zentrale Rolle der Kapital 9 und 10 für das Ijobbuch* (Forschung zur Bibel 83; Würzburg: Echter, 1998), excuses divine cruelty by elevating it to epistemology. She concludes that God did not experiment with Job's faith or love to find out what was true. He knew that already. But Job did not know (p. 293).

13. On the divine assembly, see R. N. Whybray, *The Heavenly Counsellor in Isaiah XL 13–14* (SOTSMS 1; Cambridge: Cambridge University, 1971), 39–53; E. Theodore Mullen Jr., *The Divine Council in Canaanite and Early Hebrew Literature* (HSM 24; Chico, Calif.: Scholars, 1980), idem, "Divine Assembly," *ABD* 2:214–17.

14. Rivkah Schärf Klüger, *Satan in the Old Testament* (Evanston: Northwestern University, 1967); Peggy L. Day, *An Adversary in Heaven: Satan in the Hebrew Bible* (HSM 43; Atlanta: Scholars, 1988); and Victor P. Hamilton, "Satan," *ABD* 5:985–89.

15. The Adversary introduces a visual pun on the name, *haśśāṭān*, specifically *miśśûṭ*.

16. On the assumption that this proverb derives from pre-Yahwistic ideas of Mother Earth, the narrator in Genesis 3 may move naturally from the notion of nakedness to that of mortality, both with regard to the punishment speci-

fied for disobedience and with respect to the tree of life. Perhaps the second tree is less obtrusive than interpreters think.

17. Readers must pay special attention to the meaning of the verb *bārak*, for it can mean either "bless" or "curse." For cynical speakers, it functions euphemistically to signify "curse."

18. The absence of an interrogative particle permits a different reading: "Actually we receive good from God but do not receive evil." There are at least five differences between Job's first statement in 1:21 and that in 2:10, according to van Wolde, *Mr and Mrs Job*, 25. They are: (1) the use of Yahweh versus Elohim; (2) praise and blessing versus none; (3) a statement versus a question; (4) the addition of "with his lips" in 2:10; and (5) a heavenly perspective versus an earthly one.

19. The addition of "with his lips" was understood by some rabbis as an admission that Job's true resentment remained an unexpressed thought. On rabbinic interpretation of the book, see J. Weinberg, "Job versus Abraham: The Quest for the Perfect God-Fearer in Rabbinic Tradition," in *The Book of Job*, ed. Beuken, 281–96; and Nahum Glatzer, "The Book of Job and Its Interpreters," in *Biblical Motifs*, ed. A. Altmann (Cambridge: Harvard University, 1966), 197–220.

20. See Dariusz Iwanski, *The Dynamics of Job's Intercession* (AnBib 161; Rome: Pontifical Biblical Institute, 2006). Iwanski orients the intercession to the *rîb* controversy and adopts a holistic approach to the entire book.

21. Various reconstructions of an earlier version have been put forth, but such conjecture carries little conviction. Variations in the story line occur in the later *Testament of Job*, but the changes largely concern Job's piety, his encounters with the Adversary, his wife's loyalty, and his extraordinary legacy to the three daughters. Kenneth Numfor Ngwa, *The Hermeneutics of the 'Happy' Ending in Job 42:7–17* (BZAW 354; Berlin: de Gruyter, 2005), thinks the epilogue brings together divine transcendence and immanence. See also Duck-Woo Nam, *Talking about God: Job 42:7–9 and the Nature of God in the Book of Job* (New York: Peter Lang, 2003).

22. John T. Wilcox, *The Bitterness of Job: A Philosophical Reading* (Ann Arbor: University of Michigan, 1989), emphasizes the erotic dimensions of the text relating to the daughters and Job's keen desire to return to nature (219–23). The textual basis for such a reading is meager.

23. That unpleasant thought comes home with shuddering impact in Neil Simon's play, *God's Favorite*. Here the Adversary turns to "Job's" favorite son and remarks, "Guess who is God's favorite now." The implication is that disaster will strike him just as it had his father.

24. James L. Crenshaw, "In Search of Divine Presence," *ReExp* 74 (1977): 353–69 (*UAPQ*, 481–98). See Hans-Peter Müller, "Die Hiobrahmenerzählung und ihre altorientalischen Parallelen als Paradigmen einer weisheitlichen Wirklichkeitswahrnahme," in *Book of Job*, ed. Beuken, 21–40; and Perdue, *Wisdom Literature*, 77–135. Perdue writes: "Job, the tragic hero, is engaged in an assault on God to remove him from heaven's throne, while God's attack on Job is occasioned by identifying him with the dark forces of chaos challenging divine rule" (p. 117). Susannah Ticciati, *Job and the Disruption of Identity: Reading Beyond Barth* (London: T & T Clark International, 2005), thinks that "God takes up the evil of creation onto himself in order to transform it" (p. 180). In her view, Job's God arbitrarily perverts justice, the epilogue critiques the prologue, and creation trumps law.

25. I have examined the Joban "drama" from this perspective in "The Twofold Search: A Response to Luis Alonso Schökel," *Semeia* 7 (1977): 63–69. The

epilogue is analyzed by Yohan Pyeon, *You Have Not Spoken What Is Right about Me: Intertextuality and the Book of Job* (StBL 45; New York: Peter Lang, 2003). He stresses the interrelationship between the speeches in the book of Job and other canonical literature, as well as the intricate web of citations of each friend's speech.

26. This language derives from Edwin M. Good, *Irony in the Old Testament* (Philadelphia: Westminster, 1965), 196–97.

27. David Clines, "False Naivety in the Prologue to Job," *HAR* 9 (1985): 127–36, recognizes features that imitate but exaggerate the style of a folktale, specifically symmetrical parallelism, stylized characterization, and the impression of a remote past. At the same time, he thinks, the author uses wordplays and ambiguity to indicate distance from the naiveté.

28. Michael Fishbane, "Jeremiah IV 23–26 and Job iii 3–13: A Recovered Use of the Creation Pattern," *VT* 21 (1971): 151–67.

29. Fohrer, "The Righteous Man in Job 31"; see also M. Oeming, "Hiob 31 und der Dekalog," in *Book of Job*, ed. Beuken, 363–88; M. B. Dick, "Job 31, the Oath of Innocence, and the Sage," *ZAW* 95 (1983): 31–53; Lévêque, *Job ou le drame de la foi*, 119–29; James L. Crenshaw, "A Good Man's Code of Ethics," *Prophets, Sages, & Poets*, 42–45; and J. Gerald Janzen, *Job* (Interpretation; Atlanta: John Knox, 1985), 210–16.

30. Zophar's final speech is missing, unless it has been mistakenly attributed to Job. In any case, Job speaks entirely inappropriate language in 24:18–25; 26:5–14; and 27:13–23.

31. See W. A. M. Beuken, "Job's Imprecation as the Cradle of a New Religious Discourse: The Perplexing Impact of the Semantic Correspondences between Job 3, Job 4–5 and Job 6–7," 41–78; J. E. Hartley, "From Lament to Oath: A Study of Progression in the Speeches of Job," 79–100; and Leo G. Perdue, "Metaphorical Theology in the Book of Job: Theological Anthropology in the First Cycle of Job's Speeches (Job 3:6–7; 9–10)," 129–56, all in *Book of Job*, ed. Beuken.

32. See my *Hymnic Affirmation of Divine Justice* (SBLDS 24; Missoula, Mont.: Scholars, 1975); idem, "Flirting with the Language of Prayer (Job 14:13–17," in *Prophets, Sages, & Poets*, 6–13, 201–3. Lévêque, *Job ou le drame de la foi*, 201–34 emphasizes the role of creation in the book, as well as hymnic language.

33. Von Rad, *Wisdom in Israel*, 217. See also David Penchansky, *What Rough Beast? Images of God in the Hebrew Bible* (Louisville: Westminster John Knox, 1999); and James L. Crenshaw, "The Reification of Divine Evil," *Perspectives in Religious Studies* 28 (2001): 327–32.

34. Jean Lévêque, "L'interprétation des discours de Yhwh (Job 38,1–42,6)," in *Book of Job*, ed. Beuken, 203–22; James L. Crenshaw, "When Form and Content Clash: The Theology of Job 38:1–40:5," in *Creation in the Biblical Traditions*, ed. Richard J. Clifford and John J. Collins (CBQMS 24; Washington, D.C.: Catholic Biblical Association of America, 1992), 70–84; T. N. D. Mettinger, *In Search of God* (Philadelphia: Fortress, 1988), 175–200; Robert Alter, *The Art of Biblical Poetry* (New York: Basic Books, 1985); Jürgen van Oorschot, *Gott als Grenze* (BZAW 170; Berlin: de Gruyter, 1987); Robert Gordis, "The Lord out of the Whirlwind: The Climax and Meaning of Job," *Judaism* 13 (1964): 48–63; R. A. F. MacKenzie, "The Purpose of the Yahweh Speeches in the Book of Job," *Bib* 40 (1959): 435–45; Samuel Terrien, "The Yahweh Speeches and Job's Responses," *RevExp* 68 (1971): 497–509; Kenneth Thompson, "Out of the Whirlwind," *Int* 24 (1960): 51–63; and H. D. Preuss,

"Jahwes Antwort an Hiob und die sogenannte Hiobliteratur des alten Vorderen Orients," in *Beiträge zur alttestamentlichen Theologie: Festschrift für Walther Zimmerli zum 70. Geburtstag*, ed. Herbert Donner, Robert Hanhart, and Rudolf Smend (Göttingen: Vandenhoeck & Ruprecht, 1977), 323–43.

35. The cosmological and meteorological phenomena address the issue of divine control, whereas the five pairs of creatures illustrate a strange "providential care" that permits each one to live according to its nature, even when that eventuates in violence and bloodshed.

36. This seems to be the point of the challenge to overcome the proud, a task that has been too much for God. Nevertheless, God's power over the mythological creature, Behemoth, suggests that the Deity can face the most threatening opponent known to the human imagination. The two creatures, somewhat resembling a hippopotamus and a crocodile, recall the mythological role of these animals in Egyptian thought. On mythic thinking in the book of Job, see Gisela Fuchs, *Mythos und Hiobdichtung* (Stuttgart: Kohlhammer, 1993); and Leo G. Perdue, *Wisdom in Revolt* (JSOTSup 112; Sheffield: Almond, 1991).

37. David Neiman, *The Book of Job* (Jerusalem: Massada, 1972); and Robert Gordis, *The Book of God and Man: A Study of Job* (Chicago: University of Chicago, 1965).

38. On theodicy see James L. Crenshaw, ed., *Theodicy in the Old Testament* (IRT; Philadelphia: Fortress, 1983); idem, *UAPQ*, 141–221; idem, "Theodicy," *ABD* 6:444–47; idem, *Prophets, Sages, & Poets*, 173–94, 253–61; Antti Laato and Johannes C. de Moor, eds., *Theodicy in the World of the Bible* (Leiden: Brill, 2003); and David Penchansky and Paul L. Redditt, eds., *Shall Not the Judge of All the Earth Do What Is Right? Studies on the Nature of God in Tribute to James L. Crenshaw* (Winona Lake, Ind.: Eisenbrauns, 2000).

39. M. Sekine, "Schöpfung und Erlösung im Buche Hiob," in *Von Ugarit nach Qumran: Festschrift Otto Eissfeldt*, ed. W. F. Albright et al. (BZAW 77; Berlin: Töpelmann, 1961), 213–23.

40. John G. Gammie, "Behemoth and Leviathan: On the Didactic and Theological Significance of Job 40:15–41:26," in *Israelite Wisdom*, ed. Gammie et al., 217–31; Othmar Keel, *Jahwehs Entgegnung an Ijob* (FRLANT 121; Göttingen: Vandenhoeck & Ruprecht, 1978); and Veronika Kubina, *Die Gottesreden in Buche Hiob* (FThSt 115; Freiburg: Herder, 1979).

41. For a convenient summary of the many possibilities, see Newsom, "Book of Job," 629:

1. "Therefore I despise myself and repent upon dust and ashes" (i.e., in humiliation);
2. "Therefore I retract my words and repent of dust and ashes" (i.e., the symbols of mourning);
3. "Therefore I reject and forswear dust and ashes" (i.e., the symbols of mourning);
4. "Therefore I retract my words and have changed my mind concerning dust and ashes" (i.e., the human condition);
5. "Therefore I retract my words, and I am comforted concerning dust and ashes" (i.e., the human condition).

42. Newsom, "Book of Job," 628, understands the *waw* as conjunctive, inasmuch as God has just commanded Job to listen. She translates: "I have listened to you with my ears, and now my eye sees you." For Job, sight is a consequence of attentive listening rather than a contrast to hearing. On the role of sight

and sound in ancient education, see James L. Crenshaw, "Knowledge," *NIDB*, 3:539–46; "Education," *NIDB*, 2:195–205; and *Education in Ancient Israel.*

43. The speeches by Elihu have attracted considerable attention lately, especially that of T. Mende, *Durch Leiden zur Vollendung* (TTS 49; Trier: Paulinus, 1990); and H.-M. Wahl, *Der Gerechte Schöpfer* (BZAW 207; Berlin: de Gruyter, 1993). Bruce Zuckerman, *Job the Silent: A Study in Historical Counterpoint* (New York: Oxford University, 1991), 148–53, views Elihu's youthfulness as an indication of a generation gap between the original composition and the later author of chaps. 32–37. For older studies, see Marvin E. Tate, "The Speeches of Elihu," *RevExp* 68 (1971): 487–95; and David Noel Freedman, "The Elihu Speeches in the Book of Job," *HTR* 61 (1968): 51–59. See Konrad Schmid, "The Authors of Job and Their Historical and Social Setting," *Scribes, Sages, and Seers*, 145–153, for the changing circumstances as the book of Job grew.

44. On the fear of the Lord, see David J. A. Clines, "'The Fear of the Lord Is Wisdom' (Job 28:28): A Semantic and Contextual Study," in *Job 28*, ed. van Wolde, 57–92; and J. van Oorschot, "Hiob 28: Die verborgene Weisheit und die Furcht Gottes als Überwindung einer generalisierten *ḥokmâ*," *Book of Job*, ed. Beuken, 183–202. On the entire poem, see Stephen A. Geller, "Where Is Wisdom? A Literary Study of Job 28 in Its Settings," in *Judaic Perspectives on Ancient Israel*, ed. Jacob Neusner, Baruch Levine, and E. S. Frerichs (Philadelphia: Fortress, 1987), 169–75; van Wolde, ed., *Job 28*; Alison Lo, *Job 28 as Rhetoric: An Analysis of Job 28 in the Context of Job 22–31* (SVTSup 97; Atlanta: Society of Biblical Literature, 2003). The poem is often taken as an interlude, allowing readers to assess the intensity of Job's turmoil and to prepare for the divine speeches, but Lo thinks it alerts the audience to the inadequacy of traditional theodicies and triggers Job's actions in chaps. 29–31. Edward L. Greenstein, "The Poem on Wisdom in Job 28 in Its Conceptual and Literary Contexts," in *Job 28*, ed. van Wolde, 253–80, thinks this poem is a continuation of Elihu's speech in chap. 37 and that it refers to God's activity in exploring the deep, not human achievement.

45. Although many critics interpret the book as either a debate or a lament, Katharine J. Dell, *The Book of Job as Sceptical Literature* (BZAW 197; Berlin: de Gruyter, 1991), opts for skeptical literature as its genre.

46. On warrants for the opposing views of the main speakers in the book of Job, see James L. Crenshaw, "Wisdom and Authority: Sapiential Rhetoric and Its Warrants," in *Congress Volume: Vienna 1980* (VTSup 32; Leiden: Brill, 1981), 10–29 (*UAPQ*, 326–43).

47. Such bold affirmation occurs within the Babylonian parallel to Job (*I Will Praise the Lord of Wisdom*) and in the Canaanite Baal epic.

48. The prominence of language pertaining to a lawsuit (*rîb*) within Job has been stressed by various interpreters, most notably by S. H. Scholnick, "Lawsuit Drama in the Book of Job," Ph.D. diss., Brandeis University, 1975: and "The Meaning of *mišpaṭ* in the Book of Job," *JBL* 101 (1982): 521–29.

49. Carl G. Jung, *Answer to Job* (Cleveland: World, 1970), 20. For a different psychological analysis, see Jack H. Kahn, *Job's Illness: Loss, Grief and Integration: A Psychological Interpretation* (Oxford: Pergamon, 1975).

50. Dorothea Sitzler, *Vorwurf gegen Gott: Ein religiöses Motiv im Alten Orient (Ägypten und Mesopotamia)* (SOR 32; Wiesbaden: Harrassowitz, 1995). Sitzler concentrates on eight texts, four from Egypt (*Coffin Text 1130, Merikare, Ipuwer, Words of Heliopolis*) and four from Mesopotamia (*Sumerian Job, A Man and His God = Old Babylonian Text AD 4462, Ludlul bel nemeqi [I Will Praise the Lord of Wisdom]*, and *Babylonian Theodicy*).

51. A fuller treatment can be found in my article, "The Human Dilemma and Literature of Dissent," in *Tradition and Theology in the Old Testament*, ed. Douglas A. Knight (Philadelphia: Fortress, 1977), 235–58.

52. Ludwig Schmidt, "*De Deo*": *Studien zur Literarkritik und Theologie des Buches Jona, des Gesprächs zwischen Abraham und Jahwe in Genesis 18:22f. und von Hi 1* (BZAW 143; Berlin: de Gruyter, 1976), has examined this passage and related ones from the perspective of source criticism, with highly questionable results. For considerably different analysis of Gen. 18:22–33, see James L. Crenshaw, "The Sojourner Has Come to Play the Judge: Theodicy on Trial," in *God in the Fray: A Tribute to Walter Brueggemann*, ed. Tod Linafelt and Timothy K. Beal (Minneapolis: Fortress, 1998), 83–92.

53. On the reason for Jonah's dismay over divine compassion for the hated Ninevites, see James L. Crenshaw, "Who Knows What YHWH Will Do? The Character of God in the Book of Joel," in *Fortunate the Eyes That See: Essays in Honor of David Noel Freedman in Celebration of His Seventieth Birthday*, ed. A. B. Beck et al. (Grand Rapids: Eerdmans, 1995), 185–96. For the affinities between Job and Jonah, see Bruce Vawter, *Job & Jonah: Questioning the Hidden God* (New York: Paulist, 1983).

54. James L. Crenshaw, *A Whirlpool of Torment* (OBT; Philadelphia: Fortress, 1984), 31–56.

55. Ibid., 93–109.

56. Jim Alvin Sanders, *Suffering as Divine Discipline in the Old Testament and Post-Biblical Judaism* (Rochester, N.Y.: Colgate Rochester Divinity School, 1955); Mende, *Durch Leiden zur Vollendung*; O. Leamann, *Evil and Suffering in Jewish Philosophy* (Cambridge: Cambridge University, 1995); David Kraemer, *Responses to Suffering in Classical Rabbinic Literature* (Oxford: Oxford University, 1995); Jan Lambrecht and Raymond F. Collins, eds., *God and Human Suffering* (LTPM 3; Louvain: Peeters, 1990); Richard Rohr, *Job and the Mystery of Suffering* (New York: Crossroad, 1996); Markus Witte, *Vom Leiden zur Lehre* (BZAW 230; Berlin: de Gruyter, 1994); Crenshaw, *Defending God*.

57. Johannes Hempel, "Das theologische Problem des Hiob," *ZST* 6 (1929): 638 repr. in *APOXYSMATA* (BZAW 81; Berlin: Töpelmann, 1961), 128.

58. Von Rad, *Wisdom in Israel*, 206–26.

59. Kornelis H. Miskotte, *When the Gods Are Silent*, trans. John W. Doberstein (New York: Harper & Row, 1967); and Terrien, *Elusive Presence*. In the latter work the adjective rarely functions because of the majestic cultic presence that overwhelms modern readers as it surely must have done many ancient worshipers.

60. MacLeish, *J.B.* (Boston: Houghton Mifflin, 1956).

61. Jung's lack of expertise in biblical training did not prevent him from recognizing the immense theological issues involved in the character of God as presented in Job and throughout the Bible. Those problems, which Jung treats under the shadow side of God, are irreconcilable with a moral view of deity.

62. On Ernst Bloch's interpretation of Job, see Dichter Gebracht, "Aufbruch zu sittlichem Atheismus: Die Hiob-Deutung Ernst Blochs," *EvT* 35 (1975): 223–37. For different perspectives on Job, see Dermot Cox, *The Triumph of Innocence: Job and the Tradition of the Absurd* (Analecta Gregoriana 212; Rome: Universita Gregoriana, 1978); and Philippe Nemo, *Job and the Excess of Evil* (Pittsburgh: Duquesne University Press, 1998). Nemo believes that the excess of evil destroys the world in order to reveal another world, "what is other *than* the world" (pp. 2–3). He writes: "The world is the organ by which God makes signals in the direction of souls" (p. 140). For other responses to

the book of Job, see Robert Frost's "Mask of Reason," William Blake's artistic representations (S. Damon Foster, *Blake's Job* [New York: Dutton, 1969]); and William Safire, *The First Dissident: The Book of Job in Today's Politics* (New York: Random House, 1992).

63. John Day, "How Could Job Be an Edomite?" in *Book of Job*, ed. Beuken, 392–99. Day gives four reasons for viewing Job as an Edomite: (1) the sages' internationalism; (2) a fixed tradition; (3) the representation of Job as a worshiper of Yahweh; and (4) the setting of the story in ancient times before the later hostility.

64. Samuel Terrien, "Quelques remarques sur les affinités de Job avec le Deutéro-Esaïe," *Volume du Congrès, Genève 1965* (VTSup 15; Leiden: Brill, 1966), 295–310.

65. On these similarities see my *Hymnic Affirmation of Divine Justice*, and "The Influence of the Wise upon Amos," *ZAW* 79 (1967): 42–52.

66. See n. 48; to these may be added G. Many, "Der Rechtsstreit mit Gott (*rîb*) im Hiobbuch," Ph.D. diss., Munich, 1970.

67. Particularly *The Babylonian Theodicy*, which is closer to the book of Job than *I Will Praise the Lord of Wisdom, A Man and His God*, and *A Dialogue Between a Master and His Slave*.

68. The curious doubling of Job's possessions (and children in the Septuagint) indicts God, who pays the customary price of a convicted criminal. Given this irony, it is unlikely that God speaks unambiguously for the poet.

69. For a different view, see von Rad, *Wisdom in Israel*, 210.

70. Chaim Zhitlowsky, "Job and Faust," in *Two Studies in Yiddish Culture*, ed. Percy Matenko (Leiden: Brill, 1968), 152, writes: "His emotional world suddenly assumes a different form. The clouds of darkness are dispersed. A feeling of infinite confidence in the world and its Divine Leader arises in his soul and he laughs at the thousand questions, the hungry wolves with burning eyes, and they disappear from his soul."

71. Matitiahu Tsevat, "The Meaning of the Book of Job," in *SAIW*, 341–74.

72. Interpreters have silenced Job just as God did. See T. W. Tilley, "God and the Silencing of Job," *Modern Theology* 5 (1989): 257–70; and P. Rouillard, "The Figure of Job in the Liturgy: Indignation, Resignation, or Silence?" in *Job and the Silence of God*, ed. C. Duquoc and C. Floristan (New York: Concilium, 1983), 8–12. Silence plays a different role in an article by Alan M. Olson, "The Silence of Job as the Key to the Text," in *The Book of Job and Ricoeur's Hermeneutics*, ed. John Dominic Crossan (Semeia 19; Chico, Calif.: Scholars, 1981), 113–19. David Wolfers, *Deep Things out of Darkness* (Grand Rapids: Eerdmans, 1995), offers a bold interpretation of the book, one that assumes numerous mistranslations by previous scholars.

Chapter 5

The Chasing after Meaning

Ecclesiastes

With Qoheleth[1] the ultimate goal of wisdom became considerably more ambitious than it was in Proverbs or Job. The sages who composed canonical proverbs undertook a modest task—the discovery of life-securing knowledge by which they could demonstrate fidelity to the divine will as it penetrated the universe itself. For the unknown author of Job, the single purpose that enabled the innocent sufferer to endure excruciating agony was the hope of recovering an earlier relationship with a God who had withdrawn into impenetrable silence. Both quests were accompanied by faith in the universe and its Creator, even if in Job's case the basis for such trust had crumbled. In addition, both Proverbs and the book of Job are products of a wisdom ethos that placed enormous confidence in the human intellect. The author of Ecclesiastes lacked trust in either God or knowledge. For him nothing proved that God looked on creatures with favor, and the entire enterprise of wisdom had become bankrupt.[2] The astonishing thing is that such skepticism did not prevent Qoheleth from asking the question of questions: Does life have any meaning at all?[3]

The understanding of wisdom as a search is singularly appropriate for Qoheleth.[4] Twice the name Qoheleth occurs within the body of the book; in each case the author speaks self-consciously about his goal as a sage. In both

instances he uses two words for searching, as if to say that his entire life had constituted a quest for meaning. Moreover, the first text (1:12–18) has Qoheleth
identify himself as king over Israel in Jerusalem, a literary fiction that justifies the
adjective *royal*. Here two verbs for searching occur as the focus of firm resolve
(*dāraš* and *tûr*). Qoheleth's determination to seek out and explore everything
that happens under heaven was achieved through means of wisdom. While *dāraš*
suggests ordinary searching, *tûr* connotes extraordinary measures more appropriate to spying. Together the verbs imply that Qoheleth left no stone unturned
in his relentless search for a single meaningful act on earth.[5]

The final verdict of this quest pronounces judgment upon God: "It is a grievous business God has given people with which to occupy themselves" (1:13).[*]
Small wonder Qoheleth announces the results of his search in a refrain that the
entire book echoes: "I saw every action that is done under the sun, and everything is futile and shepherding the wind" (1:14). For him divine gifts evoked no
ecstatic shout, inasmuch as one's lot could not be altered. The crooked could not
be straightened, and what was lacking could not be counted. Indeed, superior
knowledge constituted no real asset, for increased sorrow invariably accompanied expanding insight.

The other text (7:23–29) juxtaposes Qoheleth's vision of achieving wisdom
and the stark reality of its inaccessibility. No amount of desire to become wise sufficed, since the goal remained far away and very deep, beyond human acquisition.
Although Qoheleth determined to know, explore, and search out wisdom and the
sum of things, he found only one good man in a thousand; whether he found a
single woman remains a matter of debate.[6] In this context the verb that suggests
spying is coupled with a customary expression for seeking (*bāqaš*), and both are
reinforced by the oft-recurring verb for finding (*māṣā'*). Unfortunately, Qoheleth
was not able to find out anything positive. From such unhappy discoveries he
drew a painful conclusion: "God has made humankind upright, but they have
sought after numerous devices" (7:29).[7] The implication is that collectively they
have devised ways to corrupt things, a view that stands in tension with the earlier
denial that those who dwell under the sun could change their predetermined lot—
unless we should attribute perverse intentions to God. Does Qoheleth imply that
God fixed all fates in such a way that perversion naturally followed?[8]

The author of the first epilogue within the book remained true to Qoheleth
when trying to characterize his mentor's activity (12:9–11).[9] After calling his
teacher a wise man who taught the people, this admirer describes Qoheleth as
one who deliberately searched for and arranged numerous proverbs. The sense of
the rare verb (*'āzen*) is uncertain. It may mean "he listened"[10] or something like
"he weighed" in the sense of evaluating words. The second verb (*ḥēqer*) is identical with that used in Proverbs 25:2 with reference to a king's glory in *searching
out* things that are hidden.[11] As if this allusion to seeking were insufficient, the
student proceeds to reinforce the idea. Qoheleth sought (*bāqaš*) to find (*māṣā'*)

---

* Translations of Ecclesiastes are mine.

pleasing words, and faithfully wrote truth. In short, both Qoheleth and his epilogist used verbs connoting search whenever the title Qoheleth occurred.

MAJOR THESES

At the end of this search, what discoveries enriched Qoheleth's knowledge? I will attempt to clarify Qoheleth's thinking by examining five major convictions: (1) death cancels everything; (2) wisdom cannot achieve its goal; (3) God is unknowable; (4) the world is crooked; and (5) pleasure commends itself. All five of these theses flow from a loss of trust in the goodness of God, a presupposition of earlier wisdom. Even Job had secretly harbored a powerful faith that God really intended good things for devout people, despite the serious rupture in the universe at the moment. Qoheleth, however, could muster no confidence in God's disposition to reward virtue and punish vice. In his view, Job's exceptional experience of innocent suffering had become the rule, and the death angel[12] made no distinctions among creatures. Naturally, Qoheleth thus struck at the heart of the tradition in which he had been nurtured. Between him and old wisdom stretched a great abyss that was too deep for either to cross.[13]

Death Cancels Everything

The chasm separating Qoheleth from his predecessors could hardly be wider than in 2:17 ("Then I hated life, for the work that was done under the sun was grievous to me because everything was futile and shepherding wind"). Life, the highest good to earlier sages, has now become an object of loathing. This shocking discovery registers Qoheleth's conclusion to a series of experiments concerning possible meanings of life. Pretending to be King Solomon, whose wisdom was thought to have surpassed that of Eastern kings and whose power was limitless, Qoheleth tested the various answers to life's meaning: pleasure, work, wealth, renown, wisdom.[14] In the end he judged them all to be worthless since death cancels any advantage that might have accrued to the sage. Ultimately, all of these so-called meanings, for which humans strive relentlessly, amount to nothing permanent. The two images emphasize the insubstantial quality of such reward for striving. The first (*hebel*) refers to breath,[15] which is real but fleeting, while the second (*rĕ'ût rûaḥ*) alludes to "shepherding," or chasing after, wind (or even feeding on air).

In denying absolute value to feasting, toil, possessions, fame, and knowledge Qoheleth conceded that they do possess fleeting significance. Still, pleasure vanishes quickly, while time eventually erodes human achievements and obliterates all memory of outstanding individuals. Knowledge, too, bestows only relative advantage, enabling people to see the fate that encounters them. Unfortunately, a common end unfolds for the wise and the fool. Moreover, that death often benefits surviving fools who inherit the fruit of a sage's toil. Such reflection thrust Qoheleth forward into radical denial of life's goodness. After a lifetime of toil, no profit remains, and the sum of things resembles one mighty act of breathing.

In this regard humans merely participated in a futile exercise that character-ized the universe as well. While generations come and go, the world endures time's passing, but ceaseless movement of the cosmos succeeds only in going around in a circle. Streams flow to the sea, the sun pants toward its goal, and the wind blows endlessly—yet things remain unchanged. The sum of all activity, human or natural, was one huge zero, the greatest emptiness.

It follows that Qoheleth preferred the day of death to the moment of birth, since human illusions burst before the harsh reality that removes all distinctions among people. Sheer honesty compels Qoheleth to declare that it is "better to go to the house of mourning than to frequent the house of feasting, since it is the end of everyone, and the living should reflect on it." Thus he concluded that sadness was better than laughter, inasmuch as a heart is gladdened by a sorrowful countenance (7:2–3).[16] Precisely what he means by this declaration escapes us, unless he refers to the proverb that understood harsh discipline as a necessary stimulus for eventual happiness. In any case, he notes that the wise gravitate toward houses of sorrow while fools throng banquet halls (7:4).[17]

In one sense death commended itself to one and all: it brought rest from all labor. The image of death as rest functions powerfully in Qoheleth's thought. Consideration of the sorry lot experienced by those who lacked power to fend for themselves among corrupt companions moved him to startling observations: the dead were more fortunate than the living, and better than both were those who have not been born. In this context the twofold reference to an absence of com-forters indicates how close Qoheleth came to throwing off his disinterested cloak. The chiastic linking (abb'a') of rampant oppression and evil under the sun (4:1, 3) demonstrates the unusual impact social injustice achieved on this teacher.[18]

Not all cruelty originated with humans. In 6:1–6 Qoheleth moved from considering divine injustice to questioning the advantages of living when com-pared with the peace surrounding an aborted birth. This extreme judgment was not put forth without qualification; to ignore the circumstances prompting the strange conclusion would lead to gross misunderstandings. Qoheleth objects to instances in which wealth and longevity have not been accompanied by power to profit from them, however fleetingly, so that a stranger devoured the fruit of another's labor. In such instances a stillborn child was luckier than the miserable wretch who toiled in vain, for it found rest.

These two texts (4:1–3; 6:1–6) look upon death as entirely welcome under certain circumstances.[19] The first generalizes from common misery, and the sec-ond refers to a specific instance. Since wickedness thrives unchecked, death—nay, nonexistence—is better than life. The powerlessness of poor victims of society is thus taken for granted; devoid of hope, they face an intolerable existence. Some-times the unfortunate individuals are those who seem to enjoy divine favor, for all life's good things surround them. For some unexplained reason, certain persons live in luxury's lap without a moment's fulfillment of desire. When that happens, Qoheleth observes, an aborted birth is more fortunate.

For others whose experience has been different, Qoheleth concedes the natural desire to live as long as possible.[20] Thus he advises against conduct that would shorten one's days; this warning to avoid extreme virtue or vice endorses a sort of middle way, the path of least resistance.[21] Perhaps Qoheleth would have urged others to greet death with open arms if they could have discovered the right time to do so. Unfortunately, such conduct remained without meaning so long as death's proper time lay in mystery. To be sure, the debilitating effects of inevitable decay (12:1–8) hardly commend themselves to anyone. In effect, the deterioration of body and mind slowly drains away every ounce of dignity a person has accumulated in a lifetime, leaving utter emptiness. Unlike a newborn babe, this human shell has used up its potential once and for all. The shattering bowl can only presage release for one whose existence is finally canceled by death.

Even when Qoheleth seems to endorse life as intrinsically better than death, he may speak ironically. The crucial text (8:16–9:6) bristles with polemic against established wisdom.[22] In this instance Qoheleth boldly rejects claims that sages can find out what God is doing. Although human deeds, good or evil, reside in God's mighty hand, no one can determine whether God's disposition toward human beings is love or hate. With absolute certainty one thing looms before them: a single fate befalls righteous and unrighteous, clean and unclean, sacrificer and nonsacrificer, good and bad, swearer and the one who disdains oaths. Causality as put forth in Deuteronomy and taken for granted by almost everyone no longer commended itself, either as reward for virtue or punishment for vice. No wonder human hearts are filled with evil and madness, which death alone stills.

At this point Qoheleth pauses to declare that the living have hope, "for the living know that they will die, but the dead know nothing, and have no more reward, since memory of them is forgotten" (9:5). In addition, "their love, their hate, and their passions have already perished, and they no longer have any portion ever in all that is done on earth" (9:6). To demonstrate his point, Qoheleth quotes a familiar aphorism: "A living dog is better than a dead lion" (9:4b). Whatever this saying means in context,[23] it surely does not imply that knowledge that one is going to die constitutes real hope. Instead of giving hope to the living, such insight furnishes a stark reminder that all achievement is futile. At least those who have entered the land of darkness have sloughed off every vestige of passion and no longer participate in human madness.

Furthermore, death carries its victims on a journey from which none returns. Just as persons came into this world naked, so they return without anything that they accumulated in the intervening years.[24] Both people and beasts share the same fate—they return to dust. Qoheleth shrinks from the impact of this observation only far enough to qualify it with a rhetorical question: "Who knows whether human breath ascends and animals' breath descends?" (3:21).[25] Elsewhere he leaves no doubt about his own answer to this question. A god who tests human beings to show them that they are but beasts cannot be expected to separate the two in death. At that decisive moment chance reigns:

> The race is not to the swift, nor the battle to the strong, nor yet bread to the wise, and riches to the astute, nor favor to the informed, for time and mischance meet them all. (9:11)

The divine hunter's snare falls without warning, and silence ensues.

For a fleeting moment Qoheleth flirts with the remote possibility that death occasions a remarkable distinction between humans and beasts. Whereas dust returns to the earth, human breath ascends to God, who gave it. Surely this text (12:7) furnishes solid evidence for abiding hope. On the contrary, for Qoheleth proceeds to declare the meaning of the matchless poem describing old age and death: "Absurdity of absurdities, says the Qoheleth, everything is absurd" (12:8).[26] Such a conclusion would be out of place if the allusion to breath's return to God contained the slightest foundation upon which to build any hope. For Qoheleth the divine support of life has entirely vanished. In his view the final word is death's chilling summons.

The natural conclusion to the twin concepts that death offers *rest* for the weary and that the living have no *real* advantage over the dead must surely be an enthusiastic endorsement of suicide. The puzzling inconsequence of Qoheleth's thought concerns the lack of any positive attitude toward speedy termination of life. Unlike those who composed comparable works in Egypt and Mesopotamia, Qoheleth refused to view suicide as a way of resolving the immense existential anxiety in which he moved and breathed. Its lure would seem irresistible for one who hates life and who falls into despair's viselike grip. As we shall soon see, another powerful answer presented itself and etched its features indelibly into Qoheleth's heart.

Wisdom Cannot Achieve Its Goal

Death's shadow was not the only cause for Qoheleth's ennui. Another source of his negative observations about life was the recognition that wisdom could not secure existence. Earlier sages had endorsed wisdom with confidence that knowledge assured life's good things. In their view, one could know "what was good for women and men," and, knowing it, could achieve the desired end. Such optimism failed to persuade Qoheleth that individuals could control their future. Instead, he insisted that wisdom could not achieve its goal. The experience of Job has intervened between earlier wisdom and Qoheleth's skepticism.

To be sure, some insight surrendered to persistent inquiry, but that tiny bit of knowledge only complicated reality. Far from bestowing tranquillity upon those who successfully acquired a degree of wisdom, this information resulted in troubled minds and exhausted bodies. Open eyes beheld grievous injustice, both human and divine, and sought in vain for redress from wrong. In such a world, ignorance was surely a way to insulate individuals from suffering because of grievous injustices.

Random insights hardly sufficed for Qoheleth, who aspired to total knowledge. His vocabulary soars over the expanse of the universe; phrases like "under the sun," "under heaven," "everything," "the sum of things," and so forth abound. Here is a thinker who wanted to accomplish more than the mere accumulation of facts about separate entities. Indeed, Qoheleth wished to penetrate to the underlying meaning of all knowledge.[27] In the end, he lacked the key that would unlock the vault within which ultimate purpose lay untouched.

That closed door was not God's way of preventing humans from discovering that the world was their greatest enemy. On the contrary, the universe was created orderly, since everything was appropriate in its time. Qoheleth did not wholeheartedly accept the Priestly writer's enthusiasm concerning the goodness of creation; the latter uses significantly different language in Genesis 1:1–2:4a. Whereas the first account of creation repeatedly declares that "God saw that it was good," Qoheleth qualifies that declaration.

> He has made everything beautiful in its time, also he has put the unknown
> in their mind, because of which no one can find out the work God has done
> from beginning to end. (3:11)

Here one encounters theologically neutral vocabulary instead of the weighty Priestly writer's terms for "create" and "good." In addition, Qoheleth attributed a gift of dubious value to God. That difficult word I have translated "the unknown," although "eternity" is also possible. In either case, this divine gift does individuals no good, since they cannot discover it at all.[28]

Like unused wisdom, a gift that defies discovery amounts to heartless teasing. Elsewhere Qoheleth mentions a tragic instance in which a poor wise man's knowledge went to waste because no one remembered him when the city was threatened by a powerful king (9:13–16). If only someone within the besieged city had recalled the poor sage, he would have delivered the unfortunate people.[29] Since his knowledge about warfare lay dormant when survival depended upon its awakening, calamity struck a forgetful population. Even when men and women remember God's gift, it remains untouched and thus inconsequential. Indeed, such a gift actually generated anxiety, for it created a longing for full knowledge or for eternity.

This desire to achieve complete knowledge has a single purpose: to control the future. It follows that inability to find out God's activity at any point signals doom for all efforts at securing one's existence. Although Qoheleth seems to acknowledge wisdom's capacity to grant life to its owner in one instance (7:12), the context places such optimism under a heavy cloud. As so often happens in Qoheleth's thought, traditional wisdom is cited for the purpose of demonstrating its inadequacy. How can wisdom bestow life, he asks, when no one can alter what God has already shaped? Furthermore, nobody can discover anything concerning the future (7:13–14). If the twisted reality God has fashioned inevitably persists, and the future lies under a veil of ignorance, then wisdom cannot give life to those who strive for earthly security.[30]

In dealing with the inability to control the future, Qoheleth registers his own certainty through his choice of syntax; rhetorical questions function as powerful statements (6:12; 7:13; 8:7; 10:14). No one can straighten what God has made crooked! No one can predict the future! Such linguistic forms scarcely yield evidence that Qoheleth's mind fluctuated with regard to securing the future by wisdom.

Wherever the topic of an uncertain future surfaces, it invariably gives no comfort to those who endeavored to transform the wisdom enterprise into a "science of the times."[31] While we cannot be sure such a background evoked Qoheleth's sharp rebuke in 8:17, it seems likely. Sages may claim to possess knowledge of the times, but their many boasts are empty lies. That much Qoheleth knows for certain. Like the contingencies of birth and death, over which individuals have no power, the future lies in God's hands. Nobody knows what will be, for who can inform him about the future (8:7)? Ceaseless toil alone cannot enable one to find out what God is doing (8:17). Although a definite time for everyone exists, none can ascertain that fateful moment. As a result, all people blunder blindly into the net like fish and are captured like helpless birds when the trap falls (9:12).

The reason for the miserable plight of God's creatures lies in the nature of wisdom, which is beyond reach. Qoheleth's description of wisdom as a deep abyss reveals an astonishing lack of faith in human goodness. Members of the masculine minority have precious little grounds for pointing an accusing finger at women, since, in the view of the one who composed this old proverb, only one in one thousand separates the two genders where virtue is concerned (7:23–29). Elsewhere Qoheleth denies that anyone succeeds in doing right all the time, so that ultimately all who once were upright (*yāšār*) now veer from their true destination. Unable to penetrate into the depths and to retrieve the secret that unlocks one's fate, we conjure up emergency aids.

If we cannot determine our future, however much we try, God's disposition toward us becomes a matter of life and death. Happily, Qoheleth thought that God was generous beyond comprehension.[32] The only problem was that the gifts seemed to follow no identifiable pattern, so that an element of arbitrariness prevailed. Men and women possessed no control over the good that God dispensed in his own time and manner. Not even morality purchased the best gifts, and often good people waited in vain for signs of divine favor while rich rewards speedily greeted those who engaged in evil acts. In short, the trouble with gifts was that God retained control over their timing and disposition. In a sense God forced men and women to rely upon the giver for everything. Where, then, does human mastery of existence through wisdom find a toehold?

The inevitable consequence of such thinking would seem to be some form of determinism.[33] Since God's works cannot be altered, and none can discover what the Creator is doing now or intends to do in the future, the nerve of life atrophies. One is tempted to throw up the hands in despair, rather than to tackle life's enigmas with confidence. In such unhappy circumstances the perfectly natural reaction is to reject the possibility of knowing the meaning of anything (8:1).

Now if one asks what has transpired within the thought of the sage at this point, a single response resounds through the halls of learning. The urge to master life has suddenly rammed against a solid wall; the earlier assumption that wisdom could secure life has collapsed for Qoheleth. Once upon a time individuals could identify themselves as devout ones (ṣaddîqîm), inasmuch as they belonged to a particular group by virtue of their essential character. Goodness was a status, and people could recognize to which camp they belonged. Such assurance no longer existed, and nobody knew whether God smiled or frowned on him or her.

God Is Unknowable

The mystery surrounding God need not arouse consternation, for the One who fills heaven and earth is by nature invisible. Still, Israel's sages had managed to say much about this mysterious Deity whose wondrous name concealed more than it divulged. Qoheleth acknowledged God's mystery, likening it to the amazing power that forms an embryo within the womb of a pregnant woman. Instead of deriving comfort from this unknown and unknowable divine essence, Qoheleth complained that God's activity was just as hidden as the divine essence. The miracle of life occurs and no one knows how such transformation takes place; likewise God moves within the universe without leaving enough clues to permit men and women to recognize divine presence at any time (11:5).[34]

Contemporary thinkers find Qoheleth's theism somewhat puzzling, for it would seem more natural to abandon belief in God altogether. Not for a single moment did he entertain the possibility of atheism, at least in his written legacy. For Qoheleth God was a given that not even the skeptic could doubt. How perilously close he comes to depicting God as the force behind all things! Indeed, Qoheleth speaks as if God were indifferent power before which we must cower in fear, and he often equates God's will with whatever happens.

In one sense God approaches the personal, acting with malice toward creatures. On one occasion Qoheleth actually describes God as testing men and women to show them that they are beasts (3:18). In the conclusion based on the majestic poem about an appropriate time for everything, he implies that God conceals the knowledge that would enable people to take advantage of this gift (3:1–11).[35]

Such an understanding of God left no place for personal relationship, however desirable it may have been to persons who extolled their God for fidelity to a covenant. Although earlier sages had never adopted this kind of language from prophets and priests, neither had they presented God as indifferent to human conduct, except for Job's three friends, who insisted that the deeds of puny humans did not affect God in any way. In Qoheleth's mind it was impossible to tell whether God looked upon humans with interest or with disdain. As a result, Qoheleth never addresses God in dialogue, either in prayer or lament. Whereas psalmists frequently complained about the same inequities that disturbed Qoheleth, they directed their attacks to God. They did so because of a vital personal relationship with the champion of widows and orphans. Like Job, these bold defenders of justice believed that God wished to repair the rupture that had endangered a vibrant personal relationship.

Lacking any such experience with God, Qoheleth advocated prudence before absolute power. The best procedure was to avoid the limelight, but if people must approach sacred territory they should do it cautiously. Economy of speech was better than extended talk, for the more individuals speak the more likely they are to incur divine wrath. Besides, a vast distance separates worshipers and Deity. Does Qoheleth mean that God cannot hear the words, and that they are so much wasted breath? If so, his view must have changed at some time, for he also warns against taking vows if one is not absolutely certain they will be carried out. The danger posed by an angry Deity implies that God hears vows and later checks to make certain they have been kept. Apparently, the messenger from God is the death angel, who can hardly be expected to excuse foolish impulses (5:1–6 [Heb. 4:17–5:5]).[36]

With this text we arrive at one of the most vexing problems in Qoheleth's thought. Did he believe God would judge the sinner and punish wickedness? To be sure, a few texts assert the traditional understanding of retribution; however, the overwhelming impact of the book points in the opposite direction. In one remarkable case Qoheleth argues that every official owes allegiance to another, so that injustice brings no real anxiety. The inevitable conclusion of such reasoning places the responsibility for abuse of power upon God, the ultimate ruler. As the highest authority, the Deity alone can be blamed for the cruel realities that surround us daily (5:7–9 [Heb. 6–8]). In one sense Qoheleth embraced the expectation of divine judgment: God would bring every living thing into the waiting arms of death. Nevertheless, Qoheleth differed from traditional views in denying that God was likely to make moral distinctions at that time.

The discerning reader will have noted that Qoheleth seems to know far more about God than his theology of divine mystery allows. In truth, he frequently makes assertions about God's will and activity despite the protestations about God's hiddenness. In some instances these observations come rather close to the modern notion of fate, and in others they reflect an equation of God with whatever happens. Occasionally, such comments almost endorse humor with respect to God.[37]

Perhaps the most conspicuous declarations concerning God's will have to do with the gift bestowed upon humans indiscriminately. That gift can be labeled "sorry business" (1:13), but it can also be called the single answer to the endless quest for meaning (2:24–26; 3:13). Eating, drinking, and enjoying life constitute God's gift to those who make the most of their youth.[38] In one surprising text Qoheleth encourages such behavior and justifies it with the claim that God has already approved the action (9:7). Such a defense of festive living seems to presuppose that God, the supreme power, endorses whatever happens. Obviously, nothing could happen that did not meet with divine approval.

Twice Qoheleth speaks of God in highly ambiguous language (3:15; 5:20 [Heb. 19]).[39] The first instance pictures God chasing prior events as if to ensure that nothing new occurs under the sun. Here God seems preoccupied with past, present, and future—so much so that wickedness thrived on earth. The other text may allude to God's way of reducing the troubled hearts of men and women, so that joy alone impresses itself upon the memory.[40] Alternatively, it may accuse God of afflicting them with thoughts of unachieved joy. The latter of these interpretations accords with Qoheleth's understanding better than the former. Both texts therefore approach the ludicrous. God's ceaseless activity is just as meaningless and vexing as human striving. No wonder Qoheleth took the further step toward nihilism: the universe itself cannot be trusted.

The World Is Crooked

Qoheleth's predecessors made two fundamental assumptions about the nature of reality: God was moral, and the world was trustworthy. Neither presupposition survived Qoheleth's critical scrutiny. The movement of nature led to no purposeful goal (1:4–9), since nothing unexpected ever intruded upon the scene. No episodic moments when nature smiled upon good men and women brightened the horizon, and no goal beyond the sunset awaited saint and sinner. Instead, the breezes went on their daily rounds, and rivers flowed into the sea, but nothing about this circular movement suggested that an underlying purpose could be found.

Within the existential boundaries of birth and death fell many meaningful eventualities, provided that one could discover the right time for each. No such fortune befell mortals, who watched helplessly as these momentous events transpired in their own time.

> A time to give birth and a time to die,
>   a time to plant and a time to pull up what has been planted.
> A time to kill and a time to heal,
>   a time to dismantle and a time to build.
> A time to weep and a time to laugh,
>   a time of mourning and a time of dancing.
> A time to throw stones away and a time to gather stones,
>   a time to embrace and a time to refrain from embracing.
> A time to search and a time to count as lost,
>   a time to keep and a time to throw away.
> A time to rip and a time to sew,
>   a time to be quiet and a time to talk.
> A time to love and a time to hate,
>   a time of war and a time of peace.
>
> (3:2–8)[41]

Inasmuch as no one could match a moment with the appropriate deed, a certain degree of chance inevitably followed. Earlier wisdom was founded upon the conviction that one could indeed discern the right deed for the occasion.

In such a universe suffering is hardly eased by soothing thoughts that it was deserved or that it will eventually be removed by a forgiving Deity. Instead, innocent victims weep uncontrollably and nobody comes to their aid. The hopelessness of the human condition prompts Qoheleth to repeat himself when thinking about the absence of comforters. The mighty cry of oppressed individuals resounds through the heavens, but no comforting response breaks the silence of eternity.

Although humans share the responsibility for perverting the world, not a single individual does good always and escapes sin's clutches (7:20). Given Qoheleth's view about the inability to know the correct time for any act, how could it be otherwise? That is why he becomes more excited about the end of an event than its beginning; how differently it would have been if he could have faced the future with confidence that he possessed the decisive key to appropriate conduct.

Because everyone lacks important knowledge about admissible and inadmissible deeds at any given moment, society suffers from lack of vision. The social upheaval that accompanied major shifts in power had left its mark on the community within which Qoheleth found himself, but he refuses to view his own situation as qualitatively different from all others.[42] In this regard, Qoheleth resembles the book of Job, which also generalizes from personal experience. But Qoheleth lacks the comforting faith that resolves all inequities in the epilogue of Job just as he lacks the disquieting memory of better days. For Qoheleth, a depressing sameness envelops former days and those yet to unfold before his eyes.

Pleasure Commends Itself

Precisely because the world refuses to encourage goodness by dispensing rewards to those who deserve them, pleasure commends itself as the only real means of salvaging a small portion of life. Invariably, Qoheleth links the two themes of vanity and enjoyment. In doing so he calls attention to the fact that such attempts at pleasurable living constitute grasping at straws. The enjoyment of fine foods, clothing, and women was only a kind of lifeboat ethics. This conclusion can hardly be avoided, since Qoheleth claims that he made a test of pleasure and dismissed it as empty. That is why the contexts within which his so-called positive advice appears render the message somewhat hollow.

For example, Qoheleth sprinkles these bits of advice with a heavy dose of extract from bitter herbs. The reminder that enjoyment depends upon God's pleasure was Qoheleth's way of saying that not everyone can take advantage of his free advice. The power to enjoy life belonged to the category of divine gift. As such it lay outside one's grasp and made mockery of those who furtively reached for pleasure when God chose not to grant it. For this reason, Qoheleth passed judgment on life within the shadow of such pleasure. This, too, he mused, is futile (2:1–3, 24) during the brief span of time allotted everyone (5:18–19 [Heb.

17–18]; 9:7). Even youth succumbs before the severity of this judgment, for it also is empty (11:9–10).[43]

At times Qoheleth seems almost to identify toil with the pleasures of the appetite it makes available. One could even say that he understood work as one of life's genuine pleasures; however, gainful employment enabled individuals to purchase the means of pleasure, and for this reason toil belongs within the context that enjoins the pursuit of sensual gratification. Ironically, Qoheleth notes that excessive profits from toil only lead to sleepless nights, and that increased riches vanish because of the additional claim upon available funds made by a coterie of servants.

These encouragements to live with gusto occur throughout the book of Ecclesiastes and are evenly divided between the two sections that treat the theoretical foundations for Qoheleth's thought and the practical conclusions that he draws. No clear distinction in terms of subject matter is discernible in either half of the book, for the admonition possesses a remarkable repetitiveness where genuine enthusiasm should have created some examples of poetic flourish. For that reason, the theory that Qoheleth's enthusiasm knows no bounds when calling others to share in the pleasures life holds does not commend itself.[44]

Perhaps the fullest explication of what he has in mind by this counsel appears in the sequel to Qoheleth's wry observation that in some cases the dead possess definite advantages over the living (4:2). Here he specifies the good things that he envisions: eating in circumstances where joy prevails; drinking wine when the heart is free from care, since God has already approved such actions; regularly wearing fine clothes; using ointment generously; and enjoying the warmth of the woman you love.[45] All of this sounds marvelous, until one pays attention to the somber undertones: enjoy these things throughout your empty days that God has granted you under the sun all the days of your absurd life! Furthermore, all this pleasure reaches its destiny in Sheol, to which you are going (9:7–10). One cannot escape the suspicion that Qoheleth wants to assure those who grasp for pleasure that emptiness will reign regardless of their successful use of life's opium, until death seizes its prey.

When we examine the things that Qoheleth approves, however halfheartedly, we see how self-interest dominates his thought.[46] The old query, "What is good for man and woman?" is understood in a thoroughly selfish manner. Curiously, the experiment that convinced him that pleasure also fell into the category of futility was hardly adequate, for he insisted that his rational faculties governed the entire test (2:1–3). He can be faulted for refusing to let go, but we must remember that Qoheleth was, after all, a sage. The self-interest that stands out so noticeably in Qoheleth's total experiment, and that the personal pronouns punctuate dramatically, prevents him from using to best advantage the important insight that life without companions is hazardous (4:9–12). For a fleeting moment he recognizes the advantages of teaming up with another person for mutual protection from the terrain, brigands, or frigid winds. Even here, however, Qoheleth scarcely thinks about alleviating someone else's suffering.

The prophetic conscience is entirely lacking here, and *moral impotence* reigns.[47] Qoheleth may see the same kind of injustice that Israel's prophets inveighed against, but he does not seem constrained to do battle against those who perpetrate the villainy. Instead, he advises against struggling with someone who possesses superior strength and sees no value in verbal harangue. How differently Job weighed the situation, and how valiantly he waged battle against the Almighty![48]

So far nothing has been said about Qoheleth's further qualification of his positive advice that seems to reverse all values (7:2–3). Grief and mourning are adjudged to be better than festive living. Even if Qoheleth's "better" sayings cannot properly be termed "excluding proverbs," nevertheless this passage certainly places the other admonitions to pleasure under a dark cloud.

To sum up, Qoheleth's positive counsel has little cause for exhilaration. The advice invariably occurs within contexts that emphasize life's absurdity and attendant inequities, as well as those that stress God's control over human ability to enjoy life. Qoheleth's concept of divine gift is an expression for human limitation rather than an extolling of a generous God. The sources of pleasure—woman, wine, food, clothes, ointment, toil, and youth—are empty, like life itself. In the end none accompanies the dead to Sheol. In spite of the limited satisfaction such pleasure affords, it does amount to something. Like breath that cannot be seen but makes life possible, such enjoyment renders existence endurable. Still, that life-endowing breath returns to its source and leaves a corpse, and the pleasant moments disappear without a trace. Fleeting satisfaction may be conjured up through an active memory, but even that means of storing up youthful pleasure soars aloft when the death angel raises its wings and sets out with its reluctant burden on a journey into nothingness.

LITERARY CHARACTERISTICS

Form

The book of Ecclesiastes consists of personal observation and reflection. The subject doing the reflecting is not just anyone; instead, this astute observer assumes the persona of King Solomon, "the wisest of men." He uses characteristic expressions of observation and reflection ("I saw," "I know," "I said in my heart," "I gave my heart," "there is"). The overarching literary form by which Qoheleth chose to communicate his message owes its origin to ancient Egyptian Instructions.[49] Often called *royal testament*, this device readily lent itself to a literary work that purported to register King Solomon's understanding of reality. In general the pharaohs or their viziers collected their insights for the benefit of aspiring young rulers, whom they hoped to steer successfully along paths of wisdom. Such advice appeared in autobiographical form, constituting a king's legacy for his successors (cf. Eccl. 1:12–2:26).

In addition, the book preserves a number of proverbs, many of which Qoheleth quoted for the purpose of refuting.[50] Others, however, represent school wisdom that Qoheleth used in his own formulation of sapiential instruction. Together these proverbs and instructions may actually constitute Qoheleth's lectures to students,[51] who probably have composed the two epilogues rendering his unusual views a trifle more acceptable to those who endorsed traditional wisdom and thus leading to its inclusion in the canon.

Qoheleth also uses autobiographical narrative, exemplary story, anecdote, parable (often called allegorical poem), antithesis, and "better" proverbs. In addition, the proverbial sayings cover a wide spectrum: numerical sayings, traditional sayings, malediction and benediction, and the emphatic "nothing is better" sayings. He was particularly fond of "better" sayings, for they enabled him to pretend to endorse conventional wisdom but actually to challenge its veracity by introducing a wholly different consideration (cf. 4:3, 6, 9, 13; 5:5 [Heb. 4]; 6:3, 9; 7:1, 2, 3, 5, 8; 9:16, 18).

Two poems that Qoheleth either composed or borrowed from some other source (1:4–11; 3:2–8) and the final poem about the decay that accompanies old age (11:7–12:7) have already been mentioned. These exquisite poems concerning the cycles of natural events and the time that exists for everything resemble some extant Egyptian and Greek texts, but they could easily have been written by Qoheleth himself.[52] The same is true for the description of the deterioration that presages death, even if in this case an Egyptian Instruction opens with a comparable poem.[53]

Although many interpreters think Qoheleth urges listeners to remember the Creator, the context suggests that the unusual word *bôrĕ'eykā* plays on the double metaphors cistern and grave (12:1).[54] In doing so Qoheleth recalls his "positive" advice to "enjoy the woman you love" and negative warning about one's approaching death. Such remembrance stood in stark contrast to the much lamented threat of forgetfulness in Sheol and offered an appropriate introduction to the waning years that occasion entrance into that land.

> Before the sun is darkened and the light—and the moon and the stars—
> and the clouds return after the rain.
> When the keepers of the house tremble and valiant men are stooped,
> and the grinding women cease because they are few,
> and those who look through the windows are dimmed;
> and the doors on the street are closed,
> when the sound of the grinding is muted,
> and one rises at the sound of the bird,
> and all the daughters of song are brought low.
> Also they are afraid of heights,
> and terrors are in the path
> and the almond blossoms, the locust burdens itself,
> the caperberry is useless;
> for humans go to their eternal home,
> and the mourners go about the street.
>
> (12:2–5)

Structure

The outer form of the book is easily discerned. Leaving aside the superscription in 1:1, there remain a thematic refrain (1:2, perhaps also 1:3), and a poem (1:4–11) at the beginning and a poem (11:7–12:7) plus a thematic refrain (12:8) at the end. Together with the superscription (1:1), the two epilogues (12:9–12, 13–14) enclose the book in a kind of envelope. The initial poem demonstrates the aptness of the thematic statement in the realm of nature, and the final poem shows the accuracy of the theme on the human scene. Nature's ceaseless repetition illustrates the utter futility of things, as does the eventual disintegration of the human body.

Within Qoheleth's teachings bracketed by a thematic statement and a poem, a few distinct units are recognizable by means of content or formulaic refrains, either introductory or concluding. A single thread holds together the royal experiment in 1:12–2:26, while a coherent idea seems to unite 3:1–15 (a time for everything) and 4:9–12 (the advantages of teaming up with someone for mutual benefit). While a few such discrete units stand out, no unifying principle underlying the whole book has come to light.

In the absence of clear demarcations of the several units, how can one decide on the extent of each? Perhaps a clue exists in Egyptian Instructions, clearly divided into sections called chapters. Analogy with *Papyrus Insinger*, roughly contemporary with Qoheleth, may suggest that refrains mark off larger units in the Hebrew text. One refrain, the sevenfold exhortation to eat, drink, and enjoy one's portion of life's good things (2:24–26; 3:12–13; 3:22; 5:18–20 [Heb. 17–19]; 8:15; 9:7–10; and 11:7–10), indicates both the promise of such an approach and its problems. The refrain in 3:24–26 actually concludes a unit, and the formula in 11:7–10 certainly begins one. Moreover, the book has a wealth of formulaic expressions, and interpreters are obliged to take into consideration additional factors in choosing those expressions that demarcate units of text.

Perhaps the most attractive hypothesis envisions two fundamental units (1:12–6:9; 6:10–11:6) enclosed by an introductory and a concluding poem (1:2–11; 11:7–12:8).[55] The two main sections employ different refrains. Whereas the first uses "(emptiness and) chasing after wind," the second has "cannot find out" or "who can find out?" and "do not know" or "no knowledge." These refrains occur with regularity in the two sections, as if to mark off smaller units as well. In addition, a single refrain introduces and concludes the work: "Utter futility, says Qoheleth, all is futile" (1:2; 12:8). This verse functions as a motto for the whole book.

Even this analysis poses many difficulties. In one instance the formula occurs in the middle of a unit of thought rather than at the end (e.g., 11:2); moreover, certain repeated phrases do not enter into consideration ("shepherding the wind," "this is absurd," "under the sun," "I turned and considered"). Upon close inspection, the supposed objectivity reveals itself as somewhat contrived, especially the numerological presuppositions underlying the hypothesis.

Perhaps the safest procedure is to isolate textual units on the basis of content. My own analysis yields the following:

1:1	Superscription
1:2–3	Motto and Thematic Statement
1:4–11	Poem: Nothing New under the Sun
1:12–2:26	Royal Experiment
3:1–15	A Time for Everything
3:16–4:3	Tears of the Oppressed
4:4–6	Proverbial Insights about Toil and Its Opposite
4:7–12	Advantages of Companionship
4:13–16	Fickle Crowd
4:17–5:8 (Eng. 5:1–9)	Religious Obligations
5:9–6:9 (Eng. 5:10–6:9)	Disappointments of Wealth
6:10–12	Transitional Unit
7:1–14	Collection of Proverbs
7:15–22	On Moderation
7:23–29	Seeking and Finding
8:1–9	Rulers and Subjects
8:10–17	Mystery of Divine Activity
9:1–10	Shadow of Death
9:11–12	Time and Chance
9:13–18	Wasted Wisdom
10:1–20	Collection of Proverbs on Wisdom and Folly
11:1–6	Element of Risk
11:7–12:7	Youth and Old Age
12:8	Thematic Statement (Inclusio)
12:9–14	Epilogue

Qoheleth's fondness for repetition leads to remarkable recurrence of preferred vocabulary, creating a sustained tone for the entire book. His favorite expressions include: "emptiness" or "absurdity," "under the sun," "under heaven," "no profit," "one fate," "portion," "gift of God," "toil," "the whole." Furthermore, he uses several expressions as transition markers: "then I turned and saw," or "gave myself up to," "I applied my mind to understand"; "this also is emptiness and chasing after wind." Rhetorical questions abound within the book, as if in defiance of more affirming wisdom as represented in canonical proverbs.

Unity

Although the present text of Ecclesiastes has achieved a degree of unity in theme and perspective, strong evidence of supplementary glosses exists. Besides those attempts to salvage the traditional view of retribution (3:17; 7:18; 8:12–13; 11:9b), at least two epilogues are readily discerned, although their exact scope is uncertain (12:9–12 and 13–14 or 12:9–11 and 12–14). The epilogues testify to the difficulty such thought encountered, inaugurating the first of several attempts to tone down Qoheleth's theology.[56] His words are adjudged to be true, although hard to take, and readers are warned to fear God and keep the commandments, for he will judge every secret, whether good or bad.

Authorship

The literary fiction of Solomonic authorship does not persist throughout the work but disappears after the section on the royal experiment. Elsewhere Qoheleth writes from the standpoint of one who lacks power to correct human oppression and reflects about kings from the position of a subject. Even the claim of Solomonic origin seems to have been taken lightly, for the author indicates an appalling lack of vital information about the Davidic monarchy. Although only David preceded Solomon on the throne at Jerusalem, Qoheleth boasts that he excelled all those who went before him. Furthermore, he gives more information about his genealogy than necessary if he actually were Solomon.[57]

The language of the book resembles the latest Hebrew in the canon; in some respects it comes close to Mishnaic Hebrew,[58] although occasional features of early Hebrew occur. The preference for participles, use of the relative *še*, two Persian loanwords (*pitgām* and *pārdēs*), and certain Hebrew words, namely *sôp* (end), *pešer* (interpretation), *môšēl* (ruler), *šālaṭ* (govern), and *'inyān* (worry), suggest a late date, as do occasional Aramaic words. Interpreters usually consider the mid-third century the probable date of the book.[59] The fragments of the book discovered at Qumran (parts of 5:14–16 [Heb. 13–17], substantial portions of 6:3–8, and five words from 7:7–9) date from the mid-second century BCE. Although the evidence is debatable, the provenance for this skeptical work in Jerusalem has much to commend it.

The unusual title *Qoheleth*[60] is just as enigmatic as the book itself. In the opening verse the word functions as a proper name, and the identification with Solomon is provided; but 12:8 speaks of *the Qoheleth* as if the word were a common noun with the definite article. In the Septuagint of 7:27 *Ekklēsiastēs* is also a common noun, although the Hebrew can be understood as a proper name. Elsewhere the word can be translated either way. In any event, the title refers to an office or function, which explains the feminine ending and accompanying verbal form. The similarity with *hassōperet* (scribe) and *pōkeret haṣṣēbāyîm* (binder of gazelles, Ezra 2:55, 57) is readily apparent, even if the actual office to which *Qoheleth* refers cannot be determined.

On the basis of various forms of the root *qhl*, the most obvious explanation for the task designated by *Qoheleth* has something to do with assembling people for some specific purpose. This meaning has given rise to the Greek title *Ecclēsiastēs*, one who assembles people for religious purposes. In light of Qoheleth's teachings, such a translation seems entirely inappropriate. One could understand *Qoheleth* as a teacher who assembled his pupils for instruction, an interpretation that would do justice to the title without turning him into an ecclesiastical figure.

The title may derive from the literary fiction of Solomonic authorship rather than from an official function of the author. If so, at least two possibilities present themselves: it may refer to Solomon as a *gatherer of women*,[61] or it may suggest a teacher's attempt to tally the sum of things. The former interpretation may derive support from the strange allusion to "one in a thousand," which registers the opinion that King Solomon's thousand wives left much to be desired. Anyone who gathered wives as freely as Solomon did deserves a title like "the assembler."

The second alternative takes its cue from the strange expression in 7:27 ("Says Qoheleth, one to one to find the sum"). Could this unusual phrase contain a hidden clue about the use to which the author put the title *Qoheleth*? If this reference to adding up the sum of things represents the teacher's task of discovering the profit (or lack of it) in living, the title *Qoheleth* becomes intelligible. The teacher gathers together the total of individual experiences in the hope of finding some meaning in life. A remarkable irony intrudes at this point: the mathematical compilation achieved its purpose, and the gatherer announced his profit as a worthless zero. Attractive though this hypothesis may be, it depends on an extension of the root *qhl* to things in addition to humans. Elsewhere only people stand as the object of this verb. In light of the author's equation of animals and humans in God's sight, such an extension of *qhl* cannot be ruled out in principle.

Another title for the teacher occurs in 12:11, which mentions "one shepherd" as the source of the teachings of the book. The royal background for this metaphor seems undeniable,[62] although some interpreters apply the metaphor to the Deity, the supreme king. It seems more likely that the epilogist follows 1:1 in attributing these skeptical teachings to King Solomon. Even apart from the Egyptian affinities, this literary fiction functions to underscore the negative impact of the book. If one who had absolute power and unlimited riches pronounced life futile, who are we to argue with him? The rabbinic claim that Solomon wrote this book in his dotage only heightens its message, for senility and the ultimate broken pitcher fell the most avid enthusiast who vainly assembles his own version of life's bounty.[63]

NOTES

1. The name Qoheleth occurs seven times:

   1. The words of Qoheleth, son of David, king in Jerusalem (1:1).
   2. The ultimate absurdity, says Qoheleth, the ultimate absurdity; everything is absurd (1:2).
   3. I am Qoheleth, I have been king over Israel in Jerusalem (1:12).
   4. Look, I have discovered this—says Qoheleth—adding one to one in order to find the sum (7:27).
   5. The ultimate absurdity, says the Qoheleth, everything is absurd (12:8).
   6. In addition to the fact that Qoheleth was a sage, he also taught the people knowledge (12:9a–b).
   7. Qoheleth sought to find pleasing words and accurately wrote down trustworthy sayings (12:10).

   Critics have understood Qoheleth as a personal name, a nom de plume, an acronym, and a function.

2. That does not mean that Qoheleth abandoned the rational investigation of reality. Instead, he interiorized the epistemological task, giving primacy to

personal observation and feelings, the domain of human freedom. Although the world yielded no evidence of rationality, he persisted in a pursuit of meaning solely through the intellect.

3. The existential question he posed is surprisingly modern, as are his conclusions, so much so that Michael V. Fox, *A Time to Tear Down and a Time to Build: A Rereading of Ecclesiastes* (Grand Rapids: Eerdmans, 1999), 8–11, compares his thoughts with those of Albert Camus, *The Myth of Sisyphus*. Robert Gordis, *Koheleth—The Man and His World* (3rd ed.; New York: Schocken, 1968), 112–21, compares Qoheleth's thinking to modern existentialists but argues that he offers a *via tertia*, that is, the conviction that meaning exists, even though veiled (p. 116).

4. Luca Mazzinghi, "The Verbs *mṣ'* ('to find') and *bqš* ('to search') in the Language of Qohelet: An Exegetical Study," in *The Language of Qohelet in Its Context: Essays in Honour of Prof. A. Schoors*, ed. A. Berlejung and P. van Hecke (OLA 164; Leuven: Peeters, 2007), 91–120.

5. Job 39:8 refers to an animal's search for food, and Prov. 12:26 seems to imply that wise people examine their friends very closely. In both cases *tûr* is used.

6. The issue arises because of uncertainty over 7:28. Does Qoheleth cite a conclusion of earlier sages, with which he takes issue? A growing number of interpreters have reached that conclusion, thus absolving Qoheleth of the charge of misogyny. The context makes plain that Qoheleth's understanding of human wickedness indicts everyone, and even if 7:28 represents his view, women are said to be only one one-thousandth less trustworthy. On this problem, see Norbert Lohfink, "War Kohelet ein Frauenfeind?" in *Sagesse de l'Ancien Testament*, ed. Gilbert, 259–87; and Antoon Schoors, "Bitterder dan de Dood is de Vrouw (Koh 7, 26)," *Bijdr* 54 (1993): 121–40. Alternatively, woman is understood as personified Wisdom, both elusive and unattainable, and 7:28b is taken as a gloss based on a misunderstanding of the dangerous woman in 7:26. On this view, see Choon-Leong Seow, *Ecclesiastes* (AB 18C; New York: Doubleday, 1997), 264–65; and Thomas Krüger, "'Frau Weisheit' in Koh 7, 26?" *Bib* 73 (1992): 394–403.

7. Not until Ben Sira does a sage use the concept of mirroring the Deity, the idea that humans are made in God's image. Qoheleth distinguishes between the ideal and the actual; created *yāšār* (morally upright), human beings become perverse. The real tension between what God intended for humankind and its propensity for evil evoked considerable thought, eventuating in a theory of two natures, one predisposed to evil and the other inclining toward goodness. Rabbinic literature develops this concept of two inclinations in a spirited fashion, speculating on the moment when each one takes up residence in an individual. The *yēṣer hārā'* (evil inclination) begins to manifest itself in infancy, whereas the *yēṣer haṭṭôb* (good disposition) does not emerge until one reaches an age of mature choice and is thus subject to the commandments (*bar miṣwâ*). Ben Sira comes close to this idea when emphasizing the complementary pairs, or opposites, making up the universe, a concept also found in Stoic philosophy. Qoheleth's poem about a time for everything does not quite make this point, despite its use of opposites.

8. Peter Machinist, "Fate, *miqreh*, and Reason: Some Reflections on Qohelet and Biblical Thought," in *Solving Riddles and Untying Knots: Biblical, Epigraphic, and Semitic Studies in Honor of Jonas C. Greenfield*, ed. Ziony Zevit, Seymour Gitin, and Michael Sokoloff (Winona Lake, Ind.: Eisenbrauns, 1995), 159–74, identifies four expressions in Qoheleth for the concept of fate: *ḥešbôn*, *ma'áśeh*, *'ōlām*, and *miqreh*. He thinks these terms imply a more explicit con-

ceptualization and abstraction than earlier notions of fate. Qoheleth was not alone in this view of human perversion, on which see James L. Crenshaw, "Deceitful Minds and Theological Dogma (Jer 17:5–11)," in *Utopia and Dystopia in Prophetic Literature*, ed. Ehud Ben Zvi (Publications of the Finnish Exegetical Society 92; Helsinki: Finnish Exegetical Society; and Göttingen: Vandenhoeck & Ruprecht, 2006), 105–21.

9. Martin A. Shields, *The End of Wisdom: A Reappraisal of the Historical and Canonical Function of Ecclesiastes* (Winona Lake, Ind.: Eisenbrauns, 2006), thinks the epilogist points to an alternative form of wisdom to that proclaimed by Qoheleth, specifically the fear of God and obedience to God's commandments. Rami Shapiro, *The Way of Solomon: Finding Joy and Contentment in the Wisdom of Ecclesiastes* (San Francisco: HarperSanFrancisco, 2000), thinks Qoheleth teaches the illusion of permanence, separateness, and control. The problem with this reading is that it imposes modern anxieties on an ancient text and ignores basic biblical insight that body and soul are one and that an unbridgeable chasm separates humans and Deity.

10. This singular use of the verb *'zn* in the sense of weighing something prompted C. F. Whitley, *Koheleth: His Language and Thought* (BZAW 148; Berlin: de Gruyter, 1979), 102, to translate "he listened," appealing to versional support. Seow, *Ecclesiastes*, 384, concurs. The educational context, where listening was central to knowledge, lends support to this reading.

11. In its negative form, *'ēn ḥēqer* indicates the unsearchable, that which cannot be discovered. See M. Tsevat, *"ḥāqar, ḥēqer, meḥqār," TDOT*, 5:148–50 ("Far more than the synonyms *bḥn*, *nsh*, and *ṣrp*, *ḥqr* stands for a purely cognitive and analytical examination and testing; *nsh* and *ṣrp* emphasize more the practical aspect of testing or 'trying out,' and *bḥn* suggests intuitive comprehension," 149).

12. For the signal importance of death to Qoheleth, see my essay, "The Shadow of Death in Qoheleth," in *Israelite Wisdom*, ed. Gammie et al., 205–16 (*UAPQ*, 573–85); Shannon Burkes, *Death in Qoheleth and Egyptian Biographies of the Late Period* (SBLDS 170; Atlanta: Society of Biblical Literature, 1999); and Ludger Schweinhorst-Schönberger, "Vertritt Kohelet die Lehre vom absoluten Tod: Zum Argumentationsgang von Koh 9:1–6," in *Auf den Spuren der schriftgelehrten Weisen. Festschrift für Johannes Marböck*, ed. Irmtraud Fischer, Ursula Rapp, and Johannes Schiller (BZAW 331; Berlin: de Gruyter, 2003), 207–19. John J. Collins, "The Root of Immortality: Death in the Context of Jewish Wisdom," *HTR* 71 (1978): 177–92, is concerned primarily with Ben Sira and Wisdom of Solomon.

13. Walther Zimmerli, "The Place and Limit of the Wisdom in the Framework of the Old Testament Theology," in *SAIW*, 325–26, sees Qoheleth as a guardian of ancient faith concerning divine freedom and human limitation.

14. James L. Crenshaw, "Beginning, Endings, and Life's Necessities in Biblical Wisdom," in *Wisdom Literature in Mesopotamia and Israel*, ed. Richard J. Clifford (SBLSymS 36; Leiden: Brill, 2007), (= *Prophets, Sages, & Poets*, 95–103, 230–33).

15. On the meaning of *hebel*, see Fox, *Qohelet and His Contradictions*, 29–51; Klaus Seybold, *"hebhel," TDOT*, 3:313–20; Graham S. Ogden, "'Vanity' It Certainly Is Not," *BT* 38 (1987): 301–7; Diethelm Michel, *Untersuchungen zur Eigenart des Buches Qohelet* (BZAW 183; Berlin: de Gruyter, 1989), 40–51; Dominic Rudman, "The Use of *Hebel* as an Indicator of Chaos in Ecclesiastes," in *Language of Qohelet in Its Context*, ed. Berlejung and van Hecke, 121–42; Ethan Dor-Shav, "Ecclesiastes, Fleeting and Timeless,"

Azure 18 (5765–2004): 67–87; and Douglas B. Miller, *Symbol and Rhetoric in Ecclesiastes: The Place of Hebel in Qoheleth's Work* (SBLAB 2; Atlanta: Society of Biblical Literature, 2002).

16. The sense of 7:3 recalls Prov. 14:13 ("The heart is sad even in laughter, and the end of joy is grief"). This rare interest in the psychology of sadness and mirth hardly accords with the exhortations to enjoy life.

17. The intellectual stimulation provided by symposia contradicts such a statement. Perhaps this practice of making speeches at a banquet was not known in Israel until Ben Sira's day.

18. Frank Crüsemann, "The Unchangeable World: The 'Crisis of Wisdom' in Koheleth," in *The God of the Lowly*, ed. Willy Schottroff and Wolfgang Stegemann, trans. Matthew J. O'Connell (Maryknoll, N.Y.: Orbis, 1984), 57–77, downplays the element of compassion in Qoheleth, while stressing his solidarity with the wealthy.

19. From ancient Egypt *A Dispute over Suicide* likens death to the recovery of a sick man, the odor of myrrh, the return from a journey, the clearing of the sky, and the longing of a person to see home again after spending many years in captivity.

20. In Sir. 41:1–4 the sage describes two entirely different reactions to the possibility of dying, depending on one's circumstances. Those who have wealth, health, and peace feel bitterness over death's summons, whereas people who have grown old and lost their capacity for enjoyment welcome the eternal decree, "You must die." The problem often is that death will not come soon enough.

21. R. N. Whybray, "Qoheleth the Immoralist? (Qoh 7:16–17)," in *Israelite Wisdom*, ed. Gammie, 191–204, takes a different view. See also his "Conservatisme et radicalisme dans Qohelet," in *Sagesse et Religion: Colloque de Strasbourg (Octobre 1976)* (Paris: Presses universitaires de France, 1979), 65–81.

22. The negation applies to Qoheleth and to all other sages. They may intend to attain knowledge, but they cannot succeed in the quest, given the role of chance in the world. Qoheleth's sharp attack on those who thought too highly of intellectual ability, in his view, does not fit well with recent attempts to understand the epilogue as a rejection of Qoheleth's teaching. In my view, he is not presented as a convenient straw man whose teachings were easily dismissed.

23. In light of the metaphorical use of the words "dog" and "lion" in the Bible, the aphorism may constitute a response to one who registered surprise over a marriage to a person of lower social status. Its point would be: a live spouse, even of limited means, is preferable to none at all, however noble.

24. The similarity with Job's well-known remark in Job 1:21 is obvious. In short, the funeral shroud has no pockets.

25. On the rhetorical question, see James L. Crenshaw, "The Expression *mî yôdēaʿ* in the Hebrew Bible," *VT* 36 (1986): 274–88 (*UAPQ*, 279–91).

26. The only other place where the name Qoheleth has an article is 7:27, but it is the result of wrong division of an earlier manuscript with continual script yielding *ʾāmarâ qōhelet* instead of *ʾāmar haqōhelet*. The similar motto in 1:2 has no article with Qoheleth. The mixture of images in this poem has led to several interpretations; it describes a funeral, a raging storm, the destruction of a house, old age, and death. On this exquisite poem, see Maurice Gilbert, "La description de la viellesse en Qohelet XII 7 est-elle allégorique?" in *Congress Volume: Vienna 1980* (VTSup 32; Leiden: Brill, 1981), 96–109; D. C. Fredericks, "Life's Storms and Structural Unity in Qoheleth 11:1–12:8," *JSOT* 52 (1991): 95–114; J. F. A. Sawyer, "The Ruined House in Ecclesiastes 12: A

Reconstruction of the Original Parable," *JBL* 94 (1976): 519–31; Hagia H. Witzenrath, *Süss ist das Licht: Eine Literaturwissenschaftliche Untersuchung zu Koh 11,7–12,7* (ATSAT 11; St. Ottilien: EOS, 1979); Fox, *Qohelet and His Contradictions*, 277–310; and James L. Crenshaw, *Ecclesiastes* (OTL; Philadelphia: Westminster, 1987), 181–89.

27. Some interpreters have seen a beginning of Jewish philosophy in Qoheleth's investigations. See Oswald Loretz, "Poetry and Prose in the Book of Qoheleth (1:1–3, 22; 7:23–8:1; 9:6–10; 12:8–14)," in *Verse in Ancient Near Eastern Prose*, ed. Johannes C. de Moor and Wilfred G. E. Watson (Alter Orient und Altes Testament 42; Neukirchen-Vluyn: Neukirchener, 1993), 155–89; idem, "Anfänge jüdischer Philosophie nach Qohelet 1, 1–11 und 3, 1–15," *UF* 23 (1991): 223–44; idem, "'Frau' und griechisch-jüdische Philosophie im Buch Qohelet (Qoh 7, 23–8, 1 und 6, 6–10)," *UF* 23 (1991): 245–64; A. P. Hayman, "Qohelet and the Book of Creation," *JSOT* 50 (1991): 93–111; James L. Crenshaw, "Qoheleth's Quantitative Language," in *Language of Qohelet in Its Context*, ed. Berlejung and van Hecke, 1–22; and Martin Rose, "Qohelet als Philosophe und Theologe: Ein biblisches Votum für *universitas*," in *Universitas in theologia—theologia in universitate: Festschrift Hans Heinrich Schmid zum 60. Geburtstag*, ed. Matthias Krieg and Martin Rose (Zurich: Theologischer, 1997), 177–99.

28. On this difficult problem, see my essay, "The Eternal Gospel (Ecclesiastes 3:11)," in *Essays in Old Testament Ethics*, ed. Crenshaw and Willis, 23–55 (*UAPQ*, 548–72).

29. Alternatively, the text may mean that the poor sage was consulted and his advice heeded, but the rescued people soon forgot the one who delivered them from certain death. On this text, see James L. Crenshaw, "Poor but Wise (Qoh 9:13–16)," forthcoming.

30. The powerful role of omens that generated a "science of predicting the future" in Mesopotamia is missing from Jewish wisdom. The closest thing to it is mantic wisdom, at home in apocalyptic. See H.-P. Müller, "Mantische Weisheit und Apokalyptik," in *Congress Volume: Uppsala 1971* (VTSup 22; Leiden: Brill, 1972), 268–93; and Benjamin G. Wright III and Lawrence M. Wills, eds. *Conflicted Boundaries in Wisdom and Apocalyptic* (SBLSymS 35; Atlanta: Society of Biblical Literature, 2005).

31. Von Rad, *Wisdom in Israel*, 263–83, tries to relate Israel's sages with the ancient interest in determining the times which God has fixed for the universe. The argument fails to convince me.

32. H.-P. Müller, "Wie Sprach Qohälät von Gott?" *VT* 18 (1968): 507–21. The verb *nātan* (to give) occurs often with Elohim (God) as subject.

33. Dominic Rudman, *Determinism in the Book of Ecclesiastes* (JSOTSup 316; Sheffield: Sheffield Academic, 2001).

34. James L. Crenshaw, "From the Mundane to the Sublime: Reflections on Qoh 11:1–8," in *Prophets, Sages, & Poets*, 61–72, 217–22.

35. Hartmut Gese, "The Crisis of Wisdom in Koheleth" (trans. Lester L. Grabbe), in *Theodicy in the Old Testament*, ed. Crenshaw, 148–49. Human beings are wholly dependent upon God's disposition, since God alone decides what and when to give away.

36. *The Instruction of Ani* has the following advice: "and when thy messenger [i.e., Death] comes to thee to take thee, . . . do not say, 'I am (too) young for thee to take,' for thou knowest not thy death. When death comes, he steals away the infant which is on its mother's lap like him who has reached old age" (*ANET*, 420).

37. On Qoheleth's departures from empirical validation of knowledge, see James L. Crenshaw, "Qoheleth's Understanding of Intellectual Inquiry," in *Qohelet in the Context of Wisdom*, ed. Schoors, 205–24. From observation, where could Qoheleth have learned that God has appointed a time for judgment, dislikes fools, will punish rash vows, created the world good/appropriate, dwells in heaven, chases the past, tests people to make them fear God, gives human beings unpleasant business, keeps them preoccupied with joy, made men and women upright, has already approved one's actions, and rewards those who fear God? Qoheleth simply accepted many traditional teachings without submitting them to the test of experience. On Qoheleth's epistemology, see Annette Schellenberg, *Erkenntnis als Problem: Qohelet und die alttestamentliche Diskussion um das menschliche Erkennen* (OBO 188; Freiburg: Herder, 2002).

38. R. N. Whybray, "Qoheleth, Preacher of Joy," *JSOT* 23 (1982): 87–98, fails to take seriously the overwhelmingly pessimistic mood of the book, emphasized by William H. U. Anderson, *Qoheleth and Its Pessimistic Theology: Hermeneutical Struggles in Wisdom Literature* (Mellen Biblical Press Series 54; Lewiston, N.Y.: Mellen Biblical Press, 1997). The seven encouragements to enjoyment are concessions: given life's burdens, try to seize some pleasure.

39. Thomas Krüger, "Meaningful Ambiguities in the Book of Qoheleth," in *Language of Qohelet in Its Context*, ed. Berlejung and van Hecke, 63–74. Benjamin Lyle Berger, "Qohelet and the Exigencies of the Absurd," *Biblical Interpretation* 9 (2001): 141–79, thinks the ambiguities in the text turn it into an exercise in erasure, not allowing any text to compete with the claim that all is absurd.

40. Norbert Lohfink, "Qoheleth 5:17–19—Revelation by Joy," *CBQ* 52 (1990): 625–35. A positive reading of Ecclesiastes marks the recent commentary by Ludger Schwienhorst-Schönberger, *Kohelet* (HTKAT; Freiburg: Herder, 2004). Agustinus Gianto, "The Theme of Enjoyment in Qohelet," *Bib* 73 (1992): 528–32, sees an increase in this theme in the second part of Ecclesiastes. In "Human Destiny in Emar and Qohelet," in *Qohelet in the Context of Wisdom*, ed. Schoors, 473–79, Gianto discusses a text from Emar that has the teacher recommend joy in the heart. See also Stefan Fischer, *Die Aufforderung zur Lebensfreude im Buch Kohelet und seine Rezeption der ägyptischen Harfnerlieder* (Wiener Alttestamentliche Studien 2; Frankfurt: Peter Lang, 1999).

41. Joseph Blenkinsopp, "Ecclesiastes 3.1–15: Another Interpretation," *JSOT* 66 (1995): 55–64, views 3:1–8 as embedded Stoic philosophy (or a product of a stoicizing Jewish sage) and 3:9–22 as idiosyncratic commentary on it. He thinks that Qoheleth entered into dialogue with philosophical ideas about timely action, claiming that everyone is trapped in a circle of destiny. For a different interpretation, see R. N. Whybray, "'A Time to Be Born and a Time to Die': Some Observations on Ecclesiastes 3:2–8," in *Near Eastern Studies Dedicated to H. I. H. Prince Takahito Mikasa*, ed. Masao Mori et al. (Wiesbaden: Harrassowitz, 1991), 469–83.

42. On Qoheleth's social location, see C. Robert Harrison, "Qoheleth in Social-historical Perspective," Ph.D. diss., Duke University, 1991; Seow, *Ecclesiastes*, 21–36; idem, "The Socioeconomic Context of 'The Preacher's' Hermeneutic," *Princeton Seminary Bulletin* 17 (1996): 168–94; idem, "The Social World of Ecclesiastes," *Scribes, Sages, and Seers*, 189–217; Stephan de Jong, "Qoheleth and the Ambitious Spirit of the Ptolemaic Period," *JSOT* 61 (1994): 85–96; James L. Crenshaw, "Qoheleth in Historical Context," *Bib* 88 (2007): 285–99; and Christoph Uehlinger, "Qohelet im Horizont mesopota-

mischer, levantanischer und ägyptischer Weisheitsliteratur der persischen und hellenistischen Zeit," in *Das Buch Kohelet: Studien zur Struktur, Geschichte, Rezeption und Theologie*, ed. L. Schwienhorst-Schönberger (BZAW 254; Berlin: de Gruyter, 1997), 155–247.

43. James L. Crenshaw, "Youth and Old Age in Qoheleth," *HAR* 10 (1986): 1–13 (*UAPQ*, 535–47). The placing of the haunting refrain about the "vanity"/ absurdity of all things weakens Thomas Krüger's argument that Qoheleth consistently deconstructs traditional wisdom (*Qoheleth*, e.g., 22–24), for the motto implies no progress has been made during Qoheleth's journey that would indicate profit.

44. Von Rad, *Wisdom in Israel*, 231.

45. The similarities between Qoheleth and the Gilgamesh Epic thus extend beyond the framing concept of a king transmitting advice, reaching as far as the haunting theme of death's inevitability. The ale wife's advice to Gilgamesh is strikingly like Qoheleth's counsel in 9:7–10. Siduri tells Gilgamesh:

> The life thou pursuest thou shalt not find.
> When the gods created mankind,
> Death for mankind they set aside,
> Life in their own hands retaining.
> Thou, Gilgamesh, let full be thy belly,
> Make thou merry by day and by night.
> Of each day make thou a feast of rejoicing,
> Day and night dance thou and play!
> Let thy garments be sparkling fresh,
> Thy head be washed; bathe thou in water.
> Pay heed to the little one that holds on to thy hand,
> Let thy spouse delight in thy bosom!
> For this is the task of [mankind]!

(*ANET*, 90)

46. Peter Höffken, "Das Ego des Weisen," *TZ* 4 (1984): 121–35.

47. Johannes Pedersen, "Scepticisme israélite," *RHPR* 10 (1930): 348–50, saw this fact with great clarity. On sapiential ethics generally, see Miriam Lichtheim, *Moral Values in Egypt* (OBO 155; Fribourg: University Press; Göttingen: Vandenhoeck & Ruprecht, 1997); and Otto, *Theologische Ethik des Alten Testaments*, 117–74.

48. Aarre Lauha, "Die Krise des religiösen Glaubens bei Kohelet," in *Wisdom in Israel*, ed. Noth and Winton Thomas, 183–91, contrasts Job and Qoheleth as examples of the differences between religious and secular people. See also R. N. Whybray, "Conservatisme et radicalisme dans Qohelet," in *Sagesse et Religion*, 65–81; idem, *Two Jewish Theologies: Job and Ecclesiastes* (Hull: University of Hull, 1980); and Carol Newsom, "Job and Ecclesiastes," in *Old Testament Interpretation: Past, Present, and Future: Essays in Honor of Gene M. Tucker*, ed. James Luther Mays, David L. Petersen, and Kent Harold Richards (Nashville: Abingdon, 1995), 177–94.

49. Christian Klein, *Kohelet und die Weisheit Israels: Eine formgeschichtliche Studie* (BWANT 132; Stuttgart: Kohlhammer, 1994), concludes that the dominant genre is *māšāl*, by which he means a metaphorical saying that possesses paradigmatic authority. Tremper Longman III, *The Book of Ecclesiastes* (NICOT; Grand Rapids: Eerdmans, 1998), 15–20, makes a case for Qoheleth as fictional autobiography. See his *Fictional Akkadian Autobiography* (Winona Lake, Ind.: Eisenbrauns, 1991), for comparative data. Eric S. Christianson,

A Time to Tell: Narrative Strategies in Ecclesiastes (JSOTSup 280; Sheffield: Sheffield Academic, 1998), and Gary D. Salyer, *Vain Rhetoric: Private Insight and Public Debate in Ecclesiastes* (JSOTSup 327; Sheffield: Sheffield Academic, 2001), emphasize narrative strategies and rhetoric.

50. Michael V. Fox, "The Identification of Quotations in Biblical Literature," *ZAW* 92 (1980): 416–31; and R. N. Whybray, "The Identification and Use of Quotations in Ecclesiastes," in *Congress Volume: Vienna 1980*, 435–51, have demonstrated the difficulty of proving any theory of citations. Krüger, *Qoheleth*, provides a sophisticated analysis of Qoheleth's use of traditional views to reshape a worldview.

51. Walther Zimmerli, "Das Buch Kohelet—Traktat oder Sentenzensammlung?" *VT* 24 (1974): 221–30, sees evidence for both understandings of the book—a casual treatise and a careful collection of valuable advice.

52. The assumption that a single idea gave rise to all instances of that notion (monogenesis) is less likely than independent thinking about universal concerns (polygenesis).

53. *The Instruction of Ptahhotep* (*ANET*, 412). See also the Sumerian text entitled *The Old Man and the Young Girl* (Bendt Alster, *Studies in Sumerian Proverbs* [Mesopotamia 3; Copenhagen: Akademisk, 1975], 90–97).

54. Crenshaw, *Ecclesiastes*, 184–85. It follows that I believe certain words function as ciphers and connote two distinct senses. In this instance, the word usually rendered "your creator" (*bôrĕ'eykā*) alludes to an erotic usage known to us from Prov. 5:15–20, but it also provides a grim reminder of the "hole" into which everyone will eventually be laid.

55. Addison D. G. Wright, "The Riddle of the Sphinx: The Structure of the Book of Qoheleth," in *SAIW*, 245–66. The conclusions in this essay have been revised; see idem, "The Riddle of the Sphinx Revisited: Numerical Patterns in the Book of Qoheleth," *CBQ* 42 (1980): 35–51. T. A. Perry, *Dialogues with Kohelet* (University Park, Pa.: Pennsylvania State University, 1993), envisions a dialogue between an optimist and Qoheleth, a pessimist. This conversation comprises, in Perry's view, nineteen sections.

56. Holm-Nielsen, "On the Interpretation of Qoheleth in Early Christianity"; Gerald T. Sheppard, *Wisdom as a Hermeneutical Construct* (BZAW, 151; Berlin: de Gruyter, 1980), 121–29; and idem, "The Epilogue to Qohelet as Theological Commentary," *CBQ* 39 (1977): 182–89.

57. Surely readers of Ecclesiastes would have known that Solomon was David's son and that the place of his rule was Jerusalem.

58. On Qoheleth's linguistic usage, see above all Antoon Schoors, *The Preacher Sought to Find Pleasing Words: A Study of the Language of Qoheleth*, 2 vols. (OLA 41, 143; Leuven: Peeters, 1992; 2004). Compare D. C. Fredericks, *Qoheleth's Language: Re-evaluating Its Nature and Date* (ANETS 3; Lewiston, N.Y.: Mellen, 1988); Bo Isaksson, *Studies in the Language of Qoheleth: With Special Emphasis on the Verbal System* (SSU 10; Stockholm: Almqvist & Wiksell, 1987); and Seow, *Ecclesiastes*, 11–21.

59. C.-L. Seow, "Linguistic Evidence and the Dating of Qoheleth," *JBL* 115 (1996): 643–66, pushes the date back to the Achaemenid period, fifth or fourth century BCE. The evidence he adduces illuminates the socioeconomic situation in the province of Yehud during these centuries, but it is offset by strong evidence favoring the Ptolemaic era. Whitley's claim that the book was composed between 152 and 145 BCE (*Koheleth*, 119–46) has not been well received.

60. Paul Joüon, "Sur le nom de Qohéleth," *Bib* 2 (1921): 53–54; Edward Ullendorff, "The Meaning of Qoheleth," *VT* 12 (1962): 215. See also the illumi-

nating discussion by Jennifer L. Koosed, *(Per)mutations of Qohelet. Reading the Body in the Book* (LHB/OTS 429; New York: T & T Clark International, 2006), 16–33.

61. Duncan Black Macdonald, *The Hebrew Philosophical Genius: A Vindication* (New York: Russell & Russell, 1965), 36.

62. First Kings 22:17 applies the image to King Ahab. Nevertheless, the metaphor of shepherd was widely used for deities in the ancient Near East. A third possibility is that the word *'eḥād* should be understood as "any," hence any shepherd who uses goads to make animals go in the desired direction.

63. For the interpretation of Ecclesiastes, see Crenshaw, *Ecclesiastes*, 23–54; idem, "Ecclesiastes, Book of," *ABD* 2:271–80 (*UAPQ*, 499–519); idem, "Qoheleth in Current Research," *HAR* 7 (1984): 41–56 (*UAPQ*, 520–34); Agustinus Gianto, "Ecclesiastes," *NIDB*, 2:178–85; Otto Kaiser, "Beiträge zur Kohelet-Forschung," *TRu* 60 (1995): 1–31, 233–53; idem, "Die Botschaft des Buches Kohelet," *ETL* 76 (1995): 48–70; Katharine Dell, "Ecclesiastes as Wisdom: Consulting Early Interpreters," *VT* 44 (1994): 301–29; Judah Goldin, "The End of Ecclesiastes: Literal Exegesis and Its Transformation," *Lown Institute for Judaistic Studies* 3 (1966): 135–58; Schwienhorst-Schönberger, "Kohelet: Stand und Perspektiven der Forschung," in *Buch Kohelet*, ed. Schwienhorst-Schönberger, and Diethelm Michel, *Qohelet* (EF 258; Darmstadt: Wissenschaftliche Buchgesellschaft, 1988), who discusses (1) the name and author, (2) literary structure, (3) language, (4) influence of the environment, (5) Jewish tradition, (6) literary forms, (7) religious individuality of Qoheleth, (8) influence on Ben Sira and Wisdom of Solomon, (9) date and place, and (10) canonization. See also Michel, *Theologische Realenzyklopädie* 19 (1990): 345–56.

Chapter 6

The Quest for Survival

Sirach

The sages who composed Proverbs, Job, and Ecclesiastes scrupulously avoided the slightest allusion to Israel's sacred history as it unfolds within the rest of the Hebrew Bible. An openness to the world on the part of these teachers expressed itself in borrowings from realms beyond Palestine, thereby appreciably enriching canonical wisdom with regard to form and content. At the same time, those who cherished prophetic and Yahwistic traditions were convinced that an absence of particularity greatly impoverished Jewish wisdom by excluding an important dimension of daily life, however much its universalism enriched the sages' tradition. The theophany within the book of Job bears eloquent testimony to an awareness that the experience of the living God belonged to the essence of any authentic search for knowledge. Sirach advanced beyond this cautious acknowledgment to bold proclamation that true wisdom was hidden in the Mosaic law. The consequences of this conviction were far-reaching; in a word, they brought about a significant transition within wisdom.[1]

INTEGRATION OF SACRED HISTORY INTO WISDOM

Sirach's integration of sacred history into sapiential discourse was no after-thought, as one might conclude from the fact that the praise of past heroes and eulogy of a contemporary priest appear toward the end of the book (44:1–50:21). Actually, the entire work is sprinkled with explicit references and recognizable allusions to biblical persons and events, while the distinctive piety of the sages has succumbed to the powerful influence of Yahwism as it manifests itself outside canonical Wisdom literature.

The boldest move in this direction is the *actual quotation of Scripture*. In the light of the wholly unpromising theological context of the early second century BCE, the choice of that text approximates a doxology of judgment:[2]

> Let us fall into the hands of the Lord,
>   but not into the hands of mortals,
> for equal to his majesty is his mercy.
>   (2:18)

The reference to David's decision to risk divine punishment rather than human vindictiveness is grounded in the greatness of God's mercy (2 Sam. 24:14). Similarly, the allusion to the Noachic covenant in Sirach 17:12 underlines the Lord's compassion for the human race after the flood threatened to wipe it out, and many references to God's mercy for repentant individuals (e.g, 17:29) recall promises within prophetic and legal material.[3]

By far the most *allusions* derive from pentateuchal traditions concerning the primeval history in Genesis 1–11 and the narratives about the patriarchs Abraham, Isaac, and Jacob. These two kinds of allusions include Adam (Sir. 33:10; 40:1) and Eve (25:24), Lot (16:8), Sodom and Gomorrah (39:23), the fallen angels (16:7), Jacob's descendants (23:12), the flood (40:10), the tree of knowledge (38:5), the image of God (17:3), and the creation account (39:16, 23). Other biblical allusions derive from the larger canon: the six hundred thousand Israelites who perished in the wilderness (16:9–10), the divine epithet "Holy One" (4:14), the law of Moses (24:23), Zion (36:13–15), and the tree that sweetened water (38:5). Two of the last three occur within larger sections that mention components from several sacred traditions: creation by means of a heavenly mist, the pillar of cloud that symbolized God's dwelling place, Jacob and Israel, the holy tabernacle, Jerusalem, the special people of God (24:1–12), divine signs and miracles, the reciting of God's wonders, tribes of Jacob, their inheritance, people called by God's name, Israel, God's firstborn, the city of God's sanctuary, prophecies spoken in God's name, and Aaron's blessing (36:1–17).

Although Qoheleth had cautioned against hasty vows, Ben Sira went far beyond such sound advice to admonish active participation in the sacrificial rituals current in his day.[4] In his view, priests should be supported financially as Scripture commands, specifically by means of

the first fruits, the guilt offering, the gift of the
>   shoulders,
the sacrifice of sanctification, and the first fruits
>   of the holy things.
>
> (7:31; cf. 14:11)

Elsewhere Ben Sira indicates that he had been influenced by a trend toward spiritualizing cultic requirements, for he noted that deeds of kindness and almsgiving
constitute flour and praise offerings, and the renunciation of evil is an offering of
atonement, while keeping the law is a thank offering (35:1–3). He does not even
mention circumcision or the laws relating to the Sabbath. Still, Ben Sira refused
to go the next step and view actual sacrifices as dispensable. Instead, he urged the
complete performance of sacrifices that God had commanded, noting that the
Most High is pleased by first fruits, tithes, and generous gifts of fat (35:4–11).

The fervent prayer in 36:1–17 implies that Ben Sira (or more probably an
editor who lived during the time of the Maccabees) nourished strong eschatological hopes that God would manifest power once again in political events,
restoring the chosen race to its former glory. That anticipation seems also to
underly the frequent warnings that God will judge wickedness at the hour of
death, transforming that occasion into sufficient horror to offset all memory of
pleasures gained through devious means. Since radical changes can take place
between dawn and dusk, when the Lord wills it, the faithful need not be alarmed
by apparent prosperity of the wicked (18:24–26).

If one asks what principle dictated the choice of canonical material that Ben
Sira integrated into his teachings, the answer must surely be the *tension between
wrath and mercy*. Even the cultic references belong to this realm of discourse,
for the sacrificial system represented God's means of dealing with evil in such a
way that mercy would triumph. Nevertheless, God's mercy was dependent upon
human forgiveness; divine healing came only after men and women conquered
their rage toward one another (28:1–7).

The Hymn in Praise of Ancient Heroes

Within the praise of heroes belonging to Israel's history (chaps. 44–50), pride
of position falls to priestly figures—Moses, Aaron, and Phinehas. As a result,
the eulogies of Aaron and Simon represent the high point of this account, as the
poetic flourish certainly suggests. Modern interpreters marvel at Ben Sira's peculiar view of prophets as miracle workers, and wonder how anyone could have
ignored many really noble moments in Israel's past, but present standards of
judgment must not preclude this teacher's right to select his own representatives
from Israel's picture gallery. Beginning with Enoch's repentance and concluding
with Simon's pronunciation of the sacred name Yahweh on the Day of Atonement, a great host of men[5] labored to make a name for themselves and to establish the covenant with God forever. It is noteworthy that the Hebrew canon
dictated the actual progression of this praise of famous men. Ben Sira began

with the Pentateuch, moved through the Former Prophets, then mentioned the Latter Prophets, and finally touched upon three heroes of the restoration. As an afterthought, he returned to his starting point, Enoch, and recalled Joseph, Shem, Seth, and Adam.

This remarkable paean has been dubbed an epic, one that concentrates on various offices in ancient Israel in demonstrating divine control of the institutions by which life was maintained. The epic consists of three parts: (1) the establishment of covenants with the conquest of the land as transition; (2) the history of the prophets and kings, with the story of the restoration as transition; and (3) the climax in Simon the high priest. The poem resembles an encomium, with four parts: (1) a proemium in 44:1–15; (2) a genealogy in 44:17–49:16; (3) the narration of the subject's achievements in 50:1–21; and (4) an epilogue in 50:22–24. The seven components, which do not occur in every context, not even in the fuller accounts, are: (1) designation of office; (2) divine approval or election; (3) covenant; (4) the individual's character; (5) his deeds; (6) the historical context; and (7) reward.[6] The Greek genre *encomium* has been the subject of special study.[7] If the hymn in Sirach 44–50 is an encomium, it has been greatly altered.[8]

The choice of heroes has elicited much discussion, particularly Ben Sira's silence about Ezra. Various explanations have surfaced in the literature: (1) the changed socioeconomic circumstances made mixed marriage a matter of indifference; (2) the scribal profession evolved from narrow attention to the law to that of teacher; (3) Ezra's political quietism did not commend itself to Ben Sira, who wanted Simon's son and successor, Onias III, to be more like Simon; (4) Ben Sira focuses on those who actively constructed or repaired the temple, which excluded Ezra; (5) Ezra's championing of the Levites did not fit Ben Sira's elevation of the Aaronide priestly lineage.[9] The lack of any reference to Joseph (except in the textually dubious afterthought in 49:14–16) and Saul has also occasioned comment. Ben Sira's bias against the north may have prevented him from mentioning Joseph, whose blessing of Ephraim and Manasseh would seem to approve the Samaritans. Perhaps, too, Joseph's role in counseling the Egyptian pharaoh did not commend him to Ben Sira. The negative treatment of Saul in biblical traditions and his association with northern tribal groups may explain Ben Sira's silence about him. Presumably, Daniel is not mentioned because the book had not been composed by the time of Ben Sira's activity.

Some things stand out even among those persons who are mentioned. Moses is described as the recipient of the law rather than a lawgiver; the militant Joshua receives considerable attention, ten verses over against five in describing Moses; David was the recipient of an eternal covenant, despite the absence of anyone on the throne during Ben Sira's day; Elijah's main claim to fame derives from the miracles he performed; similarly, Elisha, Hezekiah, and Isaiah; Jeremiah foretold Jerusalem's fall to the Babylonians; Ezekiel's vision set him apart; Job appears among the prophets, as in Josephus.

PIETY AND WISDOM

The piety characterizing these canonical works has thoroughly infused Ben Sira's thinking. As a result the tone shifts markedly from earlier sapiential teaching. Emphasis falls upon God's compassion, which almost seems to be an obsession with Ben Sira. Insisting that delay in punishment for sin arose from God's desire to give men and women time to repent, Ben Sira rejected the sinner's audacious claim that God could not see through darkness, which concealed adulterous acts.

> His fear is confined to human eyes,
>> and he does not realize that the eyes of the Lord
>> are ten thousand times brighter than the sun;
> they look upon every aspect of human behavior,
>> and see into hidden corners.
>
> (23:19)

Such individuals were culpable first and foremost because they broke the law that God declared through Moses (23:23). Elsewhere Ben Sira associates godless persons with violation of the law, as if the norm for conduct consists of divine statutes. Accordingly, persons deserving contempt were those who failed to keep commandments, rather than foolish sluggards who had provoked earlier sages' ire.

Naturally, Ben Sira recommended the study of the law (39:1) and urged meditation upon the commandments. In his opinion, the wise never despised the law, which was fully as reliable as the sacred dice used in connection with a divine oracle. It followed that the commandments were complete, needing no further supplement. Therefore, all efforts to develop a science of interpreting dreams, visions, and omens were deemed superfluous if not outright perfidy. Ben Sira joined Qoheleth in advising people to reflect upon death and to let that imminent threat spur them on to enjoy life's innocent pleasures, but he also urged such somber thoughts on death as a motive for keeping the commandments. His reasoning is clear: since you must die, let your life be exemplary in order that God's smile may accompany death.[10]

Occasionally, Ben Sira brought together his thinking about piety and wisdom; in doing so, he subordinated wisdom to the law and to the fear of God.[11] For example, he described worship as the outward expression of wisdom and admonished sages to rely upon God-fearers who kept the commandments. To be sure, he also encouraged self-reliance as one's most dependable counselor but hastened to place such self-trust under a greater obligation, the necessity to pray for divine guidance (37:12–15). In one striking statement Ben Sira urged fighting for truth in full confidence that God would join the skirmish to assure victory. Such thinking accords with traditional interpretations of God as the champion of the poor, but earlier sages had never spoken of God as a co-combatant. Although Ben Sira advised sages to act as fathers to orphans, he warned against indiscriminate giving.[12] In his opinion, those who lavished their

goods upon others had to make intelligent choices, eliminating all persons who
did not fear God.

The truth within the claim that with Ben Sira "the teacher has become a
worshiper"[13] comes closest to surfacing in the contexts that treat the subject of
the fear of God.[14] Certain statements lend considerable support to the thesis
that the book's central theme is not wisdom but the fear of God. For instance,
Ben Sira remarked:

> Better are the God-fearing who lack understanding
>   than the highly intelligent who transgress the law.
> (19:24)

And he insisted that nothing was superior to the fear of the Lord or sweeter than
keeping the commandments (23:27).

> How great is the one who finds wisdom!
>   But none is superior to the one who fears the Lord.
> Fear of the Lord surpasses everything;
>   to whom can we compare the one who has it?
> (25:10–11)

Elsewhere Ben Sira identified all wisdom with the fear of the Lord and fulfilling
the law (19:20).

Perhaps the strongest statement subordinating wisdom occurs in 1:1–20,
which introduces readers to the two themes that recur throughout Ben Sira's discourses, namely wisdom and the fear of God. Like the comparable prologue in
Proverbs 1:2–7, this one calls wisdom's first principle the "fear of the Lord." But
Ben Sira went much further, even to the extent of saying that wisdom's garland
and root can be found in the fear of the Lord. That is why in another context he
was able to write that fear of God alone justified a sense of accomplishment.

> The rich, and the eminent, and the poor—
>   their glory is the fear of the Lord.
> (10:22)

Against this elevation of the fear of Yahweh von Rad has argued that Ben
Sira's tongue was loosened when extolling wisdom, particularly in the majestic
hymn to wisdom (chap. 24).[15] The criterion of eloquence can only point in
another direction, for Ben Sira's tongue was looser still in praising Aaron and
Simon. The exquisite details concerning priestly duties and privileges, the glowing account of their demeanor during the daily ritual, and the excitement such
thoughts engendered show clearly the precise point at which Ben Sira's heart
beat excitedly. The high priest Simon

> was like the morning star appearing through a cloud
> or the full moon on festal days;
> like the sun shining on the temple of the Most High
> or the light of the rainbow on the gleaming clouds;

like a rose in springtime
or lilies by a fountain of water;
. . . .
like an olive tree laden with fruit
or a cypress with its summit in the clouds.
                    (50:6–8, 10 REB)

What, then, did Ben Sira say about wisdom and discipline, the two themes that his grandson who translated the Hebrew work into Greek[16] singled out as noteworthy? On the one hand, Ben Sira endorsed traditions that described wisdom as a cosmic entity wholly inaccessible to men and women,[17] while, on the other hand, he maintained that human effort succeeded in grasping wisdom. The two understandings are brought together ingeniously in 24:1–23, which identifies this primordial wisdom with the Mosaic torah.[18] This marvelous account of wisdom's search for a permanent dwelling place reaches back into a variety of traditional matter (creation by the divine word; the creative mist that engendered life in a desert oasis; the pillar of cloud that accompanied the Israelites in the wilderness; the sacred tent in Jerusalem; Israel as God's special possession). The identification of this heavenly wisdom with a written document meant that she was not available to all who thirsted for knowledge. That is why Ben Sira could promise those who worked in wisdom that they would not go astray. Elsewhere he claimed that wisdom resulted from keeping the commandments or was acquired by keeping oneself pure. Anyone who mastered the law achieved wisdom as well (15:1), and students discovered genuine satisfaction in the law.

How different this view of the sages' intellectual sphere was from earlier understandings, where study of nature and human experience seemed to suffice. Nothing could be farther from the old view of free inquiry than Ben Sira's warning against probing into things that were too difficult or defied all attempts to answer. Activity that once seemed to constitute the natural domain of sages is here called meddling into God's secrets, and the intellectual enterprise is directed toward understanding divine revelation (3:21–24). Not surprisingly, Ben Sira advised against following difficult paths or swimming against the current.[19]

Nevertheless, the secondary theme of discipline forced Ben Sira to qualify this warning against heroic endeavor, for wisdom first manifests itself as a grievous yoke until the individual has demonstrated willingness to be molded in the proper manner. Then the fetters fall away and wisdom presents herself as a beautiful bride, who brings life to her beloved. Ben Sira adopted the image of sowing seeds as a convenient way to highlight the labor that must go into the acquisition of wisdom, but also to focus attention upon the joyous experience accompanying the harvesting of crops.

My child, from your youth choose discipline,
    and when you have gray hair you will still find wisdom.
Come to her like one who plows and sows,
    and wait for her good harvest.

For when you cultivate her you will toil but little,
  and soon you will eat of her produce.
She seems very harsh to the disciplined;
  fools cannot remain with her.
She will be like a heavy stone to test them,
  and they will not delay in casting her aside.
               (6:18–21; cf. 4:11–19)

To be sure, Ben Sira retained earlier authentic emphases of sages, as when he encouraged the study of ancient maxims.[20]

Do not slight the discourse of the sages,
  but busy yourself with their maxims;
because from them you will learn discipline
  and how to serve princes.
Do not ignore the discourse of the aged,
  for they themselves learned from their parents;
from them you learn how to understand
  and to give an answer when the need arises.
                    (8:8–9)

Ben Sira's own mastery of older maxims can scarcely be denied, for his teachings are filled with counsel similar to that contained in Proverbs.

AMBIGUITY

Nevertheless, a distinctive difference quickly meets the eye. Ben Sira perceived the ambiguity in life much more clearly than the earlier sages seem to have done. For example, wealth no longer indicated divine favor.[21]

Riches are good if they are free from sin,
  poverty is evil only in the opinion of the ungodly.
                    (13:24)

The rich performed a miracle by remaining free of its taint (31:8–9), while poverty offered a unique opportunity to demonstrate virtue (20:21), or it enforced goodness for lack of an opportunity to do otherwise. Extreme need also made life so miserable that death was welcome relief. Silence arose from ignorance or lack of courage, as well as from recognition that the lack of any response at all was timely. The ideal of a large family was less important than integrity, for children were not always a blessing (16:1–3). The birth of a daughter was a loss, but not every woman provoked Ben Sira's scorn. To fools education resembled fetters and handcuffs, while the wise viewed it as a golden ornament or a bracelet. Modesty commends itself in some circumstances and is out of place at other times. Almsgiving is proper action in given instances, but withholding a gift is right in others. The same ambiguity characterizes "going security" for someone.

Such kindness is meritorious, but its consequences often impoverish. Hence care must be taken lest a good deed ruin compassionate individuals through the loss of all their possessions.

Earlier teachers had recognized limits to all knowledge, but Ben Sira even distinguished between the proper use of the intellect and a cleverness that produced expertise at performing evil.

> The whole of wisdom is fear of the Lord,
>   and in all wisdom there is the fulfillment of the law.
> The knowledge of wickedness is not wisdom,
>   nor is there prudence in the counsel of sinners.
> There is a cleverness that is detestable,
>   and there is a fool who merely lacks wisdom.
> Better are the God-fearing who lack understanding,
>   than the highly intelligent who transgress the law.
> There is a cleverness that is exact but unjust,
>   and there are people who abuse favors to gain a verdict.
>   (19:20, 22–25)

Just as Ben Sira believed a rich man was nearly incapable of virtue, he also thought merchants stood little chance of resisting greed.

> A merchant can hardly keep from wrongdoing,
>   nor is a tradesman innocent of sin.
>   (26:29)

> As a stake is driven firmly into a fissure between stones,
>   so sin is wedged in between selling and buying.
>   (27:2)

To these may be compared *The Instruction of Ankhsheshonqy* 28.4, "Do not have a merchant for a friend; he lives for taking a slice."

Human ingenuity, like craftiness, could be enlisted in the service of evil. Sometimes an appropriate use of intelligence interfered with God's punishment of sinners, as when physicians successfully prescribed medicines for an individual. Ben Sira recognized a fundamental problem with the healing profession. On the one hand, the vital knowledge of medicines constituted a proper use of human intelligence and therefore represented an important step toward mastering the world. On the other hand, according to traditional teaching, sickness was one means God had chosen to punish iniquity, and any act that shortened or ameliorated the punishment placed physicians at cross-purposes with God. Unable to resolve the tension between these convictions, Ben Sira endorsed the medical profession because he considered it essential for the well-being of society, but he also insisted that physicians should pray for assistance from the genuine source of healing. In the end, however, Ben Sira reaffirmed the old view of sickness as a form of divine punishment and urged sinners to summon a physician when they fell into God's hands (38:1–15).

LITERARY ANALYSIS

Historical Context

In the case of Proverbs, Job, and Qoheleth neither the authors nor the time of composition are known. With Ben Sira, things are different. We know his name, the approximate date, and the general location of his scholarly activity.[22] His name was Jesus son of Eleazar son of Sirach (50:27), and he completed his book around 180 BCE in Jerusalem. From the prologue, which was composed by Ben Sira's grandson in Alexandria sometime after 132 BCE, we learn that the original language of the book was Hebrew and that the grandson had completed a translation into Greek. It follows from these facts that Simon II was the high priest whose performance of the holy ritual within the temple made such an impact upon his contemporary, Ben Sira. Simon was in office from 219 to 196 BCE.

The transition from Ptolemaic to Seleucid rule in 198 BCE did not bring about immediate hostility toward Jews. To express his gratitude for Jewish assistance in the struggle against Ptolemy V Epiphanes (203–181 BCE), Antiochus III the Great (223–187 BCE) made a number of concessions: (1) to help defray the cost of daily sacrifices; (2) to exempt from taxation the materials for building the temple; (3) to obligate the people to live according to the Torah; (4) to exempt from taxation the senate, priests, scribes, and sacred singers; (5) to exempt Jerusalem citizens from taxation for three years; and (6) to let the remaining citizens reduce their taxes by a third and to emancipate slaves. That positive attitude gradually gave way under the pressure of economic duress, and with the coming to power of Antiochus IV Epiphanes (175–164 BCE) Jews became subject to extraordinary abuse, which precipitated the Maccabean revolt.

The internal situation reflected the political climate abroad. Opportunists chose sides, hoping to find themselves on the side of the eventual winners in the struggle for power. Competing families, Tobiads and Oniads, strove for popular support, and old rivalries, Jews and Samaritans, extended the dissension beyond Jerusalem. Avarice and greed ran free, touching the highest office, turning the religious priesthood into a coveted prize up for grabs to the highest bidder. Jason's and Menelaus's willingness to compromise ancestral practices in favor of Greek ways demonstrates the degradation of the priesthood and explains Ben Sira's glowing praise of Simon, who stood as a sharp contrast to the weak son, Onias III, who was murdered in 173 BCE, and the hellenizing Jason, or even Onias IV, who fled to Egypt and founded a temple at Leontopolis. A few allusions in Sirach may refer to this volatile situation: 50:25–26 voices contempt for Idumeans, Philistines (hellenizers), and Samaritans; 7:4–7; 40:25–26; 50:1, 23–24 (Hebrew text) may criticize contenders for the office of high priest. The prayer in 36:1–22 envisions renewed deeds of deliverance and signs of divine leadership, suggesting that the ancient experience of divine watch-care may have been fading from collective memory.

Hellenistic Influence

For the most part, however, Ben Sira gives no indication that he had declared war against Hellenism. He adopts the Stoic phrase, "He is the All," without drawing the conclusion that the Lord is identical with the parts of the universe. He endorses the Greek culture of banquets; indeed, he even encourages readers to participate fully in them, even to the point of hosting them. He subscribed to Greek medical practice, urging people to seek such healing, inasmuch as physicians pray for divine assistance, and they use medicines that God created. He adapts the Greek form of praise, encomium, in paying tribute to men of worth, and he uses at least two Greek arguments in defending divine justice, one philosophical and another psychological.

In one sense Ben Sira was completely hellenized: his pride of authorship. At the conclusion of the majestic hymn to wisdom (24:1–29), he ventured to compare his teachings with prophecy and contemplated future generations using his own inspired work alongside prophetic utterances. Such teaching was more than an ego trip for Ben Sira, who labored to benefit those who sought wisdom. That is why he compared his discipline to a canal that brought water to a garden. Perhaps his final product far exceeded the scope he had originally contemplated, for Ben Sira seems to indicate that he took up his writing implements for a second effort, as if carried along by a mighty flood (24:30–34).

In yet another context Ben Sira acknowledged the fact that he was a latecomer, like a gleaner following grape pickers, but he insisted that his tardiness did not prevent him from achieving just as much as any predecessor. Still, Ben Sira conceded that his remarkable success was due to God's blessing. As if to explain why God looked upon him with favor, the teacher emphasized once more that the true motive for his labors was the desire to instruct others. In this instance he even named dignitaries and leaders in the assembly as those for whom he wrote (33:16–18).

On one occasion this teacher gave his name and identified his place of activity.

> Instruction in understanding and knowledge
>   I have written in this book,
> Jesus son of Eleazar son of Sirach of Jerusalem,
>   whose mind poured forth wisdom.
> Happy are those who concern themselves with these things,
>   and those who lay them to heart will become wise,
> For if they put them into practice, they will be equal to anything,
>   for the fear of the Lord is their path.
>
>   (50:27–29)

The book closes with a long defense of Ben Sira's wisdom and piety, which leads ultimately to an attempt at recruiting students for his house of learning (51:13–30). Ben Sira claims to have sought wisdom from his youth and to have kept himself pure as well. As a reward for his diligence God gave him eloquence with which to praise the Lord. Having settled the matter of his character, Ben Sira then urged all who lacked instruction to dwell in his school,[23] where their thirst would be slaked forthwith. Perhaps he realized the attraction other centers of learning offered, for he scolded his hearers for thinking they must travel some distance to find discipline. Anticipating an objection that the cost of study in his house of learning was high, Ben Sira appealed to the desire to earn a profit and reminded prospective students that their modest investment would yield huge dividends.

This latecomer in God's vineyard mastered many literary forms that his predecessors had employed. Like the author of the first major section in Proverbs, Ben Sira used the didactic essay to great advantage. A single saying no longer sufficed to encapsulate the message Ben Sira hoped to communicate concerning any given subject. Instead, exposition became the normal mode of discourse. In the oldest collections of proverbs, the teachers had been satisfied with stimulating others to think through the implications of a given saying, even at the risk of misinterpretation. Ben Sira resembles interpreters who rely upon others for the original material that they endeavor to illuminate by means of their highly trained critical faculties. Rarely did he permit a proverb to appear without interpretation. Occasionally he did set one saying alongside another to provide contrasting descriptions, for example, of poverty and wealth, in the same manner that the earliest sages had done (13:3; cf. 20:5–6; 11:11–13).

THEMES

The topics that Ben Sira chose to discuss are wide-ranging, although some subjects occur several times and give the impression of special fondness on the teacher's part. Like others before him, Ben Sira reflected often on the danger posed by *evil women*. At times he permitted this ancient tradition about foreign women to discolor his attitude toward all women, especially when declaring that a man's wickedness is better than a woman's goodness (42:14) and when announcing that the birth of a daughter was a loss (22:3). Elsewhere Ben Sira implied that he thought females occasioned too much worry over their virginity and suspected that girls opened their quiver for any arrow and drank from the nearest spring like a thirsty traveler (26:12). Nevertheless, this sage cannot be labeled a complete misogynist, for he also had words of highest praise for good women, even if indirect.[24]

> Happy is the husband of a good wife;
> > the number of his days will be doubled.
> > > (26:1)

Lacking such a wife, Ben Sira observed, a man walks around and sighs for a home (36:30).

Ben Sira was almost equally fascinated with the subject of *death*, which he treated with considerable depth and occasional humor, particularly when alluding to an inscription on a tombstone that read: "Mine today, and yours tomorrow" (38:22). Although acknowledging that all human beings stand under the same sentence, "You shall die," Ben Sira recognized that individuals experienced the anticipation of that dreaded event differently. Death in its proper time belongs to the natural process, just as trees shed their leaves and put on new ones. Accordingly, such bowing out in order to make way for new generations should occasion no tears of remorse. As Ben Sira saw it, mourning for the dead should be carefully controlled, lest such morbid thoughts lessen one's enjoyment of life's innocent pleasures. For some people, especially those whose vigor has departed, death came as solace; for others, who still possessed power to drink life's sweetest nectar, an early death brought nothing but regret.

Other topics that Ben Sira took up cover a broad spectrum, inevitably combining wisdom and piety. They include enjoyment of life's good things (14:11–19), occupations (38:24–39:11), medicine (38:1–15), discipline (30:1–13), table manners (32:1–13), duty to parents (3:1–16),[25] poverty and riches (4:1–10), drunkenness (31:25–31), dreams (34:1–8), passions (6:2–4), and friendship (6:5–17; 9:10–16, 11:29–12:18; etc.).[26] The necessity to *encourage* enjoyment must surely arise from a changed attitude among the sages, for the good life had earlier demonstrated God's favor, thus requiring no justification. Ben Sira's admonition to honor parents rather than making fun of old people probably signals a decisive shift in values resulting from the conflict between the generations brought on by Hellenism. In any event, Ben Sira's attempt at humor suggests that the issue had not yet taken on the gravity that it later manifested.

> Do not disdain one who is old,
>> for some of us are also growing old.
>> (8:6)

In several instances this inclination toward exposition of a given topic led Ben Sira to use *refrains* as a means of emphasizing continuity of subject matter. In one block of material three different refrains occur, each of which is used three times (2:7–18). The first, "You who fear the Lord," addresses persons who have begun to question God's justice as it had been proclaimed in the doctrine of exact reward and retribution. Ben Sira encouraged a wait-and-see attitude and directed the skeptics' attention to past history.

> Consider the generations of old and see:
>> has anyone trusted in the Lord and been disappointed?
> Or has anyone persevered in the fear of the Lord and been forsaken?
>> Or has anyone called upon him and been neglected?
>> (2:10)

Any *delay in retribution* was readily explained by God's compassion and mercy. At the same time, the Lord's majesty must be taken into consideration. Therefore, Ben Sira pronounced three woes upon all who had abandoned faith in the hour of trial, for they will be defenseless when God's time of reckoning breaks.

Returning to the initial refrain, although in slightly different form ("Those who fear the Lord"), Ben Sira contrasted those subjects of a curse with fortunate faithful ones who adhered to God's way, immersed themselves in the law, and humbly placed themselves in God's hands. The final quotation of Scripture suggests that Ben Sira was not willing to let his teaching validate itself by logical consistency. Instead, he appealed to the ultimate warrant for this defense of God's justice.

Another unit uses the refrain "Be ashamed" eight times, and "Do not be ashamed" twice, followed by five instances of "for fear she may" (cf. NEB). The section closes with an attempt to link the two topics under discussion, woman and shame (41:14–42:14). In this interesting section Ben Sira named numerous acts that should evoke a strong sense of shame, for example, fornication, bad table manners, following up charity with a lecture, and betraying a secret. Then he mentioned things for which one should not feel shame: the law of the Most High, using accurate weights and measures, disciplining one's children, correcting the foolish, graybeards who commit fornication, and so forth. The heavy concentration on sexual sins and disciplining children prompted Ben Sira to consider the anxiety generated by a willful daughter. In his opinion, fathers never escaped cause for worry over their daughters for fear they fail to marry, or fall out of favor with their husband, or lose their virginity, or commit adultery, or be unable to have children. Such a headstrong daughter succeeded only in shaming her father, according to Ben Sira.

> For from garments comes the moth,
>   and from a woman comes woman's wickedness.
> Better is the wickedness of a man than a woman who does good;
>   it is woman who brings shame and disgrace.
>
> (42:13–14)

Once again the teacher has appealed to a warrant for his message, but this time a popular proverb undergirds his words. The power of these observations in a culture that placed a premium on honor and shame can hardly be matched.

Some refrains adopt an entirely different principle of alternation. In 7:22–24 three questions occur, each of which is followed by a word of advice.

> Do you have cattle? Look after them;
>   if they are profitable to you, keep them.
> Do you have children? Discipline them,
>   and make them obedient from their youth.
> Do you have daughters? Be concerned for their chastity,
>   and do not show yourself too indulgent with them.

This passage may be compared to 10:19:

> Whose offspring are worthy of honor? Human offspring.
> Whose offspring are worthy of honor? Those who fear
>   the Lord.

Whose offspring are unworthy of honor? Human offspring.
Whose offspring are unworthy of honor? Those who
break the commandments.

Another pattern resembles an *aba'b'* versification scheme (19:13–17). Here "Question a friend" alternates with "Question a neighbor," and both refrains occur twice.

Not all Ben Sira's refrains exemplify this principle of alternation. Many of them simply depend upon repetition of a single phrase. For example, 6:14–16 uses "faithful friends" three times, without juxtaposition with another refrain at all. Here the value of a good friend is emphasized as a sort of second thought after a highly cynical statement concerning personal relationships.

Keep away from your enemies,
and be on guard with your friends.
(6:13)

Similarly, 22:11–12 uses the word "weep" three times, although in different expressions, and "mourning" once. By this means Ben Sira compared mourning for fools and the dead, observing that fools occasioned more bitter tears since their darkness endured for a lifetime. Finally, in 14:1–2, "Happy are those who" occurs twice, in each case followed by two grounds for his happiness, while 40:18–27 has nine uses of "better still" (cf. NEB).

PRAYER

The book of Proverbs also provided the prototype for another literary form that Ben Sira added to the sages' repertoire, namely prayer. The simple request in Proverbs 30:7–9 for a balance between poverty and wealth greatly resembles Ben Sira's modest appeal in 22:27–23:6, which happily uses a refrain twice ("Lord, Father and Master/God of my life"). The images in Sirach are exceedingly powerful, particularly those accompanying the first use of the refrain.

Who will set a guard over my mouth,
and an effective seal upon my lips?
(22:27a)

Who will set whips over my thoughts?
(23:2a)

The second occurrence of the slightly different refrain ("Lord, Father and *God* of my life") is accompanied by less graphic language, and the request reaches out to embrace as much as possible. It asks for protection from desire, passion, gluttony, and lust, which seem to flow from one's eyes as freely as tears. Elsewhere Ben Sira mentioned a greedy eye:

> What has been created more greedy than the eye?
> Therefore it sheds tears for any reason.
>
> (31:13b–c)

The restraint exercised in this prayer is eased in the other one to be examined, allowing Ben Sira or a later glossator to utter fervent nationalistic feelings (36:1–17). In this respect the reader stands before a new stage in sapiential thinking, one in which the earlier universalism surrendered to particularistic concerns. To be sure, ancient teachers had spoken of fools with similar scorn, but this text made distinctions solely on the basis of nationality, ultimately expressing a loathing for three nations—the Idumeans, Philistines, and Samaritans (50:25–26). From the sentiment exposed within this great prayer, it becomes clear that oppression of dispersed Israelites had dulled their capacity to recite God's saving deeds, and unfulfilled prophecies threatened to drown all hopes in a sea of despair. Confidence that God intended better things for his people prompted the author to invoke divine action.

> Give new signs, and work other wonders;
> make your hand and your right arm glorious.
> Rouse your anger and pour out your wrath;
> destroy the adversary and wipe out the enemy.
> Hasten the day, and remember the appointed time,
> and let people recount your mighty deeds.
>
> (36:6–8)

> Gather all the tribes of Jacob,
> and give them their inheritance, as at the beginning.
>
> (36:13, 16)

> Fill Zion with your majesty,
> and your temple with your glory.
>
> (36:19)

Like Job, who thought the Creator would eventually long for a human handiwork, Ben Sira appealed to the fact that God created Israel as basis for continued interest. In addition, he reminded God that prophets had announced an imminent restoration of the chosen people in the name of the Deity. However, the ultimate grounds for his prayer rested elsewhere than a belief in creation and revelation. They nestled in the Priestly blessing articulated in Numbers 6:23–26.

HYMNIC PRAISE

The thanksgiving hymn in Sirach 51:1–12 reiterates many themes known to us from similar psalms: rescue from death, deliverance from slander, remembrance of God's mercy, cry for help, granting of prayer, promise to praise God, and so forth. The initial epithets for God, "Lord and King," strike an unusual chord in Wisdom literature, which carefully avoids royal language with reference to God. Since the psalm of deliverance mentions slander in the king's presence, Ben Sira probably used an old hymn or built upon earlier models without bothering to alter the facts to fit the situation in his own day when no king resided in Jerusalem.

Whereas Proverbs provided justification for Ben Sira's widespread use of didactic essays and occasional bending of the knees in prayer, the book of Job paved the way for *"hymnic" praise*. Three didactic compositions within Ben Sira's teaching demonstrate his remarkable capacity for combining sapiential insights and pious inclinations (16:24–18:14; 39:12–35; 42:15–43:33).[27] The last of these erupts into a mighty crescendo of praise, a sentiment that had allowed itself to remain dormant in the other two compositions.

Sirach 16:24–18:14 is a meditation upon the facts as they are proclaimed in the story about creation in the book of Genesis. The language gives the impression of rational reflection, particularly the references to exact and accurate knowledge, but also the teacher's appeal for attention and responsive listening. The poem speaks about an order in creation and a comparable principle by which men and women must live, specifically, the life-giving law. The argument seems to run as follows: Because divine decree has assured the natural order, human conduct is subject to the same kind of authoritative command. Since the individual heavenly bodies and forces do not transgress against one another or their Maker, humans should abide by the Noachic and Mosaic covenants, which function to render life in community possible. In the case of men and women, a certain amount of power over animals is granted, and the right to make independent judgments belongs to those who bear God's image and have achieved knowledge about good and evil. Ben Sira did not stop here; instead, he claimed that God actually spoke to lowly creatures at Sinai, thereby communicating the divine will for human conduct.[28] Naturally, one who has shown so much interest in human rulers keeps constant watch over their hearts, listening for songs of praise.

Not everyone acknowledged an orderliness in the cosmos or among humans. As a result, these skeptics denied the appropriateness of natural catastrophes in a universe that was governed by a benevolent ruler. The refrain, "No one can say, 'What is this?' or 'Why is that?'" occurs twice; such questioning of an inherent order is dismissed in the second didactic composition as nonsense (39:12–35). The composition consists of an appeal for a hearing and for participation in singing God's praise (39:12–15), the hymn proper (39:16–31), and a concluding declaration that all God's works are very good (39:32–34), which leads into an invitation for everyone to praise the name of the Lord (39:35). Ben Sira subscribed to the Priestly writer's positive evaluation of all things:

> All the works of the Lord are very good,
>   and whatever he commands will be done at the appointed time.
>
>   (39:16)

But the concession that a temporal lapse exists between the divine command and its implementation suggests that the question, "Why is that?" was indeed appropriate. Admitting as much, Ben Sira promised that an answer would come at the right time. Although no one can thwart God's power, evil persons managed to rebel against their Maker, who sees all their deeds. Just as humans belong to two distinct camps, so do the elements which God created. Good things were prepared for the devout and evil things for sinners. Better still, the same times manifest themselves as beneficial to good people and destructive for sinners. In addition, certain things were created as agents of retribution from the beginning; among these are destructive winds, fire and hail, famine and deadly disease, beasts of prey, scorpions and vipers, and the avenging sword. In short, the hymn suggests that in its time the true nature of everything will be revealed, making plain the dispositions of human beings. It follows that faith enabled one to distinguish between real and apparent evil. Ben Sira believed this so deeply that he offered a personal testimony in writing:

> All the works of the Lord are good,
>   and he will supply every need in its time.
>   (39:33)

Therefore, Ben Sira concluded,

> No one can say, "This is not as good as that,"
>   for everything proves good in its appointed time.
>   (39:34)

Elsewhere Ben Sira broached the idea of opposites or complementary pairs and defended God's right to shape human beings as the Deity chose (33:7–15). Distinctions among days of the month lie within God's prerogative, Ben Sira claimed, so that through divine decree holy days became more important than ordinary ones. People, too, fell into two groups, despite a common origin, for they were like clay in a potter's hands.

> Good is the opposite of evil,
>   and life the opposite of death;
>   so the sinner is the opposite of the godly.
> Look at all the works of the Most High;
>   they come in pairs, one the opposite of the other.
>   (33:14–15)

Here, in his zeal to defend God's right to make arbitrary decisions, Ben Sira ignored the element of human choice, which he took for granted elsewhere (15:11–20).

Sirach 42:15–43:33 can be appropriately classified as a hymn, whereas the two previously discussed texts belong to the category of didactic composition. To be sure, certain affinities with the other texts stand out, particularly the emphasis upon pairs that supplement each other (42:24–25), God's all-seeing eye (42:20), and the orderliness of creation (42:21–22; 43:10). The mood differs markedly, however, despite the occasional awareness that not everyone shared the hymn's enthusiasm (42:18, 20, 23–25). This majestic attempt to describe God's glory that fills creation pauses to single out for special consideration the sun, moon, stars, and rainbow. Such masterpieces point beyond themselves to their Creator, who issues a command that speeds the sun on its course, who bends a bow in the sky, and who decrees that the innumerable stars stand at attention in their appointed places. The hymn also mentions such wonders as snow, thunder, lightning, earthquake, clouds, hailstones, winds, frost, ice, drought, and dew.

Occasionally, Ben Sira became a poet, using exquisite images (clouds fly out like birds, icicles form like pointed stakes, ice settles on every pool as though the water were putting on a breastplate). In the end he let his thoughts stray across the ocean floor and marveled at the mysteries lying beyond most people's immediate experience, secrets that have enlisted the aid of seafarers who never tire of recounting the wonders lurking beneath the surging waters. Nevertheless, God's mystery is greater still, and no one can succeed in describing the one who exceeds his works. Straining to sum up the theme of God's majesty, Ben Sira borrowed a Greek expression: He is the all. Nevertheless, Ben Sira did not understand this statement as Stoics did, for the God he revered was greater than the total creation.[29]

Surprisingly polemical notes can be heard now and again within this hymn. For example, Ben Sira seems to have rejected the notion that God consulted Wisdom before creating the world (42:21), and he most likely discounted the claim of some that God could not see through dark clouds. The idea that God's creative act was assisted by a preexistent primordial entity arose naturally from speculation about personified Wisdom, which Ben Sira squelched for the most part by identifying Wisdom with the Torah. As for the denial of God's full knowledge, Ben Sira made a strong counterclaim.

> He searches out the abyss, and the human heart,
>   he understands their innermost secrets.
> For the Most High knows all that may be known,
>   he sees from of old the things that are to come.
> He discloses what has been and what is to be,
>   and he reveals the traces of hidden things.
> No thought escapes him,
>   and nothing is hidden from him.
>   (42:18–20)

A FORM OF DEBATE

Whereas Proverbs had paved the way for the didactic essay and prayer, and the book of Job had adapted hymnic texts to sapiential ends, Qoheleth made use of an ancient form of debate that Ben Sira found particularly helpful in his struggle against those who questioned God's justice.[30]

> Do not say: "Why were the former days better than these?"
>   For it is not from wisdom that you ask this.
>   (Eccl. 7:10)

This form can be traced to wisdom literature in Egypt as well.

> Do not say, "I am (too) young for thee [thy messenger: Death] to take; for thou knowest not thy death. When death comes, he steals away the infant which is on its mother's lap like him who has reached old age." (*Ani*; *ANET*, 420)

> God is (always) in his success,
> whereas man is in his failure;
> One thing are the words which men say,
> Another is that which the god does.
> Say not: "I have no wrongdoing."
> Nor (yet) strain to seek quarreling.
>   (*Amenemope*; *ANET*, 43)

> Do not say: "I have ploughed the field but it has not paid";
> plough again, it is good to plough.
> Do not say: "(Now that) I have this wealth
> I will serve neither God nor man."
> Wealth is perfected in the service of God, the one who
>   causes it to happen.
> Do not say: "The sinner against God lives today,"
> but look to the end.
> Say (rather): "A fortunate fate is at the end of old age."
>   (*Ankhsheshonqy*; *AEL*, 3:166, 173, 168)

As in Qoheleth and several Egyptian examples, Ben Sira used the ancient form of debate overwhelmingly within contexts that treated the vexing problem of theodicy.[31] These passages throb with agony brought about by intense soul-searching.

> Do not say: "It was the Lord's doing that I fell away";
>   for he does not do what he hates.
> Do not say: "It was he who led me astray";
>   for he has no need of the sinful.
>   (15:11–12)

> Do not say: "I am hidden from the Lord,
>   and who from on high has me in mind?
> Among so many people I am unknown,
>   for what am I in a boundless creation?"
>   (16:17)

Do not rely on your wealth,
> or say: "I have enough."
Do not follow your inclination and strength,
> in pursuing the desires of your heart.
Do not say: "Who can have power over me?"
> for the Lord will surely punish you.
Do not say: "I sinned, yet what has happened to me?"
> for the Lord is slow to anger.
Do not be so confident of forgiveness
> that you add sin to sin.
Do not say: "His mercy is great,
> he will forgive the multitude of my sins";
for both mercy and wrath are with him,
> and his anger will rest on sinners.

> > > > (5:1–6)

Do not say: "What do I need,
> and what further benefit can be mine?"
Do not say: "I have enough,
> and what harm can come to me now?"
> > > (11:23–24)

In most cases the form consists of (1) the prohibition formula, (2) a direct quotation, and (3) a refutation introduced by *kî* (for). Seven times the prohibition formula (*'al tōmar*, "do not say") stands in the initial position of the sentence; twice it occurs in the second half of a verse (5:1) or in a parallel verse connected by means of a linking word in Hebrew (5:6). The *kî* also varies in two instances: once it appears in the second of two verses functioning as a refutation (11:23–26), and once it follows a prohibition that does not occupy the initial position (5:6).

What prompted Ben Sira's free use of didactic essays and hymns, prayers, and a form of debate? One can begin to answer this significant question by learning more about his antagonists.[32] From the content of these different compositions it seems that certain persons threatened to forsake Judaism because of an inability to believe in God's justice. Again and again Ben Sira turned to these dissenters with wise counsel and fervent appeal. In doing battle with these individuals, he used traditional arguments gleaned from earlier teachers, but Ben Sira also developed two wholly new responses to the problem of theodicy.

The old approaches may be conveniently summarized as follows:

1. God knows all things even before they happen and also sees them as they materialize;
2. past experience bears convincing witness to God's justice;
3. every apparent injustice will be set right at the appropriate hour;
4. surrender before the divine imperative of wonder is the ultimate response to creation's grandeur.

To these, Ben Sira added appeals to psychology and metaphysics. In his view, the real burden of existence was emotional and mental, for sinners' share of anxiety was multiplied sevenfold. For example, God sent nightmares for the wicked and thus punished them in ways not immediately apparent to outsiders. The second answer concerns the structure of the universe. Ben Sira believed that the universe itself punished vice and rewarded virtue. All things existed in pairs, good things to encourage right conduct and bad things to punish wicked behavior. Like the sages before him, Ben Sira found it necessary to depart from realms subject to verification when trying to address the problem of evil.[33]

The threat to convictions that Ben Sira treasured came from other camps too. On the one hand, traditional Yahwists eyed the Wisdom literature with suspicion because it lacked specific features that had arisen in and had given distinctive character to Israel's encounter with its God. On the other hand, another group looked on this lack as the unique strength inherent within the wisdom texts but saw no reason to prefer such literature over the Greek intellectual heritage with which they had recently come into contact. This noble attempt to find adequate responses to the two groups amounted to a search for continuity, for both Yahwism and the wisdom tradition were at stake.

Ben Sira's concession to the first group was the extensive integration of sacred traditions into sapiential thought. In this way the chasm separating sages from others became less and less wide, for teachers donned prayer shawls. At the same time, the incorporation of Israel's heroes into the teachings of sages enabled Ben Sira to defend sacred texts as God's gift to Israel, and thus to juxtapose divine words and human speculation. In his view, Greek philosophy failed to achieve the heights reached by the Hebrew Scriptures. Nevertheless, he did demonstrate willingness to enrich his own teachings from the scholarly tradition within Hellenism and by this means strengthened his appeal to those who longed for intellectual respectability in the Greek world.

Regardless of the different responses to those who partially shaped the Jerusalemite sage's thinking, one fact can hardly escape detection: theology prevailed over the experiential tradition, for a world devoid of divine compassion had been found wanting. Ben Sira's emphasis upon God's mercy set him apart from the earlier sages whose legacy he inherited; so it is singularly appropriate that his final words combine both emphases with characteristic confidence.

> May your soul rejoice in God's mercy,
>   and may you never be ashamed to praise him.
> Do your work in good time,
>   and in his own time God will give you your reward.
>   (51:29–30)

NOTES

1. Fichtner, *Altorientalische Weisheit*; Marböck, *Weisheit im Wandel*; Otto Rickenbacher, *Weisheitsperikopen bei Ben Sira* (OBO 1; Göttingen: Vandenhoeck & Ruprecht, 1973); Patrick Skehan and Alexander A. Di Lella, *The Wisdom of Ben Sira* (AB 39; New York: Doubleday, 1987); James L. Crenshaw, "Sirach,"

NIB, 5:603–867; E. J. Schnabel, *Law and Wisdom from Ben Sira to Paul: A Traditional Historical Inquiry into the Relation of Law, Wisdom and Ethics* (WUNT 2/16; Tübingen: Mohr, 1985); Adams, *Wisdom in Transition*, 153–213; Perdue, *Sword and Stylus*, 256–91; Friedrich Vinzenz Reiterer, "Review of Recent Research on the Book of Ben Sira (1980–1996)," in *The Book of Ben Sira in Modern Research*, ed. Pancratius C. Beentjes (BZAW 255; Berlin: de Gruyter, 1997), 23–59; *Treasures of Wisdom: Studies in Ben Sira and the Book of Wisdom*, ed. Núria Calduch-Benages and Jacques Vermeylen (BETL 143; Leuven: Leuven University, 1999); Passaro and Bellia, eds., *The Wisdom of Ben Sira* (BCLS 1; Berlin: de Gruyter, 2008); Georg Sauer, *Jesus Sirach/ Ben Sira* (ATD Apokryphen 1; Göttingen: Vandenhoeck & Ruprecht, 2000), 7–15 (extensive bibliography). Oda Wischmeyer, *Die Kultur des Buches Jesus Sirach* (BZNW 77; Berlin: de Gruyter, 1994), examines the cultural setting of Ben Sira, in many ways supplementing the exclusively religious studies above. John J. Collins, *Jewish Wisdom in the Hellenistic Age* (Louisville: Westminster John Knox, 1997), 23–111, discusses the developments within second-century Jewish wisdom.

2. Von Rad, "Gerichtsdoxologie," in *Schalom: Studien zu Glaube und Geschichte Israels: Alfred Jepsen zum 70. Geburtstag*, ed. Karl-Heinz Bernhardt (AzTh 1/46; Stuttgart: Calwer, 1971), 28–37. The pioneer essay on this subject was written by Friedrich Horst, "Die Doxologien im Amosbuch," *Gottes Recht: Gesammelte Studien zum Recht im Alten Testament* (Theologische Büchere: 12; Munich: Chr. Kaiser, 1961), 155–66.

3. On the significance of this increased emphasis upon divine mercy, see Rylaarsdam, *Revelation in Jewish Wisdom Literature*; James L. Crenshaw, "The Concept of God in Old Testament Wisdom," in *In Search of Wisdom*, ed. Perdue et al., 1–18 (*UAPQ*, 191–205); and Pancratius C. Beentjes, "God's Mercy: 'Racham' (pi.), 'Rachum,' and 'Rachamim' in the Book of Ben Sira," in *Ben Sira's God: Proceedings of the International Ben Sira Conference Durham— Ushaw College 2001*, ed. Renate Egger-Wenzel (BZAW 321; Berlin: de Gruyter, 2002), 101–17; and Maurice Gilbert, "God, Sin and Mercy: Sirach 15:11–18:14," in ibid., 118–35. Ben Sira's use of earlier canonical material is discussed at length in *Intertextual Studies in Ben Sira and Tobit*, ed. Jeremy Corley and Vincent Skemp (CBOMS 38; Washington, D.C.: Catholic Biblical Association of America, 2005), 89–182 (on Genesis 1–11 [Maurice Gilbert], Exodus [Friedrich V. Reiterer], Kings [Pancratius C. Beentjes], prophets[Leo G. Perdue], and Proverbs [Jeremy Corley]).

4. Leo G. Perdue, *Wisdom and Cult* (SBLDS 30; Missoula, Mont.: Scholars Press, 1977), takes a more positive view of the cult than von Rad, *Wisdom in Israel*, 186–89; and J. G. Snaith, "Ben Sira's Supposed Love of Liturgy," *VT* 25 (1975): 167–74. Helga Stadelmann, *Ben Sira als Schriftgelehrter: Eine Untersuchung zum Berufsbild des vor-Maccabäischen Sofer unter Berücksichtigung seines Verhältnisses zu Priester-, Propheten- und Weisheitslehretum* (WUNT 2/6; Tübingen: Mohr, 1981), views Ben Sira as a priestly learned scribe. See also John F. A. Sawyer, "Was Jeshua Ben Sira a Priest?" *Proceedings of the Eighth World Congress of Jewish Studies*, Div. A (Jerusalem: World Union of Jewish Studies 1982), 65–71; Saul M. Olyan, "Ben Sira's Relationship to the Priesthood," *HTR* 80 (1987): 261–86; Michael W. Duggan, "Ezra, Scribe and Priest, and the Concerns of Ben Sira," in *Intertextual Studies in Ben Sira and Tobit*, ed. Corley and Skemp, 201–10; and Johannes Marböck, "Der Hohepriester Simon in Sir 50. Ein Beitrag zur Bedeutung von Priestertum und Kult im Sirachbuch," in *Treasures of Wisdom*, ed. Calduch-Benages and Vermeylen, 215–30.

5. Although he could easily have chosen heroines for inclusion in this eulogy, Ben Sira did not do so.

6. Burton L. Mack, *Wisdom and the Hebrew Epic: Ben Sira's Hymn in Praise of the Fathers* (Chicago: University of Chicago, 1985), 18–26.

7. Thomas R. Lee, *Studies in the Form of Sirach 44–50* (SBLDS 75; Atlanta: Scholars, 1986).

8. Chris A. Rollston, "The Non-Encomiastic Features of Ben Sira 44–50," M.A. thesis, Emmanuel School of Religion, Johnson City, Tennessee, 1992.

9. See Peter Höffken, "Warum schwieg Jesus Sirach über Esra?" *ZAW* 87 (1975): 184–201; Christopher Begg, "Ben Sirach's Non-Mention of Ezra," *BN* 42 (1988): 14–18; P. J. Beentjes, "'The Countries Marvelled at You': King Solomon in Ben Sira 47:12–22," *Bijdr* 45 (1984): 6–13; idem, "Hezekiah and Isaiah: A Study of Ben Sira xlviii 15–25," *OTS* 25 (1989): 77–88; and Núria Calduch-Benages, "Fear for the Powerful or Respect for Authority?" in *Der Einzelne und seine Gemeinschaft bei Ben Sira*, ed. Renate Egger-Wenzel and Ingrid Krammer (BZAW 270; Berlin: de Gruyter, 1998), 87–102.

10. Lutz Schrader, *Leiden und Gerechtigkeit: Studien zu Theologie und Textgeschichte des Sirachbuches* (BBET 27; Frankfurt am Main: Peter Lang, 1994), focuses on the topic of suffering in the face of death. See also Friedrich Vinzenz Reiterer, "Deutung und Wertung des Todes durch Ben Sira," *Die alttestamentliche Botschaft als Wegweisung: Festschrift für Heinz Reinelt*, ed. Josef Zmijewski (Stuttgart: Katholische Bibelwerk, 1990), 203–36; and J. L. Prockter, 'His Yesterday and Yours Today' (Sir 38:22): Reflections on Ben Sira's View of Death," *JSem* 2 (1990): 44–56.

11. Josef Haspecker, *Gottesfurcht bei Jesus Sirach: Ihre religiöse Struktur und ihre literarische und doctrinäre Bedeutung* (AnBib 30; Rome: Päpstliches Bibelinstitut, 1967); Alexander A. Di Lella, "Fear of the Lord and Belief and Hope in the Lord Amid Trials: Sirach 2:1–18," in *Wisdom, You Are My Sister*, ed. Barré, 188–204; Renate Egger-Wenzel, "'Faith in God' Rather Than 'Fear of God' in Ben Sira and Job: A Necessary Adjustment in Terminology and Understanding," in *Intertextual Studies in Ben Sira and Tobit*, ed. Corley and Skemp, 211–26.

12. Victor Morla Asensio, "Poverty and Wealth: Ben Sira's View of Possessions," in *Der Einzelne und seine Gemeinschaft*, ed. Egger-Wenzel and Krammer, 151–77, writes that Ben Sira expected humans to assist God in helping the poor.

13. For the role of prayer in Ben Sira's thought, see Crenshaw, "The Restraint of Reason, the Humility of Prayer," in UAPQ, 206–21; P. C. Beentjes, "Sirach 22:27–23:6 in zijn Context," *Bijdr* 39 (1978): 144–51; Johannes Marböck, "Das Gebet um die Rettung Zions Sir 36:1–22 (G 33, 1–13a, 3b, 16b–22) in Zusammenhang der Geschichtlichen Ben Siras," in *Memoria Jerusalem*, ed. J. B. Bauer (Graz: Akademische Druck und Verlagsanstalt, 1977), 93–116.

14. Von Rad, *Wisdom in Israel*, 242–46, subordinates the theme "fear of the Lord" to that of wisdom.

15. Ibid., 246.

16. Two copies of the Greek text of Sirach have survived, a short one and an expanded version. About two-thirds of the book are extant in Hebrew, thanks to a discovery in a genizah (depository for used sacred books) in Cairo, a scroll at Masada, and a hymn about wisdom appended to the great Psalms Scroll from Qumran. On the text of Sirach, see Skehan and Di Lella, *Wisdom of Ben Sira*, 51–62; and Pancratius C. Beentjes, *The Book of Ben Sira in Hebrew: A Text Edition of All Extant Hebrew Manuscripts and a Synopsis of All Parallel Hebrew Ben Sira Texts* (VTSup 68; Leiden: Brill, 1997).

17. See Murphy, "Personification of Wisdom," 222–33; and Judith M. Hadley, "Wisdom and the Goddess," 234–43, in *Wisdom in Ancient Israel*, ed. Day et al.; and Perdue, *Wisdom and Creation*, 247–90.

18. Johannes Marböck, "Gesetz und Weisheit: Zum Verständnis des Gesetzes bei Jesus Ben Sira," *BZ* 20 (1976): 1–21; Gerald T. Sheppard, "Wisdom and Torah: The Interpretation of Deuteronomy underlying Sirach 24:23," in *Biblical and Near Eastern Studies: Essays in Honor of William Sanford LaSor*, ed. Gary A. Tuttle (Grand Rapids: Eerdmans, 1978), 166–76.

19. Crenshaw, "Qoheleth's Understanding of Intellectual Inquiry," in *Qohelet in the Context of Wisdom*, ed. Schoors, 205–24.

20. On education as understood by Ben Sira, see James L. Crenshaw, "The Primacy of Listening in Ben Sira's Pedagogy," in *Wisdom, You Are My Sister*, ed. Barré, 172–87; idem, *Education in Ancient Israel*, and Frank Ueberschaer, *Weisheit aus der Begegnung*. Ben Sira's arranging of his own teachings has been understood in directly opposing ways, as random thoughts and as carefully organized units. The most complex theory is that of Wolfgang Roth, "On the Gnomic-Discursive Wisdom of Jesus Ben Sirach," *Semeia* 17 (1980): 59–79. He thinks the original book consisted of 1:1–23:27 and 51:1–30, to which Ben Sira added three units (24:1–32:13; 32:14–38:23; 38:24–50:24, 29). A prologue introduces each new section, and an autobiographical note intervenes between the prologue and the body of the unit. In these teachings Roth sees the forerunners of both halakic and haggadic instruction. In Roth's view, the first four sections were arranged alphabetically (*'āb*, "father," in 3:1–16; *bôšet*, "shame," in 4:2–28, *gā'ôt*, "arrogance," in 7:17 and 10:5–18; and *da'at*, "knowledge," in 16:25b–23:27), and the units move from simple to more difficult issues, like education itself. More probably, poetic units are introduced by a poem or hymn in praise of wisdom, although an appearance of randomness remains. See also Georg Sauer, "Gedanken über den thematischen Aufbau des Buches Ben Sira," in *Treasures of Wisdom*, ed. Calduch-Benages and Vermeylen, 51–62.

21. Ben Sira's attitude to wealth is complex, for he certainly viewed riches favorably, refusing to disdain them the way the author of *1 Enoch* did, according to R. A. Argall, *1 Enoch and Sirach: A Comparative Literary and Conceptual Analysis of the Themes of Revelation, Creation and Judgment* (SBLEJL 8; Atlanta: Scholars, 1995), 252–54.

22. Edmond Jacob, "Wisdom and Religion in Sirach," in *Israelite Wisdom*, ed. Gammie et al., 247–60; J. Marböck, "Sirachliteratur seit 1966. Ein Uberblick," *TRev* 71 (1975): 177–84; and Daniel J. Harrington, "Sirach Research since 1965: Progress and Questions," in *Pursuing the Text: Studies in Honor of Ben Zion Wacholder on the Occasion of His Seventieth Birthday*, ed. J. C. Reeves and J. Kampen (JSOTSup 184; Sheffield: Sheffield Academic, 1994) 164–76, give a survey of research on Sirach after 1966; see also Reiterer, "Review of Recent Research on the Book of Ben Sira (1980–1996)"; Crenshaw, "Sirach," 603–37; and R. E. Murphy and B. Mack, "Wisdom Literature," in *Early Judaism and Its Modern Interpreters*, ed. Robert A. Kraft and George W. E. Nickelsburg (Philadelphia: Fortress, 1986), 371–410; Perdue, *Sword and Stylus*, 256–91; Collins, *Jewish Wisdom in the Hellenistic Age*, 23–111.

23. Some scholars understand the reference to a school as a metaphor for the book of Sirach, e.g., Wischmeyer, *Kultur des Buches Jesus Sirach*, 175–76.

24. Contra Warren C. Trenchard, *Ben Sira's View of Women: A Literary Analysis* (BJS 38; Chico, Calif.: Scholars, 1982). Claudia V. Camp, "Understanding a Patriarchy: Women in Second Century Jerusalem through the Eyes of Ben

Sira," in *"Women Like This": New Perspectives on Jewish Women in the Greco-Roman World*, ed. Amy-Jill Levine (SBLEJL 1; Atlanta: Scholars Press, 1991), 1–39, offers a more balanced perspective than Trenchard's analysis.

25. Reinhold Bohlen, *Die Ehrung der Eltern bei Ben Sira* (TTS 61; Trier: Paulinus, 1991).

26. F. V. Reiterer, ed., *Freundschaft bei Ben Sira* (BZAW 244; Berlin: de Gruyter, 1996); and Jeremy Corley, *Ben Sira's Teaching on Friendship* (BJS 316; Providence: Brown University, 2002).

27. On these hymns see Marböck, *Weisheit im Wandel*; James L. Crenshaw, "The Problem of Theodicy in Sirach: On Human Bondage," *JBL* 94 (1975): 47–64 (*UAPQ*, 155–74); and Luis Alonso Schökel, "The Vision of Man in Sirach 16:24–17:14," in *Israelite Wisdom*, ed. Gammie et al., 235–45; and Núria Calduch-Benages, "The Hymn to the Creation (Sir. 42:15–43:33: A Polemic Text?" in *The Wisdom of Ben Sira*, 119–38.

28. That is, Ben Sira supplements human inquiry with divine revelation. The Torah thus becomes material with which the sages work in their attempts to master reality.

29. On Ben Sira and Stoicism, see David Winston, "Theodicy in Ben Sira and Stoic Philosophy," in *Of Scholars, Savants, and Their Texts: Essays in Honor of Arthur Hyman*, ed. R. Link-Salinger (New York: Peter Lang, 1989), 239–49; Otto Kaiser, "Die Rezeption der stoischen Providenz bei Ben Sira," *JNSL* 124 (1998): 41–54; S. L. Mattila, "Ben Sira and the Stoics: A Re-examination of the Evidence," *JBL* 119 (2000): 473–501; and U. Wicke-Reuter, *Göttliche Providenz und menschliche Verantwortung bei Ben Sira und in der Frühen Stoa* (BZAW 298; Berlin: de Gruyter, 2000).

30. Crenshaw, "Problem of Theodicy in Sirach." See also Pancratius C. Beentjes, "Theodicy in the Wisdom of Ben Sira," in *Theodicy in the World of the Bible*, ed. Laato and de Moor, 509–24.

31. Johannes Marböck, "Kohelet und Sirach," in *Buch Kohelet*, ed. Schwienhorst-Schönberger, 275–301; discusses the similarities and differences between Ecclesiastes and Sirach. See James L. Crenshaw, "Theodicy," in *NIDB*; and "Theodicy and Prophetic Literature," in *Theodicy in the World of the Bible*, ed. Laato and de Moor, 236–55.

32. See James D. Martin, "Ben Sira—A Child of His Time," in *A Word in Season: Essays in Honor of William McKane*, ed. Martin and Philip R. Davies (JSOTSup 42; Sheffield: JSOT, 1986), 141–61, for emphasis on emerging apocalypticism in the second century.

33. Crenshaw, *Defending God*, evaluates the several approaches within the canon.

Chapter 7

The Widening Hunt

*Wisdom of Solomon, Psalms
with Affinities to Wisdom, and Beyond*

The impact of Israel's sages extended far beyond small village life, the royal court, and scribal contexts, for the major issues with which they struggled were universal ones. The author of Wisdom of Solomon endeavored to apply philosophical rigor to profoundly religious themes. Moreover, certain psalmists tried to provide adequate responses to the problem of undeserved suffering, the apparent prosperity of wicked persons, and life's brevity. In the process, the liturgical tradition slowly took over a few sapiential concepts. Beyond these two significant ventures one may discern various literary works that have been thought to breathe wisdom's atmosphere to a greater or lesser degree.

WISDOM OF SOLOMON

Unlike Ben Sira, the cosmopolitan author of Wisdom of Solomon selected the Greek language as his medium of expression. Writing in the first century BCE or CE,[1] he directed teachings to a Jewish minority living in the Hellenistic city of Alexandria. Although a number of Jews served as a kind of border patrol at Elephantine in the fifth century, many more seem to have migrated to this region during the reigns of the first two Ptolemies, for the earliest Jewish inscriptions in Egypt date from the third century. Jews of this time enjoyed a measure of self-rule but were not granted citizenship. During Caligula's rule (37 CE), they were subjected to beatings with whips ordinarily used on native Egyptians, and in 24/23 BCE the Romans imposed a poll tax on Jews, from which Greek citizens were exempt. A few Jews from prominent families (Philo and his brother, for example) may have attained citizenship, but most Jews of the area longed in vain for respect that they rightfully thought was due them. The author of Wisdom of Solomon put forth a treatise highly charged with apologetic. Here one encounters exquisite rhetoric in a philosophical vein rather than gnomic sayings. In addition, one comes up against reflective poems about personified Wisdom and historical retrospect akin to that in some psalms. The boldness of the author is astonishing, particularly the understanding of wisdom as a reflection of the divine being and the manner in which history becomes intrinsic to his thought, not just a supplement as in Sirach.

Structure

The book consists of three parts: (1) a book of eschatology (1:1–6:21); (2) a book of wisdom (6:22–10:21); and a book of history (chaps. 11–19). Its themes concern love of righteousness (1:1) and wisdom (6:9). The didactic exhortation, protreptic, appeals to listeners to follow a particular way of life. The author insists that the hope for righteousness is full of immortality, one grounded in creation itself. Moreover, the author attributes immortality to the soul. As for death, it resulted from human waywardness (1:16) and the devil's envy (2:24).

The long section on divine providence during the exodus contains five (or seven) syncrises, contrasts that compare the different ways God dealt with Israelites and Egyptians: (1) 11:6–14, thirst, in one instance quenched and in another not; (2) 11:15–16:15, small animals as plagues for Egyptians and food for the fleeing Israelites; (3) 16:16–23, heavenly gifts of destructive water and fire for Egyptians and manna for Israelites; (4) 17:1–18:4, unrelieved darkness for Egyptians and a pillar of fire for Israelites; and (5) 18:5–19:21, the massacre of Egyptian sons and escape of Jewish boys.[2]

Theological Views

Sirach's emphasis upon divine mercy is carried forward with vigor; indeed, this significant theological claim is formulated in a refrain that occurs twice within the work:

> grace and mercy are upon his elect/holy ones,
> and he watches over his elect/holy ones.
> (3:9, but with uncertain text; 4:15)

If this assertion left any question about God's willingness to forgive those who belong to the chosen people, a further declaration removed even the slightest doubt.

> But you, our God, are kind and true,
> patient, and ruling all things in mercy.
> For even if we sin we are yours, knowing your power;
> but we will not sin, because we know that you acknowledge us
>   as yours.
>
> (15:1–2)

The consciousness of belonging to an elected people pervades this work and the belief that the souls of the righteous rest in God's hand (3:1).

The idea of an elect people scarcely accords with the universalism that dominates the wisdom of ancient Israel, but Ben Sira's praise of past heroes paved the way for the adoption of particularistic thinking. Conscious that such a position could not be defended logically, the author appealed to divine sovereignty (12:1–18). No one, human or otherwise, can call the only God to task for dubious conduct.

God's compassion expressed itself upon the elect and those not favored by divine choice, according to this author. Even the wicked Canaanites were given ample warning and perished little by little so that they would have an opportunity to repent (12:3–11). The same lenience was granted the Egyptians, whom God could have slain much more dramatically than by sending the plagues (11:15–20). Still, the author seems constrained to point out that God had sufficient foresight to know that these wicked people would never abandon their folly (12:10). Now and again tension exists between this sort of thinking and a desire to emphasize God's love for everyone, particularly since the entire world is no more than a speck of dust that tips the scales (11:22)—an argument that the book of Job expressed with considerable power.[3]

It follows from this divine foreknowledge that God sees and hears everything that takes place within the created universe (1:7–8). To be sure, some people draw erroneous conclusions from divine forbearance, viewing delayed punishment as evidence that God does not maintain justice. When this suspicion is strengthened by reflection on life's brevity, it often leads to a lifestyle in which sensual gratification becomes the highest good. The author of Wisdom of Solomon attacks those who reason in this manner, accusing them of faulty logic (1:16–2:24).[4] In this connection care is taken to place the responsibility for death squarely upon human shoulders—and upon the devil's.

Human perversion expresses itself most visibly in the *worship of idols*, according to this author (13:1–15:17).[5] He even considers idolatry the beginning, cause, and end of all evil (14:27). Two explanations, perhaps three, are offered for the genesis of idol making: vanity, grief, and aesthetics. Desire to pay proper respect to faraway emperors prompted royal subjects to fashion images in the likeness of their ruler. Alternatively, a grief-stricken father may have shaped a piece of wood to resemble his dead child. Both explanations are reinforced by the desire to make images that please the eye; pride of craft turns idle carving into purposeful design.

The author goes a long way toward condoning the worship of nature, since created artifacts contain visible witness to their Creator. The error lay in a failure to move one step further from the creation to its Maker. The stupidity of those who practice idolatry becomes evident in the requests made to lifeless objects: one prays to a dead thing for life, to an inanimate artifact for health, to an idol that cannot take a single step for protection on a journey (13:18). This author finds it ludicrous that people embarking on a voyage by ship will entreat a paltry piece of wood, when God is the helmsman[6] who steers safely into harbor. Precisely at this point the symbol of God as Father surfaces (14:3), as if to emphasize providential care.

Hypostasis of Wisdom

This allusion to God as Father stands alongside mention of wisdom, by which the ship was built. In no other book does the figure of Wisdom play such a prominent role, and nowhere else does she possess such rich imagery. Here Wisdom goes beyond personification to hypostasis; she becomes a manifestation of God to human beings, an emanation of divine attributes. Furthermore, she is portrayed as Solomon's bride, who enables him to rule wisely and justly. In addition, she functions in synonymous parallelism with the divine word and even seems to be identical with God's holy spirit (6:12–9:18).

Whereas Ben Sira had identified wisdom and Torah, Wisdom of Solomon brings God even closer to humans by understanding Wisdom as

> a breath of the power of God,
>   and a pure emanation of the glory of the Almighty.
>   (7:25)

As such she mirrors God's eternal light and activity, for she is an image of God's goodness (7:26). For this reason divine attributes are ascribed to her.

> There is in her a spirit that is intelligent, holy,
> unique, manifold, subtle,
> mobile, clear, unpolluted,
> distinct, invulnerable, loving the good, keen,
> irresistible, beneficent, humane,
> steadfast, sure, free from anxiety,
> all-powerful, overseeing all,
> and penetrating through all spirits
> that are intelligent, pure, and altogether subtle.
>   (7:22–23)

What is more, she is actually called the orderer and creator of all things (8:1, 6). (Behind such thinking may lie Stoic philosophy and hymns about the Egyptian goddess Isis.) That is why she can also be described as the teacher of the Hellenistic cardinal virtues: self-control, prudence, justice, and courage (8:7).

According to 7:17–22, Wisdom was thought to have provided instruction in the fundamental subjects comprising the curriculum in a Greek school: philosophy, physics, history, astronomy, zoology, religion, botany, and medicine.[7]

> For it is he [God] who gave me unerring knowledge of what exists,
> to know the structure of the world and the activity of the elements;
> the beginning and end and middle of times,
> the alterations of the solstices and the changes of the seasons,
> the cycles of the year and the constellations of the stars,
> the natures of animals and the tempers of wild animals,
> the powers of spirits and the thoughts of human beings,
> the varieties of plants and the virtues of roots;
> I learned both what is secret and what is manifest,
> for wisdom, the fashioner of all things, taught me.
>
> (7:17–22a)

In addition, Wisdom enters holy souls, turning them into prophets (7:27).

In this capacity Wisdom guided the chosen people from the very beginning. The author traces this wondrous leadership from the first man to the memorable journey in the wilderness, referring specifically to Adam, Cain (negatively), Noah, Abraham, Lot (and his unfortunate wife), Jacob, Joseph, and Moses, in every instance without directly naming the individual being discussed. Passing by the narratives from Genesis as hurriedly as possible, the sage dwells at length on the events surrounding the exodus. Wisdom is even identified as the cloud that accompanied God's people by day and the pillar of fire by night. The final ten chapters (10–19) consist largely of a midrashic exposition on the exodus experience. From 15:18 to 19:22 the contrast between God's manner of dealing with two entities, God's people and the Egyptians, occupies center stage.

Since the book we are discussing purports to come from Solomon's hand, it elevates the *erotic relationship* with Wisdom. In King Solomon's prayer at the sacred place in Gibeon (1 Kgs. 3:6–9), he requests an understanding mind to enable him to judge his people fairly. The author of Wisdom of Solomon amplifies that request, at the same time viewing the young king's prayer as the desire to acquire Wisdom for a bride. Such a wife brings respect, companionship, and freedom from pain. Her dowry includes the finest things one can envision: immortality, wealth, joy, renown, and understanding. Like Torah, Wisdom will guard and guide those who love her.

This eulogy of the bride, Wisdom, contains some interesting self-reflections by Solomon. Despite his singular place in Israel's history, Solomon admits that he is mortal like everyone else. Lest the obvious be overlooked, he takes pains to point out that his prayer lacked every vestige of selfish interest. He preferred Wisdom to wealth, health, and beauty, but these accompanied her—to Solomon's utter surprise!

All good things came to me along with her,
and in her hands uncounted wealth.
I rejoiced in them all, because wisdom leads them;
but I did not know that she was their mother.
(7:11–12)

Perhaps the most astonishing comment concerning Solomon's unusual status is his remark that a good soul befell him since he was good.

As a child I was naturally gifted,
and a good soul fell to my lot;
or rather, being good, I entered an undefiled body.
(8:19–20)

A Greek Spirit

To this point I have refrained from identifying *Hellenistic features* in Wisdom of Solomon.[8] This acknowledgment of pervasive Greek thought does not rule out a possible use of traditions in Hebrew[9] for sections of chapters 1–9. Entirely Greek, however, are the following rhetorical features: diatribe, sorites (a chain-like list of syllogisms in 6:7–21), aporia (a philosophical problem to be explored), aretalogy (a list of virtues), and the aforementioned synchreses.

A Greek spirit issues in a different attitude toward theological doubt, which occupies a prominent place in the Hebrew Bible and functions positively, for the most part. Wisdom of Solomon allows no room for religious skepticism, asserting that Wisdom comes only to those who believe fully (1:2–5). Similarly, the Hebraic notion of progeny as an indication of God's favor flies out the window, for this author pronounces the barren, undefiled woman blessed (3:13), extends that honored status to eunuchs who are virtuous (3:14), and extols childlessness with virtue (4:1). To be sure, earlier Israelite sages would probably have agreed that virtue excels vice, even if the latter is accompanied by many children, but the very formulation of the issue in Wisdom of Solomon seems to reflect new attitudes. The same goes for the negative understanding of old age, for now the attainment of advanced years is no longer viewed as reward for a life well-lived.

For old age is not honored for length of time,
or measured by number of years;
but understanding is gray hair for anyone,
and a blameless life is ripe old age.
(4:8)

This conviction arose from attempts to understand untimely deaths; the author sees such premature departures as God's gracious removal of persons from the possibility of sinning. An early death prevents worthy persons from defiling themselves and therefore does not signify God's displeasure. Naturally, Enoch functions as a paradigm for this view, for in popular memory he pleased God and was taken up to heaven as a reward for righteous living.[10]

Another Greek concept occurs in connection with the problem of theodicy: Creation itself fights on behalf of the righteous (5:15–23; 16:24). The whole universe has been created so as to defend virtue and punish vice (16:17). The author uses this idea with stunning effect in discussing the punishment inflicted upon the ancient Egyptians and in describing God's solicitous care for the elect people. In this connection he also develops a theory concerning psychological fear, according to which the Egyptians suffered more from anxiety than from actual physical causes, whereas the holy people, clothed with impenetrable spiritual armor, confidently relied upon their God for protection.

We have by no means discussed the full extent of Greek influence upon Wisdom of Solomon. The mention of the four cardinal virtues in 8:7 suggests that the author had thoroughly immersed himself in the Greek worldview in the same way Philo mastered its language and thought. The foregoing remarks underline the significant changes that occurred once Hebraic wisdom shifted its locus to Greek soil. The different perspective appears nowhere so dramatically as it does in the following lament over limits imposed upon human knowledge.

> For who can learn the counsel of God?
> Or who can discern what the Lord wills?
> For the reasoning of mortals is worthless,
> and our designs are likely to fail,
> for a perishable body weighs down the soul,
> and this earthly tent burdens the thoughtful mind.
> (9:13–15)

Qoheleth would gladly have endorsed this sentiment—except for the explanation for this ignorance, which departed completely from the biblical conviction that all things created by God are very good. The distinction between body and soul owes its origin to the Hellenistic environment, not to Hebraic sapiential traditions. *immortal soul a reward for righteous living* .

PSALMS WITH AFFINITIES TO WISDOM

If the book of Psalms is the voice of ordinary citizens, one would expect to find in it a certain kinship with other literary products of common people. Similarities between a given psalm and the older collections in the book of Proverbs are not surprising. They do not justify the label "wisdom psalms."[11] Psalm 37 emphasizes sacral traditions such as the land as an inheritance from the Deity and the exacting punishment for sinners, but it also includes brief aphorisms that would be perfectly at home in Proverbs.

> Better is a little that the righteous person has
> than the abundance of many wicked.
> (37:16)

> Again I passed by, and they were no more;
>   though I sought them, they could not be found.
>   (37:36)

> The wicked borrow, and do not pay back,
>   but the righteous are generous and keep giving.
>   (37:21)

This psalm introduces the vexing issue of unjust suffering even while insisting that God remains in control during such adversity. Earlier sages also acknowledged cracks in the causal connection between good conduct and blessing but claimed that the fallen will get up, even seven times. The striking personal testimony in 37:25, "I have been young, and now am old; yet I have not seen the righteous forsaken or their children begging bread," resembles a genre used by Qoheleth, the "testament," which was based on his daily experience. Qoheleth, however, never derived comfort from observation, for he saw too much injustice that in his eyes demolished such creeds, the outgrowths of willful blindness.

The similarities between Psalm 39 and reflective wisdom in the books of Job and Qoheleth are close enough to suggest either dependence or folk tradition on which the authors of all three works may have drawn.[12] The psalmist uses language that functions as Qoheleth's motto signifying the fragility of existence.

> Surely everyone stands as a mere breath.
>   (39:5, 11 [Heb. 6, 12])

> Surely everyone goes about like a shadow.
>   (39:6 [Heb. 7])

Moreover, the psalmist concurs with Qoheleth that nobody can really acquire knowledge, presumably of a lasting truth (39:6 [Heb. 7]). This psalmist's experience with an oppressive Deity evoked the cry for relief that echoes Job's agonizing plea.

> Turn your gaze away from me, that I may smile again,
> before I depart and am no more.
>   (39:13 [Heb. 14]; cf. Job 7:16; 10:20)

Whereas the narrator of the prologue to the book of Job absolves the hero of any guilt from wrongful speech, the psalmist takes a solemn vow to stand guard over his tongue, even to muzzle his mouth, in order to avoid tripping over his tongue (Ps. 39:2). Warnings against loose speech abound in international wisdom, as one might expect, given the tongue's power to injure others. Like arrows, spoken words, once released, cannot be recalled.

> Conceal your heart, control your mouth.
>   (*Ptahhotep* 618; *LAE*, 1:75)

A man may be ruined by his tongue;
beware and you will do well.
>   (*Ani* 7.8; *COS*, 1:112)

Do not sever your heart from your tongue.
>   (*Amenemope* 10.16; *COS*, 1:118;
>   cf. *Insinger* 25.21)

Keep firm your heart, steady your heart,
Do not steer with your tongue;
If a man's tongue is the boat's rudder
The Lord of All is yet its pilot.
>   (*Amenemope* 18.3–5; *COS*, 1:120)

You may trip over your foot in the house of a great man;
You should not trip over your tongue.
>   (*Ankhsheshonqy* 10.7; *LAE*, 3:167)

Two realities impinged on the psalmist, who resolved to place a guard over his speech, imperiling a worldview: (1) the brevity of human existence, and (2) the heavy hand of the Deity. Divine punishment made the short sojourn on earth unbearable, and the psalmist decided to refrain from any speech at all. Such a provisional solution, a silence that was tantamount to withdrawing from life altogether, brought further agitation. In short, the psalmist moves from an awareness of personal *hebel* (emptiness) to the generalization that everyone's existence is *hebel*, which leads him to ask: "What can I expect, or hope for?" in a world lacking substance.

This interpretation of Psalm 39 rests on an assumption of literary integrity. Otto Kaiser has argued that the section on life's brevity (4–6, 11 [Heb. 5–7, 12]) constitutes an earlier didactic poem like Job 28; Ecclesiastes 3:1–8; Sirach 24:1–22; and Wisdom of Solomon 2:1–9.[13] The four instances of the asseverative particle *'ak* (surely) in Psalm 39:5, 6, and 11 (Heb. 6, 7, 12) appear to set this unit aside. In my view, the psalm consists of a three-part prayer (vv. 4–6, 7–11, 12–13 [Heb. 5–7, 8–12, 13–14]) introduced by verses 1–3 (Heb. 2–4). The three vocatives (vv. 4, 7, 12 [Heb. 5, 8, 13]), two uses of the Tetragrammaton (YHWH; vv. 4, 12 [Heb. 5, 13]) and a single use of *'ădōnāy* (Lord; v. 7 [Heb. 8]), support such a reading. Alternatively, the two occurrences of *selâ* at the conclusion of verses 5 and 11 (Heb. 6, 12) suggest a two-part structure, 1–5, 6–11 (Heb. 2–6, 7–12), plus a final plea, 12–13 (Heb. 13–14).

Normally, laments introduced by *'ad-mātay* or *'ad-'ānâ* (how long?) inquire about the duration of present suffering. This one, however, asks about the number of days remaining before the grim reaper's scythe does its work. The psalmist's enforced silence seems to have been caused by the presence of the wicked. Like the author of Psalm 73:3–14, did this poet choose mutism lest he provide ammunition for detractors?

The initial prayer that explores the voluntary silence Psalm 39:4–6 (Heb. 5–7) seeks information hidden from most people, specifically the exact time of death.

The choice of the noun *qēṣ* (end) places this poet in the same camp with Amos, who with this same word announced the downfall of a nation (Amos 8:2). Others gave thought to the days that God allotted to humans, arriving at a plausible figure of seventy or eighty years, some forty years less than the number attributed to the patriarchs. This large figure of one hundred and twenty was a topos in the ancient Near East, attested both in Egypt and at Emar.[14] Religious professionals actually turned prediction of the future into a thriving business, particularly since they claimed to derive information from above. The "science" of reading the livers of animals that had been sacrificed and of interpreting omens lay at the very heart of wisdom in Mesopotamia. No evidence of this practice has survived in biblical wisdom, although something like mantic wisdom, the interpretation of dreams, was practiced by Daniel and his friends.

Refusing to offer a mythic explanation for the short life span, the psalmist shifts from duration to the quality of existence, which he characterizes as total emptiness, a mere image devoid of substance despite every hustle and bustle. Ironically, he sees his own brief existence as nothing in Yahweh's presence, presumably because the Deity is not subject to time's erosive force.

The second prayer (vv. 7–11 [Heb. 8–12]) alternates between trust and accusation. Here the psalmist wrestles with the idea of harsh discipline and death-dealing punishment. No wonder he boldly accuses Yahweh while justifying his earlier silence. Strong emotions elicit an extreme charge leveled against the Deity: "for it is you who have done it!" The translator of this psalm into Greek found such audacity unacceptable and changed it to read: "for you made me." In this way an accusation is transformed into acknowledgment that Yahweh is creator. The harsh sentiment in the Hebrew text finds a parallel in Lamentations, a poetic reaction to the destruction of Jerusalem by the Babylonian army (Lam. 1:12). Comparing Yahweh to a destructive moth, the psalmist reduces existence to a single breath, a rare concrete sense of *hebel*.

The lone echo of sapiential language in the third prayer, actually an outburst, (vv. 12–13 [Heb. 13–14]), reminds one of Job's abandonment of hope. The request that Yahweh look away and consequently hasten the end signifies that the psalmist, too, has given up because of disenfranchisement. His existence is that of aliens who are forced to live marginally as powerless outsiders, no better than a *gēr* or *tôšāb* (resident alien or sojourner).

Psalm 39 shares some things with Psalm 62, especially the adverbial particle *'ak* and the noun *hebel*. The adverb "surely" occurs six times in Psalm 62 as over against four in Psalm 39, and human breath is said to weigh more than his essence (62:9 [Heb. 10]). The particle *'ak* reinforces a low assessment of humankind in both psalms. A similar view occurs in Psalm 144:4 without such reinforcement. The two psalms differ stylistically in that the two occurrences of *selâ* in Psalm 62 precede a comment about human transcience (vv. 1–4, 5–8 [Heb. 2–5, 6–9]), whereas they follow a refrain about humans as *hebel* in Psalm 39.

Psalmists had other ways to describe life's brevity. Psalm 90 compares people to grass that flourishes briefly and then dies. The irrevocable decree relegating humans to dust in verse 3 becomes intolerable in light of the seventy or at most eighty years granted them, particularly when divine chastisement also weighs one down. The comparison of humans to a flower in Job 14:2 is more elegant, but flowers also wither and die. Both images, grass and flowers, are combined in Psalm 103:15–17 (cf. Isa. 40:6–8), which contrasts their brief flourishing to Yahweh's steadfast love.

Resemblances between Psalm 39 and Qoheleth go beyond the use of a common noun, *hebel*, to signify breath, breeze, or vapor. *Hebel* also has the meaning "futility," as in Job 9:29; Psalm 94:11; and often in Qoheleth. In a few instances, Qoheleth uses *hebel* to express ephemerality, as in Job 7:16; Psalms 39:5 (Heb. 6); 78:33; and 144:4. In addition to *hebel*, thematic and syntactical affinities exist between Psalm 39 and Qoheleth. Both authors refer to people who accumulate things without any assurance of gathering them in permanently. For Qoheleth, it was the uncertainty of inheritance (Eccl. 2:18–23). In Psalm 39:6 (Heb. 7) the consonants in *bṣlm* (as an image) can be divided differently to yield the picture of walking in a shadow, which occurs in Qoheleth, for whom a shadow symbolizes emptiness instead of relief from the scorching sun.

A remote resemblance is the psalmist's anxiety about extinction ("before I go and am no more"), an expression that includes a form of the verb *hlk* (to go) as a euphemism for dying and the particle of nonexistence to denote extinction, both of which Qoheleth among others employs. In addition, Psalm 39:2 (Heb. 3) uses the rare verb *ḥāšâ* to indicate silence just as Qoheleth does (Eccl. 3:7). He too considers the dangers of talking too much, but Qoheleth's reason lies in the distance separating him from Elohim.

Some interpreters consider Psalm 49 a wisdom psalm, largely because its subject is the inevitability of death, and this fact is reflected on by means of riddle-like language.

> My mouth shall speak wisdom (*ḥokmôt*);
> the meditation of my heart shall be understanding.
> I will incline my ear to a proverb;
> I will solve my riddle (*ḥîdātî*) to the music of the harp.
> (49:3–4 [Heb. 4–5])

The plural form of the noun for "wisdom" is rare (cf. Prov. 1:20), and the image of opening or unlocking a riddle is more technical than the verb *bîn* (to understand) in Proverbs 1:6 (cf. Judg. 14:12–18, where *ngd* [to tell] in the causative occurs).

Psalm 49 has a variant of what has been called "a summary appraisal,"[15] although it anticipates ("Such is the fate of the foolhardy, the end of those who are pleased with their lot," 49:13 [Heb. 14]). The word here for "end" is *'aḥărît* rather than *qēṣ*. The psalmist employs an exquisite metaphor for the sorry state of humans: death is a shepherd watching over the sinner (49:14 [Heb. 15]). It is difficult to see why the psalmist considered the common fate of humans and animals a riddle,[16] if as some people think that is the insight reached by rigorous logic. Like the author of Psalm 39, this one recognizes that the dead "leave their wealth to others" (49:11 [Heb. 12]). For some, the psalmist's overriding concern, the prosperity of the wicked, marks this psalm as wisdom, but that topic alone hardly identifies a text as sapiential, else the entire book of Lamentations and numerous prophetic texts, especially the "confessions" of Jeremiah (cf. Jer. 12:1–6), have been wholly misunderstood.

What, then, justifies the inclusion of Psalm 73 in the category of wisdom psalms?[17] A near-consensus has formed around this psalm, primarily because of its treatment of the same problem lying behind the book of Job. Here too it seems preferable to speak of affinities with reflective wisdom. Just as Job's consternation elicits an answer to the problem of unjust suffering from outside sapiential discourse, the psalmist discovers an answer in the cult, again beyond the pale of wisdom prior to Ben Sira, if silence about sacred institutions in the case of Proverbs and suspicion on Qoheleth's part mean anything. It may be that the Joban poet and the psalmist blaze new trails for sages, but if so, that new departure was a lonely trek until Ben Sira's day. Whatever its source, the fresh insight into the nature of goodness that the psalmist arrived at through a harrowing test of his own presuppositions presses beyond old ways of thinking, cultic or otherwise, and achieves the sort of ethical standard demanded by the Adversary in the prologue to the book of Job. God's goodness consists of presence, not presents (Ps. 73:28).

To these four psalms (37, 39, 49, 73) have been added three others (1, 19, 119), although most interpreters acknowledge that these three are meditations about divine torah. A much more appropriate term, therefore, is "meditation on torah." Psalm 1 uses an image that also occurs in Egyptian Instructions.

> They are like trees
> planted by steams of water,
> which yield their fruit in its season,
> and their leaves do not wither.
> In all that they do, they prosper.
> (Ps. 1:3)

Here the symbol of the wise person as a fruitful tree departs from the fuller image in Egypt, where the wicked are likened to a tree without sufficient water. Instead, the author of Psalm 1 considers sinners no more substantial than chaff blowing in the wind. This picture of humans as a tree is varied in Jeremiah 17:5–8, where the one who trusts in mortals rather than the Lord is said to resemble a mere shrub while his opposite flourishes as a luxurious tree. A popular saying concludes this meditation:

> Like the partridge that gathers a brood
> which she did not hatch,
> so is he who gets riches but not by right;
> in the midst of his days they will leave him,
> and at his end he will be a fool.
> (Jer. 17:11 RSV)

One is tempted to ponder whether the author of this unit in Jeremiah 17 had in mind the sages' anthropological starting point in epistemology. Be that as it may, later sages came to raise the same issue and began to warn against too much self-reliance.

Psalm 19 appears to harbor a riddle about speech[18] that lacks any sound, a motif that intrigued various thinkers (the author of the story about Yahweh's appearance to Elijah and the accompanying stillness; the dream vision that Eliphaz experienced when the visitor was unrecognizable and an eerie silence ensued). This psalm seems to combine an earlier solar hymn with meditation on the torah. If so, the non-Israelite hymn, like so many hymns to the sun god in Egypt and Mesopotamia, is a worthy expression of a desire on the part of creation to communicate with humans. This music of the spheres discloses divine mystery to astute listeners. The ponderous acrostic that plods on and on in an effort to bestow adequate praise on the torah (Psalm 119) can only be dragged into the sapiential enclosure while kicking and screaming.

Occasionally, psalms use expressions and images that can also be found in Wisdom literature. For example, Psalm 127 elaborates upon the sages' claim that human plans often go awry due to divine intentions (127:1–2). This psalm also has the image of children as arrows in a quiver (127:4). Here and there, psalms preserve popular proverbs that could easily have found a home in the book of Proverbs.

> I will instruct and teach you
> the way you should go;
> I will counsel you with my eye upon you.
> Do not be like a horse or a mule, without understanding,
> whose temper must be curbed with bit and bridle,
> else it will not stay near you.
>
> (Ps. 32:8–9)

Similarly, Psalm 94:8–11 juxtaposes folly and wisdom in a manner highly reminiscent of sages.

> Understand, O dullest of the people;
>   fools, when will you be wise?
> He who planted the ear, does he not hear?
> He who formed the eye, does he not see? . . .
> He who teaches knowledge to humankind,
>   does he not chastise?
> The LORD knows our thoughts,
>   that they are but an empty breath (*hebel*).

The reference in Psalm 62:11–12 (Heb. 12–13) to a single-verbal disclosure on Elohim's part that evoked a response of a twofold hearing on the part of the psalmist has a ring of mystery so beloved by sages.

This delineation of psalms with affinities to wisdom uses formal and thematic criteria, as well as the overall tone that surfaces in a given text. Other readings of the data have certainly been offered, ranging from the bare admission of wisdom or learned psalmography to a hypothesis of numerous wisdom psalms. The present analysis has looked askance at certain formal and thematic considerations: 'ašrê sayings (Happy the . . .); acrostic (alphabetic) arrangement; anthological composition (made up of selected phrases from various sources); mere didactic intent; themes such as "fear of God," the fate of the righteous and the wicked; and exhortation as such. By widening the net to include such features that belong to society in general, we would have difficulty demonstrating their sapiential character. It seems best, therefore, to exercise caution with respect to the incorporation of additional passages into the category of wisdom. In any event, we have isolated sufficient evidence to suggest that a few psalms share some vocabulary and interests with Israel's sages. Still, we are not justified in taking the further step toward declaring these psalms "wisdom" and assuming that the sages had a lively interest in the cult prior to Ben Sira.

1 ESDRAS 3:1–5:3

The impact of sapiential thought was also felt in late historiography. The contest of Darius's guards in 1 Esdras 3:1–5:3 concerning the strongest thing in the world makes free use of traditions derived from Wisdom literature.[19] A case can be made for direct dependence on Sirach and Qoheleth, and the matchless description of wine's power over its hapless victims echoes similar observations in Proverbs. Although the final praise of truth has been compared to a passage in *Ptahhotep's Instruction*,[20] it represents universally acknowledged conviction that the truth alone survives time's passage.

At the same time, the larger context resembles Sirach 43:1–5 and 17:31–32 in so many respects that a direct relationship seems probable. Both Sirach and 1 Esdras praise the sun, but they note that its light pales, so that only truth lasts forever. Each passage concludes with a doxology lauding the Creator of the sun and Lord of truth. Furthermore, Sirach 17 singles out humans as masters of the earth and contrasts ephemerality and unrighteousness with that which endures, just as 1 Esdras juxtaposes eternal truth with everything that eventually decays because it is unrighteous. On the basis of these striking resemblances, together with evidence within the context itself (1 Esd. 4:2, 14, 37), it appears that a fourth speech has been displaced from the narrative. In it, human beings were depicted as strongest because they lorded it over beasts.

The kinship with Qoheleth occurs within the speech concerning the king as strongest. Here remarkable similarities with Ecclesiastes 3:1–9 have escaped notice. Only those actions not subject to external command (for example, making love, hating, and so forth) are missing from 1 Esdras. Otherwise, essentially the same polarities appear in both texts.

> If he tells them to kill, they kill; if he tells them to release, they release; if he tells them to attack, they attack; if he tells them to lay waste, they lay waste, if he tells them to build, they build; if he tells them to cut down, they cut down; if he tells them to plant, they plant. (1 Esd. 4:7–9)

The four answers to the question, "What is strongest?" are defended with considerable flourish: wine, the king, woman, and truth. The author's fondness for rhetorical questions expresses itself throughout the dialogue, as does conscious humor. Two exquisite examples of humor occur when a man is described as dropping his most cherished possession and gazing *open-mouthed* at a lovely woman, and when the king is reminded of his gazing *open-mouthed* at his playful concubine after she has just slapped him. This remarkable observation reduces the king to the level of ordinary humans, so that the final verdict appropriately comes from the people themselves.

That spontaneous celebration of truth introduces a religious dimension into the story, for all eyes turn toward the one before whom even eternal truth pales. Here entertaining dialogue functions in the service of religious instruction; furthermore, nothing demands a hypothesis of Greek origin for this exaltation of abstract truth.[21] The Israelite sages were certainly capable of praising abstract concepts like truth, righteousness, and wisdom.

BARUCH 3:9–4:4

A hymn in praise of wisdom occurs in Baruch 3:9–4:4, a text that probably originated during the first century BCE. It draws heavily on canonical language, imagery, and concepts, particularly Proverbs and Job, but it also borrows from Ben Sira. As a consequence of such extensive reliance upon earlier texts, this hymn signals no advance in sapiential reflection.

The similarity with Proverbs extends beyond the reference to the fountain of wisdom.

> Learn where there is wisdom,
>   where there is strength,
>   where there is understanding,
> so that you may at the same time discern
>   where there is length of days, and life,
>   where there is light for the eyes, and peace.
> (Bar. 3:14)

The connection between the hymn and Deuteronomy 30:12–14 and Job 28 is even more striking.

> Who has gone up into heaven, and taken her [wisdom],
>   and brought her down from the clouds?

>Who has gone over the sea, and found her,
>   and will buy her for pure gold?
>No one knows the way to her,
>   or is concerned about the path to her.
>But the one who knows all things knows her,
>   he found her by his understanding.
>   (Bar. 3:29–32a)

Although wisdom is inaccessible to humans, the God of Israel acquired her and bestowed her upon Jacob, another name for Israel, with whom she came to dwell. It follows that those people who claim to have achieved wisdom, the Edomites, for example, have not done so. The concluding verse of Job 28 lacks such a narrow understanding of wisdom as the sole possession of Israel. Like Ben Sira, this author identifies wisdom with the Mosaic torah.

>She is the book of the commandments of God,
>the law that endures forever.
>   (Bar. 4:1)

BEYOND THE APOCRYPHA

Speculation about the accessibility of wisdom increased in the intertestamental period. The author of *1 Enoch* alters Sirach's idea that wisdom searched for a place to reside until finally choosing Jerusalem; in the new version she could not find a suitable place anywhere on earth.

>Wisdom found no place where she might dwell;
>Then a dwelling-place was assigned her in the heavens.
>Wisdom went forth to make her dwelling among the children of men,
>and found no dwelling-place:
>Wisdom returned to her place,
>and took her seat among the angels.
>   (1 En. 42:1–2; *APOT*, 2:213)

This emphasis on the hiddenness of wisdom derives from a canonical text (Job 28:1–27) and finds expression in 2 Esdras 5:9b–10a.

>Then shall reason hide itself, and wisdom shall withdraw into its chamber,
>and it shall be sought by many but shall not be found.

Philo of Alexandria drew freely upon Wisdom literature; his fondness for this section of the Hebrew Bible is rivaled only by his love of the Torah.[22] The similarities between Philo's writings and Wisdom of Solomon are striking, although the resemblances occasion little surprise since both works came from the same general vicinity and date. Reflective mythology was completely at home in Philo's thought, and wisdom (*sophia*) was portrayed as mother, wife, lover, virgin, and bride; however, this heavenly hostess was also a symbol for evil, seduction, and carnal passion—as she was in Proverbs 9.

A long didactic poem from the first century BCE or CE attributed to the sixth-century philosopher Phocylides who lived in Miletus of Ionia is the work of a Jewish author.[23] *Pseudo-Phocylides* has 230 verses of gnomic wisdom, a type of saying highly valued by Hellenistic educators, especially Cynics. An introductory summary in verses 3–8 recalls the Decalogue, although it lacks any reference to the Sabbath or to idolatry but adds a criticism against homosexuality. The author emphasizes the pursuit of virtue, reflects on death and the afterlife (vv. 97–115), and addresses thematic concerns similar to those in Sirach. The cult of worship in the temple plays no significant role in *Pseudo-Phocylides*'s teaching; in this respect, the work resembles Proverbs and Ecclesiastes. The main concern, morality, links up with conventional wisdom from biblical times.

WISDOM TEXTS AT QUMRAN

The scrolls from the area of the Dead Sea contain several sapiential fragments and indicate that wisdom played an important role to the sectarians who preserved and/or composed this literature.[24] Fragments of canonical Proverbs (4Q102–3), Ecclesiastes (4Q109–10), Job (2Q15, 4Q99–101), and two Aramaic Targums of Job (4Q157, 11Q10) reveal their admiration for both types of Wisdom literature, proverbial sayings and reflective thought. In addition, fragments of Sirach (2Q18), together with Sirach 51:13–19a located in the Psalms Scroll (11Q5), as well as extensive fragments from Masada, reinforce this impression of fondness for wisdom texts. Several texts composed by the sectarians at Qumran attest to the widespread use of language commonly associated with sages: the *Rule of the Community*, *Damascus Document*, and *Thanksgiving Hymns (Hodayot)*. This use of sapiential language is remarkable, given the heightened emphasis on communal organization rather than individual virtues. Still, one should hardly be surprised to encounter such language with reference to God.

Four features of the sapiential texts composed by the sectarians of Qumran broaden the scope of interest in directions already indicated within conventional wisdom. They become more eschatological, heighten the erotic dimension associated with personified Wisdom, intensify the particularism made possible by Ben Sira's use of Israelite history as a special instance of guidance by wisdom, and attribute knowledge to revelation.

A long fragmentary text with an apocalyptic worldview, 4Q*Instruction* (1Q26; 4Q415–18, 423), uses the enigmatic expression *raz nihyeh* (the mystery that is yet to be) over twenty times. The term refers to God's control of history from beginning to end, with revealed truth limited to the elect. This deterministic text describes a final judgment as inevitable and implies a rational plan for history. Its interest in the cult does not extend to ritual purity or liturgical prayer. Surprisingly, this text addresses women (4Q415 2), but it does not appeal to personified

Wisdom. Its audience seems to be people of humble status. These farmers and artisans are promised eternal joy after death.

The *Book of Mysteries* (1Q27; 4Q299–301) has a scene in which the wicked are obliterated. Like 4Q*Instruction*, it is deterministic, emphasizes revelatory knowledge, and uses the term *raz nihyeh*. Before birth, the wicked were ordained to behave that way. By way of contrast, the good have their ears opened from above; even the punishment of the wicked is viewed as revealed knowledge. Like Qoheleth, this text uses rhetorical questions often. Its apocalyptic worldview includes a utopian transformation of the world.

The erotic dimension that was so prominent in Proverbs is continued in 4Q*Wiles of the Wicked Woman* (4Q184). This text never mentions personified Wisdom, nor does the woman ever explicitly invite lovers to sleep with her, not even to kiss her. It has little interest in teaching sexual ethics; instead, the woman represents wickedness and folly. Accordingly, she dwells in Sheol and her tents are in the midst of eternal flames. Those who escape her will enjoy astral immortality, for they resisted her efforts to keep them from observing torah. In short, "4Q184 transforms the Strange Woman from an alluring but dangerous married woman into a mythological figure of evil."[25]

The longest sapiential text from Qumran, 4Q*Sapiential Work* (4Q185), composed in six fragments, uses the threat of a fiery judgment to encourage an ethical life. Although it appears to associate wisdom with a woman, it has more interest in linking wisdom with torah. Anthological in style, it appeals to national history in a way that recalls Sirach, Wisdom of Solomon, and *Testaments of the Twelve Patriarchs*. Angels play an important role in apocalyptic literature, and the *mēbîn* (those who know) are encouraged to seize the day as in Ecclesiastes. At the same time, they are admonished to observe torah ("Listen to me, my sons, and do not rebel against the words of YHWH," 4Q185 1–2 ii 3). This use of the Tetragrammaton is rare in texts from Qumran. Extraordinary too is the language that knowledge goes forth from God, which resembles earlier views about *hokmâ* as being brought forth. Given the prominence of personified Wisdom in Proverbs 1–9, Sirach, and Wisdom of Solomon, its near-absence in 4Q185 is remarkable. Equally uncertain is the reference to Wisdom's yoke in this text despite its presence in Sirach and 4Q*Ways of Righteousness*. The wondrous deeds of salvation history do find ample space in 4Q185.

In 4Q*Words of the Maskil to All Sons of Dawn* (4Q298) the addressees are the same as those in the Damascus Document. In 4Q298 they are called "men of heart," an expression found in Job 34:10 and 34. There is no explicit claim to revelatory knowledge, and the people who are "dawning" from darkness to light seem to be completing a two-year probationary period. The use of dawn as a symbol for divine illumination in the *Hodayot* suggests, however, that the word in 4Q298 does not indicate inferior knowledge. The text is not sectarian, nor does it express interest in messianism, dualism, or halakah (legal torah).

Some interpreters consider 4Q*Ways of Righteousness* (4Q420–21) a sapiential text that brings together wisdom and halakah. No other sapiential text does. A practical wisdom text, 4Q424*Instruction*, advises on money and social inter-action. It contains twelve descriptions of negative types of people and six of positive types. The primary concern is promoting financial and social success, so much so that it is nearly devoid of theology. It has no interest in revelation, eschatology, or the angels.

The Torah is central to 4Q*Beatitudes* (4Q525), a text whose beginning resembles Proverbs 1:1–7. While the beatitudes usually appear alone or in pairs, a series of five does occur in 4Q525 2 ii + 3 just like those in Matthew 5:3–12. The erotically charged search for wisdom in Sirach is not replicated in 4Q*Beatitudes*. It has been said, "It is reasonable to suppose that if all of 4Q525 24 ii were available, it would be a wisdom poem similar to Sir 24."[26] Probably the product of an upper-class scribal milieu, 4Q525 encourages humility, a pure heart, and observance of torah.

When we pause to look at this brief account of sapiential texts from Qumran, we search in vain for collected proverbs, personified Wisdom as active speaker, mantic wisdom, and the major emphases of Job and Qoheleth, that is, theodicy and life's meaninglessness. Even the apocalyptic leanings here and there are over-shadowed by the texts that emphasize knowledge by empirical observation and the possibility of maintaining the social fabric.

RABBINIC WISDOM

The Mishnaic tractate *Pirke Aboth* (*Sayings of the Fathers*), attributed to Judah the Prince and dating around 200 CE, although containing earlier sayings, has often been compared to the book of Proverbs and Ecclesiastes because of its high number of ethical admonitions and occasional aphorisms. The fifth chapter seems weighted toward the academy. For example, 5:10 gives seven characteris-tics of a sage, stating that their absence identifies a person as uneducated. These admirable traits acknowledge the need to show deference to one who excels in wisdom, to think carefully before speaking, to follow proper protocol, and above all to maintain integrity. Types of students occasion comments in 5:15, 17, and 18. The necessity of embodying wisdom underlies the distinctions in 5:17 among students: one who merely attends the place of learning, one who exhibits wisdom without attending the house of the wise, one who both attends and embodies the teachings, and one who neither goes nor performs virtuous deeds. The similes in 5:18 describe the various capacities of students to grasp and retain what is being taught: a sponge, a funnel, a strainer, and a sieve. Similarly, 5:15 applies a temporal standard in assessing four types of students: quick to learn and quick to lose, slow to learn and slow to lose, quick to learn and slow to lose, slow to learn and quick to lose.

The fourth chapter also comments on the task of identifying the person who is truly wise. According to 4:1, a wise person realizes that every individual has something to teach others. Paradoxically, it notes that the really strong person is one who controls passions, as stated in Proverbs 16:32. The motive for learning underlies *Aboth* 4:6, which praises the one who learns in order to do the teachings over the person whose only goal is to be an instructor. The exalted status of one's teacher is affirmed in 4:15, and his heavy responsibility comes to expression in 4:16. Aphoristic wisdom occurs in 4:20 ("Be first in greeting every man; and be a tail to lions and not a head to foxes"). In 4:22 a "better" saying appears, and an admonition in 4:23 insists on doing the timely thing. The advantages of learning during youth and disadvantages of putting off education until old age form the advice in 4:25, while a more positive attitude to old age occurs in 4:26, the fact that years of experience help one attain true wisdom. Hence, it suggests, trying to learn from young people is a mistake.

At least two sayings express harsh criticism of the wise, a term in this tractate for the rabbinic teachers. "All my days I have grown up among the Wise, and I have not found anything better for one than silence; and not study is the chief thing but action; and whoso multiplies words occasions sin" (1:17). Rabbi Eliezer, who was excommunicated by his colleagues, concludes the saying in 2:15 with these words: "and warm thyself at the fire of the Wise, and beware of their glowing coal lest thou be scorched. For their bite is the bite of a fox, and their sting the sting of a scorpion, and their hiss the hiss of a serpent, and all their words like coals of fire."[27]

EARLY CHRISTIAN WISDOM

Within the New Testament, wisdom traditions made a significant impact— from Q, the oldest collection of Jesus' sayings,[28] to hymnic texts in the Pauline corpus. Although Q has been understood against the background of Hellenistic wisdom, there is no need to do so, for Jewish sapiential literature provides an adequate milieu for this material.[29] In this document Jesus and John were viewed as Wisdom's sons and prophets. Matthew develops this idea further, interpreting Jesus as the sender of prophets, wise men, and scribes. In short, for Matthew Jesus was the incarnation of wisdom and embodiment of torah. Therefore, he can speak as wisdom does in Sirach 51:26–27; "Come to me. . . . My yoke is easy, and my burden is light" (Matt. 11:28–30).[30]

In Colossians 1:15–17 the hymnic description of Jesus is indebted to the praise of Wisdom in Proverbs 8:22–31. Both Jesus and Wisdom are thought to have been the firstborn of creation; still, a difference stands out here. Wisdom observes God at work but Jesus is said to be actively involved in beginnings, the very image of the invisible God. The monumental move from *ḥokmâ* to *sophia* and eventually to *logos* made it possible to identify Jesus with *ḥokmâ* and therefore to attribute to him all former qualities of Wisdom.

The Pauline corpus implies that the negative aspects of wisdom threatened the unity of the Christian fellowship. Perhaps an organized school of wisdom at Ephesus introduced excessive rhetoric and uncontrolled speculation, prompting

Paul's assertion that God alone is wise (1 Cor. 1:18ff.).[31] In any event, Gnostic speculation certainly surfaces within the early Christian community. In the *Gospel of Thomas* from Nag Hammadi Jesus appears as a teacher of salvific knowledge. Accordingly, his teachings are introduced by the formula, "Jesus says." From the other perspective, ethical Jewish maxims undoubtedly influenced the author of James,[32] and the Johannine prologue describes Jesus as the *logos* incarnate. In Stoic philosophy the *logos* represented the rational principle of the universe, whereas in John it stands for the divine revelation itself.

How do these understandings of Jesus as divine Wisdom accord with sapiential literature? One way of answering this question is to examine the philosophical premise of sages. The principle of similarity—that humans were fundamentally like deity—was accepted by them just as it was by everyone else in the ancient world.[33] Mortals were made in the divine image, to use the language of Genesis 1:26–27 that finally entered sapiential discourse with Ben Sira. When transcendent realities were involved such belief allowed sages to use analogies drawn from what was accessible to eye and ear. A dual aspect, likeness to Deity and kinship with dust, made mortals the object of intellectual ambivalence issuing either in praise as in Psalm 8 or in satire as in Job 7:17–21. The human desire to overcome this ambivalence gave rise to legends about superhuman attempts to become gods. In Mesopotamia a certain Adapa, the most pefect of mortals, comes close to achieving membership in this exclusive club, only to be tricked by Ea, the god of wisdom, into refusing to partake of the food of the gods. Similarly, the mythic first couple in the garden of Eden lost access to the tree of life, the fruit of which would have made them immortal. Gilgamesh, too, laid aside a leaf from the tree of life long enough to go for a swim, only to watch a serpent devour it and shed its skin, now rejuvenated. Nevertheless, the challenge to be like God became a Levitical injunction (Lev. 11:44–45).

Two things render this command ironic. First, the gods themselves were believed to be subject to death, and at least one psalm reflects such a belief in ancient Israel ("I thought, 'You are gods, all of you, sons of Elyon'; therefore you will die like Adam, fall like one of the princes," Ps. 82:6–7). Second, rising above self-absorption was impossible. A low opinion of mortals was widespread, ranging from the belief that the gods of creation endowed them with lies, according to the *Babylonian Theodicy*, to the bald statement in Jeremiah 17:9 that the human mind is either sick or perverse.

These attenuations of the principle of similarity shaped theological discourse and undergirded the concept of reward and retribution. Human ideals were assumed to have been divine ones as well, although breaches of moral behavior by Yahweh brought much agitation and ultimately led to emphasis on divine hiddenness. Divine mystery thus generated various means of penetrating the cloud of unknowing.

Confrontations with an alien deity forced individuals to question that assumed principle of similarity. The sufferer in *I Will Praise the Lord of Wisdom* concludes that ignorance prevails where the will of the gods is concerned. Similarly, the

author of the book of Job has the hero experience a Deity who resembles nothing Job has ever imagined. Qoheleth goes one step further than that taken by the
Joban author. He hurls a rhetorical question into the air: "Who knows?"

Into the void created by the collapse of belief in the Deity's predictable conduct, based on analogy with humans, came mediators, variously called *ḥokmâ*,
one in a thousand, or angels. The resulting confusion created by divine mystery
provided a matrix for an emerging worldview, one not based on calculating
morality. The moral breakthrough achieved by the book of Job can be described
by a single word, first introduced by the Adversary and used later by Yahweh.
That word is *ḥinnām*, "for nothing." In short, true allegiance to God calcu-
lates neither reward nor punishment. Such love is wholly disinterested. To this
breakthrough must be added another, this one from the most unlikely source,
Qoheleth. For him, all existence is *hebel*, futile. The primary issue is not morality; it is meaning, hence philosophy. From here it is a small step to epistemological agnosticism.

Worldviews are not easily overturned; witness the efforts by Ben Sira and
Wisdom of Solomon to recover traditional understandings of reality. Even
divine mystery comes under the umbrella of eschatology at Qumran, for the
raz nihyeh (mystery that is to be) promises hope for the faithful. Moreover, the
mediating *logos* in Wisdom of Solomon, together with *ḥokmâ*, offer a way to
restore the similarity between mortals and god. What is lacking? A divine figure
in flesh and blood.

In this person as depicted by the Gospels the decisive breakthroughs do not
fare well. True, a few narratives indicate acceptance of gratuitous love (*ḥinnām*):
the innocent Galileans executed by Pilate, the eighteen unfortunates on whom
a tower fell (Luke 13:2–5), the blind man (John 9:1–3), the sun's rays that fall
indiscriminately, and the readiness of the heavenly Father to forgive. This hint
of *ḥinnām* love is dwarfed by the dominance of the retributive theme: exhortations to earn divine favor and threats of hellfire.

Hebel thinking fared no better. Qoheleth's sense of grand absurdity left no
place for manipulative behavior by humans, however selfless the act. In his view,
one could not depend on a rational response from God. In light of the passion,
such a dark view should have appealed to early Christians struggling to make
sense of Jesus' death. The marvel is that they refused to cast their eyes "under
the sun" but relied on apocalyptic hopes that abandoned locative spirituality for
the utopian.

For all they knew, Jesus was entangled in the same web that chance had
thrown over the sages. Like them, he tried to unite justice and mercy in his
understanding of God. Like them, too, he found that task impossible. However
sublime the concept of gratuitous (*ḥinnām*) love may have been, it had an unwelcome corollary: the total loss of a bargaining chip when finally ushered into the
divine presence. And however true *hebel* thinking rang in death's shadow, it left
individuals without hope. The Gospel writers believed that the God who raised
Jesus from the grave could be trusted to make all things new; they grounded

this conviction in a worldview burdened by retributive morality and a utopian escape from reality. In doing so, they cast their vote for the principle of similarity and remained oblivious to the epistemological revolution ushered in by the unknown authors of Job and Ecclesiastes.

Two early sapiential works outside the New Testament reveal the continuing appeal of this type of thinking, namely the *Sentences of Sextus*[34] and the *Teachings of Silvanus*.[35] The former consists of over four hundred proverbial-type maxims setting forth the ideal life for Christians. These nuggets of learning also functioned to inculcate morals; that is, they served as instruments of moral transformation. Unlike Sextus, Silvanus engages in mystic-theosophical reflection.[36] Both authors are non-Jewish in their inspiration, although similarities with Israelite wisdom certainly occur. Silvanus, like Philo, resembles Wisdom of Solomon; metaphysics, not experience, lies behind his motive clauses and exhortations. Such sages have come a long way from the early proverbs, which drew practical lessons from daily experience. The endless quest has widened its net to feed an unquenchable appetite like Sheol's.

NOTES

1. David Winston, *The Wisdom of Solomon* (AB 43; Garden City, N.Y.: Doubleday, 1979), 23–25, argues for a date during the reign of Gaius (Caligula) (37–41 CE). See also G. Bellia, "Historical and Anthropological Reading of the Book of Wisdom," in Deuterocanonical and Cognate Literature Yearbook 2005: *The Book of Wisdom in Modern Research*, ed. Giuseppe Bellia and Angelo Passaro (Berlin: de Gruyter, 2005), 83–111; Helmut Engel, *Das Buch der Weisheit* (Neuer Stuttgarter Kommentar: Altes Testament 16; Stuttgart: Katholisches Bibelwerk, 1998); and Maurice Gilbert, "Sagesse de Solomon (ou Livre de la Sagesse)," in *DBSup* 9:58–119.
2. James M. Reese, *Hellenistic Influence on the Book of Wisdom and Its Consequences* (AnBib 41; Rome: Biblical Institute, 1970).
3. Morna McGlynn, *Divine Judgment and Divine Benevolence in the Book of Wisdom* (WUNT 2/139; Tübingen: Mohr Siebeck, 2001), investigates what she calls a "Mercy Dialogue" in Wis. 11:15–12:27. She argues that two principles are used in it to explain God's treatment of the wicked: (1) measure, number, and weight; and (2) little by little.
4. Many interpreters think the author has Qoheleth in mind, but Skehan, *Studies in Israelite Poetry and Wisdom*, 213–36, especially 228, disputes this claim. He writes: "Ecclesiastes is not, therefore, the typical hedonist whom Wis[dom] is arraigning; nor is there any real warrant from the language employed for supposing that Wis[dom] is concerned with deliberate misuse of the doctrine of Eccl[esiastes]." If Qoheleth is the ultimate source of these ideas, the author of Wisdom has distorted his teachings.
5. Maurice Gilbert, *La critique des dieux dans le livre de la Sagesse* (AnBib 53; Rome: Pontifical Biblical Institute, 1973); and von Rad, *Wisdom in Israel*, 177–85.
6. On this image, see *The Divine Helmsman: Studies on God's Control of Human Events Presented to Lou H. Silberman*, ed. James L. Crenshaw and Samuel Sandmel (New York: Ktav, 1980). John J. Collins, "The Biblical Precedent for Natural Theology," *JAAR* 45/1, Sup. B (1977): 35–67, has perceived the

underlying idea in this discussion of the cosmos's witness to its Creator. See also James Barr, *Biblical Faith and Natural Theology* (Oxford: Clarendon, 1993).

7. See Alan Mendelson, *Secular Education in Philo of Alexandria* (MHUC 7; Cincinnati: Hebrew Union College, 1982), for discussion of Greek education.

8. See Reese, *Hellenistic Influence*; Perdue, *Sword and Stylus*, 292–355; and Collins, *Jewish Wisdom in the Hellenistic Age*, 178–221.

9. Winston, *Wisdom of Solomon*, e.g., 14–18, 62–63, makes a strong case against the thesis of Hebraic sources for the book.

10. For traditions regarding Enoch, see James C. VanderKam, *Enoch: A Man for All Generations* (Columbia: University of South Carolina, 1995). The centrality of death in Wisdom of Solomon has been shown by Michael Kolarcik, *The Ambiguity of Death in the Book of Wisdom 1–6: A Study of Literary Structure and Interpretation* (AnBib 127; Rome: Biblical Institute, 1991). See also George Nickelsburg, *Resurrection, Immortality, and Eternal Life in Intertestamental Judaism* (HTS 26; Cambridge: Harvard University, 1972).

11. I question the genre in "Wisdom Psalms?" *Currents in Research: Biblical Studies* 8 (2000): 9–17; while J. Kenneth Kuntz defends it in "Reclaiming Biblical Wisdom Psalms: A Response to Crenshaw," *Currents in Biblical Research* 1 (2003): 145–54; and idem, "Wisdom Psalms and the Shaping of the Hebrew Psalter," in *For a Later Generation: The Transforming of Tradition in Israel, Early Judaism, and Early Christianity*, ed. R. A. Argall (Harrisburg: Trinity Press International, 2003), 144–60. Manfred Oeming, "Wisdom as a Hermeneutical Key to the Book of Psalms," *Scribes, Sages, and Seers*, 154–62, attributes a decisive role to wisdom, at least by interpretation.

12. See James L. Crenshaw, "The Journey from Voluntary to Obligatory Silence (Reflections on Psalm 39 and Qoheleth)," forthcoming in a Festschrift for Douglas A. Knight.

13. Otto Kaiser, "Psalm 39," in *Gottes und der Menschen Weisheit: Gesammelte Aufsätze* (BZAW 261; Berlin: de Gruyter, 1998), 71–83.

14. Jacob Klein, "The 'Bane' of Humanity: A Lifespan of One Hundred Twenty Years," *Acta Sumerologica* 12 (1990): 57–70.

15. Brevard S. Childs, *Isaiah and the Assyrian Crisis* (SBT 2/3; London: SCM, 1967), 128–36.

16. Leo Perdue, "The Riddles of Psalm 49," *JBL* 93 (1974): 533–42.

17. Ernst Würthwein, "Erwägungen zu Psalm 73," *Wort und Existenz? Studien zum Alten Testament* (Göttingen: Vandenhoeck & Ruprecht, 1970), 161–78; Martin Buber, "The Heart Determines," *On the Bible* (New York: Schocken, 1968), 199–210; J. Luyten, "Psalm 73 and Wisdom," in *La Sagesse de l'Ancien Testament*, ed. Gilbert, 59–81; James F. Ross, "Psalm 73," in *Israelite Wisdom*, ed. Gammie et al., 161–75; and Crenshaw, *Whirlpool of Torment*, 93–109, reprinted in *The Psalms: An Introduction* (Grand Rapids: Eerdmans, 2001), 109–27.

18. Harry Torczyner (Tur Sinai), "The Riddle in the Bible," *HUCA* 1 (1924): 125–49.

19. I have discussed these traditions in "The Contest of Darius' Guards," in *Images of Man and God: The Old Testament Short Story in Literary Focus*, ed. Burke O. Long (BLS 1; Sheffield: Almond Press, 1981), 74–88 (*UAPQ* 222–34).

20. Paul Humbert, "'Magna est veritas et prevalet' (3 Esra 4:35)," *OLZ* 31 (1928): 148–50.

21. Karl-Friedrich Pöhlmann, *Studien zum Dritten Esra* (FRLANT 104; Göttingen: Vandenhoeck & Ruprecht, 1970), 37–52.

22. Jean Laporte, "Philo in the Tradition of Biblical Wisdom Literature," in *Aspects of Wisdom in Judaism and Early Christianity*, ed. Robert L. Wilken

(Notre Dame: University of Notre Dame, 1975), 135. On Philo in general, see Samuel Sandmel, *Philo of Alexandria: An Introduction* (New York: Oxford University, 1979).

23. Collins, *Jewish Wisdom in the Hellenistic Age*, 158–77; Max Küchler, *Frühjüdische Weisheitstraditionen* (OBO 26; Freiburg: Universitätsverlag, 1979), 236–302; and P. W. van der Horst, "Pseudo-Phocylides," in *The Old Testament Pseudepigrapha*, ed. James H. Charlesworth, 2:565–82 (Garden City, N.Y.: Doubleday, 1985).

24. See Daniel J. Harrington, *Wisdom Texts from Qumran* (London: Routledge, 1997); and Matthew J. Goff, *Discerning Wisdom: The Sapiential Literature of the Dead Sea Scrolls* (VTSup 116; Leiden: Brill, 2007). In discussing these texts, my indebtedness to Harrington and Goff is huge. I have followed Goff's delineation of sapiential texts with the exception of "wisdom psalms," for which the evidence is slim. Even in some others discussed above, the wisdom features are not very extensive.

25. Goff, *Discerning Wisdom*, 121.

26. Ibid., 217.

27. R. Travers Herford, *Pirke Aboth: The Ethics of the Talmud: Sayings of the Fathers* (1945; reprint, New York: Schocken, 1962), 55.

28. James M. Robinson, "*Logoi Sophon*: On the Gattung of Q," in *Trajectories Through Early Christianity*, ed. Robinson and Helmut Koester (Philadelphia: Fortress, 1971), 71–113. Also published in *The Future of Our Religious Past: Essays in Honor of Rudolf Bultmann*, ed. James M. Robinson (New York: Harper & Row, 1971), 84–130.

29. M. Jack Suggs, *Wisdom, Christology, and Law in Matthew's Gospel* (Cambridge: Harvard University, 1970), 5–29, especially 12–13.

30. Ibid., 130. Suggs writes: "The Jesus who meets us in Q as *sophos* and 'child of wisdom' brings truth to men; he is the mediator of divine revelation. The Jesus who meets us in Matthew retains his functions as teacher and revealer, but he is no longer merely a prophet (albeit the last and greatest) of Sophia. He is Wisdom and that means, as well, that he is the embodiment of Torah" (p. 127).

31. Birger A. Pearson, "Hellenistic-Jewish Wisdom Speculation and Paul," in *Aspects of Wisdom*, ed. Wilken, 43–66.

32. Luke Timothy Johnson, *The Letter of James* (AB 37A; New York: Doubleday, 1995), 33–34.

33. Karel van der Toorn, "Sources in Heaven: Revelation as a Scholarly Construct in Second Temple Judaism," in *Kein Land für sich allein: Studien zum Kulturkontakt in Kanaan, Israel/Palästina und Ebirnâri für Manfred Weippert zum 65. Geburtstag*, ed. Ulrich Hübner and Ernst Axel Knauf (OBO 186; Freiburg: Universitätsverlag, 2002), 265–77, has argued that the collapse of a worldview based on the principle that the gods resembled humans led to the idea of revelation and elitism.

34. Robert L. Wilken, "Wisdom and Philosophy in Early Christianity," in *Aspects of Wisdom*, 143–68.

35. William R. Schoedel, "Jewish Wisdom and the Formation of the Christian Ascetic," in ibid., 169–99.

36. Elisabeth Schüssler Fiorenza, "Wisdom Mythology and the Christological Hymns of the New Testament," in ibid., 17–41.

Chapter 8

The Reciprocating Touch
Knowledge of God in Wisdom Literature

The title of this chapter, "The Reciprocating Touch," is inspired by Michelangelo's painting of the creation of Adam that adorns a small but central section of the Sistine Chapel. The primary figures, God and Adam, are a lesson in contrasts, despite the similarity in bodily form. A clothed Ancient of Days, with gray hair and beard, is flanked by eleven angels, all cherubic except for a single wide-eyed and slightly older one. The divine right arm extends toward Adam, the index finger poised for the anticipated moment of touch. God's left arm rests on the neck and shoulders of the only angel who is attentive to the unprecedented appearance of a creature in God's image. Who is this nubile figure?

Students of Michelangelo's masterpiece have proposed four possibilities: (1) Lilith in late Jewish folklore; (2) Wisdom as described in Proverbs 8:22–31; (3) Eve in the divine mind; and (4) Mary the Mother of Jesus.

Some interpreters think the young girl represents a female who was linked romantically with Yahweh in popular imagination. Harsh denunciations of the worship of a goddess in the Bible did not prevent Jewish citizens on the Egyptian border at Elephantine from worshiping two different female deities alongside Yahweh. Nor did they dissuade Jews from imagining a female companion for

Yahweh at the fortified city Khirbet el-Qom in the Judean hills. Therefore the identification of the young girl as Lilith cannot be dismissed out of hand.[1]

Other critics view the girl in Michelangelo's painting as a depiction of *ḥokmâ*, a fully fleshed out persona in Proverbs 8:22–31. The erotic language of dancing before the Creator to bring delight resembles similar attributions of the Egyptian goddess of right order, Ma'at. Echoes of language pertaining to this goddess have made their way into the book of Proverbs elsewhere, strengthening this interpretation of Michelangelo's painting.[2]

Still others believe that the attentive girl among the other cherubs stands for the unformed first woman. Nevertheless, in the next frame the newly created Eve is a mature woman, not a youthful female. For this reason the identification of the girl as Eve does not seem likely.[3]

Another group of critics consider the pubescent child Michelangelo's way of introducing Mary[4] into the painting. In light of popular veneration of her during Michelangelo's lifetime, this identification of the extraordinary female has much to commend it. Whether *ḥokmâ* or Mary, the two most credible suggestions, this beautiful girl who exudes pristine innocence momentarily diverts attention from the focus of the painting, the creation of Adam. Although another angel clings to God's arm, and the divine hand rests loosely on the shoulders of a third angel, these two do not claim the attention that the other one does. A cloth enshrouds the entire heavenly retinue, almost like swaddling clothes. It is as if the angels are Purity personified.

Astonishingly, God's physique is less muscular than Adam's, whose pose is almost casual. Adam's left leg is bent at the knee, his left foot resting under his right thigh. Complete nakedness reveals genitalia and, unexplainably, given the biblical account, a navel.[5] Adam is clean-shaven and his short hair is well groomed. Most surprisingly, his left arm is relaxed, resting on his knee; the index finger droops rather than eagerly straining to touch God's extended finger. Adam's eyes match the passive stance of his posture, suggesting rousing from slumber if not outright reluctance.

This painting leaves no doubt about Michelangelo's desire to ascribe the initiative to God, which is the only way it could be when envisioning human origins. That understanding accords with the usual description of the way knowledge of God is acquired too.[6] In a word, it is believed to be entirely the result of divine self-revelation, a lifting of the veil that ordinarily hides the source of all things from view. That may well be the way most of the Bible formulates an answer to the simple question: Whence our knowledge of transcendence? In that sense, Karl Barth's emphatic no to natural theology, defended by Emil Brunner, was more biblical than the position Barth rejected with a forceful *Nein*. Their way of stating the issue is now seen as inadequate, for James Barr is undoubtedly correct that all revelation falls under the category of special.[7] That assessment applies both to sacred literature and to the book of nature.

Barth's answer is not, however, the one most scholars have gleaned from Wisdom literature.[8] In this literary corpus, a passive Adam has roused from partial slumber and has stretched his mind, if not his index finger, to illuminate the darkness of the heavens, and failing that, to make some sense of observable phenomena. The reluctance that occurs here takes place in the divine arena, with a rare exception, and a rival, Ḥokmâ, is born from God's passivity. In what follows, I shall evaluate this widespread assumption about the sages' view of how they came to know about the Creator.

What prompted this turn toward biblical wisdom? Traditional theology was, in the language of Brevard Childs, "in crisis," a word that is often used loosely.[9] Still, many considered religious belief altogether bankrupt.[10] An inability to believe in the existence of God rested uneasily with a reluctance to surrender faith entirely. That unease is illustrated beautifully in two poems by the Nobel laureate Czeslaw Milosz, whose Catholic nurturing lingered in old age, almost against his will.

Believing, like many others, that God is nothing more than a figment of a fertile human imagination, a construct exalting people as made in the divine image and little less than deity, Milosz prefers skeptical philosophy but still recites the Christian confession of faith although, to quote him, "I know that my belief has no justification." In his view, atheism brings little comfort. Instead, it imposes an obligation not to sadden others by declaring one's lack of belief. His language reveals the moral power of biblical theism, at least for him, for he insists that those who reside in a godless world are obligated to one another ethically. In his words, "He is still his brother's keeper."[11]

For Milosz, the death of God has ethical ramifications because of ordinary people's need for the comfort inherent to belief in God. The threat of nonbeing forces many who stare death in the face to imagine that their lives amount to nothing. The thought of a compassionate deity who can make their achievements permanent and validate their morality brings hope and sustains them while they await the grim reaper. In recent years, those dealing with the dying in hospitals and hospices are becoming sensitive to the power of spiritual grounding in patients.[12] In some instances, even skeptics have recognized the healing power of prayer.

The collapse of traditional biblical theology was but a pale reflection of the intellectual tradition in the West, where philosophy and the social sciences offered multiple explanations for belief in a higher being, none very flattering. With the perceived implausibility of the earlier ontological, cosmological, and teleological arguments for the existence of a higher being, the focus shifted earthward to the moral consciousness with Immanuel Kant, to the human mind with Sigmund Freud and Ludwig Feuerbach, to society at large and the prevailing culture with Emile Durkheim, and even to the collective psyche with Carl Jung. Still, the longing for God and the images concocted out of this desire were believed by thinkers like Paul Tillich and Martin Heidegger to point to a reality beyond the traditional God. To some degree God became a symbol for intentionality in a transcendent realm, a Ground of Being rather than a personal entity with whom one could enter into a meaningful relationship. For Julian Huxley, these explanations concentrated exclusively on human beings. He therefore considered nature to be the only access to any knowledge of God.[13]

Among theologians, Barth's intellectual stature and voluminous literary productivity made it virtually impossible for others to introduce the sapiential understanding of knowledge into theological discourse. Only gradually did the recovery of insights from Wisdom literature begin to challenge the dominant view. An attitude that had been cavalierly labeled idolatry eventually presented itself as worthy of consideration: the study of natural phenomena and human experience yields precious knowledge about its Creator.

We are left, then, with two grand books, Scripture and nature. Neither, however, is self-validating. For this reason, the claim that the Bible is the word of God falls into the category of testimony, necessitating a Kierkegaardian leap of faith. Scripture therefore requires interpretation no less than do the insights that the wise gleaned from observing reality. That is why so much energy throughout history has been devoted to developing a suitable hermeneutic for the synagogue and the church.

To be sure, the biblical sages differed among themselves, even when treating the matter of knowledge about God. Just as prophets held varying views on many things, and priests differed among themselves, the wise who composed Proverbs, Job, Ecclesiastes, Sirach, and Wisdom of Solomon represent both positions outlined above.[14] Nevertheless, their emphasis on the human pursuit of knowledge virtually mutes the opposite understanding of a self-revealing creator.

REVELATION OR DISCOVERY?

Job 38:1–41:34

To answer the above question, we turn to a second portrait, this one drawn with words rather than with brush, paint, and selected tints. Here too the artist focuses our attention on two figures, the combative creator of the universe and a weary Job. Weakened both physically and emotionally by cruel blows from a heavenly adversary and from erstwhile friends, he is still able to gather his last ounce of strength in order to challenge the judge of the universe to set things right.[15] Here the initiative comes from below, the response from above.

A host of created bodies, none born of woman, surrounds these two prominent figures. Some of these have no breath at all, although they have an existence of their own. In this group are the foundations of the earth, the celestial wonders—stars, sun, moon, planets—thunder and lightning, snow and ice, morning and night, the clouds, rain and the rolling sea. Other secondary figures comprise members of the predatory animal kingdom, specifically lions, mountain goats, wild asses and oxen, the ostrich and the war-horse, as well as winged creatures consisting of eagles, ravens, and hawks that soar high above. In a prominent panel, two monstrous creatures vie for the center of attention on this canvas.

They bear mysterious names, Leviathan and Behemoth, and remotely resemble the hippopotamus and the crocodile, mythic representatives of chaos in ancient Egypt.

Like the Canaanite god Baal, Yahweh the Creator rides on the wings of a tempest, its mighty winds roaring like the angry sea and reflecting the mood of its rider. The scene is overwhelmingly dark, except for a dazzling streak of light within the storm cloud. An open mouth suggests a booming voice, full of authority and intent on deflating a lowly Job, who stands with a defiant finger pointed in the direction of the whirlwind. His anguished face is flushed from rage and mortification.

In the scene the prevailing understanding of Yahweh's self-disclosure outside Wisdom literature has spilled over into the book of Job, although the content divulged here has little in common with revelation elsewhere in the Bible. Instead of demanding obedience in all realms of life, the divine speeches from the tempest communicate knowledge about meteorology and animals that have not fallen under the control of humans. The only allusions to people emphasize their ignorance of the habits of these independent creatures and inability to subdue the proud, whom the mighty Leviathan and Behemoth symbolize. The sole link between these speeches and revelation elsewhere in the Bible is the idea of the Creator.

Job 4:12–21

The gifted artist who drew the picture of the Creator and a lone subject against the backdrop of nature's fury also painted a captivating scene that describes another revelatory moment. This time, however, the two figures are less clearly delineated. In fact, the heavenly one is represented by images resembling a ghost, while the human recipient of the revelation lies in bed. In this portrait, the initiative comes from the spirit who enters the house like a thief and conceals its identity in a nightmare. The scene has two figures, only one of whom is active. The other awakes from slumber and is frightened by the ghostlike visitor. Across the whole canvas wavelike lines suggest movement, broken momentarily but nevertheless preventing observers from discerning distinctive facial characteristics.

This text could easily have appeared in prophetic literature either from the Bible or from Mari in the eighteenth century BCE.[16] The brief anecdote, shimmering with mystery, is narrated by Eliphaz to give his argument additional authority. It describes a scary moment of sleepless reflection when a specter intruded momentarily on his private space and then abruptly departed, leaving behind a whispered question: "Can a human be more righteous than Eloah, or can a man be purer than his Maker?" (4:17, my trans.).[17]

The mysterious nature of the ghostly appearance dominates the entire scene. Its language is calculated to increase the eerie nature of the visit: stolen, whisper, troubled thoughts, nocturnal visions, deep sleep, terror and dread, shaking bones, spirit gliding on the face, hair bristling, stood, form, appearance, voice.

The wholly unexpected experience rules out oneiromancy, the ancient science of interpreting dreams, and incubation, the practice of sleeping at a sacred place in the hope of receiving a secret revelation from a deity, as Solomon did at the shrine in Gibeon. Both of these efforts to obtain immediacy with a deity imply human initiative and anticipated response, neither of which applies here.

The word for "deep sleep," *tardēmâ* (v. 13), recalls other stories about an anesthetized Adam during the "birth" of Eve (Gen. 2:21), Abraham's drowsiness when Yahweh "cut" a promissory covenant (Gen. 15:12), and Jonah's heavy repose in a ship's hull during a violent storm (Jonah 1:5), all of which have this rare word for deep sleep. The word for a "silence" or hushed stillness, *dĕmāmâ* (Job 4:16), in this instance preceding a voice, evokes Elijah's experience of a theophany on Mount Carmel when Yahweh responds to a dejected prophet (1 Kgs. 19:17–18). That story, too, has the heavenly visitor dash expectations. Who would have thought that Yahweh would appear in the stillness of a whisper rather than in an earthquake, a fire, or a mighty wind?

The subtle ways by which the authors of Job and Ecclesiastes guide readers to the broader canon make it difficult to determine whether a definite allusion occurs. In them, a mere linguistic hint links their thoughts to other literature. That is not true of Ben Sira and Wisdom of Solomon. The former actually names heroes of the past,[18] whereas the latter openly refers to a number of individuals from Israel's narrative tradition without identifying them. His rhetorical technique implies familiarity with the canon on the part of readers.

Returning to the scene as reported by Eliphaz, we note that he applies the word for "deep sleep" to humans in general, but stresses the personal nature of the experience with the word *wĕʾēlay*, "and to me," in the initial position (v. 12). His choice of a passive form of the verb *gānab*, which usually indicates the action of a thief, depicts the element of surprise. It also connotes something done to him for which he has no suitable defense. The Greek translation in the Septuagint, "It rendered him immobile," varies the description to emphasize the impact of the theophany on Eliphaz. This version is hardly apt for one who is presumably lying in bed. By using *rûaḥ* (spirit), the author guards against attributing human features to the Deity, whose nature is mysterious. According to Numbers 12:8, only Moses was privileged to behold Yahweh as one confronts another being, that is, face to face.

Not everyone held this restrictive view of divine hiddenness,[19] as stories about Abraham and Jacob demonstrate. In them, Abraham entertains three visitors, one of whom is Yahweh (Genesis 18), and Jacob is said to have wrestled with God at a place that he names Peniel (Genesis 32). In all of these stories, however, mystery remains, a point made effectively by the remark about a spirit tarrying before Eliphaz but defying recognition. The resurrection appearances of Jesus in the Gospels use a similar rhetorical device to distance him from an earlier manifestation. Even his closest disciples did not recognize him in the various accounts of his appearances after the fateful events at Calvary.

The argument in Job 4:18–21 moves from the greater to the lesser, specifically from angels to mortals. The basis for Eliphaz's low opinion of supraterrestrial servants is probably a myth of fallen angels like that lying behind the story of a union between the "sons of God" and women in Genesis 6:1–4, of which later traditionists made much, or the fall of the Day Star in Isaiah 14:12–20 (cf. Ezek. 28:12–19), later identified with Satan and immortalized as Lucifer by John Milton. To some extent the characterization of the Adversary in the prologue to the book of Job accords with Eliphaz's concept of heavenly beings, even if his function in the plot can be understood to be less adversarial than is implied in the New Testament and later Jewish and Christian thought.[20] Nevertheless, Eliphaz views humans as burdened with guilt that destroys them in the span of a half day, from morning to evening. The reversal of the usual sequence, from evening to morning, carries dramatic force. In this view, the daylight hours, normally safer than the hours of darkness, when danger lurks in hidden places, are transformed into a perilous time by the power of sin.

The same order occurs in Psalm 90:5–6, where the image begins with the vulnerability during the night when dreams invade one's slumber but ends with the simile of fading grass in the evening. This phenomenon of the sun's relentless rays scorching grass that flourishes early was all too familiar in the Near East. Eliphaz mentions houses of clay, reminiscent of the Yahwistic story of the Deity's fashioning Adam from moistened clay, a form of creation also attested in Egyptian and Mesopotamian literature.[21] The juxtaposition of the words "foundation" and "dust" is oxymoronic, for dust is even less stable than sand. For Eliphaz, the return to dust is in the final analysis beyond human ken, almost in the same way his use of a moth and tent-cord defy understanding. Surely, he did not consider humans more ephemeral than a moth, and the dual sense of the word rendered "tent-cord" or "excellence" is appropriate before the expression "devoid of wisdom." Four verbs spell the end: crushed, destroyed, plucked up, die. Here is no ambiguity. Death is certain.

Curiously, Eliphaz uses the singular "word" to signify the message whispered in his ear, but this use for an oracle consisting of multiple words has prophetic precedent, for example, "The word of Yahweh that came to Hosea" (Hos. 1:1). The rhetorical question leaves an indelible print on the argument that follows, first in Job's variant, then in Eliphaz's second speech, and finally in Bildad's third discourse. The first instance of these rhetorical questions about divine justice, in Job 9:2, uses an altogether different preposition, one that implies presence with someone: "Truly, I know that it is so; how then can a person be just before ('im) El?" (my trans.). This formulation seems aimed at Eliphaz, who construed Job's complaint as proof that he considered himself more righteous than Eloah. Perhaps this deduction arises from Job's stinging attack against Eloah, charges that are justified by the narrative itself.[22]

Returning to this theme in 15:14–16, Eliphaz asks the same question that Job did in 7:17–18, which interpreters consider a parody of Psalm 8. But Eliphaz does not stop with the simple "What are mortals?" Instead, he qualifies the question with the words "that they can be clean, or those born of woman, that they can be righteous?" Here, however, Eliphaz extends the untrustworthiness to the heavens themselves, while observing that humans drink iniquity (*'awlâ*) like water. This point is made all the more emphatic by wider debates over whether Yahweh was capable of doing wrong. The prophet Zephaniah's sharp retort in 3:5 that "Yahweh is righteous in her [Jerusalem's] midst and cannot do wrong (*'awlâ*)" (my trans.) leaves no doubt about his view of the issue. Job would have rejoiced if Yahweh really dispensed judgments every morning. Significantly, the word "his servants" in Job 4:18 is replaced in 15:15 by "his holy ones." This low view of humans was also expressed in Mesopotamian wisdom, especially in *The Babylonian Theodicy*, which asserts that the gods endowed mortals with lies.[23]

When Bildad takes up the theme of human righteousness, he follows Job's version ("with God") but fuses this reading with Eliphaz's additional themes: "How then can a man be righteous before El, or how can one born of a woman be innocent?" (25:4, my trans.). Now, however, the comparison is with moon and stars, which are said to be less than pure, and humans are reduced to the swarming creatures that ultimately consume their decaying flesh (cf. Sir. 10:11). The cost of defending El's honor is high indeed, and the contrast between this assessment of Job and that proclaimed in the prologue by both God and the narrator could hardly be greater.

Elihu's Allusion to Revelation

Besides the divine speeches from the tempest, this instance of revelatory disclosure in Job 4:12–21 is the only example of direct revelation in Wisdom literature. Perhaps that is why it must make a furtive entrance through the back door. The closest thing to this mode of revelation comes in allusions that pique the imagination. For instance, the youthful Elihu refers to communication from above, almost as if reminiscent of the spirit's appearance to Eliphaz.

> For in one way El speaks,
>   indeed in two ways, one does not perceive it.
> In a dream, a vision of the night,
>   when heavy sleep falls on people,
>   while they slumber in bed.
> Then he opens their ears
>   and frightens them with warnings.
>   (Job 33:14–15, my trans.)

Revelation as Elihu perceives it serves a single purpose, to fill one with dread.[24] Two proverbial sayings approximate Elihu's sentiment, for they assert that Yahweh orchestrates decisions when lots are cast (Prov. 16:25) and guides the tongue in overriding human plans (Prov. 16:1).[25] Two other sayings suggest that Yahweh does not always adhere to a policy of hands-off in the decision-making process among humans. In Proverbs 20:24 the claim is made that one's steps are ordered by Yahweh, rendering a person incapable of understanding his way, and 20:27 insists that Yahweh's lamp, a metaphor indicating the breath or spirit, searches a person's innermost being. Precisely how the divine will was thought to have been communicated to people in these instances is not specified.[26]

MEDIATED REVELATION

Revelation need not imply communication through humans to others, as these proverbs imply. In fact, several sages conceived of mediated divine disclosure that eventually rivaled direct speech from God. This revelation, personified Wisdom, evolved over time from a mere metaphor to a divine emanation. Its exact origins are unknown, but precedent exists in ancient Egypt, where truth, justice, intelligence, and understanding were personified as Ma'at, and where the goddess Isis declared her own worth to humans somewhat like the self-revelations of ḥokmâ.[27]

Israelite poets, too, knew the dramatic effect of attributing human qualities to virtues. A psalmist announced excitedly that truth and justice were locked in passionate embrace (Ps. 85:10 [Heb. 11]). This practice of personifying various attributes was widespread, ranging from the divine face and name to agents of destruction such as famine, pestilence, and sword. The dramatic force of this mode of discourse can be observed in a twice-used anecdote within the book of Proverbs about the effects of laziness. Want enters the house like a thief when one is too lazy to work (Prov. 6:6–11; 24:30–34). The image of Sheol's limitless appetite and of her declaration that she has only heard a rumor about Wisdom carries personification beyond the human dimension to include the realm of the dead.[28]

Neither the impetus from Egyptian linguistic practice nor that from Israel's own poetic imagination fully explains the emergence of personified Wisdom. It has been argued that the perceived collapse of the traditional understanding of Yahweh's active engagement with Israelites and its replacement by a passive Deity left a void that was soon filled by the figure of Wisdom.[29] Accordingly, her function was that of theodicy, specifically to provide a means for an absent Deity to communicate with earthlings and thus to comfort those who believed that Yahweh had abandoned them.

An alternative hypothesis, that personified Folly antedates that of Wisdom,[30] implies an evolution of feminine Wisdom to counter the erotic potency of Dame Folly. Still the failure to develop those intriguing possibilities of this seductive figure beyond its initial stages in Proverbs 9:13–18 is difficult to explain. The feminization of Wisdom may have taken on this erotic component to a degree that rendered pointless such attribution to folly.

Proverbs 8:22–31

We have not yet completed our tour of the sages' gallery featuring divine disclosure. The next picture is a diptych, its two panels depicting the first act of creation and its sequel. One panel shows only Yahweh and *ḥokmâ*; everything else is an empty void. The portrait of *ḥokmâ* has the innocence of Botticelli's *Birth of Spring* and the coquettishness of Leonardo da Vinci's *Mona Lisa*. The emphasis falls on origin and primacy, both in time and in value. The other panel depicts Yahweh's subsequent creative acts, with *ḥokmâ* observing and possibly assisting. This scene describes the origin of the heavens and earth, sky and ocean, with intervening mountains. At every moment of creation, an adoring *ḥokmâ* appears beside the Creator, almost like a lover or a darling child overcome by reverent awe.

One thing stands out in the initial portrayal of Wisdom and may offer a clue about her origins: she is closely associated with cosmogony,[31] the creation of the world and its ordering. Regardless of how we read the controversial *'āmôn* of Proverbs 8:30, the rest of the poem extending from verse 22 to verse 31 makes bold claims about Wisdom's priority over everything except the Creator, before whom she dances and to whom she brings delight. Acquired or begotten by Yahweh as the first of the divine works, she is said to be either a master craftsman or a darling child, unless the noun *'āmôn* modifies the Creator, the unsurpassed artisan.[32] Her unique status as observer of Yahweh's creative work in establishing the universe is matched by a desire to bring joy to humans.

In some circles, proximity to Yahweh mitigates against her function as a mediator of divine thoughts, for she takes on the Deity's dual attributes of hiddenness and accessibility. This paradox gives birth to the poem in Job 28 contrasting human ingenuity when it is applied to the search for precious gems with a complete failure to discover wisdom, while inexplicably identifying it with a piety that is available to everyone.[33] The author of Baruch 3:1–4:4 appears to have known a myth about futile efforts to ascend to heaven in search of prized wisdom. This same myth may lie behind Agur's question in Proverbs 30:3–4 about going up to heaven and returning without knowledge.[34]

Such emphasis on Wisdom's hiddenness is carried to a logical conclusion in *1 Enoch* 42:2, which states that a descent to earth by *ḥokmâ* did not end in locating a suitable site in which to reside. Wisdom therefore returned to her point of departure and left humankind in ignorance. How differently the author of Deuteronomy 4:5–8 viewed things. The divine statutes, in his view, constituted Israel's unique wisdom that even the other nations acknowledged. For this reason, no one need go up to heaven to acquire wisdom, or even cross the sea in search of knowledge, inasmuch as it is already nearby, in mind and word (Deut. 30:11–14).

Sirach 24:1–23

The next picture that we encounter in the sages' gallery is a montage borrowed from alien portraits. The several images are brought together in a manner that highlights the sensual, for they constitute *ḥokmâ*'s self-praise. She actualizes the

Creator's speech, taking visible form in a mist that engulfs the earth. Alternatively, she assumes the shape of a pillar of cloud and eventually comes to rest in the temple at Jerusalem, where she assists with the daily liturgy.[35] Other scenes depict her as one of several majestic trees, a fruitful vine, or aromatic spices. Every single one of these unrelated scenes opens into a scroll that stands for the Mosaic torah.

The association of wisdom with divine statutes has thus culminated in Ben Sira's identification of personified Wisdom with the law of Moses (Sir. 24:1–23).[36] This identification of the Mosaic torah as an earthly manifestation of divine wisdom comes at the end of considerable enrichment of the figure inherited from Proverbs 8:22–31. We now hear about her origin in the divine mouth, her descent to earth in the mist that made the creation of man from dust possible, and taking the form of a pillar of cloud that led the enslaved people out of Egypt. She infuses people of every nation before finding a suitable dwelling place in Zion, where she flourishes like trees in the garden of Eden, producing abundant fruit and spices. In a sort of supplement, she is associated with the rivers in the story about the garden of Eden, although these have been joined by others as well. In a word, both the tree of life and that of knowledge can flourish in such a paradise.

Wisdom of Solomon 7:22b–26

The unknown author of Wisdom of Solomon views personified Wisdom in traditional ways, stressing the intimacy of lovers as the appropriate relationship between Pseudo-Solomon and Wisdom. She takes on a wholly different character, however, when her twenty-one attributes are praised, for now *ḥokmâ/sophia* appears as a pure emanation of the Creator (Wis. 7:22b–26). The word "hypostasis"[37] has been applied to this figure, who is an extension of the divine personality, just as the sun's rays participate in the nature of their source. Indeed, she even assumes the role of the spirit who guides and protects Israel from harm and thus becomes the prime mover of sacred history.

This elevated concept easily prepared the way for the later Christian understanding of Jesus as the wisdom and word of God, for the Hebrew *ḥokmâ* was translated into Greek by *sophia*, with which the philosophical *logos* was linked. By this means, the prologue to the Gospel of John identified Jesus as the divine *logos* and a hymn in Colossians 1:15–20 sings Jesus' praise in the language of Proverbs 8:22–31 about *ḥokmâ*.[38]

When we step back to reflect on this extraordinary evolution of a concept, it is important to recognize that several sociological factors were at work: (1) the lingering effects of the Babylonian conquest of Jerusalem on the understanding of Yahweh; (2) the deleterious impact of Persian satraps on the family structure itself within the province Yehud; (3) the growing influence of priests and their entrance into the scribal ranks;[39] (4) the intellectual attraction of Hellenistic philosophy,[40] and (5) an emerging monetary economy.[41] These are but some of the factors that shaped the particular features attributed to personified Wisdom.

The first, conquest in 587 BCE, underscored the need for divine presence in something more permanent than a perishable temple; and the second, Persian taxation and oppressive rule, necessitated a means of cementing the family through both eros and disciplined love, especially maternal. The third, priestly resurgence, gave rise to the incorporation of sacred traditions into the mainstream of wisdom, even to identifying *tôrâ* as the visible manifestation of *ḥokmâ*. The fourth, Hellenism, opened the way for the enthronement of wisdom as queen of the curricular disciplines, and in this way bestowed intellectual respectability on the Hebraic legacy bequeathed to the young, who were otherwise attracted to Hellenism. The fifth, a monetary economy, reinforced the emphasis on success that had been taken over from the book of Proverbs and gave it a measurable scale with far-reaching consequences.

To sum up, revelation in the traditional sense found its way into Wisdom literature. Even in the two instances of divine speech in the book of Job, sharp differences can be discerned besides the covert nature of the word that terrified Eliphaz. The third example of revelation, personified Wisdom, interposes a mediator between a silent Deity and human beings. In addition, she becomes the occasion for dispensing altogether with direct self-disclosure on Yahweh's part, specifically by the identification of written torah with *ḥokmâ*, the divine wisdom. Ironically, this distancing of Yahweh eases the perception of divine inattention, for the revealed word is now omnipresent.

DIVINE MYSTERY

It is not easy to explain the presence of revelation in Wisdom literature. After all, reason seems capable of managing quite well without resorting to faith. The total experience of the community, past and present, was a formidable depository on which to draw. Perhaps that is why modern interpreters have such difficulty integrating faith and reason in these ancient texts. Indeed, the tension between the two seems even greater today than long ago.

A new explanation for the encroachment of faith in Mesopotamian wisdom has recently appeared,[42] one that is said to apply equally to biblical wisdom. Profound differences in the Old Babylonian edition of the Gilgamesh Epic and the Standard Babylonian edition, to which a scribe has added a prologue of twenty-eight lines, provide the basis for the hypothesis. The new material identifies Gilgamesh as one who has obtained secret wisdom of the gods from Utnapishtim, the hero of the flood story that parallels the biblical account. Whereas old wisdom consisted of "human knowledge painstakingly acquired by a lifetime of experience," new wisdom is revelation. Such rarified knowledge is then associated with exorcism, astrology, and divination; all of these are domains reserved for the intelligentsia.

Why did this shift in understanding take place? The move from oral tradition to a written text brought about an encrypting in a predominantly oral culture, for only scholars had access to this material. In reality this claim amounted to no more than rhetoric, for the stories of the flood and Gilgamesh were familiar to all through oral tradition. Nevertheless, wisdom was now believed to consist of divine secrets, hence a mystery known only by the gods and the scribes to whom the knowledge had been disclosed.

If this theory correctly interprets the changed view of wisdom within ancient Mesopotamia, does a parallel development take place in biblical wisdom? Several interpreters claimed to detect a shift from early secular wisdom to a later theologization of wisdom,[43] but no one has as yet furnished a convincing time line for such a transition. In all probability, different understandings of the concept underlying wisdom existed simultaneously, even if one view may have been dominant. Historical circumstances may even have brought shifts in the prevailing perspective.

Nevertheless, the Hellenistic era ushered in an esotericism that intensified in Roman times, both in apocalyptic literature and in sapiential texts from Qumran that refer to the mystery that is to be.[44] Such thinking was undoubtedly stimulated by the identification of *ḥokmâ* with the Mosaic torah in Sirach 24:23 and Baruch 4:1. Certainly in these circles wisdom is no longer identified with the accumulated experience of a lifetime. Instead, wisdom consists of revelation to a select group of people, and this secret knowledge is contained in writings that only a few can read. In such an intellectual environment the emergence of esoteric lore and its defense in 2 Esdras 14:46–47 is natural. Here one reads: "But keep the seventy that were written last, in order to give them to the wise among your people. For in them is the spring of understanding, the fountain of wisdom, and the river of knowledge" (RSV). Remarkably, canonical literature is here contrasted unfavorably with apocryphal texts.

ALTERNATIVE VIEWS OF REVELATION: CONSCIENCE AND NATURAL LAW

We turn now to consider two other forms of revelation within Wisdom literature: (1) an innate conscience and (2) natural order. Within the sages' gallery, these two portraits have been hung in a remote corner. The first consists of a hastily drawn cerebral cortex, standing for a conscience, in the foreground with the faint outline of kidneys, the source of feelings or emotions in biblical thought, in the background. The second portrait features a fruit tree at harvest time. Beneath its branches lie several apples that have fallen to the ground, while another is in midair on its way to the earth below, predictably drawn by gravitational pull. The sun rises in the east, and another day dawns as it has for eons as promised in Genesis 8:22 ("As long as the earth endures seedtime and harvest, cold and heat, summer and winter, day and night will not cease").

Conscience

Only a hint of the first has survived in canonical texts, and it takes back with one hand what it gives with the other. I refer to Ecclesiastes 3:11, a notoriously difficult verse in the strangest book in the Bible:

> Everything he [Elohim] has made appropriate for its time, he has also placed *h'lm* in their minds, yet so that a person cannot find out the work God does from beginning to end (my trans.).

The difference between this assessment of the created work and that in the Priestly account of creation is hardly surprising, even if one erases some of the difference by translating *yāpeh* as "beautiful" rather than "appropriate." Still, Qoheleth states that an innate endowment at birth serves no useful purpose, for Elohim has blocked access to it. For this reason, I understand the crucial word, left untranslated above, as *hā'elem* and render it either "mystery" or "the unknown."[45] Others choose to follow the Masoretic pointing *hā'ōlām* and translate it as a temporal expression indicating a desire for "eternity," which they think best fits the context dealing with a time for everything.[46] Regardless of how one views this crux, the verse clearly states that humans are given an innate quality but that it does them no good because they cannot locate it. This mysterious gift is hardly revelatory, except in the sense that it reminds individuals of finitude, as if such a reminder were needed. Calling this attribute a conscience is a bit of a stretch, especially in light of the debate over nature or nurture as the basis for an inner monitor.

Norbert Lohfink has argued that yet another text in Ecclesiastes mentions divine revelation.[47] In 5:18–20 (Heb. 17–19) Qoheleth states, like several Greek philosophers before his time, that the divine gift of food and drink is a good "portion," as is the ability to enjoy it. In this context, he remarks that a person will not much remember daily experience, for God does something (*ma'aneh*) with joy in his mind. The exact meaning of the Hebrew participle *ma'aneh* is much debated, for the verb *'ānâ* has at least three possible senses: (1) to answer, respond; (2) to afflict; and (3) to occupy oneself with, keep busy. If Qoheleth's fundamental message transcends the pessimism that runs throughout the book, verse 20 can be viewed as revelation by joy. In other words, God instills joy within human hearts.

Those interpreters who reject an optimistic reading of Qoheleth construe the verse differently.[48] In a word, God afflicts the mind with unachieved joy. Such an interpretation accords with the other revelatory statement that God placed a sense of either eternity or mystery in the mind but prevented humans from discovering it and consequently benefiting from such a gift. I therefore do not believe that this verse refers to revelation.

Qoheleth's enigmatic observation about an innate quality is almost matched by the three obscure sayings in the book of Proverbs referred to above. The same fatalism permeates Qoheleth's thinking as well as Egyptian wisdom literature from roughly the same time.[49] These sayings suggest that God works unobtrusively, directing human lives. Indeed, the image of a divine puppeteer comes to mind,[50] for strings are being pulled that control actions and their consequences. This language, and that of Qoheleth, must have struck Ben Sira as excessively deterministic,[51] for he insists on freedom of the will. Without freedom of choice, he argues, humans can easily lay the blame for their errors on God.

An occasional saying in the book of Sirach comes close to Qoheleth's belief that the Creator endowed humans with a special quality at birth. For instance, Sirach 1:14 states that *ḥokmâ* is created with trustworthy persons in the womb. In 17:6 it is said that the Creator equipped individuals with a mind, along with tongue, eyes, and ears. This reference to three senses (taste, sight, and sound) is extraordinary, although the focus falls on the capacity of the intellect to discern between good and evil. The function of the eyes in observing, the ears for hearing, and the tongue for tasting goes unspoken. Instead, even these three senses are subsumed under the category of understanding. The eyes observe how things function, the ears take in knowledge as it comes from others, and the tongue transmits to others insights gleaned from sight and sound. This function of the tongue is rare; usually in pedagogical texts the tongue conveys knowledge to others.

According to Sirach 17:11 God bestowed knowledge on humans, allocating to them the law of life. The exact meaning of "the law of life" is unclear, but it seems to claim that people have an innate quality that guides them in safe directions. To label these innate qualities "revelation" may not accord with traditional views, but they certainly belong to any discussion of the sages' understanding of the knowledge of God.

Natural Law

Natural law, the other form of revelation, is less controversial, although biblical interpreters have for the most part overlooked it. Perhaps the emergence of Roman Catholic scholarship has contributed to the recent change of perspective, although two of its leading expositors are Presbyterian and Anglican.[52] The sages believed that the natural order held important clues about its origin, together with hints about how to get along successfully by living in harmony with nature. The stamp of its Creator was thought to be discernible, and this trace assisted astute observers in negotiating difficult terrain.

This belief explains why sages paid so much attention to nature, for they hoped through analogical reasoning to glean valuable lessons from the study of natural phenomena. Indeed, Psalm 19 seems to say that nature speaks in its own way, proclaiming *without words* the divine glory day after day, night after night. Alternatively, the poet insists that no single utterance of the heavenly bodies goes unheard, either from clarity of speech or because of astute perception on the part of those who are attuned to nature.[53] Several interpreters identify this psalm as sapiential,[54] although a more accurate descriptor is "torah psalm," given its second strophe that shifts attention from nature to the torah.

Let me illustrate from personal experience the way nature informs religious reflection. The discovery of a beautiful luna moth in my garden engaged my mind to reflect on the fragility of human existence. This is what resulted from such thinking.

A Fragile Presence

Clinging beneath a purple celosia,
the winged beauty finds shelter
from the scorching sun,
    oblivious to admiring eyes.

What kind Chance
led this token of love's wonder to my flowers,
and who guards her white form,
    suspended among predators
    ready to devour a fragile presence?

If only my garden
were your permanent abode,
then I would not search in vain
for you another day.
    Sleep, my vulnerable visitor
    from heaven's door,
    and these eyes will watch over you
    'til your metamorphosis is complete.[55]

Then when my spirit
breaks free from its earthly wrap
and wends its way to a distant garden,

Will the Keeper of that refuge—
on seeing a fragile presence
    clinging to a leaf on the tree of life—

Be touched by its vulnerability
to unaccustomed radiance
and protect it from harm?

Here a wonder of nature became the catalyst for letting thoughts soar and coming to rest on the Creator of all things. At the same time, they never forget the human condition.

In grounding my thoughts on the Creator I have aligned myself with the sages, who moved from creation to the concept of the fear of God as both the beginning and the highest principle of knowledge. The exact sense of fear varied with the author using the concept, at times approximating dread, as in Qoheleth's use, but always bearing an element of awe. To some extent, the term is equivalent to "religion" in modern usage.

The sages' understanding of natural order achieved greater significance under the influence of Stoic philosophy. Both Ben Sira and the author of Wisdom of Solomon emphasize the order of the universe that perfectly balances opposites. This symmetry functioned as theodicy,[56] for apparent evil had a place in such an ordered universe. Not everyone saw nature's grandeur as pointing to the Creator, according to Wisdom of Solomon. Instead, the adoration of nature propelled the Egyptians, this author's word for arch-villains, into the worship of idols, a practice that the apostle Paul applied more generally to humans standing outside the protection of the Christian umbrella (Rom. 1:18–25). Perhaps a few sages shared the pessimistic view of the intellect that is found elsewhere in the Bible and more widely in the ancient world. These individuals, too, may have considered the mind both perverse and sick (Gen. 6:5; Jer. 17:9),[57] desperately in need of being replaced by a purer one (Jer. 31:33).

Moving Beyond the Evidence

I dare not conclude this discussion of revelation as sages conceived it without commenting, at least obliquely, on a peculiar feature of sapiential literature. Without exception, they seem to know far more about God than can be gathered by the means examined thus far. Even Qoheleth, who emphasizes the experiential nature of his insights, claims all kinds of knowledge about the Deity that cannot derive from personal observation.[58] Precisely how did the composers of maxims learn that humans propose but God disposes or that Yahweh disciplines beloved children? How did Qoheleth know that God is in heaven, that he has given humans a sorry business to keep them occupied, or that he will eventually judge everyone? We could multiply examples like this almost ad infinitum, and this extraordinary claim to be privy to much information about the Deity cries out for an explanation. Did sages endorse some traditional teaching, or did they deduce this knowledge about God from daily experience? I suspect a combination of both answers best explains the scope of theological assertions throughout Wisdom literature. This small concession mandates yet a larger one: contemporary interpreters may exaggerate the empirical aspect of sapiential knowledge.

CONCLUSION: SOME ETHICAL IMPLICATIONS

If the answer I have tentatively put forth is correct, it means that the sages believed that knowledge of God resulted from mutual giving and receiving. Therefore the image with which we began that suggests a reciprocal touch is useful because it depicts simultaneous reaching out in search of the other. At least a few biblical sages appreciated the notion of a self-revealing Deity who used various means to communicate with living vessels of clay. Others, possibly the majority, preferred to think in terms of human initiative that resulted in fuller knowledge about the world and its Maker. Either way, an act of intellectual appropriation occurs that puts to shame Adam's drooping index finger and relaxed pose. One can even hazard the suggestion that Yahweh's withdrawal from interacting with people in popular perception was used by the sages as an invitation to embark on a quest to discover divine presence and to make it meaningful once again. In this regard, as in many others, not a few citizens in the modern world are at one with biblical sages—forced by perceived absence of transcendence to search for the Divine in a silent and at times cruel universe where even a lifetime of experience no longer assuages intellectual curiosity.

This understanding of the knowledge of God in biblical wisdom as the reciprocal action between humans and God has profound implications for ethics.[59] The dominant view of ethics as obedience to a divine will revealed in Scripture does not fit the situation in Wisdom literature, where conformity to natural order is the prevailing view until Ben Sira, who supplements this understanding with Scripture. Moreover, shaping their lives by insights derived from the order of the universe, sages developed a broad concept of virtue that consisted of commitment to a particular code of conduct, arising from a moral vision, and an active formation of character. Their understanding of virtue was also the product of communal experience with all its particularities.

It is true that the sages valued success, but only in the context of a society in which honor determines worth can it be properly appreciated. Greed, a natural consequence of a morality grounded in success, was nevertheless considered a vice, as was unchecked aggression. A premium fell to societal demands for order, even within an ethic that favored autonomy over heteronomy. Only when individuals have a well developed self-esteem can a proper balance between social responsibility and right order be sustained. In all likelihood, a strong bond with the larger family cemented this positive relationship with others who were not kin.

Central to this sapiential ethic was the belief that an individual was born with innate qualities that were later developed through experience. Both nature and nurture contributed to a virtuous life, although the heart was at the same time the most significant organ of the body and the most problematic, an idea also found in Egyptian thought.[60]

Foremost of the cardinal virtues was eloquence, for speech disclosed the innermost workings of the mind and therefore one's essential character. After eloquence came timing, a recognition of the right word or deed for every given occasion. Then came restraint, the suppression of passion's ugly manifestations that led to violence. Integrity completes the virtues, as it were uniting them into a single one and guaranteeing truth. These four virtues nicely combine being and action, character and conduct. Guiding them all is the intellect or *ḥokmâ*, dear to sages, consisting of intelligence, knowledge, recognition, and understanding.

We must not overlook revelation when discussing the ethics of the sages, for they considered the natural order one form of divine disclosure. Its beauty lay in the requirement placed on the intellect to recognize hidden principles for governing one's daily experience, perhaps also in its availability to every human being. In this way disputable claims about the possession of private revelation were avoided, at least until Ben Sira.[61]

Throughout this analysis of sapiential ethics,[62] I have been reminded of a single factor that could require a different interpretation of the texts. What if they reflect a past ethos rather than that of the sages' own time, or an ideal ethos instead of an existing one? Be that as it may, I suspect that every ethical construct combines a little of all three: past, present, and a hoped-for future. I, for one, am eternally grateful that Israel's sages did not abandon reason for faith but tried to the best of their ability to actualize a reciprocating touch that even Michelangelo did not envision when depicting the origin of humankind.

NOTES

1. Originating as a malevolent lesser deity in Mesopotamia, Lilith entered the Jewish arena as especially dangerous to men sleeping alone. The four references to her in the Talmud describe her as a winged female who gives birth to demons. Midrashic and kabbalistic traditions treat her as both benign and demonic (Lowell K. Handy, "Lilith," *ABD* 4:324–25). Other goddesses were also worshiped by some Israelites; the most recent evidence comes from Khirbet el-Qom. Ziony Zevit, "The Khirbet el-Qôm Inscription Mentioning a Goddess," *BASOR* 255 (1984): 39–47, translates the crucial lines as follows: "I blessed Uryahu to YHWH. And from his enemies, O Asherata, save him."
2. Samuel Terrien, *Till the Heart Sings: A Biblical Theology of Manhood and Womanhood* (Philadelphia: Fortress, 1985), emphasizes the erotic features of *ḥokmâ* in Prov. 8:22–31.
3. Gary A. Anderson, *The Genesis of Perfection: Adam and Eve in Jewish and Christian Imagination* (Louisville: Westminster John Knox, 2002), 75–97, poses an intriguing question: "Is Eve Mary?"
4. Anderson, ibid., 97, concludes that Eve is both the exact opposite of Mary and the one who anticipates her in the divine plan.
5. As envisioned by the Yahwist, Adam was created de novo, thus without an umbilical cord. Scoffers over the centuries have made much of this peculiar feature of a human anatomy that is said to be in the divine image.
6. James L. Crenshaw, "Knowledge," *NIDB*, 3:539–46. Fuller treatments are given in Sigmund Mowinckel, *Die Erkenntnis Gottes bei den alttestamentlichen Profeten* (Tilleggshefte Til Norsk theologisk Tidsskrift; Oslo: Grondahl, 1941); Robert C. Dentan, *The Knowledge of God in Ancient Israel* (New York: Seabury, 1968); and Schellenberg, *Erkenntnis als Problem*.
7. James Barr, *Biblical Faith and Natural Theology.*
8. Cf. von Rad, *Wisdom in Israel.* Because Wisdom literature in the Bible lacked the unique features of Yahwism, Preuss, *Einführung in die alttestamentliche Weisheitsliteratur*, labeled it paganism.
9. Brevard Childs, *Biblical Theology in Crisis* (Philadelphia: Westminster, 1970). Wishing to counter the customary negative understanding of crisis, Martin Rose, "De la 'Crise de la Sagesse' à la 'Sagesse de la Crise,'" *Revue de théologie et de philosophie* 131 (1999): 115–34, emphasizes the sages' creative response to challenges.

10. The "Death of God" theology in the 1960s and 1970s echoed Friedrich Nietzsche's well-known announcement of the Deity's demise and the human role in it.

11. "To Spite Nature," *Second Space: New Poems* (New York: HarperCollins, 2004), 19–20; "Second Space," ibid., 5.

12. This recognition presents a challenge to physicians, who in their desire to help patients may forget that their training has not equipped them to deal with spiritual issues.

13. Julia Mitchell Corbett, ed., *Through a Glass Darkly: Readings on the Concept of God* (Nashville: Abingdon, 1989).

14. The shift in perspective that takes place with these two works has been brilliantly analyzed by Marböck, *Weisheit im Wandel*; Collins, *Jewish Wisdom in the Hellenistic Age*; and Adams, *Wisdom in Transition*. During this period, the tension between particularism and universalism becomes acute, especially for the social class of upwardly mobile, as Collins has recognized ("Natural Theology and Biblical Tradition: The Case of Hellenistic Judaism," *Encounters with Biblical Theology* [Minneapolis: Fortress, 2005], 117–26).

15. Crenshaw, *Defending God*, especially 183–90.

16. For this literature, see Karel van der Toorn, "From the Oral to the Written: The Case of Old Babylonian Prophecy"; and Martti Nissinen, "Spoken, Written, Quoted, and Invented: Orality and Writtenness in Ancient Near Eastern Prophecy," *Writings and Speech in Israelite and Ancient Near Eastern Prophecy*, ed. Ehud Ben Zvi and Michael H. Floyd (SBLSymS 10; Atlanta: Society of Biblical Literature, 2000), 219–34 and 235–71, respectively.

17. In contrast to the KJV and NIV, the alternative translation of this verse in RSV ("Can mortal man be righteous before God? Can a man be pure before his Maker?") ignores the normal comparative sense of the preposition *mem*. Cf. NRSV margin.

18. Mack, *Wisdom and the Hebrew Epic*, highlights the Hellenistic influence on the author of this poem.

19. Samuel E. Balentine, *The Hidden God: The Hiding of the Face of God in the Old Testament* (Oxford: Oxford University Press, 1983), explores the language for divine concealment.

20. Elaine Pagels, *The Origin of Satan* (New York: Oxford University Press, 1995); and Ruth Nanda Anshen, *The Reality of the Devil: Evil in Man* (New York: Harper & Row, 1972).

21. Man is clay and straw,
    And the god is his builder.
    Amenemope 25.13–14
    (*AWET*, 424)

    Enlil, king of the gods, who created teeming mankind,
    Majestic Ea, who pinched off their clay,
    The queen who fashioned them, mistress Mami,
    Gave twisted words to the human race,
    They endowed them in perpetuity with lies and falsehood.
    Babylonian Theodicy 26 (*COS*, 1:495)

22. Terence E. Fretheim, *God and World in the Old Testament: A Relational Theology of Creation* (Nashville: Abingdon, 2005), 233–47, defends the basic goodness of God as responsive to Job, but this emphasis runs counter to the portrayal of Yahweh in the prologue, where human life is cheap. The same criticism applies to the recent article by André LaCocque, "The Deconstruction of Job's Fundamentalism," *JBL* 126 (2007): 83–97.

23. See n. 21.
24. Carol A. Newsom, "The Book of Job," *NIB*, 4:568, recognizes the allusion in Elihu's comment about fear to Job's earlier request that God not overcome him with dread (13:21b).
25. The sages believed that ultimately human lives rested in God's hands, although the responsibility for particular destinies was largely theirs.
26. Nevertheless, a psalmist cannot imagine anywhere that can place one outside Yahweh's gaze, a sentiment shared by the prophet Amos (Ps. 139:7–12; Amos 9:1–4).
27. Miriam Lichtheim, *Maat in Egyptian Autobiographies and Related Studies* (OBO 120; Freiburg: Universitätsverlag, 1992). Christa Bauer-Kayatz, *Einführung in die alttestamentliche Weisheit* (BS 55; Neukirchen-Vluyn: Neukirchener, 1969), applied many ideas from Ma'at to the biblical description of personified Wisdom, although real differences exist between the two figures, chief of which is that Ma'at does not speak about herself.
28. Theodore J. Lewis, "Dead, Abode of the," *ABD*, 2:103; and Nicholas Tromp, *Primitive Conceptions of Death and the Nether World in the Old Testament* (BibOr 21; Rome: Pontifical Biblical Institute, 1969), e.g., 107–10.
29. Sinnott, *Personification of Wisdom*, 53–87, accepts my suggestion about the impact of a catastrophic historical event on the sages.
30. Boström, *God of the Sages*, 56.
31. Richard J. Clifford and John J. Collins, eds., *Creation in the Biblical Traditions* (CBQMS 24; Washington, D.C.: Catholic Biblical Association of America, 1992); and Leo G. Perdue, *Wisdom and Creation: The Theology of Wisdom Literature* (Nashville: Abingdon, 1994).
32. Michael V. Fox, *Proverbs 1–9* (AB; New York: Doubleday, 2000), 285–89, lays out three possible meanings as follows: (1) artisan and related concepts, (2) constantly, faithfully, and (3) nurturing (pedagogue, ward, growing up with).
33. Van Wolde, ed., *Job 28*, especially David J. A. Clines, "'The Fear of the Lord Is Wisdom' (Job 28:28)," 57–92, and Carol A. Newsom, "Dialogue and Allegorical Hermeneutics in Job 28:28," 299–305.
34. Raymond C. Van Leeuwen, "The Background to Proverbs 30:4a," in *Wisdom, You Are My Sister*, ed. Barré, 102–21.
35. Ben Sira's priestly leanings have been emphasized by various scholars, especially John F. A. Sawyer, "Was Jeshua Ben Sira a Priest?" in *Proceedings of the Eighth World Congress of Jewish Studies*, Div. A (Jerusalem: World Union of Jewish Studies, 1982), 65–71; Saul M. Olyan, "Ben Sira's Relationship to the Priesthood," *HTR* 80 (1987): 261–86; and Helge Stadelmann, *Ben Sira als Schriftgelehrter* (WUNT 6; Tübingen: Mohr, 1980).
36. The initial stage of this identification of wisdom and torah occurs in Deut. 4:5–8. A transitional moment takes place in Eccl. 12:13–14, according to Sheppard, *Wisdom as a Hermeneutical Construct*, 120–29.
37. In Prov. 8:22–31 and Sir. 24:1–23 the language about ḥokmâ is metaphorical. The twenty-one attributes of wisdom in Wis. 7:22b–23 indicate perfection (7 x 3). Do they move beyond metaphor to actual hypostasis? The answer is made more difficult by the author's characterization of ḥokmâ as Solomon's bride.
38. Alan P. Winton, *The Proverbs of Jesus: Issues of History and Rhetoric* (JSNTSup 35; Sheffield: JSOT, 1990), 18–22.
39. Israelite scribes have remained for the most part obscure and anonymous, on which see Crenshaw, *Education in Ancient Israel*; and Carr, *Writing on the Tablet of the Heart*.

40. Uehlinger, "Qohelet in Horizont"; and Reinhold Bohlen, "Kohelet in Kontext hellenistischer Kultur," in *Buch Kohelet*, ed. Schwienhorst-Schönberger, 249–73.

41. Elias Bickerman, *Four Strange Books of the Bible: Jonah/Daniel/Koheleth/Esther* (New York: Schocken, 1967), 158–67.

42. Van der Toorn, "Sources in Heaven."

43. Von Rad, *Wisdom in Israel*, 57–73; McKane, *Proverbs*; idem, *Prophets and Wise Men* (SBT 1/44; London: SCM, 1965). Dell, *Book of Proverbs*, 124, thinks the secular and religious sayings existed side by side.

44. Goff, *Discerning Wisdom*, 9–103; and Harrington, "The *Raz Nihyeh* in a Qumran Wisdom Text (1Q 26, 4Q 415–418, 423)," *RevQ* 17 (1996): 549–53.

45. Crenshaw, "The Eternal Gospel (Ecclesiastes 3:11)," in *Essays in Old Testament Ethics*, ed. Crenshaw and Willis, 23–55 (*UAPQ*, 548–72).

46. Seow, *Ecclesiastes*, 172–73 ("God is responsible for giving both time and eternity, and the human being is caught in the tension between the two," p. 173); Krüger, *Qoheleth*, 87–88 ("distant time"); and Schwienhorst-Schönberger, *Kohelet*, 268 (*Ewigkeit*, such that it goes beyond divine activity in a mythic *Urzeit [creatio prima]* to the present moment [*creatio continua*], p. 263).

47. Lohfink, "Qoheleth 5:17–19—Revelation by Joy."

48. Fox, *Time to Tear Down*, 239 ("Pleasure dulls the pain of consciousness . . .").

49. "The plans of the god are one thing, the thoughts of [men] are another" (*Ankhsheshonqy*, 26.14; *AEL*, 3:179); and "The fate and the [fortune] that come, it is the god who sends them" (*Papyrus Insinger* 7.19; *AEL*, 3:191).

50. Von Rad, "Joseph Narrative and Ancient Wisdom," *UAPQ*, 292–300.

51. Rudman, *Determinism*.

52. Barr was a Scottish Presbyterian, "a Scott whose intellectual lineage should be traced to David Hume rather than to John Knox" (Collins, "Natural Theology and Biblical Tradition," 117), and Barton is Anglican. He has emphasized the ethical dimensions of natural law (*Understanding Old Testament Ethics*, 32–44).

53. Brown, *Seeing the Psalms*, 81–103.

54. But see my "Wisdom Psalms?" 9–17.

55. Metamorphosis is finally complete at death!

56. Crenshaw, "The Problem of Theodicy in Sirach: On Human Bondage," *JBL* 94 (1975): 47–64 (*UAPQ*, 155–74).

57. Crenshaw, "Deceitful Minds and Theological Dogma (Jer 17:5–11)," 105–21.

58. Crenshaw, "Qoheleth's Understanding of Intellectual Inquiry," 205–24.

59. Otto, *Theologische Ethik des Alten Testaments*, 117–74.

60. Shupak, *Where Can Wisdom Be Found?* 297–311.

61. Fichtner, *Altorientalische Weisheit*, e.g., 28, describes Ben Sira's thinking as "nationalizing wisdom." That may well be, since Ben Sira incorporated Israel's sacred tradition into his discussion of wisdom; however, by locating wisdom in the Mosaic torah, he brought out the universal dimensions of the Mosaic legislation.

62. These reflections on ethics have benefited from reading Lichtheim, *Moral Values in Ancient Egypt*; Barton, *Understanding Old Testament Ethics*; Otto, *Theologische Ethik des Alten Testaments*; and Joseph Jensen, *Ethical Dimensions of the Prophets* (Collegeville, Minn.: Liturgical, 2006).

Chapter 9

Wisdom's Legacy

The sages of Israel have bequeathed a valuable legacy to posterity. That legacy cannot easily be summarized in the scope of a chapter, but I wish to emphasize three areas in which wisdom made a contribution to ancient Israelite thought. Naturally, these aspects of the sapiential heritage include countless other important contributions, which I shall discuss here only by implication.

Perhaps the most noteworthy feature of wisdom's legacy is the capacity to recognize the limits imposed upon human reason and to face reality honestly, submitting every claim about knowledge to this rigorous judgment. That awareness of human limits applied above all to claims regarding revelatory knowledge. The result was the *growth of skepticism* in ancient Israel. That phenomenon merits careful analysis and will therefore constitute the bulk of this chapter.

The sages also proclaimed a worldview that offered a *viable alternative to the Yahwistic one*. According to the sapiential legacy, creation was the occasion for God's contact with those who bore the divine image, that is, everyone. Revelation was pushed back to the beginning, and human beings possessed the necessary means of discovering truth. This positive view of women and men contrasts greatly with the dominant Yahwistic emphasis upon sin and guilt, a sentiment that the author of the book of Job endeavored to squelch.

A third feature of wisdom's legacy is its *ability to cope* with reality, be it favorable or threatening. In a real sense, this aspect of wisdom embraces the other two, for skepticism was wisdom's way of dealing with experienced ambiguities, and the formulation of a new worldview grew out of the actual practice of coping with events that had rendered traditional religious convictions obsolete.

THE BIRTH OF SKEPTICISM IN ANCIENT ISRAEL

"The deepest, the only theme of human history, compared to which all others are of subordinate importance, is the conflict of scepticism with faith."[1] The author of this astonishing observation, the poet Wolfgang von Goethe, described that antipathy between doubt and a vision of a transformed society with extraordinary power in Faust's final surge of humanitarianism, which elicited the fateful request, "Stay, thou art so fair," signaling the loss of his wager with Mephistopheles and, by a curious non sequitur, the ultimate triumph of virtue. In this chapter we will examine that conflict between faith and doubt in ancient Israel.

THE SKEPTIC'S VISION

To begin with, we must distinguish between *skepticism, pessimism,* and *cynicism.* In my view, skepticism includes both a denial and an affirmation. The negative side of a skeptic's mental outlook consists of doubting thought, whereas the positive affirmation of a hidden reality indicates that it is altogether inappropriate to accuse skeptics of unbelief.[2] This powerful vision of a better world inherent within skepticism prompted Blaise Pascal to write that "there never has been a real complete skeptic."[3] The matrix formed by the disparity between the actual state of affairs and a vision of what should be in a perfect universe both sharpened critical powers and heightened religious fervor. Doubt, it follows, is grounded in profound faith.[4]

Once skeptics lose all hope of achieving the desired transformation, *pessimism* sets in, spawning sheer indifference to cherished convictions. Pessimists believe chaos has the upper hand and will retain control forever; they lack both a surge for transcendence and faith in human potential. Because they own no vision that acts as a corrective to the status quo, pessimists can muster no base on which to stand and from which to criticize God and the world. The inevitable result is a sense of being overwhelmed by an oppressive reality.[5]

Cynics go a step further; by their disdain for creaturely comforts and sensual pleasure they show contempt for everything life has to offer. No vision moves them to reject an imperfect present reality while awaiting a more perfect one that God and humans bring into being, and no feeling of helplessness makes them throw up their hands in despair. Instead, they demonstrate an amazing capacity for survival despite outward circumstances to which they are inwardly indifferent.[6]

Skeptics freely raise their voices within the Hebrew Scriptures, and pessimists occasionally add their cry; but we listen in vain for cynics' sighs. The reason is easily perceived: the presupposition of cynicism, contempt for the material world, is wholly alien to Hebrew thinking. In what follows, the area of concentration will be skepticism, though rare expressions of pessimism may surface as well.

Now doubt may be what Jean Jacques Rousseau called "reverent doubt," and skepticism, "unwilling skepticism."[7] That is why Tennyson was on target when observing that there is more faith in honest doubt than in half the creeds. For some reason not yet fathomed by flesh and blood, certain eras lend themselves to wholesale skepticism, eliciting the painful admission that "we of this generation are not destined to eat and be satisfied as our fathers were; we must be content to go hungry."[8] Such deprivation resulting from a complete breakdown in cultural values offers a unique opportunity for fresh breakthroughs[9] that rejuvenate society. Once dogma freezes, traditions become lifeless fetters and can only be thrown off by a resurging vital faith that dares to challenge the most sacred belief in the name of a higher truth.[10]

It has been said that "skepticism without religion is impossible but also that religion without skepticism is intolerable."[11] Admittedly, the skeptic's faith does not necessarily name God as its object. For example, the French Enlightenment was an age of skepticism in which faith sought new outlets—first nature and after that, men and women. Unwilling to sanction the tyranny of the church any longer, these skeptics found a new and wondrous object of trust in nature, particularly when epoch-making geological discoveries cast serious doubt on established views about divine providence and the supposed date of creation. Furthermore, the complexity of human beings approached the mystery formerly relegated to God as the individual emerged into the limelight and fresh knowledge of previously unknown cultures stirred the imagination. Contemporary skeptics have substituted science for religion as the truth in which they place their trust. Long before corrupt ecclesiastical officials aroused strong resolve to crush the infamous thing, religion, Israelites too chafed under an oppressive yoke. The name of Job suffices to remind readers that religion can easily become an instrument of cruelty unless it is tempered with a skeptic's honesty.

By assisting religion in its endless struggle to prevent belief from becoming hollow testimony to a reality belonging only to the past, skepticism functions as religion's handmaid. Many of Israel's noblest insights resulted from the interplay between faith and doubt. Confronted with the void, Israel's skeptics fought to sustain their vision of an eternal order where justice prevails. Here and there we hear a triumphant shout when skeptics affirm their faith while walking in utter darkness. Perhaps the most moving expression of confidence occurs in the unparalleled seventy-third psalm, where the poet ultimately feels the touch of a father's hand and knows that God is present to one who has honestly faced doubt.[12]

Skepticism's indispensability may be seen in the fact that the great ideologies correspond to three syntactic moods.[13] *Theology affirms the declarative, humanism informs the imperative, and skepticism supplies the interrogative.* The prominence of narrative in the Hebrew Bible derives from the basic truth that theology is essentially affirmation. Once that declarative statement imposes strong demands upon men and women, humanism intrudes to maintain the dignity of persons on whom the divine imperative has fallen. Skepticism dares to penetrate beneath the statement and consequent demand; it inquires about the ultimate basis for the declaration and presses toward determining motivation for obedience. Self-knowledge emerges largely through interrogation; for example, the question, "Why am I suffering?" early became a means of dealing with guilt and eventually revolutionized Israel's understanding of reality itself.[14]

Ironically, this Joban onslaught fought against a worldview that resulted directly from the first decisive breakthrough in our intellectual history.[15] That is the principle of universality—the ideal of rationality according to which no individual possessed the truth, the universe was orderly, and human beings were spectators of a powerful drama that God directed toward a distant goal. The assumption of order precipitated crises in Mesopotamia, Egypt, and Israel, as is well documented in the relevant literature.[16] One need not envision mass distribution of these texts in Israel and elsewhere[17] to recognize the revolutionary impact of such thinking, for the doubting thought surfaced throughout recorded memory.

DOMINANT HYPOTHESES

From this observation it follows that one cannot subscribe to the theory that the decisive breakthrough in Israel coincided with the Solomonic empire and constituted a complete break with sacral thinking.[18] Skepticism within the canon can hardly be restricted to an understanding of the manner in which God governs history. Failure to recognize this important fact has seriously distorted analyses of the extent and complexity of Israelite skepticism.[19] This narrow understanding of skepticism has produced three significant half-truths that have dominated most discussion of intellectual development in ancient Israel: (1) skepticism signifies a worn-out culture;[20] (2) such rejection of established views is an elitist phenomenon;[21] and (3) skepticism arose as a consequence of historical crises.[22]

Skepticism Signifies a Worn-out Culture

To be sure, centuries of affirmation precede significant doubt. Society's givens accumulate slowly; in the beginning sanctions are consciously formulated, and later their acceptance becomes almost as natural as breathing. In this way a worldview takes shape,[23] and legitimations reinforce it from every side. Cherished beliefs are promulgated consciously and unconsciously, and daily experience seems to support such values. Only after sanctions for life have evolved and demonstrated their dependability under certain circumstances can doubt about their legitimacy arise as circumstances change. Ancient rabbis perceived this fact and applied it to their paragon of wisdom. According to them, Solomon wrote Song of Songs in his youthful days when desire surges, Proverbs during mature years, and Qoheleth when senility had settled in for good. Like individuals, civilizations grow old and cast off their youthful garments in order to don funeral shrouds.

The denigration of postexilic Israel as a burned-out culture may have coincided with prevailing interpretations of postexilic Judaism. Such a reading of Israelite history belongs inherently to certain streams of canonical tradition. The Deuteronomistic understanding of events as one great failure on Israel's part, with rare exceptions, and the apocalyptic notion of successive ages whose very names imply gradual decay—gold, silver, bronze, iron—must surely be responsible for the widespread belief that Israelite skepticism arose in the midnight hour of canonical history.

Skepticism Is an Elitist Phenomenon

The claim that skepticism is a malaise suffered only by the well-to-do builds upon an assumption about the leisure class as guardians of Israel's intellectual tradition.[24] Acceptance of this plausible hypothesis about the authors of the sapiential corpus may permit one to make significant observations concerning Job and Qoheleth, but the skeptical voice reaches far beyond these dissenting cries. Parallels with neighboring cultures, particularly the Egyptian, are informative, but Israel's sages functioned in an entirely different context from that represented by Egyptian counselors to the pharaoh.[25]

Skepticism Resulted from Historical Crises

The third misconception, that political catastrophe generates skepticism, possesses an element of truth, as a cursory reading in prophetic literature confirms. Still, various answers to the problem occasioned by defeat on the battlefield readily present themselves and secure faith intact: Israel has sinned; God is testing his people; foreign powers function as God's agents; external events do not accurately reflect true reality.[26] The amazing resiliency of faith enabled men and women to survive events that had the capacity to shatter fondest dreams. Even Josiah's dark fate precipitated no discernible religious revolt against providence.[27]

OPPOSING CLAIMS

Having acknowledged the partial truth in each of the three statements, I wish to formulate opposing assertions: (1) skepticism belongs to Israel's thought from early times; (2) it extends far beyond the intelligentsia; and (3) it springs from

two fundamentally different sources, which we may call theological and epistemological. In short, skepticism is intrinsic to biblical thinking rather than an
intruder who took Israel by surprise; this rich heritage of doubt often took up
willing residence among ordinary people in Judah and Ephraim; and skeptics
turned their attention toward human ability to know anything as well as toward
theories about God's works.

Skepticism Arose Early

Occasional texts confirm the relative antiquity of skeptical outbursts.[28] For
instance, Isaiah pronounces a woe upon those who say:

> Let him make haste,
>   let him speed his work
>   that we may see it;
> let the plan of the Holy One of Israel hasten to fulfillment,
>   that we may know it!
>
> (Isa. 5:19)

Similarly, Zephaniah accuses his contemporaries of thinking that God "will not
do good, nor will he do harm" (Zeph. 1:12). Furthermore, an old account of
Gideon's encounter with a heavenly visitor bristles with skepticism and describes
Gideon as nearly laughing in the angel's face (Judg. 6:11–13). When tested in
the crucible of experience, the people's miserable circumstances hardly accorded
with religious convictions that God actively worked to sustain Israel.

> But, sir, if the LORD is with us, why then has all this happened to us?
> And where are all his wonderful deeds that our ancestors recounted to us?
> (Judg. 6:13)

In this case the interrogative mood threatened to swallow up the declarative,
and youthful rebellion placed paternal teaching under a dark cloud. A full-
fledged pragmatist, Gideon insisted on incontrovertible proof for theological
statements. Naturally, such a one refused to surrender before the divine imperative until convincing demonstration of faith's assertions lay within his grasp. As
Jeremiah 44:15–19 shows, such empirical tests cut two ways: here the Jewish
refugees residing in Egypt inform Jeremiah that they had prospered so long as
they worshiped the queen of heaven but fell victim to destructive forces when
they abandoned their goddess. In their eyes, as in Gideon's too, devotion to
Yahweh did not pay sufficient dividends.

Even without this evidence that skeptics came upon the stage long before Job
and Ecclesiastes were written, we could reasonably conjecture that certain features of Yahwism made such doubt extremely probable. To begin with, Israel's
understanding of God as one who withholds his name at the very moment of
self-revelation openly invites skepticism.[29] Mystery clothes the one who freely
makes the divine self known, whether to Moses as "I AM WHO I AM" (Exod. 3:14)

or to Manoah as "wonderful" (Judg. 13:18).[30] In the last resort, Israel's sovereign refuses to bow before human manipulation, and thus retains freedom in all circumstances. As a result, this God gains a reputation as one who comes to assist oppressed peoples, although an occasional suspicion that God is demonic also lingers in the hearts of those who encounter stark mystery.[31] Inherent within such conviction is the belief that God dwells afar off, so that one can know only what humans are permitted to perceive. Like Adam long ago, one merely observes the surgeon's finished work. Even the celebrated "mighty acts of God," which generation after generation recited in the sacred assembly and in the family circle, were inferences drawn from footprints in the Judean hills, for no eyes ever penetrated the veil shielding God from creatures of flesh and blood.

Naturally, such theology gives rise to emphasis upon creaturely finitude. Between humans and God stretches a vast chasm, and no bridge spans the abyss. The defiant postdiluvian generation was not the only one that dreamed of linking heaven and earth. A favored two, Enoch and Elijah, were thought to have walked hand in hand with God into the sunset or to have ridden a heavenly chariot on the clouds, but for most mortals access to God was completely circumscribed. It consisted of the divine image, which included, among other things, verbal communication; by this means imagistic links occurred in the form of poetic inspiration, prophetic visions, and the sage's intuition. The walls of God's heavenly castle were so steep that even "thoughts slipped below," to quote Goethe once again, and the entire enterprise that aimed at uniting the two realms crashed to the ground like the ill-fated tower of Babel. Those who live on borrowed breath can hardly boast about their strength, especially when events overwhelm human victims and crush them indiscriminately.

The earliest sages also knew that their knowledge came up against limits beyond which it could not go.[32] Careful plans could always clash with God's secret intentions, and in such cases human beings proposed but God disposed. When the Deity's glory consists in hiding things, the stage is already set for anxiety in the face of apparent injustice. That worry intensifies the moment true wisdom is placed outside human reach, for men and women inevitably ask why God retains wisdom for God's private possession.

Given these two extraordinary facts, a God who hides and creatures who are dependent, skepticism's appearance in Israel occasioned no great surprise. Some texts seem almost to encourage expostulation with the Deity as if God longed to have probing questions directed at the divine self. For example, the narrative concerning the Lord's destruction of Sodom and Gomorrah pictures the Deity standing before Abraham in open invitation to discuss the moral implications of the decision to demolish entire cities (Genesis 18). Obviously, God is not the only one who has qualms about wholesale slaughter, for the author of the prose tale allows Abraham to utter his own weighty objections. A single question gathers together the entire moral dilemma facing God: "Shall not the Judge of all the earth do what is just?" The skeptic's criticism appeals to a vision of right conduct to which even God's deeds are subject.

Skepticism Enjoyed Popular Support

This intrinsic nature of skepticism means that it refused to become the exclusive property of an intellectually elite group of people. Admittedly, breakdowns often fail to achieve decisive breakthroughs for lack of popular support. Such aristocratic revolutions abort because they do not succeed in capturing the imagination of common people. The mere presence of potentially revolutionary thoughts cannot alter the human situation unless the idea seizes the minds of those who alone can implement lasting change.

Revolutions can be attempted without popular support, but the outcome is predictably disappointing. In Egypt Akhenaton's remarkable break with the past achieved no permanence, despite the powerful sanctions accompanying the reform, and Egypt soon reverted to pre-Amarna thinking. Similarly, the French experiment to eradicate religion in recent times was weakened by a lack of enthusiasm among the masses.[33] For these people religious belief survived the devastating attack upon faith launched by the intelligentsia. Even widespread clerical corruption failed to convince ordinary churchgoers that the reality to which they prayed did not deserve their supreme devotion.

Perhaps the most astonishing failure in this regard occurred in ancient Babylonia, where the revolutionary idea of linearity surfaced but became a victim of a more powerful belief in divine caprice. Lacking faith in God's control of human events so as to bring them to a distant goal envisioned by the deity, Babylonian religion failed to achieve the idea of purpose (*telos*) that shines with such dazzling splendor in the Hebrew Scriptures. No vision of the *eschaton* transformed Babylonian cultic dominance, and no linear purposive progression put an end to circular thinking. Divine caprice turned these people into what has been called the most pessimistic civilization in history.[34]

For several reasons, the hypothesis that Israel's skepticism was elitist misses the mark. Such a restriction of the doubting thought to the perimeters of wisdom ignores the widespread phenomenon of skepticism throughout Israelite society. Numerous instances of skeptical defiance confronted canonical prophets, prompting in them intemperate language and considerable soul-searching.[35] Not all of these antagonists challenged prophetic utterances on the basis of enduring visions of transcendence,[36] but many of them undoubtedly protested against bogus promises and insisted on complete honesty in assessing the theological situation.

In this respect compilers of canonical psalms displayed considerably more appreciation for those who uttered the perennial interrogative: "How long, O Lord?" In these expressions of lament and praise occurs a mighty crescendo of expostulation with the Deity concerning justice above all. It seems that the most devout worshiper cannot decide whether to acknowledge God's justice in the face of evidence to the contrary or to concede divine blindness, nay indifference, as irrefutable fact. Even when the psalmist cites such low opinions of God and attributes them to fools, the very articulation of skeptical views satisfies a need for honesty on the part of the worshiping community.

Within the wisdom corpus itself certain bits of evidence suggest that the skeptical mood threatened to overwhelm the entire sapiential enterprise. The sheer bulk of the skeptical literature, including Job and Qoheleth, must surely have suggested to many that the proper scholarly pursuit comprised the study of comparable texts. More importantly, Ben Sira feels constrained to enter into lively dialogue with a group of skeptics[37] who offered his own students a viable alternative to the confessional theology he had lately interpolated into wisdom's repertoire. In attempting to refute their arguments, he borrowed an old form of debate and used it freely. One element of that literary device, the actual quotation of an opponent's argument, permitted skeptical views wide audience, particularly for those who viewed Ben Sira's teachings as canonical. Even though the doubting thought is dismissed for one reason or another, it continues to sink deeply into the minds of all who read Sirach. Perhaps an awareness of this persuasive whisper moved the author of Wisdom of Solomon to register the opinion that doubt's mere presence renders one incapable of receiving divine revelation (1:2). Such a warning can only mean that skepticism posed a real threat in the eyes of this sage, and that makes the hypothesis of minimal impact by skeptical literary works wholly unacceptable.

Skepticism Flowed from Two Separate Springs

My third assertion, that skepticism arose in two distinct contexts, requires considerable elaboration. On the one hand, skepticism addresses itself to a specific theological situation; in short, it signified a perceived non sequitur, a diminishing of faith in God. On the other hand, the skeptic also isolates a wholly different kind of bankruptcy—the loss of faith in human beings. It will not do to label one stream Yahwism and the other wisdom, although the inclination to do so arises from a valid intuition. Nevertheless, the two streams converge at decisive locations, and in the end both tributaries flow into the same reservoir.

The starting point for an analysis of these streams must surely be the conviction that the cosmos was essentially orderly, which we have earlier called the first decisive breakthrough in the spiritual history of Western civilization. Without a firm sense of predictability, Israel could never have developed certain legitimations that undergirded society. The declaration that the universe could be relied upon (Gen. 9:8–17) bursts on the scene precisely when the deluge seemed to render life utterly perilous; its formulation constitutes a mighty expression of confidence in God's goodness despite the memory of raging waters. Over the years that optimism yielded further affirmations, especially the claim that virtue bore rich fruit, just as vice produced its own unwanted harvest. To be sure, minor fissures occurred here and there, but skillful hands nearly always filled those cracks with reliable cement.[38]

Alongside this belief in a calculable universe stood an equally compelling conviction that Israel was a people of the covenant who enjoyed God's favor. No task was too great, no enemy too powerful, to frustrate this desire on God's part to bestow life upon Israel at any cost. Other nations fell like flies before this God linked to Israel by a covenant, and not even sin by the favored people could thwart God's purposes. Having established the covenantal relationship in the first place, Israel's sovereign was not about to let anything frustrate eternal designs for Israel.

The principal arena in which God carried out hopes for Israel was political, and the decisive medium was the Davidic dynasty. To a large degree, the prophetic witness coincided with the period of the monarchy, a fact that has not been sufficiently appreciated in critical research. Both corporate and individual existence achieved significance in the course of history, upon which the divine word worked with matchless success. Israel's enemies fled when the Lord lifted a mighty arm, and God's people marched joyously from bondage into liberty. Valiant soldiers wasted away when the death angel spread its wings and flew into the midst of God's enemies. So ran the embellished account of Israel's history,[39] a story so far from the truth that it sowed seeds of skepticism at almost every telling. The disparity between present reality and grandiose confessions of God's mighty deeds in the past demanded an adequate explanation lest wholesale abandoning of the Lord take place.

The response to this need succeeded in reducing divine sanctions of society to a scroll, Deuteronomy. This single event paved the way for crystallized dogma and precipitated a sharp attack on a closed cosmos, an offensive that eventuated in outright skepticism. In Deuteronomy life stands over against death, and individuals are exhorted to choose which of the two they wish to embrace. Any intermediary position has vanished from sight, and the earlier dynamic juxtaposition of the one and the many has likewise disappeared altogether. In the process a decisive shift in ethos occurs. Slowly the family loses its hold over allegiances,[40] and individuality surfaces in a way hitherto unknown. Ownership of disposable property, urban concentration of the population, religious syncretism, political violence, and the like both brought this change about and shaped new attitudes that soon became widespread through conscious and unconscious dissemination.

The Deuteronomistic theory of exact retribution encouraged the rapid growth of skepticism by emphasizing human corruption, a theme that permeates the Yahwistic primeval history. Paradoxically, the canonical prophets also stimulated a sense of moral defeatism by repeated denunciations of the people as depraved, a *massa damnationis*. Perhaps to a certain extent such indictments became self-fulfilling, and moral impotence resulted because all self-esteem had been stripped away by well-intentioned prophets. Precisely where such thinking leads can be seen in 2 Esdras's lament that it would have been better not to have been born.

"Blind" bards, like the unknown author of Psalm 37, who had never seen the righteous forsaken or his descendants begging bread, tried desperately to withstand the tide of skepticism within the populace, and others wrote and rewrote actual history to remove the discrepancy between celebrated story and real fact. In the process the Deuteronomistic national focus vanished in favor of rigid emphasis on retribution at the individual level.[41] Long before the Chronicler engaged in an effort to formulate an adequate account of earlier history, individual choice played a prominent role in determining destiny. Indeed, in the Yahwist's view, the original sin introduced an alien force that even God could not eradicate. Its irresistible effect on the human will meant that no righteous person existed throughout the land. Subsequent thinkers like Jeremiah and Qoheleth agreed wholeheartedly with this low estimate of human beings. Lacking both the will and the power to achieve virtue, individuals have no choice but to rely on God's mercy. Accordingly, they praise God for accomplishing what men and women cannot do. As human potential decreases, divine power increases; nothing exists outside God's sovereignty. Naturally, the appropriate human attitude is submission before the Almighty.

The ultimate step is to deny knowledge to humans. Thus we come to the second aspect of my assertion that skepticism has two distinct sources. Theological claims about God that conflict with reality and about humans that degrade them are matched by an epistemological view that encourages skeptical thoughts. The knowledge that humans acquire is limited to terrestrial affairs, for Wisdom dwells with God, and none born of woman can approach her house. Once reason surrenders its throne to an alien power, the best the human intellect can do is to teach men and women "to bear in an understanding silence what must be borne." In such a situation, Agur's opening lament functions as a suitable motto: "There is no God at all, and I am powerless" (my trans.).[42]

Since the discussion of theological sources for skepticism has addressed issues as they arose in Yahwism generally, this analysis of the epistemological crisis will concentrate on Israelite wisdom. The earliest collection in Proverbs requires an acknowledgment that the terms "theological" and "epistemological" are inadequate, for the sages' subsequent admission concerning a bankruptcy of knowledge rests ultimately on convictions about God that surface in the very beginning. For example, human preparations for warfare may abort, because the battle belongs to the Lord. All efforts to master the universe labor under a single unknown factor—God's freedom. Thus an element of surprise hovered over every attempt to control fate, and no means of fathoming that secret ingredient presented itself. Still, the sages saw no great threat in that unknown quantity so long as they believed in God's goodness.

A decisive shift occurs in the book of Job, which wrestles with an awareness that God sometimes becomes an enemy to the one who faithfully trusts the Deity. Job complains that God cannot be found, for the Deity is unfathomable and so remote that sin does not affect God in the least. The same note is sounded with greater volume by Job's three friends and by the youthful intruder, Elihu. In their view, both humans and heavenly beings are unclean, and God alone possesses innocence. Everyone accepts this fact except Job, who would prove God guilty in order to demonstrate his own purity. Job's predicament forces him to abandon the rational principle, although his argument presupposes the truth of exact retribution for good and evil. The divine speeches remind Job of fixed limits that have been imposed upon human knowledge and powers.

Qoheleth advances in yet another direction; in his opinion, God is wholly indifferent to human beings, a thesis that picks up one aspect of the theology enunciated by Job's friends. In addition, knowledge is limited to earthly things, and even there it does not amount to anything permanent, for death cancels everything,[43] rendering all human striving a chasing after wind and utterly meaningless. A twisted world mocks all human effort, since none can straighten what God has made crooked; mystery clothes the beautiful creation and prevents men and women from making use of God's gift implanted in their hearts.[44] Moral impotence naturally flows from such a thoroughly pessimistic view.[45]

Ben Sira internalizes the burden that weighs heavily upon one and all; anxiety functions as a powerful means of equalizing things that otherwise appear to refute any belief in justice. Confronted by divine control over the inner life as well as outward events, men and women rely more and more upon God's mercy. Accordingly, Ben Sira seems never to tire of praising the Lord for compassionate dealings with sinful creatures who repent of their deeds. Earlier sages had remained silent on this theme, for they believed sufficient knowledge and power belonged to them to secure life.[46]

By far the most extreme statement of pessimism comes from Agur (Proverbs 30), who boldly rejects the theistic hypothesis and concedes that the consequence is devastating.[47] That confession stands at the polar position from earlier optimism; its simplicity and brevity electrify. In a word, "I cannot." Nevertheless, this foreign sage stopped short of the ennui gripping the author of the Babylonian *Dialogue of Pessimism*. In his chaotic world nothing commends itself sufficiently to stave off a desire to terminate life. Agur, however, resorts to rhetorical questions underscoring human frailty and ignorance.

> Who has ascended to heaven and come down?[48]
>   Who has gathered the wind in the hollow of the hand?
> Who has wrapped up the waters in a garment?
>   Who has established all the ends of the earth?
> What is the person's name, and what is the name of the person's child?
>   Surely you know!
>   (Prov. 30:4)

Such cognitive dissonance[49] brings about a wholly new situation with regard to persuasive discourse. The impossible question, saying, and task rapidly come to the forefront in Wisdom literature.[50]

> Can fire be carried in the bosom
>   without burning one's clothes?
> Or can one walk on hot coals
>   without scorching the feet?
>   (Prov. 6:27–28)

> Can papyrus grow where there is no marsh?
>   Can reeds flourish where there is no water?
>   (Job 8:11)

Here the sages argue from what is universally acknowledged to be true; ironically, they focus upon human inability. In these instances rhetorical questions function as strong assertions: no one can carry fire in his clothes without suffering the consequences of stupidity. The choice of such rhetorical questions as the appropriate language for God when finally addressing Job springs from the authority pervading this type of speech. No stronger statement can be imagined, particularly since the questions place Job in the unpleasant role of a student who has stirred up the teacher's ire.

Concomitant with an increasing awareness of human frailty runs the growing use of such impossible questions, especially in Qoheleth and 2 Esdras.

> How many dwellings are in the heart of the sea,
> or how many streams are at the source of the deep,
> or how many streams are above the firmament,
> or which are the exits of Hades,
> or which are the entrances of paradise?
>
> (2 Esd. 4:7)

> Consider the work of God;
> who can make straight what he has made crooked?
>
> (Eccl. 7:13)

> That which is, is far off, and deep, very deep, who can find it out?
>
> (Eccl. 7:24)

Similarly, impossible tasks isolate vast areas in which human strength and ingenuity fail miserably.

> Go, weigh for me the weight of fire,
> or measure for me a blast of wind,
> or call back for me the day that is past.
>
> (2 Esd. 4:5)

> Count up for me those who have not yet come,
> and gather for me the scattered raindrops,
> and make the withered flowers bloom again for me;
> open for me the closed chambers,
> and bring out for me the winds shut up in them,
> or show me the picture of a voice.
>
> (2 Esd. 5:36–37)

Occasionally, it seems that a numerical proverb has been altered to conform to this linguistic usage.

> The sand of the sea, the drops of rain,
> and the days of eternity—who can count them?
> The height of heaven, the breadth of the earth,
> the abyss, and wisdom—who can search them out?
>
> (Sir. 1:2–3)

Impossible *sayings* function in the same way that impossible *questions* and *tasks* do.

> But a stupid man will get understanding,
>   when a wild ass is born human.
>   (Job 11:12)

> My son, if the waters should stand up without earth, and the sparrow fly without wings, and the raven become white as snow, and the bitter become sweet as honey, then may the fool become wise. (*Ahiqar* 2:62; *APOT*, 2:737, 739)

Such texts could easily be multiplied, but these suffice to demonstrate their power to render a negative judgment on all human striving. Impossible questions, sayings, and tasks went a long way toward impressing on ancient Israelites the futility of trying to steer their course on the high seas once the divine helmsman had relinquished his post.

Conclusion

In summary, Israel's skeptics severed a vital nerve at two distinct junctures. They denied God's goodness if not the very existence of the Divine, and they portrayed men and women as powerless to acquire essential truth.

> Then I saw all God's work—that a person is not able to fathom the work that is done under the sun, on account of which he works to seek, but will not discover; and even if a wise man claims to know, he is not able to find it. . . .
>   For all this I took to heart, and I examined all this, that the righteous and the wise and their works are under God's control; no one knows whether it is love or hate. Everything is before them. (Eccl. 8:17–9:1, my trans.)

Faced with this formidable onslaught, God's defenders removed the Deity from the human scene altogether, or they placed sufficient emphasis on divine mercy to eclipse "the human deed in a time of despair."[51]

What, then, did these skeptics accomplish? Precisely this: they inscribed a huge question mark over the first great revolution in human thinking, turning the spotlight on the cognitive act. That is, they refused to take confessional statements concerning divine control of human events at face value, while insisting that boasts about human ingenuity also be taken *cum grano salis*. Pressing the interrogative mood thus placed linearity in jeopardy, as the quotation from Qoheleth in the preceding paragraph demonstrates with crushing finality, but it also showed the inadequacy of the critical tool by which divine purpose was discarded.[52] Reason thus was dethroned.

A VIABLE ALTERNATIVE TO YAHWISM

A second aspect of wisdom's legacy concerns its understanding of the relationship between God and the universe, including its human inhabitants. The sages offered an alternative mode of interpreting reality to the Yahwistic one in which God was actively involved in guiding history toward a worthy goal. The claim that God chose a particular people, fought on their behalf, called prophets, issued legal codes, sent angels to maintain contact with humans, enlisted foreign powers to discipline the chosen race, and promised to bestow a new covenant upon inveterate sinners for the sake of God's honor represents a way of looking at the human situation that is wholly alien to the sapiential one.

This Yahwistic affirmation of faith encountered considerable objection from those who failed to discern evidence that God actually controlled history, on the one hand, and from individuals who preferred a more tolerant religious spirit, on the other. Both criticisms possessed enormous weight, inasmuch as Israel's political history depended in large measure on the strength or weakness of the superpowers in Egypt and Mesopotamia, while religious syncretism inevitably occurred as a result of Israel's vulnerable geographical setting, if for no other reason.

The prophetic understanding of God as actively involved in the life of the people imposed a weighty burden on ancient Israel, since few individuals possessed the moral integrity to achieve the high demands laid on them, in the view of Old Testament "historians." Defeat on the battlefield easily led to abandonment of faith, for theological conviction had failed to accord with reality. The easy solution to this problem arose early: God was punishing Israel for their sins. That sort of theological improvisation had a permanent effect on the psyche of the elect people, who soon lost self-confidence and depended more and more upon divine assistance.

Perhaps the most vexing problem arising from this Yahwistic view concerns the validation of divine communication with humans. Two opposing messages, each claiming divine origin, left the people confused because they lacked a valid means of determining truth from falsehood. In such a situation the people found it necessary to put an end to this form of communication between God and humans. Thus they discredited prophecy and silenced God's voice.

The sages understood God's relationship with the world quite differently. In their view, revelation took place at the moment of creation, and when the human capacity to discover this hidden mystery seemed inadequate, God continued to make known the divine will through personified Wisdom. In other words, truth was planted within the universe, and humans searched diligently for it by using their intelligence. Still, truth was not entirely disinterested; in some mysterious fashion divine mystery declared itself to the inquiring mind.

The sages of Israel did not speak often about creation, although the notion undergirds much of what they say about the human situation. The earliest proverbs acknowledge a common creator for rich and poor, and the late sayings of Agur recall, probably mockingly, a mythic tradition about the Deity's victory over a creature representing chaotic forces. This popular myth also surfaces in the divine speeches attributed to Yahweh in the book of Job. In Proverbs 8:22–36 personified Wisdom boasts of her unique role during creation, one that places her on the scene at the beginning in some capacity—counselor, artisan, admiring "child"—although as the first of God's created acts she is careful not to detract from the honor due the Creator. Hymns within the book of Job restrict themselves to cosmology, focusing at length on the establishing of heaven and earth. These hymns almost join together the twin concepts of creation and providence. The poet stands in awe before majestic power capable of setting boundaries to the sea's restless waves, commanding the constellations and stars to shine, and controlling thunder and lightning. That awe is also felt over divine wisdom manifest in the providential sending of rain, snow, and frost.

Qoheleth's allusion to creation lacks a hymnic mood, replacing it with the somber note of a stacked deck. Having created everything appropriate in its time, or beautiful, God proceeded to implant something positive in the human mind but fixed things so that it would never be discovered (Eccl. 3:11). Another reference to the Creator, in the view of some interpreters, serves as a stimulus for chastened conduct (12:1), although the Hebrew word probably serves metaphorically for grave and cistern (wife). Ben Sira returns to the hymnic tradition in the book of Job (Sir. 43:1–33), advancing beyond that to emphasize the creation of opposites (33:15), and with that, placing providence on an equal footing with creation. At times Ben Sira's mathematical precision distances the reader from the awe-inspiring phenomena under discussion, turning the creative act into a matter of head rather than heart. At other times, Ben Sira echoes the account of creation in the first chapter of Genesis, even to specifying one's origin and destiny in dust as well as the divine image (17:3). In Wisdom of Solomon the dominant role of wisdom in Israelite history places the emphasis on providence rather than creation.

The close relationship between a theology of creation and personified Wisdom, which manifests itself in unforgettable fashion within Proverbs 8:22–36, becomes even more noticeable in Sirach 24:1–24. Here a personified Wisdom does not distance herself from the Creator as the first of many creative acts; instead, she claims to have issued from the divine mouth. In effect, Wisdom is a divine utterance; however, she covered earth in the same way a mist settled on a desert oasis in the Yahwist's version of creation (Gen. 2:4b–25). Her journey in search of a resting place resembles that of former slaves in Egypt (note the pillar of fire), but that ambitious journey over heaven's vault and into the abyss enabled her to claim possessions among all peoples. Accordingly, she receives an order from her creator—now she concedes that she was created—to make her residence among those who escaped from Egyptian bondage. This figure even does priestly duty in Zion and flourishes in that capacity. Here the imagery shifts to the natural realm—palms, roses, olives, vines, and spices—and Wisdom invites everyone to come and eat. Her abundant fruit possesses a special power to generate additional desire. Hunger and thirst for knowledge will know no end. At this point a shift occurs, one that locates this precious food in the Mosaic torah. Its abundance reconstitutes the garden of Eden, with its four rivers now becoming five, like the separate scrolls in the Torah. Appropriately, the five leading terms denoting wisdom occur here along with the rivers: wisdom, understanding, instruction, knowledge, and counsel. Ben Sira then personalizes the text, as if to explain his own attempt to communicate wisdom in the form of his scroll. The author of Baruch seizes Ben Sira's answer to the true locus of wisdom, while castigating Israel for an inability to find her, which explains its present misery, and praising God as the one who knows her (Bar. 3:9–4:4).

A further step is taken in Wisdom of Solomon 7–9, one that is bold beyond belief. True, she is a personification, with its erotic overtones, which occur in reference to Solomon's bride, wisdom, but chapter 7 describes her as an extension of divine essence, a virtual if not actual hypostasis. Her twenty-one attributes add up to supreme purity, an emanation of the glory of the Almighty, and an image of divine goodness (7:22–26). Divine wisdom and spirit unite, and wisdom functions as a providential power at work in the life of the covenantal people. The images of relationship with God dazzle the reader: breath, outpouring of divine glory, eternal light, mirror of divine activity, and God's image.

Israel's sages apparently believed in an eternal principle of rationality that exists in an undefinable relationship with the Creator. Furthermore, mere mortals mysteriously appropriate her insights into reality, and in that rare process Wisdom is not a reluctant teacher. Through it all, knowledge remains a mystery, one fraught with erotic tension.

With the exception of Sirach and Wisdom of Solomon, this sapiential view makes no claim about divine control of history; instead, the sages' understanding of reality rested upon a universal base. Everyone could make contact with transcendent reality regardless of the historical situation. Religious claims were modest ones, and no link existed between God and a particular people or ruling dynasty.

A consequence of this attitude toward reality is its orientation toward immediate experience. Nothing within human experience lacked revelatory capacity. No vision of past glory or future hope robbed the present moment of its importance. For this reason every encounter afforded a bridge into the transcendent realm. The slightest act by an insect, or the behavior of humans, concealed a secret worthy of discovery. In this way all of life became an arena in which divine truth unfolded, and God's truth coincided with human insight.[53]

ABILITY TO COPE

This observation about the intrinsic relationship between human and divine truth marks the arrival of the third facet of wisdom's legacy that I will emphasize: Wisdom enabled people to cope. The secret of Wisdom's wide appeal lay in the reward that she bestowed upon those who followed her path.

Few occasions arose in which the sages found themselves unprepared, for the paradigmatic situations they studied provided a substantial basis for broader interpretations achieved by means of analogy. The goal was to know what to do or say on any given occasion. To this end they gathered information and perfected their powers of drawing analogies between different realms and categories. Through centuries of experience the sages acquired valuable insight into personal relationships and human character.

That the sages had proverbial insights for almost every circumstance does not mean that they reduced life to the little things that could be managed successfully. Life's deepest mysteries constantly drew the sages' attention and refused resolutely to succumb to rational resolution. Nevertheless, the sages' struggle to understand the problem of suffering and death stands as living testimony that the human spirit can indeed cope, and humans need not despair when kingdoms crumble and temples vanish in flames.

If we keep in mind these three areas in which wisdom's legacy manifested itself, we shall not marvel that the sapiential literary corpus stands in the Hebrew Bible alongside torah and prophecy. The mere attribution of Proverbs and Ecclesiastes to Solomon hardly assured these works a place in the canon. Instead, Job, Proverbs, and Ecclesiastes gave authentic voice to the sages' fundamental understanding of reality, and in so doing, functioned to orient generation after generation with regard to the world into which they had been thrust.

Changing historical circumstances and theological perspectives effected comparable shifts of emphasis within the sapiential corpus itself, as we have seen. Such transitions occurred without suppressing earlier religious views. Although the result lacks uniformity in important respects, the positioning of opposing perspectives and the free use of interpretive statements (for example, the epilogue to Ecclesiastes) permitted later viewpoints to make maximal impact.

Just as private experience confirmed the veracity of innumerable proverbs, encounters with life's ambiguities demonstrated ever anew the essential truth within Job and Ecclesiastes. Undeserved suffering and the specter of death were inescapable realities for which no more satisfactory responses presented themselves than those put forth by the unknown authors of Job and Ecclesiastes.

The situation is hardly different with respect to Sirach, in spite of Ben Sira's pride of authorship. Apparently, this bold attempt to bring together two distinct traditions, wisdom and Yahwism, addressed a genuine need in the second century BCE. Wisdom of Solomon, too, serves to preserve a heritage by transmitting it in a different language and thus a new worldview. That later Jewish leaders limited the age of inspiration to the period from Moses to Ezra, thus excluding Sirach and Wisdom of Solomon from the Hebrew Bible, has nothing to do with the adequacy of the two books, but derives from altogether different circumstances.

In summary, the literary corpus of the sages was placed alongside the Pentateuch and the Prophets precisely because wisdom's legacy was no mean achievement. Proverbs enabled the people to cope in society; Job and Qoheleth empowered them to face life's enigmas, especially sickness and death; Sirach introduced hymnic praise as an essential ingredient in the discussion of evil; and both he and Wisdom of Solomon added an erotic dimension to the search for knowledge.

NOTES

1. Wolfgang von Goethe, *Wisdom and Experience*, trans. and ed. Hermann J. Weigand (New York: Pantheon, 1949), 72; quoted by Franklin L. Baumer, *Religion and the Rise of Scepticism* (New York: Harcourt, Brace & World, 1960), 3. If this claim approaches the truth, as I think it does, the silence of contemporary Old Testament theologies with regard to religious doubt represents a serious oversight, for we have not taken the dialogue with doubt half as seriously as Israel's thinkers did. See G. Buccellati, "Wisdom and Not: The Case of Mesopotamia," *JAOS* 101 (1981): 35–47.

2. Baumer, *Religion and the Rise of Scepticism*, 11.

3. Ibid.

4. Robert Davidson, *Courage to Doubt* (London: SCM, 1983); idem, "Some Aspects of the Theological Significance of Doubt in the Old Testament," *ASTI* 7 (1970): 412–52, takes a significant step toward clarifying the contribution skeptics made to the Hebrew Scriptures. Concerning the Psalms, Davidson writes: "The confession of confidence again and again springs out of a situation where life has called such confidence into question, and where a man or a community has had to walk in a darkness which has all but overwhelmed faith. . . . Is there, for example, no evidence that the very challenge to faith is a creative element in the development of faith?" (44).

5. Two canonical texts, the teachings of Agur and Qoheleth, belong to the category of pessimism. From this observation it follows that I concur in John Priest's judgment: "The skepticism of Koheleth ends, however much some commentators cry to the contrary, as pessimism pure and simple" ("Humanism, Skepticism, and Pessimism in Israel," *JAAR* 36 [1968]: 323–24).

6. Johannes Pedersen, "Scepticisme israélite," *RHPR* 10 (1930): 360–61 contrasts Qoheleth's exhortation to fear God with world renunciation, and rightly interprets this submission as wholly devoid of love.

7. Baumer, *Religion and the Rise of Scepticism*, 66.

8. Ibid., 139–40 (The quotation comes from Olive Schreiner, *The Story of an African Farm*, 2nd ed. [London: Chapman and Hall, 1883], 151).

9. Eric Weil, "What Is a Breakthrough in History?" *Daedalus* 104 (Spring 1975): 21–36. The title of this volume is *Wisdom, Revelation, and Doubt: Perspectives on the First Millennium B.C.*

10. See my essay, "Human Dilemma and Literature of Dissent."

11. Priest, "Humanism, Skepticism," 326.

12. Buber, "The Heart Determines"; and Crenshaw, *Whirlpool of Torment*, 93–109.

13. Priest, "Humanism, Skepticism," 326.

14. Paul Ricoeur, *The Symbolism of Evil*, trans. Emerson Buchanan (New York: Harper & Row, 1967), sheds fresh light on this significant issue.

15. Weil, "What Is a Breakthrough in History?" 22–24. For my view of two revolutions in Israelite intellectual history, see "Love Is Stronger than Death: Intimations of Life beyond the Grave," in *Resurrection: The Original Future*

of a Biblical Doctrine, ed. James H. Charlesworth (New York: T & T Clark, 2006), 53–78. A move toward acceptance of universality produced monotheism, and intimacy with the divine resulted in belief in a future life.

16. Hans Heinrich Schmid, *Wesen und Geschichte der Weisheit*.

17. Contra von Rad, *Wisdom in Israel*, 237–39.

18. Although the hypothesis pervades von Rad's literary corpus, it was first expressed in "The Form-Critical Problem of the Hexateuch," *The Problem of the Hexateuch and Other Essays*, trans. E. W. Trueman Dicken (Edinburgh; Oliver & Boyd, 1966), 1–78.

19. In addition to the aforementioned essays by Pedersen, Priest, and von Rad, one may also consult Martin A. Klopfenstein, "Die Skepsis des Qohelet," *TZ* 28 (1972): 97–109; Robert H. Pfeiffer, "The Peculiar Skepticism of Ecclesiastes," *JBL* 53 (1934): 100–109; Charles Forman, "The Pessimism of Ecclesiastes," *JSS 3* (1958): 336–43; and Hartmut Gese, "The Crisis of Wisdom in Koheleth," in *Theodicy in the Old Testamnent*, ed. Crenshaw,141–53.

20. Pedersen, "Scepticisme israélite," 331.

21. Von Rad, *Wisdom in Israel*, 237–39.

22. Pedersen, "Scepticisme israélite," 347; von Rad, *Old Testament Theology*, trans. D. M. G. Stalker, 2 vols. (New York: Harper & Row, 1962–65), 1:453–59.

23. See *Gerhard von Rad*, 138–60; and Kovacs, *Sociological-Structural Constraints*.

24. Von Rad, *Wisdom in Israel*, 15–23; Whybray, *Intellectual Tradition*, passim; Gordis, "Social Background of Wisdom Literature," 77–118.

25. Humphreys, "Motif of the Wise Courtier," 177–90.

26. For discussion and bibliography, see my "Theodicy," 895–96; idem, ed., *Theodicy in the Old Testament*; idem, *UAPQ*, 141–221; and idem, *Prophets, Sages, & Poets*, 173–200, 253–64.

27. Stanley B. Frost, "The Death of Josiah: A Conspiracy of Silence," *JBL* 87 (1968): 369–82.

28. Von Rad, *Old Testament Theology*, 1:453, concedes that skepticism crops up now and again as early as the eighth century; in his view, the historiography that produced the Joseph narrative and the Succession Narrative removed God from daily events so as to conceal his manipulation of the strings that governed human destiny. Von Rad writes that "the thought of God's eternity [in Psalm 90] was so overwhelming that it swept the imagination away to even greater distances, back to creation and beyond it" (453). But the powerful skepticism in Qoheleth is seen as a marginal note on the farthest frontier of Yahwism approaching the tragic dimension (455–59).

29. Davidson, "Some Aspects," 50.

30. See my *Samson*, 44–46, 76–77.

31. I developed this idea in *Prophetic Conflict* and *Defending God*. It has also been treated by Miles, *God: A Biography*.

32. Von Rad, *Wisdom in Israel*, 97–110.

33. Baumer, *Religion and the Rise of Scepticism*, 42.

34. Besides Weil's essay, "What Is a Breakthrough in History?" see in the same volume of *Daedalus* Benjamin I. Schwarz, "The Age of Transcendence," 1–8; A. Leo Oppenheim, "The Position of the Intellectual in Mesopotamian Society," 37–46; and Paul Garelli, "The Changing Facets of Conservative Mesopotamian Thought," 47–56. Bertil Albrekston, *History and the Gods* (ConBOT 1; Lund: Gleerup, 1967), has shown that Mesopotamians did, however, think the gods shaped the course of history to benefit their favored king and people.

35. Crenshaw, *Prophetic Conflict*, 23–38.

36. Baumer, *Religion and the Rise of Scepticism*, 33, distinguishes various moods in skeptics: in some "righteous indignation predominates, in others triumphant doubt and a sense of emancipation, and in still others sheer indifference or else the reverse, a longing for a religious faith which seems intellectually unattainable." Similarly, Davidson observes that Old Testament thinkers recognized that some skepticism was inappropriate, for example, the fool in Ps. 14:1 who denies God's existence ("Some Aspects," 51).

37. I have examined this confrontation in some detail in "Problem of Theodicy in Sirach."

38. Jerry Gladson, "Retributive Paradoxes in Proverbs 10–29," Ph.D. diss., Vanderbilt University, 1978.

39. One need only mention the controversy surrounding von Rad's emphasis upon salvation history to see how modern interpreters have also stumbled over the disparity between Israel's celebrated story and actual history. On this problem, see D. G. Spriggs, *Two Old Testament Theologies* (SBT 2/30; Naperville, Ill.: Allenson, 1974); and Martin Hönecke, "Zum Verständnis der Geschichte in Gerhard von Rad, Theologie des Alten Testament," *EvT* 23 (1963): 143–68.

40. Pedersen, "Scepticisme israélite," 357.

41. Both Ezekiel's atomistic thinking and Ben Sira's claim that a single act determined one's destiny carried such individualism to an intolerable extreme, despite good intentions on their part.

42. I follow Scott, *Way of Wisdom*, 166, in interpreting Agur's enigmatic opening words ("I have no God") but depart from his reading of the sequel ("but I can [face this or survive]").

43. James L. Crenshaw, "The Shadow of Death in Qoheleth," in *Israelite Wisdom*, ed. Gammie et al., 206–16; and Priest, "Humanism, Skepticism," 324 ("The real crux of his pessimism [is] the immutable fact of death which brings an end to all human aspiration, striving, and realization").

44. See my article, "The Eternal Gospel (Ecclessiastes 3:11)," in *Essays in Old Testament Ethics*, ed. Crenshaw and Willis, 23–55 (*UAPQ*, 548–72).

45. Pedersen, "Scepticisme israélite," 347–49. Many psalms emphasize human frailty (e.g., 14; 39; 44; 49; 103).

46. Rylaarsdam, *Revelation in Jewish Wisdom Literature*, and Crenshaw, "The Concept of God in Old Testament Wisdom," *UAPQ*, 191–205.

47. E. J. Dillon, *The Sceptics of the Old Testament* (London: Isbister & Company Limited, 1895), 155, writes that negations in metaphysics were compensated for amply in Job, Qoheleth, and Agur by *ethics*. I find no such compensation in Agur and Qoheleth.

48. Raymond C. Van Leeuwen, "The Background to Proverbs 30:4a," in *Wisdom, You Are My Sister*, ed. Barré, 102–21, examines the ancient topos of heavenly ascent and descent separating the gods from humans.

49. Although I do not wish to pursue Festinger's categories in this connection, the idea of cognitive dissonance seems to apply nicely to Israel's skepticism. R. P. Carroll, *When Prophecy Failed: Reactions and Responses to Failure in the Old Testament Prophetic Traditions* (London: SCM, 1979), has demonstrated the usefulness of Festinger's concepts in understanding biblical prophecy.

50. I have examined these extraordinary forms in "Impossible Questions, Sayings, and Tasks in the Old Testament," in *UAPQ*, 265–78.

51. This sentence alludes to Lou Silberman's contribution to *Essays in Old Testament Ethics*, ed. Crenshaw and Willis, "The Human Deed in a Time of Despair: The Ethics of Apocalyptic," 191–202. The present discussion of

skepticism also appears in "The Birth of Skepticism in Ancient Israel," in *Divine Helmsman*, ed. Crenshaw and Sandmel, 1–19.

52. Samuel Terrien, "The Sceptics in the Old Testament and in the Literature of the Ancient Near East," Th.D. diss., Union Theological Seminary, New York, 1941, was not available to me.

53. Perdue, *Wisdom Literature*, emphasizes the role of creation in the theology of the sages.

Chapter 10

Egyptian and Mesopotamian Wisdom Literature

Israel's ceaseless search for knowledge, divine presence, meaning, and survival was part of a larger quest in the ancient Near East. Scattered allusions within the Hebrew Bible to the wisdom of the easterners and the Egyptians (Gen. 41:8; Exod. 7:11; 1 Kgs. 4:30–31 [Heb. 5:9–10]; Isa. 19:11–15) have assumed greater force again and again as literature from Egypt and Mesopotamia has come to light. Similarities between Israelite wisdom and that of its powerful neighbors to the south and east abound, but decisive differences also exist.

Those features that distinguish Egyptian and Mesopotamian wisdom literature from similar Israelite texts have prompted caution in using the term "wisdom" with regard to extra-Israelite material. A leading authority on Egyptian wisdom literature has noted that the biblical notion of *ḥokmâ* (wisdom) is less appropriate than the descriptive term "instruction" when applied to Egyptian texts.[1] Similarly, the author of the standard treatment of Babylonian wisdom in English writes, "'Wisdom' is strictly a misnomer as applied to Babylonian literature."[2] He goes on to explain: "Generally 'wisdom' refers to skill in cult and magic lore, and the wise man is the initiate."[3] Both specialists do recognize, however, a significant area of common subject matter, literary form, and worldview in Israelite wisdom and in that of Egypt and Mesopotamia.

Inasmuch as at least one ancient writer compared Solomon's wisdom with that of Egypt and "eastern sages," by which Edomites may have been meant, it seems appropriate here to examine extrabiblical wisdom. When one considers the direct contact between various sections of Proverbs and Egyptian wisdom literature, as well as the amazing resemblances between Mesopotamian wisdom on the one hand, and Job and Ecclesiastes on the other, exploration of noncanonical sapiential literature becomes imperative. Proper comprehension of biblical wisdom depends on an understanding of related texts in Egypt and Mesopotamia. Only by this means will the distinctive features of Israelite wisdom come to prominence.

EGYPTIAN WISDOM LITERATURE

For convenience, Egyptian sapiential literature may be divided into texts that consciously endeavor to inculcate traditional morals and practical lessons from experience, and those that challenge society's givens because of adverse social changes that have rendered life hazardous at best.[4] Into the former category falls a significant body of literature with a special title, *seboyet* (teaching), although this title covers considerably more than wisdom literature. To these may be added various texts that treat the scribal profession as inherently superior to all other tasks and that deal with aspects of that exalted vocation. The second category consists of pessimistic literature in which weightier questions about life's meaning and the conflict between truth and falsehood prompt radical rethinking of established intellectual positions.

Instructions and the Scribal Tradition

The Instructions span the period from 2800 to 100 BCE and function as a barometer by which one can determine the religious and social values of ancient Egypt. Except for a tendency to become shorter (monostichs), their external form remains remarkably consistent throughout this long period; in general, a father offers advice to his son, although these two terms "father" and "son" may also designate a teacher and his student. Occasionally, the court setting of this counsel is highlighted by attributing the teaching to a pharaoh. Where this is not the case, emphasis falls on the teacher's role as advisor to the ruler. In short, many of the teachings are directed at actual or potential bureaucrats.[5] Naturally, certain themes came into prominence as a consequence of this elite clientele, although other people would also profit from such advice: the art of correct speech, proper relations with women, correct dealing with one's inferiors and superiors, rules of etiquette, truthfulness, and the like.

The fundamental concept underlying these Instructions is *ma'at*,[6] which may be translated as "justice, order, truth." No distinction exists between secular and religious truth for this literature as it does often in modern society. In Wisdom literature God's will can be read from the natural order, social relations, and political events. Life in accordance with that principle of order paid off in tangible blessings, just as conduct at variance with *ma'at* brought adversity. It follows that pragmatism enjoyed religious grounding; for this reason the utilitarianism characteristic of this literature constitutes an appropriate response of faith. Alongside purely utilitarian motivations for conduct lie positive reinforcement in terms of God's will and warnings that emphasize divine wrath arising from certain abominable practices.

A fundamental *conservatism* pervades these Instructions. The teacher transmits to his students the intellectual tradition that has accumulated over the years. This world of thought leaves no place for the creative thinker who charts new paths for the imagination. Personal experience that cannot be repeated by everyone rarely surfaces in these texts. The operative word seems always to have been "tradition." Nevertheless, discernible changes do manifest themselves, primarily as a result of widespread political unrest that alters the understanding of divine order itself.[7] In time overt piety of a self-conscious kind penetrates the teachings, whereas the earliest instructions had a powerful religious impulse that lay hidden within the concept of *ma'at*. In a word, for the ancient teachers no chasm separated divine truth from ordinary knowledge.

The goal of this instruction was to enable students to master their lives; the ideal sage was called "the silent one," although this title also applied more generally to all virtuous people. Those who *heard* their teachers acquired the art of self-control; whoever refused to listen to the voice of experience gave free rein to passions. Naturally, such persons were known as hotheaded or uncontrolled individuals.

Since paternal instruction, and that of teachers generally, could be spurned by rebellious sons, the Instructions were presented as attractively as humanly possible. Unable to rely on supernatural revelation, teachers expended considerable effort toward making their words both pleasing to the ear and intellectually cogent. In addition, appeal was made to paternal authority and to self-interest, for the status of officials within the court was a lofty one indeed when compared with ordinary work in society at large.

Turning to the Instructions, I shall attempt to summarize the distinctive characteristics of each. From the period of the Old Kingdom three texts have survived: *Hardjedef*, *Kagemni*, and *Ptahhotep*.

The earliest teaching from the Old Kingdom, *The Instruction of Hardjedef*, has perished except for a few lines that advise the reader to prepare a burial place and to choose a wife. Frequent mention of this sage in later literature bears witness to the impact of his teaching, a fact that the surviving instruction under the name Hardjedef would hardly have suggested.

Only the ending of *The Instruction of Kagemni* has survived. Its contents cover some of the themes already discussed: proper table manners and the pleasing character of the wise teaching. Here one is instructed to curb the appetite when dining with a glutton, and the person who pays heed to wise counsel is called a "silent one."

The opening lines of *The Instruction of Ptahhotep* strike readers as remarkably similar to the final description of old age in Ecclesiastes.

> O sovereign, my lord! Oldness has come; old age has descended. . . . The eyes are weak, the ears are deaf, the strength is disappearing because of weariness of heart, and the mouth is silent and cannot speak. . . . Good is become evil. All taste is gone. (*ANET*, 412)

To be sure, Qoheleth expresses himself much more felicitously, choosing exquisite poetic images to portray time's ravages on the human body. But the bottom line is the same: old age is truly an unwelcome guest.

Thirty-seven maxims follow the prologue. In them Ptahhotep counsels eloquence among other things, but warns that it is hidden and must be diligently sought after. Moreover, he concedes, persuasive speech can be found in wholly unexpected places.

> Good speech is more hidden than the emerald, but it may be found with maidservants at the grindstones. (*ANET*, 412)

Still, mastering the art of correct speech is no minor task, and eloquence is more difficult than any craft. Success in this important endeavor has its own reward, for courtiers inspire respect by the scope of their knowledge and the persuasiveness of their speech.

Correct speech implies truthfulness as well as eloquence. According to Ptahhotep, truth alone endures time's passage. Convinced of this intrinsic connection between truth and permanence, Ptahhotep denies any future to wrongdoing. Fraud may acquire riches temporarily, but "wrongdoing has never brought its undertaking into port."

The courtier must know when to be silent, particularly in the presence of powerful individuals. Ptahhotep offers advice on the right way to deal with various types of relationships. He seems to consider proper deference at table to be particularly important. The operative word seems to be "caution," and an ability to stay in one's place appears essential, especially in a setting where ambition thrives and suspicion lurks within the minds of rulers who seek to preserve their power in the face of aspiring underlings.

Courtiers seem to have been especially vulnerable on the erotic front; for this reason Ptahhotep issues a sharp warning against making overtures toward women.

> One is made a fool by limbs of fayence, as she stands (there), become (all) carnelian. A mere trifle, the likeness of a dream—and one attains death through knowing her. (*ANET*, 413)

Like Qoheleth, Ptahhotep thinks women have destroyed huge numbers of men; both teachers chose to express the devastating power of women with reference to the number "a thousand." Nevertheless, Ptahhotep recognized the great worth of a wife, whom he likened to a profitable field, a popular metaphor in the ancient world.[8]

The Instruction of Ptahhotep concludes with a lengthy discussion of the two possible responses to such advice. Naturally, hearing is the desired response; those whom God loves will listen attentively and obey their father's advice. On the other hand, failure to hear is an abomination to God; those who refuse to hear find themselves in an existential paradox: "dying while alive every day." Such a one is a fool, and "guilt is his food." The hearer, however, will eventually pass along the teaching to his son, thereby renewing the instruction.

From the period of the Middle Kingdom two Instructions merit our consideration, although a third has been preserved. These works are *The Instruction of King Merikare*, *The Instruction of King Amenemhet*, and *The Instruction of Sehetepibre* (or *Loyalist Instruction*).

Whereas Ptahhotep was a vizier to the pharaoh, and his teaching was directed to his own son, the unknown author of the partially preserved instruction *Instruction of Merikare* was a pharaoh writing for his son who reigned in the twenty-second century. Alongside repeated emphasis on silence and eloquence stand words of counsel concerning royal responsibility to ensure justice. At the same time, a certain ruthlessness appears.

> Do not kill a man when thou knowest his good qualities, one with whom thou didst once sing the writings. (*ANET*, 415)[9]

The implicit becomes entirely explicit in another connection, where Merikare is advised to kill talkers, presumably spreaders of political unrest, and to banish all memory of excitable persons.

The powerful sanction for behavior inherent within belief in a final judgment at death presents itself for the first time in this teaching, although Ptahhotep's silence in this regard does not appear to be overly significant. A new note is also struck by the claim that "good speech is more valorous than any fighting." In short, self-mastery requires far more effort than conquering enemy soldiers.

The bulk of this instruction concerns advice for the king's conduct with regard to the daily affairs of state. For one brief moment the pharaoh confesses to having done something wrong; such admission of misconduct by a divine ruler was a rarity in ancient Egypt. Perhaps it is significant that this teaching values human character above ritual performance.

> More acceptable is the character of one upright of heart than the ox of the evildoer. (*ANET*, 417)[10]

Such exalted thinking does not lead beyond self-interest, for the author proceeds to advise careful attention to oblations so that God will be disposed to return the favor. In this teacher's view, the hidden creator whose might repelled the chaos monster is attentive to the tears of human beings. Perhaps it is noteworthy that the scribe who copied this instruction identified himself as the "truly silent one," suggesting that the epithet has already become a technical term.

It should be noted that a new tone can be heard in this text: life's shadow side lurks nearby. God hides from humans, who sin unwittingly if not consciously. Although a judgment is set, one's fate cannot be altered through magical acts that aim at controlling the gods. In addition to this theological shift, another change occurs in the character of teaching, which assumes explicit political ends approaching propaganda.

The Instruction of Amenemhet consists of advice given by King Amenemhet I to his son about 1960 BCE. Since the pharaoh died as a result of conspiracy within his harem, the counsel is decidedly pessimistic.[11] In short, Amenemhet warns against placing trust in anyone. Despite his good works, which the king parades before his son, calamity befell him from trusted servants. Once again private experience provides the lesson by which others may profit; to that end the king tells about the fatal hour when he slept, oblivious to danger from his intimates.

The Loyalist Instruction, or *Sehetepibre*, enjoins loyalty to the king and recommends a strong workforce. Two other fragmentary instructions from this early period are *The Instruction of a Man for His Son*, which concerns speech, the king, silence, and discretion; and *Papyrus Ramesseum II*, which has four sayings about servants and mentions the sage, the fool, the silent man, and the ignoramus.

During the New Kingdom a different religious ethos took shape, largely because of the collapse of divine order. Whereas earlier sages thought they experienced God indirectly in the political state, law, and daily life, scribes now sought to make contact with God more directly through prayer and worship in general. Two instructions from this period manifest this new spirit magnificently: *The Instruction of Ani* and *The Instruction of Amenemope*. A third, *The Instruction of Amennakhte*, is too fragmentary to throw further light on the picture that these two teachings paint.

The scribe responsible for *The Instruction of Ani* was a minor official; a unique feature is an epilogue consisting of a dialogue between father and son. In it the son, Khonshotep, promises that he will tender an obedient response to his father. The instruction strongly endorses passivity, holiness, and religious duty. Considerable attention falls to preparation for marriage and proper conduct toward a wife, as if this instruction were actually written for a young man about to venture forth on his own. Ani's firm reminder that the lad's mother had made innumerable sacrifices in his behalf, particularly by providing daily beer and bread while he was in school, may strengthen this interpretation.

In this text a warning against foreign women occurs, a theme that assumed prominence in biblical proverbs as well.

> Be on thy guard against a woman from abroad, . . . a deep water, whose windings one knows not, a woman who is far away from her husband. "I am sleek," she says to thee every day. She has no witnesses when she waits to ensnare thee. (*ANET*, 420)

While active resistance of foreign women is necessary, one should not object to *God's* decisions, even when they entail an early death. At all times care should be taken lest God become angry; special attention belongs to the act of transporting the statues of gods in ritual processions. Indeed, the ideal is to be silent, pray, and show respect for older people. Such a cautious lifestyle implies a certain kind of secretiveness, together with a fleeing into one's own inner sanctuary.

The Instruction of Amenemope consists of thirty chapters, which exhibit parallelism and four-line strophes. The introduction has a series of infinitives that underscore the purpose of the teaching; in this respect the text resembles the introduction to the first collection in the book of Proverbs (chaps. 1–9). The final chapter of *Amenemope* describes the contents as entertaining, instructive, and powerful.

> See thou these thirty chapters;
>> They entertain, they instruct;
> They are the foremost of all books;
>> They make the ignorant to know.
> If they are read out before the ignorant,
>> Then he will be cleansed by them.
>> > (*ANET*, 424)

The fourth chapter contrasts the heated one and the silent one; the former resembles a tree growing in the open and experiencing rapid destruction, while the latter is like a tree growing in a garden. Naturally, that tree with such fortunate surroundings flourishes, yielding sweet fruit and pleasant shade. The same imagery occurs in Psalm 1 and Jeremiah 17:5–8.

The similarities between *Amenemope* and Proverbs 22:17–24:22 are so close that borrowing seems highly likely. Those affinities can be seen in the following comparisons.[12]

> Never make friends with an angry man
> nor keep company with a bad-tempered one.
>> (Prov. 22:24 NEB)

> Do not associate to thyself the heated man,
>> Nor visit him for conversation.
>> (*Amenemope* 11.13–14; *ANET*, 423)

> Do not move the ancient boundary-stone
> which your forefathers set up.
>> (Prov. 22:28 NEB)

> Do not carry off the landmark at the boundaries of the
> arable land.
>> (*Amenemope* 7.12; *ANET*, 422)

> You see a man skilful at his craft:
> he will serve kings, he will not serve common men.
>> (Prov. 22:29 NEB)

As for the scribe who is experienced in his office,
    He will find himself worthy (to be) a courtier.
                    (*Amenemope* 27.16–17; *ANET*, 424)

Do not wear yourself out to get rich;
    be wise enough to desist.
When your eyes light upon it, it is gone;
    for suddenly it takes wings to itself,
    flying like an eagle toward heaven.
                    (Prov. 23:4–5)

Do not strain to seek an excess,
When thy needs are safe for thee.
If riches are brought to thee by robbery,
. . . .
(Or) they have made themselves wings like geese
And are flown away to the heavens.
                    (*Amenemope* 9.14–11.5; *ANET*, 422)

Do not eat the bread of the stingy;
    do not desire their delicacies;
        for like a hair in the throat, so are they.
                    (Prov. 23:6–7a)

Be not greedy for the property of a poor man,
Nor hunger for his bread.
As for the property of a poor man, it (is) a blocking to
    the throat.
                    (*Amenemope* 14.5–7; *ANET*, 423)

In light of these striking similarities, the rendering of Proverbs 22:20 in terms of
Amenemope 27:7–10 seems firmly established.

Here I have written out for you thirty sayings,[13]
full of knowledge and wise advice,
to impart to you a knowledge of the truth,
that you may take back a true report to him who sent you.
                    (Prov. 22:20, my trans.)

See thou these thirty chapters:
They entertain; they instruct;
They are the foremost of all books;
They make the ignorant to know.
                    (*ANET*, 424)

We have by no means exhausted the possibilities of similarities between this
text and Proverbs. Elsewhere we read that humans propose but God disposes;
men and women may make elaborate plans, but God's will works itself out even
when it goes against human calculations. Again we confront cautious advice not

to empty one's soul to every Tom, Dick, and Harry, but to guard one's innermost thoughts against profanation. In addition, we encounter the usual pleas for responsive listening and obedient action, and we experience the zeal with which instructions were given. To be sure, we must not discount the possibility that some of these similarities between Proverbs and *Amenemope* represent universal concerns, but this explanation hardly suffices for all the resemblances above.

With *Amenemope* we sense a heightening of piety beyond *Ani*. Worship and morality lie at the heart of the instruction in these thirty chapters. Ethical motivation transcends selfish concerns, for right conduct is enjoined because of love for God. At the same time, God's ways are inscrutable, even if he has given *ma'at* for the ordering of life. Despite the fact that all are sinners, lacking essential knowledge, God sails the ship successfully into harbor. Since the all-knowing One has compassion, human beings should practice hospitality toward one another and engage in acts of love that demonstrate self-mastery.

So far we have focused on instructions from the Old, Middle, and New Kingdoms. Two texts in the language of everyday speech, Demotic, continue the teaching tradition: *The Instruction of Ankhsheshonqy*[14] and *Papyrus Insinger*. The former teaching resembles the Aramaic *Sayings of Ahiqar* in that it represents instructions transmitted by a wise man who has fallen out of favor with the ruler. The opening narrative states that Ankhsheshonqy was implicated in a palace revolt and underwent a long imprisonment, during which time he saved the potsherds in which he received his daily food and managed to copy down on them the teachings that he considered worth preserving. Two things stand out about these sayings: (1) they make use of a simple gnomic form resembling biblical proverbs that have traditionally been considered quite early, and (2) they seem to have been addressed to the populace as opposed to an elite circle.

The scope of *Ankhsheshonqy* is quite extensive; it contains more than 550 sayings, many of which are syntactically simple and make up only one line. Synthetic parallelism occurs with greater frequency than antithetic, in sharp distinction from the biblical book of Proverbs. Synonymous parallelism seems to be totally missing from the Demotic text; once again the biblical book of Proverbs differs greatly. The rural background of *Ankhsheshonqy* is evident in many of the sentences, as is a deep religious sentiment. Again and again these religious and moral statements resemble Proverbs and Ecclesiastes.

The following aphorisms exemplify the tone and scope of this instruction.

> The wealth of a wise man is his speech (8.23).
> You may trip over your foot in the house of a great man;
>   you should not trip over your tongue (10.7).
> Do not laugh at your son in front of his mother,
>   lest you learn the size of his father (11.19).
> Say "Good Fate" at the end of old age (11.22).
> Instructing a woman is like having a sack of sand whose side
>   is split open (13.20).
> He who is bitten of the bite of a snake is afraid of a coil
>   of rope (14.14).

Do not drink water in the house of a merchant;
  he will charge you for it (16.5).
Do not disdain a small document, a small fire, a small
  soldier (16.25).
Do a good deed and throw it in the water;
  when it dries you will find it (19.10; cf. Eccl. 11:1).
The hissing of a snake is more effective than the braying
  of the donkey (20.9).
There is no Nubian who leaves his skin (21.5).
He who violates a married woman on the bed will have his
  wife violated on the ground (21.19; cf. Job 31:9–10).
The way of the god is before all men (but) the fool cannot
  find it (23.12).
Man is more eager to copulate than a donkey;
  his purse is what restrains him (24.10).
The plans of the god are one thing,
  the thoughts of [men] are another (26.14).
Do not have a merchant for a friend;
  he lives for taking a slice (28.4; cf. Sir. 27:2).
                              (*AEL*, 3:159–84)

Papyrus Insinger, perhaps in its original form from the Ptolemaic period
(fourth and third centuries), comprises twenty-five teachings, each of which bears
a superscription. The religious grounding of these instructions, which make use
of the gnomic form, is pervasive. The earlier ideal of silence is replaced by a concept of equilibrium, by which is meant self-mastery that avoids every extreme.
Naturally, sin is a force that disturbs the equilibrium, and God punishes such acts
that endanger the balance. Even apparent prosperity of sinners is deceptive, for
God patiently allows sufficient time to elapse for retribution to become effective.
As the author nears the end of each chapter, he introduces a paradox that under-
mines the earlier teaching, suggesting that one cannot predict the future, which
lies in the deity's hands. People fall into one of two camps, the wise or fools.

The aphorisms cover a wide range of topics.

He who thrusts his [chest] at the spear will be struck by it (4.3).
He who raves with the crowd is not called a fool (4.11).
[The] evil that befalls the fool, his belly and his phallus bring it (6.1).
The fate and the [fortune] that come, it is the god who sends them (7.19).
No instruction can succeed if there is dislike (8.24).
Thoth has placed the stick on earth in order to teach the fool by it (9.6).
There is one who knows the instruction, yet he does not know
    how to live by it (9.17).
Before the god the strong and the weak are a joke (11.20).
One does not ever discover the heart of a woman anymore than
    (one knows) the sky (12.22).
Better a serpent in the house than a fool who frequents it (13.10).
Law and justice cease in a town when there is no stick (14.16).
He who has passed sixty years, everything has passed for him (17.11).
Death saves from prison because of prayer (20.6).
The counsel that occurs to the fool is as weightless as the wind (22.19).

Old age is a good time in life because of (its) gentleness (23.13).
The little bee brings the honey (25.2).
What comes from the earth returns to it again (30.6).
When you walk along the street, leave the way to him who is old (33.24).

(AEL 3:184–217)

The Scribal Tradition

One further Instruction belongs to those texts in which the scribal profession is singled out as more honorable than all other occupations. I have already referred to it in connection with the discussion of Sirach 38:24–39:11. This Egyptian text, *The Instruction of Khety, Son of Duauf* (also called *The Satire of the Trades*), paints a miserable picture of work in the period between 2150 and 1750. Only the scribal trade is a pleasant one, according to this satire, whereas all other forms of labor are debilitating to mind and body. Among those mentioned, the author spares no single occupation, but with almost brutal force describes the unwelcome features of the following professions, among others: stoneworkers, goldsmiths, carpenters, barbers, reed cutters, potters, bricklayers, vintners, weavers, arrow makers, field hands, sandal makers, fowlers, and fishermen. The scribe alone carries out assigned tasks without the hostile eyes of a supervisor nearby, Khety argues, and it follows that nothing surpasses writing—not even affection for one's mother.

A similar note is struck in a number of scribal texts that have survived the ravages of time. *In Praise of Learned Scribes* (c. 1300 BCE) concedes that ancient scribes were unable to construct for themselves lasting pyramids or to preserve their names in progeny, but "they gave themselves [*the papyrus-roll* as a lector] priest, the writing-board as a son-he-loves, (books) wisdom (as) their pyramids, the reed-pen (as) their child, and the back of a stone for a wife" (*ANET*, 431–32). The author proceeds to call books more effective than houses or inscriptions on stone (stelae), since the constant recitation of scribes' names constitutes a kind of immortality. This text even allocates a magical power to the teachings and attributes to sages an ability to look into the future with uncanny clarity.

Similarly, *The Instruction of a Man for His Son* mentions the incredible power within the teacher's grasp. In this author's words a scribe "teaches the mute to speak, and he opens the ears of the deaf." Despite this exalted status that befell scribes, considerable evidence points to a certain hesitancy on the part of some students to devote themselves fully to learning. *Papyrus Sallier* (I, 6.9–7.9; *LAE*, 343–44) alludes to a scribe who has neglected the writings and urges him to look at the sorry lot of field hands. This choice of alternative labor is a clever hint that the lazy scribe will soon be performing such manual work if he does not amend his ways soon. *Papyrus Anastasi* (IV, 9.4–10.1; *LAE*, 346–47) describes the miserable treatment a soldier undergoes and pleads with a certain Inena to reconsider his claim that a soldier fares better than a scribe. The argument that lessons are often too difficult fails to convince the author of *Papyrus Anastasi* (V, 8.1–9.1; *LAE*, 344–45), who observes that even apes can be taught to dance and horses can be tamed. All else failing, prayer to Thoth for skill in writing is appropriate (*Papyrus Anastasi* V, 9.2–10.2; *LAE*, 345). The ultimate goal is that scribes will embody the traditions they preserve; this sentiment must surely underlie Amunnakhte's admonition to his student: "Become like a chest of writings" (*LAE*, 342).

We know very little about the actual learning experience in ancient Egypt, although repetition seems to have characterized that setting.[15] Students recited texts from memory, copying ancient instructions over and over. This method of learning probably continued even after the meaning of the ideograms had long since faded from memory, resulting in copious scribal errors. Perhaps, too, examinations were given similar to the Akkadian "Dialogue between an Examiner and a Student" (COS, I, 592–93). Pride of accomplishment sometimes produced sarcasm about less astute fellows (cf. the Egyptian letter from one scribe to another in *ANET*, 475–79). In addition, noun lists (onomastica) were compiled, consisting of current encyclopedic knowledge concerning the different professions, flora, fauna, and so forth.

Discussion Literature

Radical social changes within the structure of Egyptian life gave birth to a significant protest against earlier expressions of confidence in the way things were. Ranging from pessimistic utterances, complaints, and protests against dominant social forces to hedonistic grasping after life's pleasures at any cost, this literature also manifests a tamer spirit now and again, particularly in debates and fables.

Such pessimism as can be found in *The Prophecies of Neferti, The Lamentations of Khakheperre-sonbe, The Admonitions of Ipuwer*, and *The Dispute of a Man with His Soul (Ba)* carries a strong element of political propaganda. *Neferti*, for example, maintains the literary fiction of prophecy, whereas it actually looks back upon the immediate past. Accordingly, this text describes the times prior to Ammenemes as chaotic and thereby justifies that king's usurpation of the throne for the purpose of establishing order. Similarly, *Ipuwer* emphasizes the calamities that had befallen the land and lauds the reigning monarch for the restoration of beneficent rule. Things had become so intolerable that the "great and small" exclaimed: "'I wish I might die.' Little children say, 'He should not have caused <me> to live.'" The proverbial hot-tempered man responded to such chaos with a blasphemous retort: "If I knew where God is, then I would serve Him" (*LAE*, 215–16).

The Lamentations (or *Complaints*) *of Khakheperre-sonbe* is couched in the form of a discourse between a man and his other self. The author complains of his own inadequate vocabulary, inasmuch as words have become ineffective through constant use.

> Would that I had unknown speeches, erudite phrases in a new language which has not yet been used, free from the usual repetitions, not the phrases of past speech which (our) forefathers spoke. (*LAE*, 231)

The following comment that "whatever has been said has been repeated, while what has been said, has been said" recalls Qoheleth's complaint that there was nothing new under the sun, since everything had already been spoken. Nevertheless, Khakheperre-sonbe ventures to utter something new, specifically that things are deteriorating throughout the land. Because of such dire straits the author wishes for additional knowledge, together with an enlarged capacity for suffering. Such endurance is necessary, since "every day one wakes to suffering. . . . Everyone is lying in crookedness. Precision in speech is abandoned" (*LAE*, 233). Once again the resemblance with Ecclesiastes is striking, for Qoheleth complained that perversion had occurred so that none did right.

This comparison with Ecclesiastes may extend even further. The opening words of *Khakheperre-sonbe* sound remarkably like the beginning lines of the epilogue to Ecclesiastes.

> The gathering together of sayings, the culling of phrases, the search for words by an inquisitive mind, which . . . wrote. (*LAE*, 231)

> In addition to being a wise man, Qoheleth also taught the people knowledge, and he weighed, searched out, and arranged many proverbs. Qoheleth sought to find pleasing expressions, and he faithfully wrote trustworthy words. (Eccl. 12:9–10, my trans.)

Once more we are compelled to ask: Could the enigmatic title *Qoheleth* have something to do with collecting, that is, gathering together, words of truth?

The Dispute of a Man with His Soul or *The Dispute over Suicide* registers some of the same points I have already alluded to, but it moves one step further to describe death as highly desirable.

> Death is in my sight today
>   (Like) the recovery of a sick man,
>   Like going out into the open after a *confinement*.
> Death is in my sight today
>   Like the odor of myrrh
>   Like sitting under an awning on a breezy day.
> Death is in my sight today
>   Like the odor of lotus blossoms,
>   Like sitting on the bank of drunkenness.
>   . . . .
> Death is in my sight today
>   Like the longing of a man to see his house (again),
>   After he has spent many years held in captivity.
>   (*ANET*, 407)

This text constitutes a dialogue between a man and his soul. Weary of life, the man contemplates suicide, but the soul objects at first because of anxiety lest there be no mortuary service for him. As an alternative course of action the soul encourages hedonistic abandon. In the end the soul seems to agree to remain with the man regardless of his ultimate decision.

Echoes of this pessimistic mood can be heard in *The Tale of the Eloquent Peasant,* an entertaining story about abuse of power and its eventual punishment.[16] The simple plot about a corrupt official who robbed a peasant and lived to regret his hasty action against so eloquent an individual, provides an occasion for elaborate discussions of justice's demands. The imprisoned peasant's articulate defense of his cause provided excellent entertainment at the royal court. At the same time, the discourses served as models for conduct in office, for they reminded rulers that they had a responsibility for executing justice in behalf of every citizen regardless of social status.

The Song of the Harper urges enjoyment while life lasts, for no one takes anything into the next world and none returns from that place. The author argues that ancient worthies who built elaborate chapels to assure survival after death wasted their time, for those edifices now lie in ruins. The natural consequence of this unhappy disclosure is to seize life's bounty in the present moment.

> Follow your desire while you live.
> Place myrrh upon your head,
> Clothe yourself in fine linen,
> Anointed with real wonders
> Of the god's own stores.
> (*LAE*, 307)

Such reflection on self-gratification leads the poet to utter the shocking bit of advice: "Do not control your passion until that day of mourning comes for you." How far this thinker has departed from the ancient teacher's admonition to acquire self-control above all else!

In the light of such passionate literature of protest, those fables and disputes that discuss the advantages and disadvantages of various trees, for example, strike readers as tame indeed. What does a dispute between the heart and stomach have to do with pessimistic literature of the sort we have been discussing? Perhaps the most that should be said is that both kinds of literature manifest a contentious spirit. To be sure, they highlight the negative aspects of existence, and for that reason the inclusion of fables and disputes in this discussion of protest literature is not entirely inappropriate.

What impact did ancient instructions and literature of protest have on Egyptian society? If we can answer that question on the basis of citations within biographical literature and royal inscriptions, the teachers must have wielded unusual power in their own day and for generations afterward. The very preservation of the names of these ancient teachers, together with their concepts, for more than fifteen hundred years bears convincing testimony to the signal importance of Egyptian teachers. But an even more telling indication of the impact of the Instructions can be seen in the adoption of the concept of "the silent one" as paradigmatic for "ideal biographies." In a word, the teachers instructed society with regard to the art of living; that is no small contribution.

MESOPOTAMIAN WISDOM

Unlike the Egyptians, Sumerian scribes arranged proverbs in separate anthologies.[17] At least twenty-four collections have survived, although their meaning is not yet as clear as one could wish. One important text, *The Instructions of Šuruppak*,[18] the survivor of the flood in Sumerian lore, resembles Egyptian teachings, even to the formal feature of father and son as teacher and instructed one.

> My son, let me give you instructions,
>> May you pay attention to them!
>>> (*IS*, 15)

> The instructions of an old man are precious,
> May you submit to them.
>> (*IS*, 35)

The counsel pertains to some of the same themes that we have isolated in Egyptian Instructions.

> [My] son, do not sit (alone) in a [chamber] with someone's wife.
>> (*IS*, 37)

> [A man installs] a good woman for a good field.
>> (*IS*, 16)

Disputations between two scribes, a schoolboy and his supervisor, two women, a bird and a fish, summer and winter, and various gods resemble the debates in Egyptian literature, although in Sumerian texts a god resolves the issue. Noun lists also were drawn up by these Sumerian scribes, together with satires—for example, those concerning a thief, a lame man, and a drunkard. In addition, considerable discussion of the scribal profession has survived. These *edubba* (tablet house) texts describe the various situations accompanying school days in ancient Sumer.

The similarities between Egyptian and Sumerian wisdom extend even farther than use of the same literary forms. Common themes also occur; one Sumerian text gives a powerful description of the aging process. This account is closer to Ecclesiastes than to Ptahhotep in its use of poetic imagery.

> (I was) a youth (but now) . . . my black mountain has produced white gypsum . . . my teeth which used to chew strong things can no more chew strong things. . . . (*SSP*, 93)

But we turn to another biblical narrative to find a closer parallel to the Sumerian text in its entirety, for the emphasis falls on the mysterious power young girls possess for revitalizing old men. The same assumption underlies the attempt to restore King David's waning life force by allowing him to sleep with the youthful Abishag (1 Kgs. 1:1–4).

One important departure from Egyptian wisdom occurs in the Sumerian variation to the biblical Job.[19] At least two significant reasons prevented the problem of theodicy from unduly occupying the Egyptian sages' thoughts.[20] Belief in life after death softened any experience of innocent suffering, for everything would be set right in the next life, and the absence of legal codes in Egypt meant that humans were less likely to try to subject their gods to rules that applied among men and women. In ancient Sumer the problem of unjust suffering elicited an early protest, in this case an objection that the gods made human beings with a basic flaw.

> They say—the sages—a word righteous (and) straightforward:
> "Never has a sinless child been born to its mother,
> . . . a sinless *workman* has not existed from of old."
>
> (*ANET*, 590)

Nevertheless, the god eventually looked favorably upon the sufferer, granting joy once more as a reward for proper conduct during suffering.

The same theme is taken up again and pursued at great depth in *I Will Praise the Lord of Wisdom* (*BWL*, 21–62). In this version a member of the nobility undergoes a complete reversal in fortune and becomes a social outcast. As if this loss of social status were not sufficient misery, the man also becomes seriously ill. While struggling to understand the reason for this sudden antagonism on God's part, the sufferer dares to think the unthinkable.

> I wish I knew that these things would be pleasing to one's god!
> What is good for oneself may be offense to one's god,
> What in one's own heart seems despicable may be proper to one's god,
> Who can know the will of the gods in heaven?
> Who can understand the plans of the underworld gods?
> Where have humans learned the way of a god?
>
> (*ANET*, 597)

As a consequence of this conviction that values must be reversed where gods are concerned, resignation seizes the sufferer. He attempts a cure through exorcism, wherein he tries to name every conceivable disease, and thus to drive the evil spirit out, and finally confesses abiding trust in his eventual restoration. At this point he experiences three suprahuman visitations that bring about a complete recovery.

Although the appropriateness of viewing this text as a Babylonian Job has been contested in favor of a kind of *Pilgrim's Progress*,[21] there can be no question at all about the pertinence of the next text, *The Babylonian Theodicy*, to the book of Job. Cast in the form of a friendly dialogue between a sufferer and his companion, this acrostic text consists of twenty-seven stanzas of eleven lines each. Dating from about 1000 BCE, it too emphasizes the remoteness of the gods and the inscrutability of their ways, complaining that they made human beings prone to injustice.

The mind of the god, like the center of the heavens, is remote;
Knowledge of it is very difficult; people cannot know it.
. . . .
Narru . . .
And majestic Zulummar . . .
And goddess Mami . . .
Gave twisted speech to the human race.
With lies, and not truth, they endowed them forever.

(ANET, 604)

In the initial stages of the dialogue the companion offers reasonably adequate responses to problems raised by the sufferer, but as the argument intensifies the answers become less satisfactory. At one point he even admits that god-fearing persons may lack sumptuous spreads on the table; nevertheless, he insists that they will not starve to death. Although the sufferer stoutly denies having done anything deserving of such harsh treatment from the gods, he eventually lowers his head and utters a prayer for help from the god who has temporarily abandoned his cause.

These three attempts to find a satisfactory response to unjust suffering stop short of considering the termination of life, and for that reason they are somewhat tame when compared with *The Dialogue of Pessimism*. This conversation between a master and his servant culminates in a radical answer to the supreme question that sages posed: What is good for men and women? That answer was: "To have my neck and yours broken and to be thrown into the river" (*ANET*, 601). Regardless of how we understand this text—as burlesque (comedy) or as deadly serious (satire)—it testifies to a crippling ennui that renders all action totally meaningless.[22] No persuasive argument favors a particular course of action over its exact opposite, and all incentive for behavior vanishes. The result is complete irreverence.

Do not sacrifice, master, do not sacrifice. You get your god to follow you about like a dog. (*ANET*, 601)

Small wonder a similar disrespect occurs where women are concerned.

["Do not] make love, master, do not make love. A woman is a pitfall, a hole, a ditch, a woman is a sharp iron dagger that slits a man's throat." (*ANET*, 601)

Such pessimistic literature was by no means the only voice to be heard in Akkadian circles. The *Counsels of Wisdom* urges love for one's enemies and enjoins benevolence in language—or silence.

Do not return evil to your adversary;
Requite with kindness the one who does evil to you,
Maintain justice for your enemy.
. . . .

Do not speak ill, speak (only) good.
. . . .
 Do not express your innermost thoughts even when you
are alone.

(ANET, 595)

Among the many disputes, that between the tamarisk and date palm possesses a feature that occurs far more frequently in biblical proverbs than in Akkadian literature.

 I am better than you. Six times I excel, seven times I [. . .] (*ANET*, 593)

This numerical heightening[23] occurs also in *The Words of Ahiqar*, a seventh-century sealbearer under two Assyrian kings, Sennacherib and Esarhaddon.

 Two things [which] are meet, and the third pleasing to Shamash: one who dr[inks] wine and gives it to drink, one who guards wisdom, and one who hears a word and does not tell. (*ANET*, 428)

This advice from a counselor who had been implicated in a palace revolt has numerous features in common with biblical proverbs, especially the necessity of using the rod in disciplining children and the impossibility of recovering a spoken word.

 For a word is a bird: once released no man *can re[capture it]*. First *co[un]t the secrets of the* mouth; then bring out thy [words] by *number*. For the *instruction* of a mouth is stronger than the *instruction* of war. (*ANET*, 428)

 Withhold not thy son from the rod, else thou wilt not be able to save [him from *wickedness*]. (*ANET*, 428)

Ahiqar's advice ranges widely.

 My son (?), do not utter everything which comes into your mind, for there are eyes and ears everywhere. But keep watch over your mouth, lest it bring you to grief! (#14b).

 How can logs strive with fire, meat with a knife,
 (or) a man with a king? (#21)

 I have carried straw and lifted bran,
  but there is nothing taken more lightly than a
  foreigner (#30).

 Do not be too sweet lest you be [swallowed];
 do not be too bitter [lest you be spat out] (#59).

 [Do not sh]ow an Arab the sea or a Sidonian the st[eppe],
 for their occupations are different (#110).[24]

Thus far we have not considered a whole series of texts that represent these sages' attempt to cope with everyday circumstances—omen literature.[25] The search for auspicious signs and the wish to isolate inauspicious omens as completely as humanly possible arose from the magical base on which Mesopotamian religion was founded. Such omen collections functioned as a means of safeguarding royalty and thus secured order and continuity from which the populace prospered. The *Advice to a Prince* goes one step further in protecting the rights of the citizenry with respect to taxation, forced labor, and appropriation of personal property. By imitating the style of omens, the author warns the king that retribution will become operative if he abuses his power.

Gleanings from the wisdom of Mari have been meager,[26] consisting of a few popular proverbs, some similes, and the like. These tablets date from 1815 to 1760 BCE.

> The bitch, in her passing back and forth (?)
>   gave birth to lame (?) (puppies).

> The fire consumes the reed,
> and its companions pay attention.

> Under the straw the water flows.[27]

> Let him go up to heaven,
> let him go down to the netherworld;
> nobody must see him![28]

The first proverb seems to mean that attention to matters of secondary importance during a time for decisive action inevitably leads to unfortunate consequences. The second observes that misfortune does not go unnoticed by those threatened by its presence, and may constitute astute political advice: "Kill deserters promptly and others will be less likely to raise their voices against the ruler." The third proverb makes the point that appearances often deceive, while the fourth, which is nothing more than a conventional saying, makes use of polarities to express totality.

From this rapid survey of Sumerian and Babylonian wisdom literature one can understand the reasons for viewing wisdom as an international phenomenon. The amazing similarities in the thinking of sages throughout the Fertile Crescent do not demand a hypothesis of borrowing, for most resemblances occur when the teachings address universal problems. Still, the increasing religionization of wisdom in Egypt and Mesopotamia may say something about the inability to sustain a high degree of self-confidence in the wake of a disintegrating society.

In Mesopotamia, once moral categories replaced natural ones the stage was set for a sharp conflict, for humans confronted the problem of death—an experience that was denied the gods. This fact alone points to gross inequity, and when unjust suffering becomes a reality as well, protests inevitably follow. The astonishing thing is the heightening of religious fervor precisely at a time when one would expect wholesale abandonment of religion.

The close connection between schools and temples is instructive, particularly since learning seems to have been the handmaid of religion during the Kassite period (c. 1600–1200 BCE). The scholars of the day were also priestly functionaries. For this reason even the strongest protests against divine conduct occur within the context of eventual submission to God's will. In a real sense, therefore, these texts, such as *I Will Praise the Lord of Wisdom*, function paradigmatically by demonstrating the way anyone undergoing extreme suffering should behave.

Although the moral ethos in ancient Mesopotamia seems to have made room for cultic prostitution and religious ritual rooted in magic, certain texts like *The Šamaš Hymn* achieve a high level, both in religious sentiment and in ethical sensitivity.

> You stand by the traveller whose road is difficult,
> To the seafarer in dread of the waves you give [. . .]
> . . . .
> A man who covets his neighbour's wife
> will [. . .] before his appointed day.
> A nasty snare is prepared for him.
>
> (*BWL*, 131)

It is becoming increasingly clear that wisdom literature from Mesopotamia spread to scribes on the Phoenician coast, Lebanon, and Syria. An Instruction from father to son, *Hear the Advice*, has been found both at Ugarit and Emar (Tell Meskene). Like the Egyptian Ani, it consists of a dialogue between a teacher and a student. Another text attested in both sites is a *Ballad of Heroes Long Gone*, for which a Babylonian recension exists. From Emar comes a text resembling Qoheleth, *Enlil and Namzitarra*, a Sumero-Akkadian bilingual text, which views human destinies as fixed and immutable, so that mortals who think they can shape their future are deluded. Consequently, the text insists, they ought to seize the day, in light of life's brevity.[29]

Similarities between the Kirta legend from Ugarit and the book of Job have been recognized,[30] and the numerical proverb stating that Baal hates two feasts, indeed detests three, has been compared to Proverbs 6:16–19. So far, however, examples of wisdom literature in Canaan and Syria are sparse, even if one adds proverbial sayings in correspondence such as the one in a letter from Tell el-Amarna stating that ants will bite the hand that strikes them, a clever bit of political advice.[31] At Emar there is also a *Debate between the Palm Tree and Tamarisk*, familiar from wisdom in Mesopotamia. A text from Ugarit gives a father's advice to his son, who is about to embark on a journey, symbolizing life itself. The father describes the consequences of obedience or disobedience and discusses in great detail the dangers confronting the young man: the hazards of travel, the risks of the city, the problems accompanying human relationships, and so forth. The father concludes by recalling life's brevity.[32]

The Hebrew Bible mentions Edomite wisdom as a well-known fact (Jer. 49:7), but none has survived to substantiate that tantalizing bit of information. To be sure, Job and certain features of the Yahwistic epic have been viewed as remnants of Edomitic wisdom,[33] but supporting evidence is scant. Perhaps the choice of a geographical setting for Job bears indirect testimony to a vibrant Edomite wisdom tradition.

According to 1 Kings 4:30 (Heb. 5:10) Solomon's wisdom surpassed that of the easterners and Egyptians. This adulation of Solomon proceeds to name some famous sages (Ethan the Ezrahite, Heman, Calcol, and Darda, the sons of Mahol), the first two of whom are alluded to in the superscriptions to Psalms 88 and 89. First Kings 10:23 states that Solomon's wealth and wisdom surpassed those of all other kings. On the basis of our discussion of Egyptian and Mesopotamian wisdom, it seems altogether proper that Israel reckoned itself among the nations of the earth in producing wisdom literature. To be sure, our survey of the evidence suggests that the Israelite author's enthusiasm threatened to distort the situation greatly, for the facts mandate considerably more modesty. Nevertheless, Israel's sages did not need to hang their heads in shame, for they made a distinctive contribution to ancient sapiential literature.

NOTES

1. Brunner, "Die Weisheitsliteratur," 90.
2. Lambert, *BWL*, 1.
3. Ibid. Lambert also thinks "a case could be made for including many of the Babylonian epics in the Wisdom category, because they deal with cosmological problems." The Epic of Gilgamesh explores the problem of human mortality, but the similarities with Qoheleth are dwarfed by the many differences.
4. Brunner, "Die Weisheitsliteratur"; and Williams, "Wisdom in the Ancient Near East."
5. In several instances the addressee is already grown, a fact that has a bearing on the actual social location of wisdom literature. Even in Egypt, the school may not have been the most important context for instruction.
6. Aksel Volten, "Der Begriff der Maat in den ägyptischen Weisheitstexten," in *SPOA*, 73–99; Schmid, *Wesen und Geschichte der Weisheit*; and Miriam Lichtheim, *Maat in Egyptian Autobiographies and Related Studies*.
7. Eberhard Otto, "Der Vorwurf an Gott," *Vorträge der orientalistische Tagung in Marburg, 1950* (1951): 1–15.
8. See my *Samson*, 118–20.
9. That is, a former school companion.
10. This text has often been compared with Samuel's rebuke of Saul in 1 Sam. 15:22.
11. Note the literary fiction of posthumous advice.
12. The pertinent texts can be seen in parallel columns in *ANET*, 424. Glendon E. Bryce, *A Legacy of Wisdom: The Egyptian Contribution to the Wisdom of Israel* (Lewisburg, Pa.: Bucknell University, 1979), has examined this material at great length.
13. The difficult Hebrew word is thus rendered as *šelōšîm*.

14. Berend Gemser, "The Instructions of 'Onchsheshonqy and Biblical Wisdom Literature," in *SAIW*, 134–60.

15. R. J. Williams, "Scribal Training in Ancient Egypt," *JAOS* 92 (1972): 214–21; Benno Landsberger, "Scribal Concepts of Education," *City Invincible: A Symposium on Urbanization and Cultural Development in the Ancient Near East*, ed. Carl H. Kraeling and Robert M. Adams (Chicago: University of Chicago, 1960), 94–122.

16. *LAE*, 31–59; *AEL*, 1:169–84; *ANET*, 407–10; *COS*, 1:98–104.

17. Edmund I. Gordon, *Sumerian Proverbs: Glimpses of Everyday Life in Ancient Mesopotamia* (Philadelphia: University Museum, University of Pennsylvania, 1959); idem, "A New Look at the Wisdom of Sumer and Akkad," *BO* 17 (1960): 122–52; idem, "Sumerian Proverbs and Fables," *JCS* 12 (1958): 1–21, 43–75.

18. Bendt Alster, *The Instructions of Suruppak: A Sumerian Proverb Collection* (Copenhagen: Akademisk, 1974); idem, *Studies in Sumerian Proverbs* (Copenhagen: Akademisk, 1975).

19. Samuel Noah Kramer, "'Man and His God': A Sumerian Variation on the 'Job' Motif," in *Wisdom in Israel*, ed. Noth and Winton Thomas, 170–82.

20. R. J. Williams, "Theodicy in the Ancient Near East," *CJT* 2 (1956): 14–26, especially 18–19.

21. *BWL*, 27.

22. Von Rad, *Wisdom in Israel*, 248 and 311, takes *both* views!

23. W. M. W. Roth, *Numerical Sayings in the Old Testament* (VTSup 13; Leiden: Brill, 1965).

24. Lindenberger, *Aramaic Proverbs of Ahiqar*, 73, 87, 99, 149, 209. On Ahiqar, see Ingo Kottsieper, "The Aramaic Tradition: Ahiqar," *Scribes, Sages, and Seers*, 109–124.

25. Bryce, "Omen Wisdom in Ancient Israel."

26. Angel Marzal, *Gleanings from the Wisdom of Mari* (STP 11; Rome: Biblical Institute, 1976); cf. Henri Cazelles, "Les nouvelles études sur Sumer (Alster) et Mari (Marzal) nous aident-elles à situer les origines de la sagesse israélite?" in *Sagesse de l'Ancien Testament*, ed. Gilbert, 17–27.

27. Jack M. Sasson, "Water beneath Straw: Adventures of a Prophetic Phrase in the Mari Archives," in *Solving Riddles and Untying Knots: Biblical Epigraphic, and Semitic Studies in Honor of Jonas C. Greenfield*, ed. Ziony Zevit et al. (Winona Lake, Ind.: Eisenbrauns, 1995), 599–608.

28. Marzal, *Gleanings*, 16, 23, 27–28, 59.

29. Agustinus Gianto, "Human Destiny in Emar and Qohelet," in *Qohelet in the Context of Wisdom*, ed. Schoors, 473–79.

30. Ed Greenstein, "The Ugaritic Epic of Kirta in the Wisdom Perspective," *Te'uda* 16–17 (2001): 1–13 (in Hebrew). Ignacio Márquez Rowe, "Scribes, Sages, and Seers in Ugarit," *Scribes, Sages, and Seers*, 95–108, does not think scribes at Ugarit composed Wisdom literature.

31. James L. Crenshaw, "A Proverb in the Mouth of a Fool," in *Seeking Out the Wisdom of the Ancients*, ed. Troxel et al., 103–15, discusses several proverbial sayings that appear in various genres, none of which belongs to Wisdom literature.

32. Gianto, "Human Destiny in Emar and Qohelet," 473–79.

33. Robert H. Pfeiffer, "Edomitic Wisdom," *ZAW* 44 (1926): 13–25; idem, "Wisdom and Vision in the Old Testament," in *SAIW*, 305–13.

Conclusion

This pursuit of wisdom began with an analysis of the distinctive sapiential feature of the moral code in Job 31. On the basis of that discussion, the conviction that humans possess the essential means of securing their existence surfaced as characteristically wisdom. Three ingredients went into the definition of wisdom offered in this treatment: a literary corpus, a way of thinking, and a tradition.

The focus upon the world of wisdom yielded evidence that sages, who first drew heavily on popular sayings transmitted by parents, later saw themselves as a professional class. As such, they developed certain literary forms that functioned to communicate their special traditions. The reader has examined these literary types, without being immersed in the waters that threaten to flood the entire Hebrew Bible, specifically the trend to label everything "wisdom."

The consideration of the traditions concerning Solomon, the central figure in the wisdom tradition, to whom at least three sapiential works are attributed, uncovered meager evidence supporting his actual participation in the enterprise devoted to wisdom. His reputation for wealth may have given rise to the further legend concerning extraordinary wisdom. The development from wisdom of the clan through the royal court and ultimately to scribal schools has seemed to merit considerable discussion. The theme for the analysis of the wisdom corpus came from the sages, for they envisioned their task as the search to uncover hidden mystery.

The pursuit of knowledge gave rise to various collections of proverbial sayings that encapsulate truths derived from experience. These sentences and more elaborate instructions reveal a great deal about the values of ancient Israelites, particularly with respect to those things that both enhance life and threaten existence. Although theological reflection occurs unevenly throughout the several independent collections, dominating the latest unit, religious sayings probably existed from the very beginning. Eventually, however, Wisdom was personified and became a sort of heavenly mediator. Her opposite, Folly, was also given some consideration, but this idea seems not to have caught on the way personified Wisdom did, except among the sectarians at Qumran.

The search for God's presence testifies to the sages' willingness to pose profound questions. In Job two issues burn themselves into human consciousness: Does disinterested righteousness actually exist? And, How does one explain innocent suffering, indeed, how should individuals conduct themselves during such misfortune? The arguments put forth by Job and his friends have astonishingly similar presuppositions and grounding, despite their apparent differences. Only the heavenly speaker sees no need to offer warrants for the speeches from the tempest, even if on the moral plane God's conduct raises painful issues. Perhaps Job's final submission was inevitable, especially if the living God came out of hiding for a fleeting moment.

The transience of such experiences impressed itself upon Israel's sages, who eagerly sought permanence in human relationships. This chasing after meaning inevitably aborted, inasmuch as Qoheleth never transcended self-interest even when forced by cruel reality to look on oppression. Death's centrality forever pressed itself on his thoughts, darkening his countenance at those rare moments when positive advice fell from his lips. The perversion of the universe and rottenness at the core of society convinced Qoheleth that life was empty, as purposeless and futile as chasing the wind. Neither knowledge nor pleasure made a decisive difference in this situation, since the former could not be attained and the latter was fleeting.

The awful ordeal through which God put Job and the lonely voice of Qoheleth touched Ben Sira deeply, but he also heard ringing testimony from another source: the sacred traditions of Israel. Convinced that the traditions that nourished him belonged together regardless of their separate origins, Ben Sira embarked on a quest for continuity and survival. The attractive Hellenistic context prompted him to demonstrate the intellectual rigor of his own national traditions and to seek answers to the problem of divine injustice from Greek philosophical treatises. A means of linking Torah and sapiential literature in general presented itself to Ben Sira in the idea of personified Wisdom, who was identified with divine revelation.

This personification of Wisdom advanced further still in Wisdom of Solomon, a Hellenistic work from the very first. In it Wisdom functions in the same way the spirit was thought to have guided and protected the Israelites when they escaped from Egyptian bondage. In Wisdom of Solomon Israel's search widens to embrace alien concepts such as an immortal soul, the dualistic separation of body and soul, barrenness as virtue, and so forth. Greek style prevails in this work, from the literary genre of the entire book to individual chainlike units (sorites). This widening hunt examined certain psalms with affinities to wisdom. The authors of these psalms wrestled with the problems of innocent suffering, divine justice, and life's ultimate meaning in light of its brevity. In addition, the search extends to other apocryphal literature, like the contest of Darius's guards in 1 Esdras 3:1–5:3, and beyond that to *Pseudo-Phocylides*, the Dead Sea Scrolls, and the rabbinic tractate *Pirke Aboth*. That open-ended pursuit pried into doors within the New Testament and early Christian literature, if only momentarily. The aim was to discover what effects, if any, the revolutionary teaching of the books of Job and Qoheleth had on the Gospels' portrayal of Jesus.

The prevailing view that sages based their teachings on what they observed in daily existence rather than on revealed knowledge has recently come under scrutiny, for even Qoheleth made claims about knowledge that could not have been acquired empirically. It has seemed worthwhile, therefore, to examine the place of revelation in Wisdom literature.

From time to time I have made theological observations about the evolution of sapiential thought in Israel. It seemed proper, therefore, to attempt to trace the final outcome of such reflection, especially since that intellectual development implies a bankruptcy of the mind and heart. Thus I have examined the birth of skepticism, taking care to indicate the chief factors that led to belief that God could not be known and humans could not secure their existence. In truth, the old conviction that wisdom was wholly inaccessible bore its special kind of fruit. Still, such skepticism was a means of coping for those who proposed a viable alternative to traditional Yahwism. Even during a perceived crisis of spirit, wisdom's representatives demonstrated remarkable resiliency and confidence in the power of the intellect, however restricted in scope.

Israel's sages participated in a phenomenon that enveloped the entire Fertile Crescent. Egyptian and Mesopotamian wisdom preceded canonical sapiential literature by nearly two millennia. Furthermore, the nonbiblical wisdom influenced Israel's thinking in clearly discernible ways. For this reason, we have taken a close look at Egyptian and Mesopotamian wisdom literature, hoping all the time to allow Israelite wisdom to stand out as a distinct entity. My aim has been to clarify, not to elevate canonical materials at the expense of texts that inspired Egyptian and Sumero-Babylonian sages for millennia.

In short, we ourselves have pursued knowledge, searched for divine presence, chased after meaning, engaged in a quest for survival, and widened the hunt at every juncture. In doing so, we have labored to carry on the quest that our remote ancestors began. Like them, we encounter the limits of knowledge precisely at the point where ultimate issues impinge on the intellect. Like them, too, we confess an inability to know anything that would enable us to master the universe for human good, for God excels at concealing things. Still, we have learned some things—and that valuable link connects us through the centuries with Israel's sages. For the opportunity to think their thoughts, and thus to enrich our own, we owe an immense debt to the wise men and women who ventured forth on an endless search more than three thousand years ago.

Bibliography
(Selected and Annotated)

Texts, Translations, and Notes

Alster, Bendt. *The Instruction of Surrupak: A Sumerian Proverb Collection.* Copenhagen: Akademisk, 1974.

——. *Proverbs of Ancient Sumer: The World's Earliest Proverb Collection.* Bethesda, Md.: CDL, 1997. Original analysis of form and structure, with attention to word play.

——. *Studies in Sumerian Proverbs.* Copenhagen: Akademisk, 1975.

Brunner, Hellmut. *Die Weisheitsbücher der Ägypter.* Zurich: Artemis, 1991. Seventeen Instructions from several millennia.

Charlesworth, James H., ed. *The Old Testament Pseudepigrapha.* 2 vols. Garden City, N.Y.: Doubleday, 1983–85. Translation, with notes, of texts, e.g., *Pseudo-Phocylides.*

Foster, Benjamin R. *Before the Muses: An Anthology of Akkadian Literature.* 2 vols. Bethesda, Md.: CDL, 1993. (Abridged in *From Distant Days.* Bethesda, Md.: CDL, 1995.) Lively translation of numerous texts, with important interpretation.

Hallo, William W., ed. *The Context of Scripture.* 3 vols. Leiden: Brill, 1996–2003. Excerpts of texts that throw light on the Bible.

Harrington, Daniel. *Wisdom Texts from Qumran.* London: Routledge, 1996. Examines the evidence for interest in wisdom by the residents of Qumran.

Lambert, W. G. *Babylonian Wisdom Literature.* Oxford: Clarendon, 1960. Classic and pioneering work with lasting value.

Lichtheim, Miriam. *Ancient Egyptian Literature.* 3 vols. Berkeley: University of California, 1973–80. Indispensable because of its scope and judiciousness.

Lindenberger, James M. *The Aramaic Proverbs of Ahiqar.* Baltimore: Johns Hopkins University, 1983. Translation and notes, with an important introduction to the text.

Marzal, Angel. *Gleanings from the Wisdom of Mari.* StP 11. Rome: Biblical Institute, 1976. An apt title.

Pritchard, James B., ed. *Ancient Near Eastern Texts Relating to the Old Testament.* 3rd ed. Princeton: Princeton University, 1969. Comprehensive, although with minimal notation.

Römer, Willem H. Ph., and Wolfram von Soden. *Weisheitstexte I.* Texte aus der Umwelt des Alten Testaments 3/1. Gütersloh: Gerd Mohn, 1990. Comprehensive and essential reading.

Simpson, W. Kelly, ed. *The Literature of Ancient Egypt.* 2nd. ed. New Haven: Yale University, 1973. Limited selections, but useful.

277

Anthologies and Collected Works

Ballard, W. Wayne, and W. Dennis Tucker, eds. *An Introduction to Wisdom Literature and the Psalms: Festschrift Marvin E. Tate*. Macon, Ga.: Mercer University, 2000.

Barré, Michael L., ed. *Wisdom, You Are My Sister: Studies in Honor of Roland E. Murphy, O. Carm., on the Occasion of His Eightieth Birthday*. CBQMS 29. Washington, D.C.: Catholic University of America, 1997. Focuses on canonical books, with minor exceptions.

Brenner, Athalya, ed. *A Feminist Companion to Wisdom Literature*. Feminist Companion to the Bible 9. Sheffield: Sheffield Academic Press, 1995. Important essays by feminist scholars, including one man, who ironically writes on the strange woman.

Crenshaw, James L. *Prophets, Sages, & Poets*. St. Louis: Chalice, 2006. Collected essays on wisdom, psalms, and prophecy.

———. *Urgent Advice and Probing Questions: Collected Writings on Old Testament Wisdom*. Macon, Ga.: Mercer University, 1995. Thirty-eight articles on the wisdom corpus, theodicy, education, method, and the wisdom books.

———, ed. *Studies in Ancient Israelite Wisdom*. New York: Ktav, 1976. Covers the following topics: ancient Near Eastern setting, structure of wisdom thought, theology, literary features, and the larger biblical canon.

Day, John, et al., eds., *Wisdom in Ancient Israel: Essays in Honour of J. A. Emerton*. Cambridge: Cambridge University, 1995. Covers the ancient environment, specific biblical and apocryphal texts, as well as several themes.

Fischer, Irmtraud, Ursula Rapp, and Johannes Schiller, eds. *Auf den Spuren der schriftgelehrten Weisen: Festschrift für Johannes Marböck*. BZAW 331. Berlin: de Gruyter, 2003. Ranges widely over the canon.

Gammie, John G., and Leo G. Perdue. *The Sage in Israel and the Ancient Near East*. Winona Lake, Ind.: Eisenbrauns, 1990. Exhaustive treatment of sages, social locations and functions, sages within the canon, postbiblical developments, and the symbolic universe of sages.

Gammie, John G., et al., eds. *Israelite Wisdom: Theological and Literary Essays in Honor of Samuel Terrien*. Missoula, Mont.: Scholars, 1978. Essays primarily on canonical texts and themes derived from them.

Gilbert, Maurice, ed. *La Sagesse de l'Ancien Testament*. 2nd ed. Gembloux: Duculot, 1990. Papers from the colloquium in Louvain, August 29–31, 1978.

Hoglund, Kenneth, G., et al., eds. *The Listening Heart: Essays in Wisdom and the Psalms in Honor of Roland E. Murphy, O. Carm*. Sheffield: JSOT, 1987. Mostly by students from Duke University demonstrating affection and expertise.

Kaiser, Otto. *Gottes und der Menschen Weisheit*. BZAW 261. Berlin: de Gruyter, 1998.

Leclant, J., ed. *Les Sagesses du proche-orient ancien*. Paris: Presses universitaires, 1963. Papers from a colloquium in Strasbourg in 1962.

Noth, Martin, and D. W. Thomas, eds. *Wisdom in Israel and in the Ancient Near East*. VTSup 3. Leiden: Brill, 1955. Essays honoring H. H. Rowley prior to renewed interest in wisdom.

Perdue, Leo G., ed. *Scribes, Sages, and Seers: The Sage in the Eastern Mediterranean World*. FRLANT 219. Göttingen: Vandenhoeck & Ruprecht, 2008. A collection of essays by specialists in the several cultures of the ancient Near East.

Perdue, Leo G., Bernard Brandon Scott, and William Johnston Wiseman, eds. *In Search of Wisdom: Essays in Memory of John G. Gammie*. Louisville: Westminster/John Knox, 1993. Includes several articles on wisdom in the New Testament, along with significant studies on older literature.

Troxel, Ronald L., Kevin G. Friebel, and Dennis R. Magary, eds. *Seeking out the Wisdom of the Ancients: Essays Offered to Honor Michael V. Fox on the Occasion of His Sixty-fifth Birthday*. Winona Lake, Ind.: Eisenbrauns, 2005.

Introductions and Related Matters

Bauer-Kayatz, Christa. *Einführung in die alttestamentliche Weisheit*. Neukirchen-Vluyn: Neukirchener, 1969. Emphasizes the influence of *ma'at* on biblical wisdom.

Bergant, Dianne. *Israel's Wisdom Literature: A Liberation-Critical Reading*. Minneapolis: Fortress, 1997. Views wisdom from the perspective of creation; good analysis of Wisdom of Solomon.

Berry, Donald K. *Introduction to Wisdom and Poetry of the Old Testament*. Nashville: Broadman, 1995. Traditional investigation, although more broadly based than most introductions to wisdom literature.

Clifford, Richard. *The Wisdom Literature*. Interpreting Biblical Texts. Nashville: Abingdon, 1997. An excellent introduction for laity, clearly written and solidly grounded in research.

————, ed. *Wisdom Literature in Mesopotamia and Israel*. SBLSymS 36. Atlanta: Society of Biblical Literature, 2007.

Collins, John J. *Jewish Wisdom in the Hellenistic Age*. OTL. Louisville: Westminster John Knox, 1997. An excellent analysis of developments within wisdom beginning with Ben Sira, both in Jerusalem and in the Diaspora.

Dell, Katharine. *"Get Wisdom, Get Insight": An Introduction to Israel's Wisdom Literature*. Macon, Ga.: Mercer University, 2000.

Dubarle, A. M. *Les Sages d'Israël*. Lectio divina 1. Paris: Cerf, 1946. Good analyses of biblical content, but dated otherwise.

Duesberg, H., and I. Fransen. *Les Scribes inspirés*. 2 vols. Paris: Desclée, 1939. Comprehensive discussion of intrabiblical relationships between wisdom and other types of literature.

Fichtner, Johannes. *Die altorientalische Weisheit in ihrer israelitisch-jüdischen Ausprägung*. BZAW 62. Giessen: Töpelmann, 1933. A classic reference, still quite valuable for its systematic treatment of concepts such as God and retribution.

Hunter, Alastair. *Wisdom Literature*. London: SCM, 2006. A useful beginner's survey of biblical wisdom.

Küchler, Max. *Frühjüdische Weisheitstraditionen*. OBO 26. Fribourg: Universitätsverlag, 1979. Traces developments in the sages' thinking from Hellenistic times, through rabbinic sources, to Christian views.

Melchert, Charles F. *Wise Teaching: Biblical Wisdom and Educational Ministry*. Harrisburg: Trinity Press International, 1998.

Murphy, Roland E. *The Tree of Life: An Exploration of Biblical Wisdom Literature*. 2nd ed. Grand Rapids: Eerdmans, 1996. A good survey of contemporary scholarship, coupled with sound analyses of biblical literature.

Paffenroth, Kim. *In Praise of Wisdom: Literary and Theological Reflections on Faith and Reason*. New York: Continuum, 2004. A provocative study of biblical wisdom in light of literature (King Lear, Moby Dick, etc.).

Perdue, Leo G. *Wisdom Literature: A Theological History*. Louisville: Westminster John Knox, 2007. Emphasizes the rich theological tradition of sages.

Preuss, Horst-Dietrich. *Einführung in die alttestamentliche Weisheitsliteratur*. UT 383. Stuttgart: Kohlhammer, 1987. A valuable introduction, although marred by ideology, specifically that biblical wisdom borrows too heavily from pagan concepts of God.

Rad, Gerhard von. *Wisdom in Israel*. Translated by James D. Martin. Nashville: Abingdon, 1972. A monumental achievement, even if flawed by an assumption of a Solomonic enlightenment and of wisdom's origins in apocalyptic.

Rankin, O. S. *Israel's Wisdom Literature*. Edinburgh: T & T Clark, 1936. Emphasizes the concept of retribution as central to wisdom.

Schmid, Hans Heinrich. *Wesen und Geschichte der Weisheit*. BZAW 101. Berlin: Töpelmann, 1966. Finds a common development in Egypt, Mesopotamia, and Israel, namely a flourishing of theology that hardens into dogma and evokes a crisis in belief.

Weeks, Stuart. *Early Israelite Wisdom*. Oxford Theological Monographs. Oxford: Clarendon, 1994. A thorough examination of the hypothesis that wisdom was associated with the royal court and professional schools, reaching a negative conclusion on both counts.

Westermann, Claus. *Forschungsgeschichte zur Weisheitsliteratur 1950–1990*. AzTh 71. Stuttgart: Calwer, 1991.

———. *Roots of Wisdom: The Oldest Proverbs of Israel and Other People*. Translated by J. Daryl Charles. Louisville: Westminster John Knox, 1995. Emphasizes the origins of early proverbs in small villages among ordinary people.

Whybray, R. N. *The Intellectual Tradition in the Old Testament*. BZAW 135. Berlin: de Gruyter, 1974. Denies that a professional class of sages existed in Israel, proposing instead a group of well-to-do thinkers.

Social Location, Theology, and Tradition

Boström, Lennart. *The God of the Sages: The Portrayal of God in the Book of Proverbs*. ConBOT 29. Stockholm: Almqvist & Wiksell, 1990. Discusses creation and order, as well as the sages' understanding of human relationships with God.

Brown, William P. *Character in Crisis: A Fresh Approach to the Wisdom Literature of the Old Testament*. Grand Rapids: Eerdmans, 1996. Uses character as the lens through which to view ancient wisdom, specifically the way character is formed, deformed, and reformed.

Clements, Ronald E. *Wisdom for a Changing World: Wisdom in Old Testament Theology*. Berkeley: Bibal, 1990. Treats wisdom's internationalism, concept of health, and its locus at the royal court.

———. *Wisdom in Theology*. Grand Rapids: Eerdmans, 1992. Emphasizes worldly pursuits among the sages: politics, health, family.

Crenshaw, James L. *Defending God: Biblical Responses to the Problem of Evil*. New York: Oxford University, 2005. Evaluates the various explanations for evil in the Bible.

———. *Education in Ancient Israel: Across the Deadening Silence*. New York: Doubleday, 1998. Studies the evidence for schools in Israel, the nature of pedagogy, resistance to learning, and epistemological assumptions of sages.

Davidson, Robert. *Wisdom and Worship*. Philadelphia: Trinity Press International, 1990. Relates wisdom to the Psalms, but also looks at the problem of theodicy, death, and Ben Sira's contribution to worship.

Doll, Peter. *Menschenschöpfung und Weltschöpfung in der alttestamentlichen Weisheit*. SBS 177. Stuttgart: Katholisches Bibelwerk, 1985.

Eaton, John. *The Contemplative Face of Old Testament Wisdom in the Context of World Religions*. Philadelphia: Trinity Press International, 1989. Refreshing analysis of biblical wisdom's affinities with the sacred literature of various religions.

Gese, Hartmut. *Lehre und Wirklichkeit in der alten Weisheit*. Tübingen: Mohr, 1958. Provocative investigation of the tension between belief and reality within the books of Job and Qoheleth.

Golka, Friedemann W. *The Leopard's Spots: Biblical and African Wisdom in Proverbs*. Edinburgh: T & T Clark, 1993. Rejects the hypothesis of schools and court wisdom in favor of popular origins of proverbs, on analogy with African proverbs.

Hausmann, Jutta. *Studien zum Menschenbild der älteren Weisheit*. FAT 7. Tübingen: Mohr, 1994. Discusses actual types of people, their roles and ideals in the oldest canonical proverbs.

Heaton, E. W. *The School Tradition of the Old Testament*. Oxford: Clarendon, 1994. Assumes that schools existed in Israel and examines the canon in this light.

Lang, Bernhard. *Wisdom and the Book of Proverbs: An Israelite Goddess Redefined.* New York: Pilgrim, 1986. Finds the origins of personified Wisdom in an Israelite goddess.

Lemaire, André. *Les écoles et al formation de la Bible dans l'ancien Israël.* OBO 39. Fribourg: Editions Universitaires, 1981. Innovative hypothesis of extensive schools throughout ancient Israel based largely on inscriptions.

McKinlay, Judith E. *Gendering Wisdom the Host: Biblical Invitations to Eat and Drink.* JSOTSup 216. Sheffield: Sheffield Academic, 1996. Examines the theme of "host" in Proverbs, Sirach, and the Gospel of John.

Passaro, Angelos, and Giuseppe Bellia, eds. *The Wisdom of Ben Sira: Studies on Tradition, Redaction, and Theology* (DCLS 1; Berlin: de Gruyter, 2008). Provocative essays by leading specialists.

Penchansky, David, and Paul L. Redditt, eds. *Shall Not the Judge of All the Earth Do What Is Right? Studies on the Nature of God in Tribute to James L. Crenshaw.* Winona Lake, Ind.: Eisenbrauns, 2000. Mostly essays on theodicy.

Perdue, Leo G. *The Sword and the Stylus: An Introduction to Wisdom in the Age of Empires.* Grand Rapids: Eerdmans, 2008. An exhaustive study of the historical context of the sages.

———. *Wisdom and Creation: The Theology of Wisdom Literature.* Nashville: Abingdon, 1994. Indispensable exploration into the metaphors for creation, with excellent attention to biblical texts.

———. *Wisdom and Cult.* SBLDS 30. Missoula, Mont.: Scholars, 1977. Valuable examination of the sages' attitude to the cult, which is viewed as positive.

Rylaarsdam, J. Coert. *Revelation in Jewish Wisdom Literature.* Chicago: University of Chicago, 1946. Traces the emergence of a concept of divine compassion in Wisdom literature.

Sheppard, Gerald T. *Wisdom as a Hermeneutical Construct.* BZAW 151. Berlin: de Gruyter, 1980. Examines various canonical texts from the perspective of wisdom.

Shupak, Nili. *Where Can Wisdom Be Found? The Sage's Language in the Bible and in Ancient Egyptian Literature.* OBO 130. Fribourg: University Press, 1993. The most comprehensive study of sapiential language available, with special attention to Egyptian parallels.

Wilken, Robert, ed. *Aspects of Wisdom in Judaism and Early Christianity.* Notre Dame: University of Notre Dame, 1975. A collection of articles on developments of wisdom during Hellenistic and Greco-Roman times.

Wisdom and the Larger Canon

Blenkinsopp, Joseph. *Sage, Priest, Prophet: Religious and Intellectual Leadership in Ancient Israel.* Louisville: Westminster John Knox, 1995. Illuminates social conditions in ancient Israelite society.

———. *Wisdom and Law in the Old Testament: The Ordering of Life in Israel and Early Judaism.* Rev. ed. Oxford: Oxford University, 1995. Studies the relationship between law and wisdom, with primary attention to law.

Morgan, Donn F. *Wisdom in the Old Testament Traditions.* Atlanta: John Knox, 1981. A linear examination of wisdom influence from premonarchical Israel to postexilic times.

Steiert, Franz-Josef. *Die Weisheit Israels—ein Fremdkörper im Alten Testament?* FThSt 143. Freiburg: Herder, 1990. Argues against the view that wisdom is an alien body within the Hebrew Bible.

Weinfeld, Moshe. *Deuteronomy and the Deuteronomic School.* 1972. Reprint Winona Lake, Ind.: Eisenbrauns, 1992. Views Deuteronomy as a product of the sages, giving special attention to the vocabulary of wisdom.

The Book of Proverbs

Commentaries

Alonso Schökel, Luis, and J. Vilchez. *Proverbios*. Madrid: Cristiandad, 1985. Attention to literary features marks the commentary, which is preceded by a long survey of research in the area of ancient wisdom.

Barucq, André. *Le livre des Proverbes*. SB. Paris: Gabalda, 1964. Somewhat sketchy, but strong on the Greek text of Proverbs.

Gemser, Berend. *Sprüche Salomos*. 2nd ed. HAT 16. Tübingen: Mohr/Siebeck, 1963. Brief and given to summarizing the overall content of chapters 10–31.

McKane, William. *Proverbs: A New Approach*. OTL. Philadelphia: Westminster, 1970. Extensive analysis of ancient Egyptian Instructions, combined with careful investigation of the Septuagint, and dubious theories about early secular proverbs.

Oesterley, W. O. E. *The Book of Proverbs*. Westminster Commentaries. London: Methuen, 1929. Valuable insights give this commentary staying power.

Plöger, Otto. *Sprüche Salomos (Proverbia)*. BKAT 13. Neukirchen-Vluyn: Neukirchener, 1984. An exemplary commentary, rare in searching for larger entities within the book of Proverbs.

Toy, Crawford H. *The Book of Proverbs*. ICC. New York: Scribner's, 1902. Attention to linguistic features and textual variants.

Waltke, Bruce K. *The Book of Proverbs*. 2 vols. NICOT. Grand Rapids: Eerdmans, 2004–2005. A conservative commentary with strong philological emphasis.

Whybray, R. N. *Proverbs*. NCB. Grand Rapids: Eerdmans, 1994. Judicious, perhaps the most useful commentary in English.

General Works

Baumann, Gerlinde. *Die Weisheitsgestalt in Proverbien 1–9*. FAT 16. Tübingen: Mohr/Siebeck, 1996. Exhaustive analysis of the figure of Wisdom in Proverbs 1–9.

Bryce, Glendon E. *A Legacy of Wisdom: The Egyptian Contribution to the Wisdom of Israel*. Lewisburg, Pa.: Bucknell University, 1979. Discusses the relationship between Amenemope and the book of Proverbs.

Camp, Claudia. *Wisdom and the Feminine in the Book of Proverbs*. BLS 11. Sheffield: Almond, 1985. Timely discussion of the role of female imagery among sages.

Dell, Katharine J. *The Book of Proverbs in Social and Theological Context*. Cambridge: Cambridge University, 2006. A careful analysis of the evolution of the canonical book and its religious views.

Fontaine, Carole R. *Traditional Sayings in the Old Testament*. BLS 5. Sheffield: Almond, 1982. Studies the function of proverbial sayings in various cultures as a means of clarifying their use in ancient Israel.

Hermisson, H.-J. *Studien zur israelitischen Spruchweisheit*. WMANT 28. Neukirchen-Vluyn: Neukirchener, 1968. Emphasizes the learned, or literary, aspect of older proverbs, hence their setting in a school sheltered within the temple.

Maier, C. *Die "fremde Frau" in Proverbien 1–9*. OBO 144. Fribourg: Universitätsverlag, 1995. Discusses the "foreign woman" in Proverbs 1–9.

Perry, T. A. *Wisdom Literature and the Structure of Proverbs*. University Park: Pennsylvania State University, 1993. An untraditional approach, emphasizing quadripartite structure.

Sandoval, Timothy J. *The Discourse of Wealth and Poverty in the Book of Proverbs*. BIS 77. Leiden: Brill, 2006. An exemplary analysis.

Schroer, Silvia. *Wisdom Has Built Her House*. Collegeville, Minn.: Liturgical, 2000. An excellent analysis of personified Wisdom.

Sinnott, Alice M. *The Personification of Wisdom*. SOTSMS. Aldershot: Aldersgate, 2005. Views personification as the result of a crisis.

Van Leeuwen, Raymond C. *Context and Meaning in Proverbs 25–27*. SBLDS 96. Atlanta: Scholars, 1988. Searches for larger units; often original.

Washington, Harold C. *Wealth and Poverty in the Instruction of Amenemope and the Hebrew Proverbs*. SBLDS 142. Atlanta: Scholars, 1994. Valuable analysis of Egyptian society and the status of scribes.

Whybray, R. N. *The Book of Proverbs: A Survey of Modern Study*. Leiden: Brill, 1995.

———. *The Composition of the Book of Proverbs*. JSOTSup 168. Sheffield: Sheffield Academic, 1994.

———. *Wealth and Poverty in the Book of Proverbs*. JSOTSup 99. Sheffield: Sheffield Academic, 1990. Indispensable studies, filled with clear discussion and valuable insights.

Williams, James G. *Those Who Ponder Proverbs: Aphoristic Thinking and Biblical Literature*. BLS 2. Sheffield: Almond, 1981. Full of philosophical insights about aphoristic speech and its power to reorient society.

The Book of Job

Commentaries

Alonso Schökel, Luis. *Job*. Madrid: Cristiandad, 1983. Sensitive to literary theory and rhetoric.

Andersen, Francis. *Job*. Tyndale Old Testament Commentaries. Downers Grove, Ill.: InterVarsity, 1976. Conservative viewpoint, and attentive to Hebrew vocabulary.

Balentine, Samuel E. *Job*. Macon, Ga.: Smyth & Helwys, 2006. A fine analysis of the book of Job in light of literature and art.

Clines, David J. *Job 1–20*. WBC 17. Dallas: Word, 1989. Daring, comprehensive, and at times original.

Dhorme, Eduard. *A Commentary on the Book of Job*. Translated by Harold Knight. Nashville: Nelson, 1967. Detailed discussion, particularly of grammar and syntax.

Fohrer, Georg. *Das Buch Hiob*. KAT 16. Gütersloh: Gerd Mohn, 1963. Strongest in treating form-critical issues.

Good, Edwin M. *In Turns of Tempest: A Reading of Job, with a Translation*. Stanford: Stanford University, 1990. Excellent use of literary criticism, with frequent insights and numerous options.

Gordis, Robert. *The Book of Job*. New York: Jewish Theological Seminary of America, 1978. Good use of Jewish tradition about the book of Job.

Habel, Norman. *The Book of Job*. OTL. Philadelphia: Westminster, 1985. The best commentary in English; strong literary and theological analyses.

Janzen, J. Gerald. *Job*. Interpretation. Atlanta: John Knox, 1985. Perceptive, pastoral, and filled with literary allusions.

Newsom, Carol A. "Job." *New Interpreter's Bible*, edited by Leander E. Keck, 4:317–637. Nashville: Abingdon, 1996. Clear, innovative, insightful, and theologically profound.

Pope, Marvin. *Job*. 3rd ed. AB 15. Garden City, N.Y.: Doubleday, 1973. Unmatched in its use of Ugaritic literature.

Rowley, H. H. *Job*. NCB. 1970. Reprint Grand Rapids: Eerdmans, 1980. Contains extensive documentation from an earlier time.

General Works

Beuken, W. A. M., ed. *The Book of Job*. BETL 114. Leuven: Leuven University, 1994. Current research as exemplified in these papers at the Biblical Colloquium in Louvain, August 24–26, 1993.

Dell, Katharine J. *The Book of Job as Sceptical Literature*. BZAW 197. Berlin: de Gruyter, 1991. Strong on the history of interpretation and on form-critical issues.

Gutiérrez, Gustavo. *On Job: God-Talk and the Suffering of the Innocent*. Translated by Matthew J. O'Connell. Maryknoll, N.Y.: Orbis, 1987. Liberation theology, with emphasis on the problem of speaking about God in difficult times.

Hoffman, Yair. *A Blemished Perfection: The Book of Job in Context*. JSOTSup 213. Sheffield: Academic, 1996. Provocative discussion of irony, catalogs, language, and theory.

Iwanski, Dariusz. *The Dynamics of Job's Intercession*. AnBib 161. Rome: Pontifical Biblical Institute, 2006. A holistic approach that links intercession to the covenant lawsuit (*rîb*).

Lévêcque, Jean. *Job et son Dieu*. 2 vols. Paris: Gabalda, 1970. Wordy but sensitive to theological issues.

Lo, Alison. *Job 28 as Rhetoric: An Analysis of Job 28 in the Context of Job 22–31*. VTSup 97. Atlanta: Society of Biblical Literature, 2003.

Mende, T. *Durch Leiden zur Vollendung*. TTS 49. Trier: Paulinus, 1990. Theological discussion of the role of suffering.

Müller, Hans-Peter. *Das Hiobproblem: Seine Stellung und Entstehung im alten Orient und in Alten Testament*. EF 84. Darmstadt: Wissenschaftliche Buchgesellschaft, 1978. Succinct discussion of the essential problems associated with the book.

Nemo, Philippe. *Job and the Excess of Evil*. Translated by Michael Kigel. Pittsburgh: Duquesne University, 1998. Philosophical, ethical, and psychological insights abound.

Newsom, Carol A. *The Book of Job: A Context of Moral Imaginations*. New York: Oxford University, 2003. A pioneering study.

Ngwa, Kenneth Numfor. *The Hermeneutics of the 'Happy' Ending in Job 41:7–17*. BZAW 354. Berlin: de Gruyter, 2005. Emphasizes the merging of retribution and its suspension.

Perdue, Leo G. *Wisdom in Revolt: Metaphorical Theology in the Book of Job*. JSOTSup 112. Sheffield: Almond, 1991. Emphasizes the many different metaphors in the theology of the book.

Pyeon, Yohan. *You Have Not Spoken What Is Right about Me*. StBL 45. New York: Peter Lang, 2003. A study in intertextuality.

Sitzler, Dorothea. *Vorwurf gegen Gott*. SOR 32. Wiesbaden: Harrassowitz, 1995. Analyzes the texts from the ancient Near East that reproach the deity.

Ticciati, Susannah. *Job and the Disruption of Identity*. London: T & T Clark International, 2005. A theological treatise on obedience.

Wahl, A.-M. *Der Gerechte Schöpfer*. BZAW 207. Berlin: de Gruyter, 1993. Stresses the concept of a just creator.

Weiss, Meir. *The Story of Job's Beginning*. Jerusalem: Magnes, 1983. Literary and psychological analysis of the prologue to the book of Job.

Westermann, Claus. *The Structure of the Book of Job*. Translated by Charles A. Muenchow. Philadelphia: Fortress, 1981. Views the book as a lament; contains a survey of research, written by Jürgen Kegler.

Wilde, A. de. *Das Buch Hiob*. OTS 22. Leiden: Brill, 1981. Attentive to linguistic niceties.

Wolde, Ellen van, ed. *Job 28: Cognition in Context*. BIS 64. Leiden: Brill, 2003. A collection of articles from the perspective of cognitive linguistics.

The Book of Ecclesiastes

Commentaries

Bartholomew, Craig G. *Ecclesiastes*. Baker Commentary on the Old Testament Wisdom and Psalms. Grand Rapids: Baker Academic, 2009. Conservative and thorough.

Barucq, André. *Ecclésiaste*. Verbum salutis 3. Paris: Beuchesne, 1968. Often perceptive, but brief.

Crenshaw, James L. *Ecclesiastes*. OTL. Philadelphia: Westminster, 1987. Attends to the history of research, offers a fresh translation, and provides a rationale for the interpretation.

Fox, Michael V. *Qohelet and His Contradictions*. JSOTSup 18. Sheffield: Almond, 1989. Very good treatment of Qoheleth's language and thought, emphasizing epistemology and the absurd.

Galling, Kurt. "Der Prediger." Pages 73–125 in Ernst Würthwein, Kurt Galling, and Otto Plöger, *Die Fünf Megillot*. 2nd ed. HAT 1/18. Tübingen: Mohr/Siebeck, 1969. Learned but brief.

Gordis, Robert. *Koheleth—The Man and His World*. 3rd ed. New York: Schocken, 1968. Excellent use of rabbinic sources and a good sense of style.

Hertzberg, H. W. *Der Prediger*. 2nd ed. KAT 17/4. Gütersloh: Gerd Mohn, 1963. A thorough commentary, often traditional.

Krüger, Thomas. *Qoheleth*. Translated by O. C. Dean Jr. Hermeneia. Minneapolis: Fortress, 2004. One of the strongest commentaries available today—the emphasis falls on deconstruction as a means of creating something credible.

Lauha, Aarre. *Kohelet*. BKAT 19. Neukirchen-Vluyn: Neukirchener Verlag, 1978. Traditional and theological, sometimes problematic.

Lohfink, Norbert. *Qoheleth*. Translated by Sean McEvenue. Continental Commentary. Minneapolis: Fortress, 2003. Perceptive, innovative, with emphasis on Greek influence.

Michel, Diethelm. *Qohelet*. EF 258. Darmstadt: Wissenschaftliche Buchgesellschaft, 1988. Good treatment, solid, and balanced.

Murphy, Roland E. *Ecclesiastes*. WBC 19A. Dallas: Word, 1992. Traditional commentary, useful, and informed.

Podechard, E. *L'Ecclésiaste*. EBib. Paris: Gabalda, 1912. Exhaustive and learned.

Robinson, James T. *Samuel Ibn Gibbon's Commentary on Ecclesiastes* TSMEMJ 20; Tübingen: Mohr Siebeck, 2007. Fascinating study, with translation from the twelfth-century Arabic text.

Schwienhorst-Schönberger, Ludger. *Kohelet*. HTKAT. Freiburg: Herder, 2004. Thoroughly theological, with emphasis on the positive message of Qoheleth.

Seow, Choon-Leong. *Ecclesiastes*. AB 18C. New York: Doubleday, 1997. Excellent use of ancient Near Eastern literature, well documented, and judicious.

Towner, W. Sibley. "Ecclesiastes." *New Interpreter's Bible*, edited by Leander E. Keck, 5:265–360. Nashville: Abingdon, 1997. Brief and pastoral.

Whybray, R. N. *Ecclesiastes*. NCB. Grand Rapids: Eerdmans, 1989. Succinct, useful, and positive.

Zimmerli, Walther. "Das Buch des Predigers Salomo." Pages 123–253 in Helmer Ringgren and Walther Zimmerli, *Sprüche/Prediger*. 3rd ed. ATD 16/2. Göttingen: Vandenhoeck & Ruprecht, 1980. Theologically astute.

General Works

Berlejung, A., and P. van Hecke, eds. *The Language of Qohelet in Its Context: Essays in Honour of Prof. A. Schoors on the Occasion of His Seventieth Birthday*. OLA 164. Leuven: Peeters, 2007.

Burkes, Shannon. *Death in Qoheleth and Egyptian Biographies of the Late Period*. SBLDS 170. Atlanta: Society of Biblical Literature, 1999. Examines the pathos of death in Qoheleth and similar literature.

Christianson, Eric S. *A Time to Tell: Narrative Strategies in Ecclesiastes*. JSOTSup 280. Sheffield: Sheffield Academic, 1998.

Fredericks, Daniel C. *Qoheleth's Language: Re-evaluating Its Nature and Date*. ANETS 3. Lewiston, N.Y.: Edwin Mellen, 1988. Argues for an early date for the book.

Klein, Christian. *Kohelet und die Weisheit Israels*. BWANT 12. Stuttgart: Kohlhammer, 1994. Thorough study of Qoheleth from the standpoint of form.

Koosed, Jennifer L. *(Per)mutations of Qohelet*. LHB/OTS 429. New York: T & T Clark International, 2006. Lively examination of "body" in Qoheleth's discourse.

Lange, A. *Weisheit und Torheit bei Kohelet und in seiner Umwelt*. EHS Theologie Reihe 433. Frankfurt: Peter Lang, 1991. Examines the function of the opposites, wisdom and folly.

Loader, J. A. *Polar Structures in the Book of Qoheleth*. BZAW 152. Berlin: de Gruyter, 1979. Emphasizes interconnecting opposites as thematic unity.

Longman, Tremper III. *The Book of Ecclesiastes*. NICOT. Grand Rapids: Eerdmans, 1998. A good conservative commentary with theological emphasis.

Loretz, Oswald. *Qohelet und der Alte Orient: Untersuchungen zu Stil und theologischer Thematik des Buches Qohelet*. Freiburg: Herder, 1964. Focuses on *topoi*, vocabulary, and parallels with ancient Near Eastern literature.

Miller, Douglas B. *Symbol and Rhetoric in Ecclesiastes: The Place of Hebel in Qoheleth's Work*. Society of Biblical Literature Academia biblica 2. Atlanta: Society of Biblical Literature, 2002.

Perry, T. Anthony. *Dialogues with Kohelet*. University Park: Pennsylvania State University, 1993. Arranges the text as a dialogue between Qoheleth and an opposing voice.

Rudman, Dominic. *Determinism in the Book of Ecclesiastes*. JSOTSup 316. Sheffield: Sheffield Academic, 2001. The role of destiny in Qoheleth.

Salyer, Gary D. *Vain Rhetoric: Private Insight and Public Debate in Ecclesiastes*. JSOTSup 327. Sheffield: Sheffield Academic, 2001.

Schellenberg, Annette. *Erkenntnis als Problem: Quohelet und die alttestamentliche Diskussion um das menschliche Erkennen*. OBO 188. Göttingen: Vandenhoeck & Ruprecht, 2002. Qoheleth's epistemology in the larger canonical context.

Schoors, Antoon. *The Preacher Sought to Find Pleasing Words*. 2 vols. OLA 41, 143. Leuven: Peeters, 1992, 2004. Superb analysis of Qoheleth's language.

———, ed. *Qohelet in the Context of Wisdom*. BETL 136. Leuven: Leuven University, 1998. Papers delivered at the Colloquium Biblicum Lovaniense in 1997.

Shields, Martin A. *The End of Wisdom: A Reappraisal of the Historical and Canonical Function of Ecclesiastes*. Winona Lake, Ind.: Eisenbrauns, 2006. Views Qoheleth as the death knell of wisdom.

Whitley, C. F. *Koheleth: His Language and Thought*. BZAW 148. Berlin: de Gruyter, 1979. Argues unsuccessfully for Qoheleth's dependence on Ben Sira.

Sirach

Commentaries

Crenshaw, James L. "Sirach." *New Interpreter's Bible*, edited by Leander E. Keck, 5:601–867. Nashville: Abingdon, 1997. Extensive introduction, documentation, and concern for literary and theological features of the book.

Oesterley, W. O. E. *Ecclesiasticus*. Cambridge Bible for Schools and Colleges. Cambridge: Cambridge University, 1912. Valuable, especially for Jewish sources.

Sauer, Georg. *Jesus Sirach/Ben Sira*. ATD Apokryphen Band 1. Göttingen: Vandenhoeck & Ruprecht, 2000. An excellent commentary.

Skehan, Patrick, and Alexander Di Lella. *The Wisdom of Ben Sira*. AB 39. New York: Doubleday, 1987. Textually strong, less attuned to literary and theological issues.

General Works

Adams, Samuel L. *Wisdom in Transition: Act and Consequence in Second Temple Institutions*. JSJSup 125. Leiden: Brill, 2008.

Beentjes, Pancratius C., ed. *Ben Sira in Modern Research*. BZAW 255. Berlin: de Gruyter, 1997.

Calduch-Benages, Núria, and Jacques Vermeylen, eds. *Treasures of Wisdom: Studies in Ben Sira and the Book of Wisdom*. BETL 143. Leuven: Leuven University, 1999. Essays in honor of Maurice Gilbert.

Corley, Jeremy. *Ben Sira's Teaching on Friendship*. BJS 316. Providence: Brown Judaic Studies, 2002. Close reading of texts in Sirach on friendship.

Corley, Jeremy, and Vincent Skemp, eds. *Intertextual Studies in Ben Sira and Tobit: Essays in Honor of Alexander A. Di Lella*. CBQMS 38. Washington, D.C.: Catholic Biblical Association of America, 2005.

Haspecker, Josef. *Gottesfurcht bei Jesus Sirach*. AnBib 30. Rome: Biblical Institute, 1967. Elevates the fear of the Lord over wisdom as the interpretive clues for understanding Sirach.

Hengel, Martin. *Judaism and Hellenism*. Translated by John Bowden. 2 vols. Philadelphia: Fortress, 1974. Exhaustive study of the relationship between Judaism and Hellenism.

Lee, Thomas R. *Studies in the Form of Sirach 44–50*. SBLDS 75. Atlanta: Scholars, 1986. Interprets the book as an encomium.

Mack, Burton L. *Wisdom and the Hebrew Epic: Ben Sira's Hymn in Praise of the Fathers*. Chicago: University of Chicago, 1985. Argues that the author turns Israelite history into an epic, emphasizing various offices and covenants.

Marböck, Johannes. *Weisheit im Wandel: Untersuchungen zur Weisheitstheologie bei Ben Sira*. BBB 37. Bonn: Peter Hanstein, 1971. Excellent examination of the transition wisdom undergoes in the second century.

Middendorp, Th. *Die Stellung Jesu ben Siras zwischen Judentum und Hellenismus*. Leiden: Brill, 1973. Exaggerates the extent of Hellenistic influence on Ben Sira.

Sanders, Jack T. *Ben Sira and Demotic Wisdom*. Society of Biblical Literature Monograph Series 28. Chico, Calif.: Scholars, 1983. Stresses the influence of the Egyptian Insinger Papyrus on Ben Sira.

Schnabel, Eckhard J. *Law and Wisdom from Ben Sira to Paul*. WUNT 16. Tübingen: Mohr/Siebeck, 1985. Comprehensive examination of the relationship between wisdom and law in the two centuries before Paul and in his thought.

Schrader, Lutz. *Leiden und Gerechtigkeit: Studien zu Theologie und Textgeschichte des Sirachbuches*. BBET 27. Frankfurt: Peter Lang, 1994. Studies the themes of suffering and righteousness in Ben Sira.

Stadelmann, Helga. *Ben Sira als Schriftgelehrter*. WUNT 6. Tübingen: Mohr, 1980. Emphasizes the scribal aspects of Ben Sira's office.

Trenchard, Warren C. *Ben Sira's View of Women: A Literary Analysis*. BJS 38. Chico, Calif.: Scholars, 1982. Overstresses Ben Sira's suspicion of women.

Ueberschaer, Frank. *Weisheit aus der Begegnung: Bildung nach dem Buch Ben Sira*. BZAW 379. Berlin: de Gruyter, 2007. A fine story of personal growth in character according to Ben Sira.

Wischmeyer, Oda. *Die Kultur des Buches Jesus Sirach*. BZNW 77. Berlin: de Gruyter, 1995. Excellent analysis of society in Ben Sira's time.

Wisdom of Solomon

Commentaries

Engel, Helmut. *Das Buch der Weisheit*. Neuer Stuttgarter Kommentari Altes Testament 16. Stuttgart: Kathologisches Bibelwerk, 1998. A brief yet solid commentary.

Kolarcik, Michael. "Wisdom of Solomon." *New Interpreter's Bible*, edited by Leander E. Keck, 5:435–600. Nashville: Abingdon, 1997. Brief, with good analysis of the author's religious views.

Larcher, C. *Le livre de la Sagesse ou la Sagesse de Salomon*. 3 vols. Paris: Gabalda, 1983–85. Often wordy, but valuable.

Schmitt, A. *Weisheit*. Neue Echter Bibel 23. Würzburg: Echter, 1989. Compact and useful.

Winston, David. *The Wisdom of Solomon*. AB 43. Garden City, N.Y.: Doubleday, 1979. Learned, especially strong on Hellenistic thought.

General Works

Bellia, Giuseppe, and Angelo Passaro, eds. *The Book of Wisdom in Modern Research: Studies on Tradition, Redaction, and Theology*. Deuterocanonical and Cognate Literature. Berlin: de Gruyter, 2005. Essays on Wisdom of Solomon.

Gilbert, Maurice. "Sagesse de Salomon." *Dictionnaire de la Bible, Supplément*, edited by J. Briend and E. Cothenet, 11:58–119. Paris: Letouzey et Ané, 1986. Excellent survey of secondary research.

Kolarcik, Michael. *The Ambiguity of Death in the Book of Wisdom 1–6: A Study of Literary Structure and Interpretation*. AnBib 127. Rome: Pontifical Biblical Institute, 1991. Perceptive examination of a major theme in the early chapters of Wisdom of Solomon.

Larcher, C. *Études sur le livre de la Sagesse*. EBib. Paris: Gabalda, 1969. Stresses the relationship between Jewish and Hellenistic thought.

McGlynn, Moyna, *Divine Judgment and Divine Benevolence in the Book of Wisdom*. Tübingen: Mohr Siebeck, 2001. Examines the "Mercy Dialogue" in Wis. 11:15–12:27.

Reese, James. *Hellenistic Influence on the Book of Wisdom and Its Consequences*. AnBib 41. Rome: Pontifical Biblical Institute, 1970. Useful treatment of Greek influence on the author.

Dead Sea Scrolls

García Martínez, Florentino, ed. *Wisdom and Apocalypticism in the Dead Sea Scrolls and in the Biblical Tradition*. BETL 168. Leuven: Peeters/Leuven University, 2003.

Goff, Matthew J. *Discerning Wisdom: The Sapiential Literature of the Dead Sea Scrolls*. VTSup 116. Leiden: Brill, 2007.

———. *The Worldly and Heavenly Wisdom of 4QInstruction*. STJD 50. Leiden: Brill, 2003.

Macaskill, Grant. *Revealed Wisdom and Inaugurated Eschatology in Ancient Judaism and Early Christianity*. JSJSup 115. Leiden: Brill, 2007.

Index of Ancient Sources

Index of Authors

Index of Hebrew and Greek Words

GREEK WORDS

*verb root
**consonant

Index of Subjects